a fireside book

PUBLISHED BY SIMON & SCHUSTER

New York   London   Toronto   Sydney   Tokyo   Singapore

BREAKING IN TO THE MUSIC BUSINESS

ALAN H. SIEGEL

Simon & Schuster/Fireside

Rockefeller Center
1230 Avenue of the Americas
New York, New York 10020

Designed by Black Angus Design Group
Manufactured in the United States of America

11 13 15 17 19 21 20 18 16 14 12

Library of Congress Cataloging in Publication Data

Siegel, Alan H., (date)
Breaking In to the music business / Alan H. Siegel.
p.   c.m.
Rev. ed. of : Breakin' in to the music business. 1986.
"A Fireside book."
Includes index.
1. Music—Vocational guidance—United States.   2. Popular music—
United States—Writing and publishing.   I. Siegel, Alan H., date
Breakin' in to the music business.   II. Title.
ML3790.S55   1991
780'.23'73—dc20   91-9884
                                                          CIP
                                                          MN

ISBN 0-671-74257-4
      0-671-72907-1   PBK

ACKNOWLEDGMENTS

I wish to acknowledge with deepest gratitude and no small degree of pride the help and contributions of the following:

Nikolas Ashford

Michael Barackman

Clive Davis

Jean Dinegar

Bob Fead

Shep Gordon

Elizabeth Granville

Valarie Greco

Josh Grier

Don Grierson

Marvin Hamlisch

Steve Karmen

Chuck Kaye

Michael Lefferts

Miles Lourie

Barbara Mandrell

Billy Meshel

Doug Morris

Milton Okun

Rupert Perry

Mary Beth Peters

Bud Prager

Saul Pryor

Irwin Robinson

Larry Rosen

George Schiffer

Irwin Schuster

Howard Siegel

Valerie Simpson

Russ Solomon

Denny Somach

David Sonenberg

John Stix

Jerry Weintraub

Bill Wyman

Maury Yeston

I also wish to acknowledge my special debt and appreciation to my editor, Barbara Gess, who rediscovered *Breaking In,* gave it a new life, and made it a better book in the process.

To Peter Primont and all of my friends at the Cherry Lane Music Group, thanks for your loyalty to me and to *Breaking In* and for your uncommon grace in permitting both of us to seek a wider audience.

—AHS

This edition of *Breaking In* is dedicated to the memory of Peter Ivers, a much-loved friend, and a uniquely talented musician, composer, and performer who was cruelly wrenched from us before his promise could be fulfilled. As an epitaph Peter would have appreciated Milt Okun's comments on page 78.

For those of us who knew him, his loss leaves us inconsolable. For those of you who can never know him, or his music, his loss is even more sad.

To Charlotte

CONTENTS

FOREWORD

As you will learn, hopefully in the not too distant future, no matter how many good notices and reviews you and your work receive, the few that linger in your mind are the others. When the first edition of this book was published the many reviews were very gratifying indeed. Only one, although generally positive, harbored a reservation. That reviewer thought the book too pessimistic in assessing the neophyte singer-songwriter's chances of success. The reviewer was wrong! Nothing has happened in the ensuing years to cause me to alter my views or the tone of this book.

Alphonse Karr said "The more things change, the more they are the same." Karr said this in 1849, he said it in French, and he didn't say it about the record business. Clive Davis, president of Arista Records and a legendary record man, said just about the same thing last month. I had offered Clive an opportunity to update the interview he gave me in 1982. His response was, "Frankly, it seems as current today as it did back in 1982. In response to the questions asked, I would give the same answers."

In the foreword to the last edition (1986) I painted a rather grim picture of record industry trends as they affected your chances of breaking in. Although industry profits have soared, and album releases have risen, these can be countered by other statistics and rationalizations which militate against your success. A lot of the industry profits can be ascribed to the success of the CD. CDs, in addition to providing the record companies with a higher margin of profit, also provided a bonanza in the form of huge sales of old catalogue recordings rereleased on the new media. Album-Oriented Rock, not usually your market, has also proliferated, and accounts for a part of now rosier record company balance sheets. Since the last edition the major record companies have been acquiring every available smaller label. Now six large record companies account for over 90 percent of sales of recorded music. I intuit that such consolidation cannot augur well for innovation . . . and that means you.

But as one becomes older, one hopefully also becomes wiser. I now realize that it is possible to find and manipulate statistics and authorities to espouse any position. With all of the above duly stated, whatever happens or doesn't happen in the record industry won't much affect your chances of success. They will still be lousy! You don't need statisticians to tell you that 40, as in "Top 40," divided by hundreds of thousands isn't a large number! In any case, as far as you are concerned, it means that you have to work harder than ever, persevere longer than ever, know more than ever, and be luckier than ever, in order to see your name on a record label. Remember, the tougher it is out there . . . and it's tougher than ever before . . . the more important it is for you to acquire all of the knowledge that is available to you.

Sprucing up and updating a book for a new edition is rewarding in several respects. The obvious is the pride one takes in the fact that the book has remained in print long enough to require a third edition. Another reward is to be able to correct mistakes, technical and editorial, that eluded you the first time around. A third and rather unusual one is to be able to pass on to your readers feedback gathered from the previous edition, and last but perhaps not least, to self-administer a little pat on the back.

Adhering to the old adage, "If it ain't broke, don't fix it," I anticipated relatively few changes in the original text. As I now stare at the blossoming garden of yellow Post-its emerging from the edges of the original edition, I realize that I was perhaps overly optimistic. A lot of developments have taken place in a short period of time. New material, especially in the video and compact disc areas, has been added and integrated into the existing text. In addition, contact (sometimes touching) with your brethren during the years the book has been out has sensitized me to your frustrations and perhaps led me to crusade a little more than might otherwise be my wont. I'll administer the pat on the back shortly.

All of the mistakes were corrected (I hope) during the second printing, but one of them deserves some ink, because there's a message for you in it. Publishers, I am told, are not above including intentional typos in their books as a means of readily proving infringement should their works be pirated. The original printing of the first edition of this book contained errors in arithmetic in Table 22 (since corrected) which were not intentional, and which escaped my eye, the eye of the editor, and of the proofreader. The gaffe was picked up by a colleague shortly after publication. With anxiety I awaited the scorn of the reviewers, and bags of mail from irate readers. To this day I have not heard from anyone! I do not mention this because I believe that confession is good for the soul, but rather to underscore how important I believe the economics of your business are to you and, unfortunately, the devotion with which you apparently avoid exposure to it. Master Table 22 and the like material. If the book is too exciting for you to stop to do arithmetic, if the sexy parts have you turning pages too fast, remember that this book doesn't self-destruct after one reading . . . go back and do your homework.

This book was intended for neophyte and aspiring songwriters and recording artists . . . it still is. But a funny thing happened on the way to the marketplace and *Breaking In* has been chosen as a text for law school classes on entertainment law, and by colleges for their music business courses. Nature does abhor a vacuum! Nevertheless, it is with gratitude and no small degree of pride that I thank those perspicacious educators and institutions.

So once again, good luck! See you on the charts!

ALAN H. SIEGEL

Scarsdale, New York
October 1990

PREFACE

Few fields of endeavor boast neophytes less prepared for what lies ahead than does the music business, and the least prepared of all are those seeking reward and fulfillment as songwriters and recording artists.

Although during the thirty-plus years I have practiced entertainment law the record contracts I have used grew from two pages to sixty pages, and although the recording-studio board has evolved from a four-track to a sixty-four-track digital, the vast majority of aspiring songwriters and performers cling stubbornly to their abject ignorance of the business in which they seek success.

Why is this lack of knowledge endemic to novice songwriters and artists? Perhaps it is because there are few, if any, formal opportunities to obtain training. If you wish to pursue a career in motion pictures, television, advertising, drama, writing, or any other creative vocation, there are a slew of universities and professional institutions where you can seek training. For songwriters and recording artists, the school is "the business" and the street, and too often the lessons are learned too late, if at all.

Whatever its cause, ignorance spells disaster for the aspiring songwriter and performing artist. It prevents him from getting a start, and if he finally gets a toe in the door, he often succeeds in fouling up whatever opportunity may have been available to him, or ends up paying unnecessarily heavy dues. Ultimately, the pressures of family and the need to make a living, coupled with disappointment and frustration, drive many of them out of "the business" and into medical school, the local service station, domesticity, or to wherever else would-be "stars" fade.

"Why the lament?" you may wonder. Isn't that why they invented lawyers, managers, and accountants—so that the "creative" can be free to create? Ideally, yes, but few things evolve ideally. Too often artists and songwriters do not seek the aid of the attorneys, accountants, and managers they need until it is too late. When they finally seek the aid of experts, they are, because of a lack of understanding, unable to state articulately the business terms they have discussed, or, even worse, what they have "agreed to." Why does this state of affairs exist, considering that artists and songwriters are, on the whole, bright and eager to learn?

The core of the problem is, I believe, a failure of communication on a technical and on a human level. The technical aspect involves the mastery of a new language. The vernacular of the music industry is studded with words that seem to have a simple and clear meaning, but which mean something more or something different in the parlance of the industry, and with words and phrases that are unique to the music business and hence totally alien to the uninitiated. The human component is more nebulous. Most neophyte writers and artists are young. Because of their youth and general eagerness to please, they are relatively easily intimidated. This, in turn, leads to shyness and a consequent reluctance to ask questions or to ask for explanations. Too often, they nod affirmation rather than ask the questions they have on their minds.

What, then, is the answer? Time and experience will take care of many of the problems for those who hang in long enough, and I hope this book will take care of many more. Knowledge is power, and power builds confidence.

Mastery of the contents of this book will provide you with a working knowledge of the language of the music business, how the business and the basic deals work, and how to acquire the professional help you will need. It will also afford you the benefit of learning from mistakes made by others, and will provide you with the answers the best professionals in the business have given me to the questions you are or should be asking yourself.

This is not the book I started to write back in 1983. That book was to be a short, gemlike, pithy masterpiece intended solely for the aspiring songwriter and recording artist. Well, I either had more to say than I thought or was unable to say it succinctly enough. This is a much bigger book than I contemplated, and a much more complete one, which may well be of help to anyone associated with or interested in the music business. I hope it is one of those rare instances where more *is* more, rather than less.

If it helps you launch your career, or increases your understanding, or helps you avoid a mistake, it will have served its purpose.

Good luck! See you on the charts!

Scarsdale, New York
January 1991

Merry Christmas! May I see your ASCAP License?

one

PENNIES FROM HEAVEN

Music by Arthur Johnston, Lyrics by Johnny Burke © 1936
Chappell and Co., Inc.

It is an inescapable fact that it is essential to have at least a rudimentary comprehension of the economics of the music industry in order to understand the forces at play while you try to break in. This is true no matter how idealistic you may be, no matter how devoted you may be to your music, and no matter how insignificant financial reward may seem relative to your hunger to be heard or to have your songs heard. So find an uncomfortable chair and listen up.

Never easy, it is now more difficult than ever to break in as a songwriter or recording artist. In the late 1970s, after enjoying an unprecedented boom and expansion during the sixties and early seventies, the record industry experienced the fall for which it had been riding. Earlier, with no end to the good times in sight, clever managers and lawyers had been able to seduce or coerce record companies into bidding wars for established artists, which resulted in low-profit, high-risk deals. Whether it was due to a lack of new and exciting talent, record piracy, the facility with which home taping could be accomplished, or just inflation and a failing economy, record sales plummeted. The low-margin deals made with the artists who were still selling records didn't provide enough ballast for many record companies to ride out the storm. Record companies folded, independent producers closed their doors, and a lot of good people, from company presidents on down, found themselves seeking new employment. As a natural result, the market for new songs dried up, and the music publishers, especially those without catalogues of established copyrights, often suffered the fate of their colleagues in the record industry. Retailers searched their basements, warehouses, and shelves for salvation in the form of records to return to the record companies for credit against their accounts payable. Many of the records thus returned were excellent recordings by established stars, which, in the halcyon days gone by, would have been retained in inventory in the valid belief that they would ultimately be sold. But the wolf was at the door, and returns inundated the record companies. In one year, returns approaching one year's total industry output found their way back to the record companies' warehouses. Desperate for cash, many record companies dumped their returns into the marketplace at ridiculous prices. Sometimes this was done even though prohibited by contract. In one instance, thousands of eight-track cartridges of an established artist were sold by a major record company for a nickel apiece.

Thus, the suicide cycle was completed. An abundance of high-quality product was available to the consumer at bargain prices. With money tight, many record buyers took advantage of the plethora of records by established artists at bargain prices rather than risk their shrunken dollars on new and still unproven artists.

Apparently flies, boils, and pestilence were not enough. As in the case of the Egyptians of biblical times, another plague was deemed necessary to drive the message home to the record companies. The locusts were provided by the radio stations, the arbiters of what music is played, what we listen to, what sells, and, consequently, who will be the stars of tomorrow. The radio stations' already limited play lists were further trimmed. Stations that were already down to forty or fifty records a day reduced their lists until some were playing only twenty-five songs a day. And these cuts reflected a trend toward conservatism. The stations "got on" the "A" sides of super groups and established artists—the records they were sure their audiences and therefore their advertisers would appreciate. There was damn little room to take a shot on a new artist. The competition for the few available slots for new artists was brutal, and a lot of good artists and a lot of good songs never had a chance to win acceptance. The situation was further aggravated by the advent and apparent success of stations with a format exclusively of "oldies but goodies" records.

The record companies were taking a beating on new artists, and many, exercising business prudence, felt that their promotion dollars were better spent "bringing home" records by established artists, where the odds were more favorable.

Having reaped what they had sown, the record industry took stock. A wave of conservatism engulfed the industry, and signings of new artists dropped dramatically. For a new act to be signed, almost universal agreement by the A&R department and a high degree of company-wide excitement and enthusiasm had to be present. Whereas in the past a "could be" artist often got a record deal, now he had to be a "sure." Even with signings limited to what the record companies believe to be sures, it remains to be seen whether the record companies' batting average will rise much above the 18 percent success rate they enjoyed in the past.

"Things are better now," you say. Yes, you're right. Things are better for the record executives and for the lawyers, and for the promotion people. CDs gave the industry a terrific kick in the butt. Revenues soared and the industry prospered. How does this affect you? Not a whole hell of a lot. You still have the same ridiculously difficult row to hoe! So what! It's been that way always. Let's assume you have the "right stuff" and get down to business!

Tempted to break your pencils or sell your guitar? Well, if you are, perhaps you should. It is clear that the laws of natural selection are going to be more heavily enforced. Only the best *and* the strongest will emerge as the stars of tomorrow. Note the "and." It is not going to be enough for you to be talented. You will also have to be incredibly hungry for success, tough as nails, and uncommonly tenacious and determined to make it in today's music business.

Frustrated by hours of fruitless listening, a record company A&R man once slammed a cassette to the floor of his office and exclaimed, "When the hell are they [meaning you] going to realize that this isn't a hobby!" He was registering frustration over the welter of "garbage" he had to wade through in the course of a day. A litany of complaints followed, including: tapes so bad technically that if they contained a great "standard" there would be no way of knowing; tapes containing such patently impoverished pap that he couldn't hit the eject button fast enough; the good idea stillborn; the lyric in search of a melody, and the melody bereft of a worthy lyric. What he was really saying was that there is a pervasive lack of professionalism demonstrated by those aspiring to be recording artists and songwriters.

Well, if it isn't a hobby, it must be a business. Business means money. Perhaps a businesslike attitude can be inspired by discussing money, music money, as it relates to you.

Myopia, the inability to focus on distant objects, is not a condition that confronts only ophthalmologists. In its nontechnical context, shortsightedness is also a concern to those who deal with not yet established artists and songwriters. Very often an artist can't understand why a record company won't risk the modest advance and meager recording budget it would take to give him his chance. Looking through the wrong end of the telescope, he doesn't realize that those expenditures are just the tip of the iceberg for the record company. The artist is oblivious to the costs the record company must incur in order to transform the masters he records into the records he eyes enviously in the racks of the local record store.

Each released album by a new artist involves an investment in excess of $250,000 by the record company. On top of the advance (if any) and recording costs, there are the costs of pressing an initial quantity of CDs and/or cassettes (usually 30–50,000), and the obligatory single, preparing the cover art, manufacturing jackets, shrink-wrapping, packing and shipping the records, distribution, and, last but not least, promotion—without which a record, like the tree falling in an uninhabited forest, doesn't make any noise. Of course some costs diminish relatively when amortized over large sales. The cost of a one-time item such as cover art becomes of small moment when it is for a platinum album, but one must appreciate the considerable risk a record company takes whenever it commits itself to an album for an untried artist—especially when they bet wrong 80 percent of the time. Why do the record companies take such risks? The question is almost rhetorical. The answer is obvious. When they bet right, the profits are large enough to cover the wrong bets and still pay a dividend to the stockholders.

As interesting as the problems of the record companies may be, I suspect you are more interested in how your income is going to be derived from your activities as a singer and/or songwriter.

Let's turn the clock ahead and assume you are a singer-songwriter whose first LP has been out about six weeks. Your recording contract is with a small label, which, because of its size, didn't have to worry about antitrust problems and therefore was able to extract half of your publishing interests, which you assigned to the label's affiliated publishing company as a condition of getting the record deal. Your record royalty is 7 percent of the retail selling price; the packaging deduction is 15 percent on discs and tapes; the free goods allowance is 15 percent; your LP bears 10 songs (all of which were written by you), and its suggested retail selling price is $9.98. Though you have surrendered half of your publishing interests, your attorney had not been able to withstand the record company's insistence on a mechanical rate, and it has agreed to pay only 75 percent of the statutory mechanical royalty of 5.7¢ per song (and only on records with respect to which they must pay a record royalty, that is, not on free goods). The recording costs were $75,000 (you learned the folly of rehearsing in the studio), and your lawyer, to make sure his fee is paid, negotiated a $10,000 advance for you.

Go to the Lexicon in the back of the book and study it till you understand your deal. I'll wait.

Well, your first LP didn't go gold, in spite of the assertions by all your friends and relatives that it couldn't miss. But you are getting over your disappointment as you realize that your sale of 250,000 units was very respectable indeed for a first album. Besides, you've noticed that the president of the record company is taking your calls and the promotion people have stopped being rude to your manager.

Your first royalty statement and check are due in a few weeks, and you enter your accountant's office to get a handle on how much money you may anticipate. While in his waiting area you clip an ad for a Porsche. The accountant sees the ad in your hand, and you hear him mutter through clenched teeth, "Here we go again." He treats you to fifteen minutes of Toyota talk (at $150 an hour). Fiscal responsibility is his game, and he knows from experience that you're not yet inclined to play.

He suggests that you work up the figures with him. First he warns you that the record company will probably hold a reserve against returns of 30 percent; therefore your sales of 250,000 units must be reduced, at least for the present, to 175,000 units. He demonstrates this for emphasis:

250,000	units	250,000	units
× 30%		− 75,000	reserve units
75,000		175,000	units

"Easy come, easy go," you quip, still smiling. After all, 175,000 units isn't chopped liver either.

He then performs the following bit of arithmetic:

175,000	units		175,000	units
× 15%			− 26,250	
26,250			148,750	units

"Wait a minute," you protest. "You already deducted thirty percent for the reserve against returns. Give me back the fifteen percent."

"You don't understand," he responds. "This fifteen percent is for free goods. They *always* take the fifteen percent for free goods, whether in fact there are any or not."

Your smile has now waned but you manage a firm "Oh."

He now explains to you that the $9.98 retail selling price has to be subjected to the 15 percent packaging deduction provided for in your contract. Out comes his pencil again.

$9.98		$9.98	suggested retail selling price
× 15%		− $1.50	packaging deduction
$1.50		$8.48	net retail selling price for royalty computation

Since your royalty rate is 7 percent, your accountant now multiplies:

$8.48	net retail selling price for royalty computation
× 7%	royalty rate
.594	royalty per record

Your Porsche is looking good. What color? you wonder. You follow your accountant's next operation with pleasure.

148,750	units
× .594	royalty
$88,357.50	royalty due

You're home! You're trying desperately to think of where the nearest Porsche showroom is. As you rise triumphantly from your chair, your accountant motions you to sit down. "You forgot a few things," he says. "Like your $10,000 advance and your recording costs of $75,000." Here comes that damn pencil again, you think. He doesn't disappoint you.

$88,357.50
− 85,000.00
$3,357.50

You realize you're barely in the black ("recouped," in the parlance of the business; see "Recoupable" in the Lexicon, please) to the tune of $3,357.50. What the hell, owning a Porsche would be pretentious anyway!

As the tears stream down your cheeks, the accountant relents and reminds you that you are also the writer of the songs and that your lawyer managed to retain half the publishing for you. (He's paying back your lawyer for having recommended you to him. Otherwise there might have been an "only" before the word "managed.") Out comes the pencil again. This time it looks friendlier. He scribbles:

      5.7¢   per song
    <u>× 10</u>   songs
     57¢   mechanical royalty per record

You understand that half of that is yours in your capacity as songwriter:

   148,750   units
<u>×   28.5¢</u>   writer mechanical royalty per unit
$42,393.75   net writer mechanical royalty

You're feeling better. Of the remaining 28.5 cents (the publisher's share), half goes to your own publishing company and half goes to the record company's affiliated publishing company. Thus another 14.25 cents per unit can be added to your coffers.

   148,750   units
<u>×   14.25¢</u>   your share of publisher's mechanical royalty
$21,196.88   net publisher's mechanical royalty

You borrow the accountant's calculator and rapidly punch in the numbers:

$ 3,357.50   net record royalty
 42,393.75   writer mechanical royalty
 <u>21,196.88</u>   publisher mechanical royalty
$66,948.13

"Not bad," say you proudly (you're thinking that an Audi isn't bad either).

Now you notice your accountant is sporting a malevolent leer. "You forgot the "Controlled Composition" clause in your record contract, whereby the record company need only pay three-fourths of the statutory mechanical rate on musical compositions directly or indirectly owned or controlled by you. Your writer mechanical royalty ($42,393.75) and your publisher mechanical royalty ($21,196.88) must therefore be reduced to . . . hmm . . ." He takes back the damn calculator. His fingers are but a blur, "$31,795.31 and $15,897.66, respectively." The leer lingers! "That knocks your $66,948.13 down to $51,050.47."

You find yourself muttering aloud. "Maybe a BMW or a Turbo Saab?" "What about your manager?" he says. "What about him?" you respond defensively. "According to your contract with your manager, I have to deduct twenty-five percent and pay it directly to him." That damn pencil again.

$51,050.47			$51,050.47		
×	25%	manager's	− 12,762.62		manager's
		percentage			commission
$12,762.62		manager's	$38,287.85		your net
		commission			(perhaps)

"Must we pay him?" you ask, knowing what the answer will be.

"Only if you don't want him to cut your heart out!" Once again you rise, extend your hand cheerfully to the accountant and offer gamely, "Well, they make some good-looking Toyotas." He doesn't release your hand. "Indeed they do," he responds. "But you will have more income this year from performance royalties, and your price for personal appearances will rise substantially. We'd better put $20,000 in a money-market fund as a hedge against taxes." His hand feels cold as he releases yours. As you turn to leave, you hear him say, "And then there is my fee . . ."

In the lobby of the building you find a pay phone with a directory. Your fingers do the walking . . . Su . . . Suz . . . Suzuki.

Actually, as you think of your assorted creditors, who have waited patiently for your first success, you realize that your dreams can wait a while. You take comfort in the knowledge that finally you no longer have to worry about breaking in. The Rolls isn't far off.

The above scenario is subject to many variables. If your lawyer had not excluded recording costs from commissionable income under your management contract, as was presumed above, you would have owed your manager another $18,750 (75,000 × 25 percent). If your record company's affiliated publishing company had insisted on a 10 percent gross administration fee, your publisher's share of mechanical royalties would have been lighter by $4,239.38. Puzzled? Don't fret about it now, we'll work out the math in the chapter devoted to publishing.

If it's of any comfort, you now know more about your business than 99.9 percent of the lawyers in the USA. If you reread and master the Lexicon, you can raise that to 99.95 percent. There's a chapter on lawyers, too.

two

I WRITE THE SONGS

Music and lyrics by Bruce Johnston © 1974 by
Artists Music, Inc.

Once upon a time songwriters only wrote songs, singers only sang songs, dinosaurs roamed the earth, dodo birds and virgins were in abundance, and a nickel pack of Kleenex cost five cents. There was also a time when record companies hounded and badgered music publishers for their best songs.

Today many singers write their own songs, music publishers hound and badger record companies to record their songs, a nickel pack of Kleenex costs 50¢, and we all know what happened to dinosaurs, dodos, and virgins.

There are many knowledgeable people in the music industry who feel that the songwriter who does not perform (a euphemism in this context for record) his own songs is well along the path taken by the extinct species cited above. To adopt this position would cost me half my readers and undoubtedly my publisher. In fact, I do not subscribe to it, but to discount it entirely would be akin to the behavior of ostriches, who bury their heads in the sand when being overtaken by pursuers, because they cannot distinguish between seeing and being seen.

Anyone who denies that the writer who performs his own songs has an edge over the writer who cannot or does not do so is similarly out of touch with reality. If you are a writer who doesn't perform, should you throw up your hands and abandon songwriting as your profession? Perhaps, for if one quintessential trait necessary for success as a writer or artist became apparent to me in the course of preparing to write this book, it was commitment. Each and every one of the experts interviewed, formidable individuals all, whether publisher, record executive, manager, artist, or songwriter sooner or later hit on "character," "persistence," "drive," or a similar quality as being the indispensable element in the success formula. For you, writing must be what winning was for Vince Lombardi—everything!

If it isn't, see if you can't exchange this book for a novel—before it becomes too dog-eared.

Still with me? Good! Get a cup of coffee and stick a bookmark in the Lexicon; you've got a lot to absorb and master in these pages. Although this chapter will be of equal importance and spellbinding interest to the singer-songwriter and the writer who doesn't perform (to whom I may allude from time to time as the "naked" writer—"naked" in the medieval sense of being without a weapon), the focus may well be on the latter, since the singer-songwriter already has his ability to perform as a vehicle to drive down the road to recognition.

It's a cold world out there, Mr. Naked Songwriter. Let's get some clothes on. Mr. Singer-Writer, don't gloat; we'll put things in perspective for you in Chapter 3.

How often have you heard someone you know say, "I ought to write a novel," or "I could write a better movie than the clinker we saw last night," or words to that effect? Well, when the first sheet of paper is in the typewriter or on the table, and it's still half blank after several hours, enthusiasm wanes. Eventually, the realization dawns that there are about three hundred and ninety-nine more sheets to go, and *that* literary masterpiece invariably comes to an end. All is not lost, however, for at the next cocktail party there is an "unfinished novel" or a "work in progress" to dazzle people with. Just the awesome bulk of a novel, the climb to the top of a mountain so high that its peak is shrouded in clouds and unattainable, is enough to discourage most amateur novelists and abort their efforts. Ah, but a song, one lousy page, a little ditty easily completed, a mere anthill as opposed to the Annapurna (26,503 ft.) of a novel, lends itself to completion, satisfaction—and incredible competition. That kind of competition, though not formidable or threatening in the quality sense, is nevertheless a killer when it is for the ear or attention of a publisher or other professional user of songs. When the amateurish (note the "ish," because most of you are probably still amateurs in the dictionary sense) cassette arrives at a publisher's office, there is no way to distinguish it from the cassette containing songs of professional and commercial quality. If you could invent a device, such as the metal detectors used at airports, that, when receiving a cassette, would announce either "BS" or "BINGO," your fortune would be assured. The demo cassette that sings "BINGO" is the subject of Chapter 4; be patient. The singer-songwriter has the same problem, but he experiences it at the record companies rather than at the music publishers. The singer-songwriter usually doesn't start hitting on the music publishers until after he feels he has struck out, at least for the time being (the hunger never dies), at getting a record deal. For the singer-songwriter, the music publisher is ofttimes thought of as the back door. For the naked songwriter, it is the front door, indeed, pretty much the only door—and the trick is to open it.

Unfortunately, I am not unique in harboring the belief that the emergence of and subsequent domination of the pop-music scene by the singer-songwriter and self-contained groups has so diminished opportunity available to the naked songwriter as to eclipse the possibility of substantial success for all but the most talented and hardy.

Some time ago a talented young singer-songwriter was referred to me. I listened to his tape and loved it. The songs were literate and melodic and his voice was inordinately good. In addition, he was charming and extremely attractive. His previous attorney had "shopped" him without success and had apparently lost interest.

I sent his tape to six record-company executives who had not previously heard him. The results were uniform, six for six—all "passes." The responses represented a typical cross section of passes:

one "wimpy"
one "nice but too MOR for us"
one "would take a shot if business were better"
one "I'd sign him if we were signing—but we're not signing.
       . . . I would be interested in one of the songs for another artist"
two "thanks, but not for us, at this time . . . try again"

Actually, there was cause for a little encouragement. I felt that the two companies that indicated that under different circumstances they would have signed the artist meant it. To the artist, however, after a while a pass is a pass, and encouraging words become just so much rhetoric.

At this point we had exhausted our supply of record companies. To the artist's credit, he had no intention of folding. I must confess I might not have been as stalwart had he not set an example by his courage and perseverance.

It was decided to work on the songs. Perhaps if he could break in as a songwriter and attain some recognition in that capacity, a record deal might follow. I arranged to play the demo for a major music publisher. The interest was real and immediate. An exclusive songwriter deal was discussed which involved a modest weekly advance. A meeting was set up, and the publishing company's people met with the artist. Enthusiasm abounded. The artist conceded on the last open issue and agreed to give all of his publishing interest to make the deal (we had tried to retain a half-interest). The publisher indicated that it was going to send the tape to a producer with whom it was just about to close a deal. Great—we might get a record deal too! We left the publisher's offices buoyed by the belief that in principle we had a publishing deal and the possibility of a record deal *too*. The publisher maintained phone contact with the artist, but nothing was "happening." After several weeks I called and was told that the publisher's deal with the producer had foundered, and that without it, the publisher was not prepared to go forward. Sorry!

Shortly after this disappointment, the artist's demo was played for the president of a newly founded record company, who appreciated it. Happily, a deal was negotiated between the artist and the record company and its publishing affiliate, and the record company announced the signing of the artist in the trades.

The day after the deal was announced in the trades, the publishing-company executive who had aborted the deal we thought we had struck called and asked, "Are you interested in doing a publishing deal?" "Where were you when we needed you?" I queried.

All of the elements one would think necessary for a publishing deal had been present: a talented and reasonable writer willing to make whatever concessions were demanded of him, and an established and well-funded publisher having great enthusiasm for the writer's songs. How come no deal?

I believe that because of the shrinking need for new songs due to the self-contained nature of most of today's artists, many publishers have lost faith in their ability to nurture and develop a new writer to the point where the investment in time and money is economically justified—unless there is a built-in record outlet for the material. I say this not in a pejorative sense. I am not implying that their lack of faith is indicative of a lack of courage or, indeed, unjustified. More ominously, I am fearful that it is well placed and that it is reflective of experience and considered judgment. The publishers realize something most of you don't yet appreciate. Without a successful record to popularize it and make it a viable economic commodity, even the best of songs may as well not have been written. Even if you are fortunate enough to have a song "accepted" by a publisher, its only immediate value to you is as encouragement. The advance, if any, will be just enough to constitute consideration necessary to sustain the contract in the eyes of the publishing company's attorney. Not one additional penny will inure to your benefit until and unless the song is recorded. No song is printed today unless it is a hit or part of a matching folio. There are no performance royalties until the song enjoys air play, which obviously it cannot have till it is recorded. If the publisher can't place it soon after its acquisition, while it is "in mind," it will probably turn to dust in the publisher's archives.

The following *Cash Box* excerpt, although dated January 30, 1982, is equally applicable now in 1991. It is from a feature entitled "*Cash Box* Spotlights Music Publishing." "*The predominance of the self-contained artist and slumping unit sales have brought about the current trend wherein publishers negotiate sub-publishing and split copyright deals with artists and production companies. Artists who perform solely outside material like Steve & Edie Gorme* [sic] *and Andy Williams have diminished 60–70% over the past 15 years, and the striking of administration and subpublishing deals has become a necessity.*"

The article was really about how the publishers were reacting to the diminished need for new songs caused by slumping record sales, paucity of new record acts, and the prevalence of the self-contained artist. Each publishing executive contributing a quotation to the article waxed enthusiastic about the health of publishing's future and indicated that the slack, if any, would be taken up either by exploiting existing catalogue through the new technology, such as video software; through repackaging; through increased efforts to revitalize underutilized areas of exploitation, such as motion pictures, commercials, and print; or through liaisons with writer-performers who have been or could be groomed for record or video-software exploitation. Unbeknownst to them at the time, the advent of the CD was about to legitimize their optimism . . . at least temporarily.

I couldn't help think, just a little, of the time-honored concept of whistling aloud to buoy one's courage while passing a graveyard.

You naked guys seem to be left out simply because the publishers can't find outlets for the material they already have stockpiled. Theirs is not an irrational position, especially when they've been trying to soothe a bunch of writers who are asking in rather strident tones, "What the hell are you doing with my songs?"

Before we both become despondent, I should state that I soon came to the realization that, as in everything else, the difficulties of the naked songwriter are relative, and that a lot of us were spoiled rotten during the sixties and seventies, when music and records were a dominant influence in our society. During those years a lot of chaff went gold and platinum, along with some wheat. More winnowing took place in the eighties, and will take place in the nineties, but a lot of "bread" is still going to be made.

The second realization was that real songwriters, ones with the right stuff (to borrow from Tom Wolfe), are going to write songs whether there are a thousand publishers or ten publishers; whether naked or armed; indeed, whether their music is commercial or not. Considering all the great standards that were written during the Great Depression, when opportunities for success were almost nil, I shudder at my presumption in thinking that my words might discourage a writer of merit. Enough apologia—back to work.

Let's turn back for a moment to my client with the aborted publishing deal. In the context of all of the above, do you perceive what was happening? I didn't, until I started putting this chapter down on paper. My attempt to create a marriage between that particular writer and that particular publisher was preordained to be a failure. As perceived by the publisher, the writer was naked. "No!" you say. "He was a singer-songwriter—not naked according to your definition." Right, but wrong. The publisher knew that he had failed to get a record deal notwithstanding many attempts. So, for all practical purposes, from the publisher's vantage point he was naked. Remember, the publisher itself was trying to cover its nakedness by closing a deal with a record producer, thus assuring an outlet for its product. Had the publisher succeeded, it could, it felt, have handled my writer. When the production deal fell through, everybody was still naked; hence no deal. When my client's record deal was announced, he became clothed, and, even though its situation had not changed, the publisher felt it could handle a contract with my client, because as a signed record artist he represented an assured albeit temporary record outlet for the songs he wrote.

About now a light bulb should appear over your head, as in a cartoon. Naked plus naked, although terrific in bed, doesn't produce progeny in today's music business.

It's a brand-new theory. Congratulations! You helped formulate it. I suspect everyone in the business has known it for years, but nobody ever said it before, out of either self-interest or lack of focus.

Okay, so what now? You singer-songwriters can skip a few pages and wait for us where we talk about the various kinds of publishing deals. I want to work a few minutes with the nonsingers.

Let's assume, as you must, that notwithstanding all adversity, you have the magic and will ultimately prevail. No harm in giving destiny a hand, is there?

Sometime in 1990, in Los Angeles, I managed to arrange a meeting with a well-known and long-established singer-songwriter—a real star! The meeting took place during a rehearsal break, and its purpose was to solicit an interview for the last chapter of this book. The meeting started badly and got worse rapidly. I had sought the interview because my past experiences with the performer indicated to me that he was an extraordinarily intelligent and articulate man from whose experience you might profit. The fate of the interview was sealed when I mentioned, perhaps unwisely, that one of the things I was exploring was the effect of the singer-songwriter on songwriters "coming up." His reaction was immediate, passionate, and defensive. Paralleling Marie Antoinette's rejoinder "Let them eat cake!" when advised that the citizens of France had no bread, our star responded, "Let them learn to sing!" Although his imperious tone belied any constructive motivation, he may unwittingly have been of great help—at least to some of you.

You needn't be a Placido Domingo to sing in the pop idiom. Perhaps some of you might give this some thought. A certain unique and indefinable majesty is often bestowed upon a song when sung by its creator. It's worth a try—and it is certainly the least expensive way to make a demo.

I would be a Pollyanna if I did not impart to you the following anecdote. An extraordinarily handsome writer of uncommon talent sought my services. I immediately had visions of sugarplums, platinum albums, and a TV career. I asked if he could sing—after all, I thought, anyone who could write a song should be able to carry a tune. His response was a forlorn negative shake of the head. He was adamant; I was insistent. Persuasion is my business, and I ultimately persuaded him to do a demo tape. A week or so later he brought in a tape. We put it on the deck. Two choruses later, I hit "Eject." I looked at him gravely and intoned, "You were right." We both laughed good-humoredly. Ultimately, one of his co-writers secured a record deal, and he is now looking forward to the release of an album that, though it doesn't bear his voice, contains several of his songs. A classic example of a naked writer finding a way to secure some cover. And he didn't even have this book!

Let's see, having propounded this super theory, how it can be put to use by you.

As you will learn in a later chapter, naked recording artists (artists who do not write and who are not equipped with a source of material) have an even tougher time getting their foot in the door than naked songwriters. It would therefore seem of mutual benefit for a songwriter and an artist of complementary talents to merge forces—object, synergism and a simultaneous withdrawal from the nudist population. An apt example was the classic triple platinum album *Bat Out of Hell*, which resulted from the writing strength of Jim Steinman and the performing power of Meatloaf.

Similarly, you can scout local performing groups whose ability and style is compatible with your songs. Every town and city has bar bands or groups that have a local following and big-time aspirations. Work on having them perform some of your songs. Usually, a lack of good original material is their main weakness. An audience's reaction, or the absence thereof, is a good teacher and will greatly aid in honing your abilities and enhancing your professionalism. Such an alliance will also provide exposure for your material and enlarge your chances for success. Besides, you may cadge a ride on their coattails.

If you play well enough, and have the disposition for it, you may attempt to join a performing group or, indeed, form one, with you and your songs as its nucleus.

Another possibility is to think in terms of specific projects rather than random songs. Perhaps you are equipped to write for the musical theater. Try working on a theater idea. If you are in college, ample access to would-be book writers (and lyricists) is available. Cast about (no pun intended).

In 1694, William Congreve said in *The Double Dealer*, albeit in a different context: "As to go naked is the best disguise."

If you wish to disguise your talent, going naked is as good a way as any. You see, I practice what I preach: I would feel very naked without a copy of Bartlett's *Familiar Quotations* at my side.

If you resolve that you are a songwriter pure and simple, and that you have neither the inclination nor the ability to utilize any of the foregoing devices, or to conjure up your own, you will have to go naked. Please keep in mind while doing so that the random broadcasting of cassettes, like the random sowing of seeds, in addition to being very expensive is sure to be less fruitful than careful planting in the right soil and climate. Till the soil of the clothed publishers first, those with record outlets for your material. Virtually all of the successful individual producers of artists who don't write have publishing satellites and are searching for hit songs that are suitable for their acts and that they can own (not necessarily in that order of priority).

Although it would be logical to assume that a music publisher that is part of the same corporate family as a major record company is not naked, it would more often than not be an erroneous assumption. The larger the corporate family, the less likely there is to be a close and productive interrelationship between the music-publishing and the recording branches of the family. Not unlike brothers and sisters in most families, jealousies and rivalries seen endemic to the relationship. They seem to vie for paternal recognition and their respective shares of the family budget. The larger the respective operations are, the larger the gulf between them seems to grow. This natural rivalry, when coupled with the omnipresent specter of antitrust prosecution, serves to maintain the separation. There are, however, exceptions, but the nuances are subtle and you will have to do a great deal of research to appreciate them.

How do you, operating out of Duluth, Terre Haute, or Oshkosh, garner the information and expertise necessary to make a choice? It would be easiest to refer you to the myriad little books and pamphlets of a "how-to-do-it" nature which sport lists of record companies, music publishers, managers, etc. (I have suspected that such lists are promulgated by the U.S. Postal Service in order to bolster the sale of stamps.) The lists are often out of date by the time the book is on sale, are undifferentiated, uninformative, and misleading. What is the benefit of sending a tape to a "music publisher" culled from the rolls of ASCAP and BMI which exists only as a repository for songs written by a particular writer (who is struggling, as are you, to have his songs recorded) and whose address is a file drawer in some accountant's office? A rhetorical question, to be sure.

I'm afraid you are going to have to earn the knowledge. Having songs placed is not a shotgun operation; it requires research and targeting. Not only do you have to beat the competition musically, you have to beat them in a business sense. You must learn not only your profession, but also the business in which you hope to ply it. The research sources are available to you wherever you are located. A prime source is your local record shop. Album jackets are loaded with information of use to you. Zero in on artists for whom you believe your songs are suitable but who don't write their own material. How do you know who does and who doesn't? Check the album cover and the label. On one or the other you will find the names of the writers of the songs and the names of the publishers. Don't be dismayed or discouraged if you find that the artist is a co-writer of several of the songs. It doesn't necessarily mean that he wrote them. There is a very strong possibility that the acknowledgment of the artist as a co-writer was merely a "cut in," a quid pro quo for recording the song. A slightly changed lyric or the turn of a musical phrase is often utilized as a rationale and permits both the "cutter" and "cuttee" to sleep better.

Let's assume you've targeted a likely artist. Study the artist's albums. (Don't worry about the proprietor of the record shop; when you're famous, you can come home and do a promotion for him.) The chances are that one publishing company's name will come up with curious frequency. Find a bookie and make a wager that that publisher is owned by either the artist or the producer. Guess where to send your demo!

The other research tool that you must avail yourself of is a trade magazine. If your local library doesn't have a subscription to either *Cash Box* or *Billboard*, you should subscribe to one of them. They are both excellent but to some extent duplicative, and either one should suffice your needs. An annual subscription (about $100) is not cheap, but quite reasonable in the context of "professional equipment." It is not sufficient for you to just read or browse through them. Study them and absorb each issue, especially the charts—not just the song titles and the artists, but the publishers and the writers. You must learn the music business if you are going to enjoy so much as a whisper of success.

Did you notice that in the parenthesis above dealing with the record-shop proprietor I used the words "come home"? Well, it was intentional. This brings me to a subject I have put off because of the potential havoc it could wreak if not handled by you maturely, and from a proper perspective. What we have really been discussing up to now is "cassette roulette." For most of you, it's as far as you will go. In any profession there is attrition along the road to success. In the "glamour" fields such as music, theater, and motion pictures, the attrition is most severe. When recognition and remuneration are high, the field is large but the winner's circle is small. The race therefore goes to the swift, the strong, and, most of the time, to the talented.

Playing cassette roulette through the mails can be fun for a while, but a little piece of you goes into the mailbox along with each demo, and it doesn't always come back along with the package marked "Return to Sender" (all the makings of a Country-and-Western song). If you have great good fortune, you may place a song or two this way. This doesn't necessarily mean that the song will ever be recorded or heard by the public—merely that a publisher thought there was a possibility of having it recorded sometime, somehow.

If you ultimately determine that songwriting is to be your lifework, that it is through songwriting that you are going to support yourself and your family, pay for your kids' braces, put them through college, and amass your retirement fund, you aren't going to do it out of Duluth, Terre Haute, or Oshkosh. Sooner or later you are going to have to go to one of the music centers, New York, Los Angeles, or Nashville, hang out, make the rounds, get to know the publishers, producers, and artists, become known by them, and otherwise pay your dues. This is one of the rare instances where I firmly believe later is better than sooner. Don't go to write songs; you can write songs in Duluth. Go when you know you have something to sell. Study your business. Know it as thoroughly as you can before you make the pilgrimage. Don't go if you're still a "kid" either chronologically or emotionally. Go when you've done everything possible to learn your craft that can be learned without leaving your own turf.

One other thing: successful writers don't seem to be very young. The art of writing requires, besides a pencil and paper, something to write about. It takes time to store up the knowledge and experience you will have to draw on in order to write. It's akin to a reservoir that needs replenishing if it is to continue to supply water. Any would-be writer, whether he be novelist, poet, screenwriter, or songwriter, who gives up a minute of education he might otherwise obtain in order to get a head start on his career is very foolish indeed. Stay in school (play cassette roulette if the need is irresistible). Then, when you are ready, really ready—good luck!

Sooner or later, if you are as talented as you think you are, and if you have worked harder and been more persevering than you thought yourself capable of, someone, somewhere, is going to want one of your songs, or your services as a songwriter. At that point you may rely on receiving a contract with an accompanying letter indicating where you should affix your signature. Before doing so, there are several things you should do. First, revel in the feeling of accomplishment and vindication it brings to you. Enjoy it enormously; it is a feeling that comes but rarely in a lifetime. Flash it a lot to friends and family and develop an "I told you so" look, so you won't have to utter the words. Second, abandon any thoughts of an immediate or even distant dramatic change in your financial status. Third, read the contract. Fourth, read it again. Fifth, find this book, wherever you may have stowed it, and reread the chapter on entertainment lawyers, and this chapter. Now, remove the contract from under your pillow and let's take a look at it.

At this stage of your career as a songwriter, there are four situations that may confront you, three of which will entail a contract with a music publisher, one of which will not—necessarily.

Situation One: You've played cassette roulette and the little steel ball landed on one of your songs. This has resulted in your being proffered a simple *songwriter contract* for that one song.

Situation Two: Your talents as a master songwriter of the future have been recognized and a publisher wants to tie up you and your songs for the long haul. The book-length contract you receive is called an *exclusive songwriter contract*.

Situation Three: Your talent is so awesome and your bargaining position is, accordingly, so strong that the publisher in situation two above is willing to allow you to retain half the publishing of your songs. The likely scenario giving rise to Situation Three is that the publisher is the arm of a small record company or independent production company with which you are making a simultaneous record deal. The publishing here is a spin-off of and a condition precedent to the record deal. The leverage you have as a desired recording artist, while probably not strong enough for you to retain all your publishing, may very well be strong enough for you to walk away from the table with half your chips. The contract covering the split of the publishing is called a *co-publishing agreement*. To work out the logistics of the relationship, it is usually accompanied by an exclusive songwriter contract.

Situation Four: This is the most blessed of all. You have secured a recording contract with a major record company which through benevolence or fear of antitrust prosecution has not hit on you for all, or even a piece of, your publishing. No contract, except an "internal" one, need evolve immediately. Any relationship with a publisher in Situation Four will be voluntary, advantageous, and probably, at least initially, lucrative.

All of the contracts alluded to above have much in common. It will be helpful to underscore the universal themes and clauses, thereby letting the differences speak more loudly. Not unlike a good song, which universally exhibits a beginning, a middle, and an ending, a good songwriting or music-publishing contract also boasts a certain universality of structure. They all contain the following elements:

1. A grant of rights of a complete or partial interest in a song, and the copyright thereof, to a publisher. This is what you give.

2. A promise to pay to the grantor of the rights in Number 1. above a portion of the income earned by the song. This is the royalty you've been dreaming about. This is what you get. There are several sources from which royalties are derived and which are subsumed in that general term. They include mechanical royalties, print royalties, performance royalties, foreign royalties, etc. It's Lexicon time again! When royalties are paid before they are earned, they are called "advances."

3. Warranties, which are affirmations that the grantor of the rights granted in Number 1. above owned them and was capable of granting them to someone else.

4. A term. This is the period of time for which the rights in the song are granted. At your stage of the game, subject to certain caveats we will discuss, the term is often for the duration of the copyright. If the contract is for a writer's exclusive services as a songwriter, there is an additional term, which is the period of years for which the writer is bound to the recipient of his services. The two terms are mutually exclusive. For example, if a writer enters into a five-year exclusive songwriter's contract with a publisher, the term of that contract is five years, at the end of which period the writer is free and may enter into another exclusive songwriter's contract with a different publisher. The songs written during the five-year term of the exclusive songwriter's contract will continue to be owned by the initial publisher for the term of the grant of rights, which probably was the duration of the copyright in each song (presumably, the life of the author plus fifty years). Thus, even though the writer may leave after five years, he cannot take the songs with him.

   Note the following well, and point it out to your attorney if you use one. The duration of copyright is now pretty much the same throughout the world: the life of the author plus fifty years. Therefore, if you grant the rights to your song to a publisher for the duration of copyright throughout the world, it's gone forever . . . right? Wrong! Under the U.S. Copyright Act you, as author, have an indefeasible right to terminate your grant to the publisher after thirty-five years! Then all of the rights come back to you, right? Wrong again! Your right of termination applies only to the U.S. Copyright. Your publisher, and his assignees, will have the rights to your songs for your life plus fifty years everywhere in the world outside of the United States. I suspect that even a Situation One writer would prevail if he were to request of the publisher that the term be for the "duration of the publisher's rights in the United States copyright of the song."

5. An accounting provision that states when and how often the royalties must be accounted for (explained) and paid; the period of time after receipt during which the recipient can protest that the royalties thus

paid were less than should have been received (there is yet to be demonstrated a single recorded instance of a royalty recipient complaining
of an overpayment); and usually, but not always (so be careful), when
and under what circumstances the royalty recipient's accountant can
audit the publisher's books to make sure the royalties are accurate.
6. Lots of boilerplate, which should be your lawyer's concern and which is
   beyond the scope of this book.

Now, let's perform an experiment. Close the book and hold it before you,
right side up, with the unbound long edge pointing at your nose. Do you
perceive that about a ³/₁₆-inch section of pages on the right is a few shades
darker (dirtier, if you will permit the indelicacy) than the remainder of the
pages? No? Well then, you either are playing Lady Macbeth or you aren't
using the Lexicon. Use it, dammit! If you don't you've wasted your money
and my time.

With the foregoing in mind, let us look a little closer at the contracts begat
by the "situations" alluded to above. It would be perhaps more prudent of me
to shunt you off to an entertainment attorney at this point and move on to
something else. Indeed, with respect to the exclusive songwriter contract and
the co-publishing agreement engendered by Situations Two and Three respectively, I shall do just that—after you have a little more awareness of the
issues involved. Let's, however, spend some time on the Situation One contract, the so-called simple songwriter contract. Why single this one out for
attention? For several reasons. It involves only a song or two, not years of
your life. Moreover, it is the type of contract that you are apt to receive while
you are still situated in Duluth or Oshkosh, where entertainment lawyers do
not abound. Since the advance, if any, will be minimal, the trip to an entertainment center and the retention of an entertainment lawyer are neither
economically practical nor justified. (Of course, if you are already in an
entertainment center, it's a fine excuse and opportunity to start lawyer-
shopping.) It is the simplest contract to understand and negotiate, and it
serves as the basis for all the music contracts, which are, for the most part,
extensions, expansions, and embellishments of the basic songwriter agreement. Finally, the Situation One writer is not in a position to extract major
concessions from a publisher even if represented by the ablest of entertainment counsel. Remember, this book is for you now, not when you have
become established and your songs are in demand. At that career stage, even
a contract for one song can become quite esoteric.

Every contract has to be read in a dual context. First, it must be read for
what it contains, then, for what it doesn't contain. It's relatively simple to
read it for the former and very difficult to read it for the latter. In the first
instance, red flags pop up after each comma. In the second, the silence is
deafening. It takes a great deal of experience with many different contracts
dealing with the same subject matter before your brain develops an intuitive
checklist and the little white flags of omission begin to wave at you. Although

most attorneys prefer their adversaries to prepare a "first draft" (it's a lot of work), we who are more insecure (or devious) volunteer to do it—exercising along the way our "rights of omission." If your songwriter contract provided that you would deliver your first-born child to the publisher, all of you would pick that up immediately, and would probably consider it a bit overreaching. (Of course, those of you with the requisite drive for success would probably start packing the kid up unhesitatingly.) If, however, it stated that you will receive a royalty on "X" and "Z" but was silent on "Y," I can guarantee that you will be oblivious to the omission. I can also guarantee that you won't receive a royalty on "Y." How could you be expected to perceive the omission? At this stage of the game, you don't even know "Y" exists. Even when you are more experienced and know that "Y" exists, you probably won't pick it up because your business is writing songs and you will never read enough contracts to develop a white-flag-intuitive checklist—nor should you.

Songwriter contracts come in all shapes, sizes, and, indeed, colors. They can be typed double-spaced on letter-size paper, in which case they are "fat"; or commercially printed in tiny type on two sides of a long sheet of paper, in which case they are intimidating. They can be in the form of a letter that is kind of folksy and friendly, or they can be in strict forbidding legalese. Pastel-colored paper is sometimes used, which the more cynical think is part of a publisher's plot to lull the reader into somnambulance (which is unnecessary, since the text effectively accomplishes that). Sometimes a songwriter contract bears the word "STANDARD" in its title, which term's only significance is as a palliative to induce the recipient to believe that the contract in question is the same one "everyone" receives and signs and hence it is unnecessary and fruitless to attempt to tamper with it. Whatever the form, color, or label, they are all going to say pretty much the same thing. "Why are the damn things so long?" you may wonder. Well, you have company. Publishers and record companies are constantly asking their attorneys the same question and beseeching them to shorten the contract. They believe, quite logically, that the shorter the contract is, the easier and cheaper it will be to close a deal. The beleaguered attorneys' response is simple: "Guarantee that the song or artist involved will be a 'flop' and I'll give you a short contract!" Songwriting and recording artists' contracts are not unlike insurance policies which start out as very concise documents but which have annexed pages and pages of riders to cover each unanticipated contingency with respect to which the insurance company was at some time required to pay. The same is true of songwriting and record contracts. Each time the publisher or record company got "burned," a new clause had to be added to cover the situation. In addition, as the music industry prospered and grew more sophisticated, more possibilities had to be anticipated and conjured with.

Be that as it may, whatever the size, form, or style of your contract, it is not immutable. All contracts are negotiable under certain circumstances.

The first principle (and the second and third as well) of contract negotiation was perhaps best stated by Archimedes, to whom is ascribed the statement "Give me a lever and I'll move the world." Want to see a "great" lawyer? In any given situation, he's the one with leverage, the one representing the client who has the guns, the client who is less in need of the deal and more prepared to "walk" if his requirements are not met. Alas, the Situation One songwriter has relatively little leverage. If it were economically feasible, and you were to retain an entertainment attorney, he would, if he were worth his salt, attack the Situation One contract as if you were Paul Williams or Billy Joel, asking for every concession ever made by a publisher to a writer, including a demand that you retain half of the publishing. He will at all times, however, have in the back of his mind the fact that you aren't Paul Williams or Billy Joel and he will be ever sensitive to the necessity of pulling back just short of "blowing the deal." If you are able to enjoy the luxury of professional aid in this situation, so much the better, but the most important thing at this stage of your career is that you "blood your sword," "break the ice," "open the door," or whatever other expression suits your fancy but means "get started." For the moment, assume that your first basic songwriter agreement is going to be a "do-it-yourself" negotiation. Accompany me on a walking tour through the highlights of a typical songwriter's contract for a single song and spot the red and white flags that may indicate contract changes that a reasonable and benevolent publisher may be willing to make for the asking. After all, you do have a little leverage—you have written a song the publisher believes may make money. What if the publisher says, "That's the deal; it's not negotiable. Take it or leave it"? My gut reaction is sign the damn thing and get on to your next song. As you prove yourself, your contracts will become more and more "negotiable."

First stop on the tour is the very beginning of the contract, which we'll call the preamble. This identifies you as the "writer," your song as the "composition," and the publishing company as the "publisher." Poke around a bit. If you see yourself characterized as an "employee" or "employee for hire" of the publisher, or, indeed, if you see any word beginning with E-M-P-L-O-Y, you have found your first red flag. Although I do not believe that a Situation One contract can be legally sustained as an employment-for-hire contract within the context of the Copyright Act, you don't want to risk losing your right to terminate the contract thirty-five years hence. Since courts are somewhat unpredictable, you should try to secure deletion of any employment language. Confused? Look up "Employee for Hire" and "Termination, Right of" in the Lexicon, and all will become clear.

Pretty soon we come upon your warranties and representations. This is the part of the contract where, in perhaps rather formal language, you state the song was created by you, was original, and that you haven't given any rights in it to anybody else. Any red flags here will be those hoisted by your conscience.

The paragraph dealing with your grant of rights to the publisher will probably soon appear. This is where you give all rights in the song to the publisher for the full length of copyright, for the entire world! Publishers' lawyers seem to compete to compound the most comprehensive all-inclusive grant of rights possible. With characteristic paranoia, the clause usually says the writer grants all rights . . . including but not limited to all copyrights, renewal copyrights, etc., etc., etc. There follows a litany of every conceivable right. Occasionally overzealousness backfires. From time to time, there may be included in the rights granted, the right to use the music of the composition with another lyric, or the lyric with different music. It's conjectural whether the broad general grant would give this right anyway, but when you see the specific language, it earns a red flag, and deletion of the provision should be requested. It's much more desirable to pick, and work with, your collaborators than to have them visited upon you.

Now we start walking uphill. The royalty provisions loom before us. Philosophically, or perhaps I should say theoretically, the publisher and the writer are supposed to share in the income from the song equally. Although most songwriter contracts attempt to deal fairly with writers in this regard, there is one area where all publishers seem to take an "edge" and another where some take a contractual edge whether or not they actually intend to avail themselves of the possibilities it affords them to unbalance the theoretical equation. The first involves a red flag: the second, a white flag. You are going to have to use the Lexicon if you are to appreciate and understand what follows. Usually the compensation provisions of a songwriter contract consist of several paragraphs setting forth the royalties to be paid. These paragraphs are either preceded by or followed by a sentence or paragraph that in more elegant prose says that all that the writer is entitled to are the specific royalties set forth. What you see is what you get!

Royalties are usually broken down into three general categories.

The first is print royalties, which are royalties from the sale of printed copies of the composition. These, in turn, are divided into a "¢" royalty for sheet music and a percentage of wholesale selling price for folios and other editions. The ¢ royalty is the red-flag edge the publishers universally (in my experience) take. Most songwriting contracts are sent out by the publisher with a 10¢ or 12¢ sheet-music royalty. Twenty-five years ago, the royalty was 3¢ to 5¢. Not a hell of a change! And notwithstanding the fact that the publisher's royalty from his print licensee is 60¢ to 70¢, depending on the retail selling price. If you question whether the publisher will raise your royalty to the theoretical "half," the answer is "No," but the publisher may blush and raise it to 12¢ or 15¢. The usual royalty on the folios and other editions is a proportionate share of 10 percent of the wholesale price, and there is little chance of improving this. Your share of the royalty with respect to a folio containing your song and nine other songs would be 1/10th of the 10 percent, or 1 percent. There is a white-flag situation here that is worth a shot. To illustrate the point, I am going to use an admittedly unrealistic hypothetical situation. Assume your song is a big hit. The publisher, seizing on your song's popularity, combines it with nine public-domain songs (songs he can use without paying a royalty). The total writer royalty the publisher has to pay on this folio is 1 percent, and the success of your song is being used to peddle the folio. If you were to ask the publisher to modify the contract to provide that your 10 percent royalty be prorated only with copyrighted songs, the publisher might just agree; they do so quite often. Granted this concession, your royalty in the hypothetical situation above would be the full 10 percent instead of 1 percent.

The next general categories of royalties are those emanating from mechanical rights and performance rights. They are traditionally 50 percent of all net royalties actually earned by the composition from those sources. This is usually quite straightforward and is not fertile ground for you to till. The contract will provide that the publisher need not pay you performance royalties with regard to those performances with respect to which you receive a writer's share of performances directly from ASCAP or BMI. This is fair, usual, and consonant with industry practice and should not be a cause for alarm or anxiety. Sometimes the language goes a bit too far and uses ASCAP and BMI payments directly to writers to exculpate the publisher from any obligation to pay performance royalties, notwithstanding the fact that there are performance areas that ASCAP and BMI won't deal with, such as the performance element of a motion-picture-use license. This does not occur too often, and, in all candor, if you are talking to a publisher rather than his lawyer, you might be thought of as a bit overzealous.

This is perhaps the appropriate time to deal with the major white-flag edge taken by publishers that was alluded to earlier. I am now referring to what, for want of a more legal term, is generally referred to as a "catchall" clause. Keeping in mind the concept that the publisher and the writer are to share equally in the earnings of the song, there must be royalty language that provides for the sharing of the myriad income sources that are not usually listed with specificity in a songwriter contract because they are too "minor," too "numerous," too "rare," too "unimportant," too "obscure," or, indeed, not yet invented or evolved. What might some of these be? Well, the title and the theme of songs may be licensed as the basis for motion pictures or television programs. "Ode to Billy Joe" and "Harper Valley P.T.A." are two examples that come to mind. If a song is licensed for use in a TV commercial, in what pigeonhole does the income nest? When satellite transmission of music and the so-called new technologies burgeon, will the income sources fit the existing royalty categories? If a catchall clause is in your contract, you can revel in each new exploitation device rather than stew about whether you are going to get your fair share of the income. Few publishers will balk at a request for a contract provision providing a royalty of *"Fifty (50%) percent of any and all net income earned by the composition and not otherwise provided for herein."* You will sleep better.

The third and last major royalty category involves income from uses of the composition outside the United States and Canada. Foreign royalties are traditionally 50 percent of what the publisher receives and usually need little touch-up except for the addition of "source" language, which is dealt with extensively in the Lexicon.

Phew! The hill has been crested, and the rest of our ramble has the aid of gravity. Now that we know what the royalties are, how do we get them? The contract will have an accounting clause. Usually the publisher will account to the writer twice a year, or semiannually. Quarterly accountings are rare but not unheard of. If you ask for quarterly accountings, you will be told that the computer is programmed for semiannual accountings. I forget what the excuse was before the advent of computers. Oh, well, you can't win 'em all. Your contract's accounting provision may or may not grant you an audit right. That is the right to have your accountant examine the publisher's books to ascertain the accuracy of your accountings. If an audit right is not included, ask for it; it will not be denied and it is a white-flag point that should not be passed over. Without an audit provision, it will be necessary to institute a lawsuit to verify your royalties. Even if you are successful, absent a huge hit song, the expense of the litigation will render your victory a Pyrrhic one.

There remain but two more stops on our tour, one of which isn't on the contract map, and one of which may or may not be. Let's look for the latter first. If your contract provides for an advance payable to you on signing, the problem is solved. You may not rejoice in its amount, but looking at your cup as half full rather than half empty, you must revel in the fact that you really did sell a song. What, however, if you see what was conceived as an advance clause on the publisher's form contract, but it has been crossed out? Ask for an advance! Many publishers feel that they will probably have to invest in a demo, and the risk of not earning back demo costs and an advance is too great to take. If you are persuasive, perhaps the publisher will relent and reinstate the clause with a modest sum inserted in the appropriate blank. How modest? One hundred to 250 dollars seems to be the range in Situation One contracts. The actual amount will depend upon whether the publisher believes he can use your demo rather than have to produce one. The crossed-out advance clause is a red flag. The nonexistent advance clause is a white one. The more artful publishers (or, more likely, their attorneys) have two sets of form contracts, one with and one without an advance clause, thereby avoiding the red-flag reflex of a "cross-out." Red flag, white flag, the bottom line is the same; if there is no advance provided, ask for one—politely, of course.

The last stop on our tour is a traditional white flag. Few, if any, Situation One contracts have this provision, yet, if requested, it is usually granted. It is a clause whereby if, after a specified period of time, the publisher has not caused the composition to be recorded, or effected some other substantial use of it, all rights in the composition revert to the writer. That's right, you get it back! The time period varies. Of late, publishers are requesting more time

because they say it is harder to get a song placed. They are right. The times
for reversion vary from two to five years. Take what you can get, gratefully.

Let's take a moment to distill the above and formulate a little checklist.

1. Employment for hire—red flag
2. Sheet-music royalty—red flag
3. Prorate print royalty with copyrighted songs only—white flag
4. Catchall clause—white flag
5. Foreign royalties, at the source—white flag
6. Audit clause—white flag
7. Advance—white flag or red flag
8. Reversion if no activity—white flag

These are the points publishers are familiar with and which, whether you are
victorious or not, will not cause you to appear unreasonable or "difficult."
Moreover, it is extremely unlikely that any contract will be deficient in all
eight areas.

We will not, thank God, go through Situation Two and Situation Three
contracts in the same way. Such an exercise would be beyond the scope of this
book. When faced with Situation Two and Situation Three contracts, you are
in lawyer country. The most we can hope to do is arm you with a smattering
of ignorance, or, phrased more positively, enough knowledge to keep you out
of deep trouble until you find the help you must have.

Okay, master songwriter of the future, you got your demo listened to, and
much to the publisher's surprise (of course not to yours) it was found to
contain not just one but three good songs. The publisher called you and asked
if you had more material. You sent another demo, and the promise of the first
demo was fulfilled—three more good songs. The publisher thinks you could
be a "winner" and proposes an exclusive arrangement. Welcome to Situation
Two! The word "exclusive" should charge you with emotion. You're not a
"one-night stand"; they're talking about "going steady." Much as it would in
a personal relationship, this opportunity must engender mixed emotions. You
have to be flattered that you're wanted, yet there is a gnawing anxiety about
being tied up. I know that right now you can't contemplate the slightest
hesitancy. You believe I am out of touch with reality (a polite euphemism).
Wait till you have the slightest affirmation that the world is aware of the
burden of that massive talent you have been bearing. See how rapidly the
manure of flattery can nourish the garden of your dreams, and, let us hope,
you will entertain the following considerations with appropriate solemnity.

Exclusivity is not to be taken lightly. It means what it implies. Every song
you write during the term of the exclusive songwriter agreement will belong
to the publisher. Indeed, all the songs you have theretofore written will also
belong to the publisher. The agreement may in rare instances take the form
of a true employment agreement, whereby you receive a salary, work space

("office" is usually too grandiose to be an accurate description), and are expected to maintain regular working hours and work under the direction of a supervisor. It may, on the other hand, be a very loose arrangement whereby the publisher lays claim to whatever, if anything, you write, during the term. Regardless of the form it takes, the following factors must be reckoned with:

How long is your commitment for? How long is the term? Is it a firm commitment or is it an option deal? How much of an advance will you receive? Will you receive a monthly or weekly stipend? Will it be just a guarantee, that is, will the publisher agree to pay you just the difference between some annual sum and what you have earned at the end of the year? Will the advance be enough for you to survive on, enough to enable you to pursue your writing without worrying about eating?

Are you satisfied that the publisher has the capacity and willingness to "work" your songs so that they will be recorded? Is the publisher one with access to producers and artists? Is it "naked"?

Will the publisher undertake, in your contract, to professionally demo your songs?

Will the publisher entertain your retaining a partial interest in the publishing?

If you are a singer-songwriter, is it a propitious time for you to enter into an exclusive arrangement? Is a record deal sufficiently remote for you to abandon the co-publishing or self-publishing options it will make available?

Do you respect and believe in the abilities of the publishing company's personnel? Can they polish your talent? teach you your craft? And, most important, will you have access to them?

You will have to ponder all of the above; you will have to spend time with the people with whom you will be dealing; you will have to ask questions, consult with your attorney (who may be familiar with the publisher in question), and make a decision. "Act in haste, repent in leisure" is the aphorism that comes to mind.

Situation Three contracts involve "co-publishing," which is defined in the Lexicon. These are the most complex of all publishing agreements, not necessarily by virtue of their length or intricacy, but by virtue of the many possibilities engendered in their conception. There are just too many ways to skin the cat. Although you are going to have the help of a lawyer on this one, let's give that poor soul a little help by preventing you from giving the store away before he is on the scene. There is nothing more disheartening for an attorney to hear in response to a proposal than "Sorry, Counselor, that's not negotiable; your client already agreed . . ."

There are two main issues that have to be resolved before a co-publishing deal can be concluded, and they are both concerned with administration. The first issue is which of the two publishers is to administer the copyrights. This one is relatively simple. Your publishing company is not. The other publishing company is presumably the more established, knowledgeable, and competent of the two. "Wonderful," you say. "They do the work and we get half the money." Almost correct. Two factors militate against this. The first is the question of advances from publishing-income sources. Remember the usual scenario. You are retaining half of your publishing because your career as a recording artist is about to be launched. In the usual co-publishing situation, the nonadministering publisher receives half of the net *earned* income of the compositions involved. The word "earned" excludes advances. Furthermore, your compositions will be commingled with the rest of the administering publisher's catalogue, and when it makes foreign deals for substantial advances there will be no way of apportioning a share of those advances to your songs, with the net result that the administering publisher will keep the advances, enjoy the use of the money at 10 percent, and pay your share as *if*, and when earned. If your records should take off, the advances from foreign licensing can be substantial. The only viable solution to this problem is to insist that your compositions be segregated from the rest of the administering publisher's catalogue (in a separate joint company) and be dealt with separately, as a unit. Whether you and your attorney can pull this off will depend on your leverage at the time the deal is "talked," on the "buzz" that exists about your record potential at the time, and, in no small part, on your being able to insinuate the concept of segregating your catalogue early on in the discussions, as early as possible.

It is traditional for the administering publisher to charge a fee for administering the catalogue. This is the second factor militating against an equal split between co-publishers. It is appropriately called an administration fee. It is usually 10 percent to 15 percent. The concept of an administration fee is not an immutable law, and it has been successfully challenged. The degree of success in such a challenge once again depends on leverage and, to a large extent, on timing and negotiating skill. If you hang back on acquiescence to a co-publishing arrangement in general, ofttimes the deletion of the administration fee can be won as a "clincher" in making the deal. It is always best for a neophyte to decline to discuss these esoteric details until he has the benefit of knowledgeable counsel. Too often I have had clients announce that they have agreed to an administration fee of 10 percent. When I ask, "ten percent of what?" the only response is a questioning stare. What I am trying to determine is whether it's 10 percent of gross income or 10 percent of the publisher's share of income after the writer's royalties are paid. If it hasn't been discussed, you may be sure that the first draft of the agreement proffered by the administering publisher will provide for an administration fee of 10 percent of gross income. What in effect has happened is that the deal that was sold to you as an equal-sharing 50/50 deal has, through a "bookkeeping" clause, been converted to a 60/40 deal, with you on the short end. Let's see how this works. Assume that one of your songs was recorded and the administering publisher receives a mechanical royalty check from a record company of $1,000:

	No administration fee	10% of gross administration fee	10% publisher's share adminis- tration fee
You as songwriter	$500.00	$500.00	$500.00
Administering publishing company	$250.00	$300.00	$275.00
Your publishing company	$250.00	$200.00	$225.00

TABLE 2.1

In the course of a long and successful career, we are talking about a great deal of money. It is therefore important that you understand the stakes in this poker game.

Where the co-publishing deal is part of a record deal, which we will assume is the case here, two things must be established immediately. They can be won if raised and disposed of immediately. If they are left till later on, they become chips in the negotiation and will have to be paid for. They are the term of the co-publishing contract and the question of cross-collateralization. Assume that your record contract is for five years. The co-publishing deal with the record company's publishing arm should also be for five years. You can bet that's what it will stipulate. What you may have forgotten is that the record deal is traditionally an option deal whereby the record company has the right to end the contract at the end of each year. Unless the co-publishing contract provides that it is coterminous with the record deal, you will find yourself in the unhappy position of being tied into the record company's publishing company after you are no longer signed to the record company. That's not good! Especially when you have a subsequent record opportunity that is contingent upon a co-publishing deal. The problem is even more important when you are signing a straight exclusive songwriter contract (no share of publishing) with a record company's publishing company.

Unless you are very vigilant, you will find that the record contract and the co-publishing agreement are cross-collateralized. (It is time to hype you about the Lexicon again.) That is to say, any advances paid you under one will be recoupable out of income from the other. Recording costs under your record contract are treated as advances to you. Therefore, if you are still in the red under your record contract, any earnings from the co-publishing agreement will be paid to the record company to diminish the unrecouped advances, including recording costs under the record contract. This is particularly vexing if the publishing income being thus applied is not even from your record!

As stated briefly above, each co-publishing arrangement also requires, as part of the package, an exclusive songwriter agreement in order to tie you as a writer to one of the publishing companies involved as co-publishers. It is desirable that your contract be with your own company. This is best effected if that agreement is presented as a *fait accompli.*

It is unlikely that you, as a somewhat awed, intimidated, and anxious novice, will sit down with the record company president or the publishing company president and negotiate these points. What is hoped is that by studying this material, you will acquire enough knowledge, enough buzz words, enough red flags, at least to deter you from acquiescing to some of the more distasteful contract provisions that have been visited upon your predecessors. Your job is to fight a holding action until the Mounties (your entertainment attorney) arrive. So much for Situation Three.

It should be pointed out that in the late eighties, attorneys for writers made considerable inroads into the publisher's traditional grant of rights language. But remember, there's no free lunch! Situation Three is becoming more and more common. No, the publishers are not becoming more generous . . . actually, it's just the opposite. Now, they rarely make a deal unless the writer is a singer-songwriter *with a record deal*. What is really happening is that they are trading bucks for less risk. It is now possible, if the publisher believes in your talent, *and* you have a record contract, for you to cut a deal whereby not only will you retain half of your copyrights, but whereby the publisher's half of the copyrights will revert to you after a negotiated period of time. So, it is now possible to receive a handsome advance, retain half your copyrights and get the other half back, in say ten years! As one publisher mournfully said to me, "Alan, we're now in the rent-a-copyright business!" The deal I just outlined would make some of my old publisher bosses turn in their graves. Why do publishers now make these deals which do not in the long term build their catalogs? Most of the publishers that have the resources to fund these high advance deals are components of large conglomerates. Their executives are less interested in building something for their heirs or egos, as were publishers of yore, than in aggrandizing their "bottom lines" upon which their incentive compensation and their shimmy up the corporate ladder are contingent.

Another brand-new wrinkle you (and your attorney) ought to be aware of is the possibility of extracting print rights from your publishing deal and dealing with and for them as a separate bundle of rights. If you have the leverage to pull this off, and if there is a buzz about you as a recording artist, you may well be able to do it; the result is a separate additional advance and a higher royalty. Most publishing companies have neither the expertise nor the facilities with which to do their own print, hence they must license the rights they received from you to one of the few companies that specialize in printed music. The licensee print company will pay an advance to your publisher against what is a pretty standard royalty. Your publisher in turn pays roughly half of what it receives (advance and royalty) to you, as your share. Clearly, if you extract print rights and license them directly to the print company you stand to make twice as much, plus the "edge" on sheet music that we spoke of before. Refer to Michael Lefferts' interview on page 87 for an informative and entertaining discussion of this new phenomena. If you are a Situation Two writer, I'd say you had a shot at pulling this off. If you are a Situation Three or Four writer, I'd be surprised if you didn't!

Incidentally, if you are cutting this kind of deal make sure that the contract provides for a 5 percent "name and likeness" royalty to you for the use of your picture on the matching and personality folios that are printed . . . after all, now you're a STAR and your picture sells folios as well as beer. This royalty can be paid to you directly or funneled through your publishing entity.

We'll make short shrift of Situation Four. You have a brand-new record deal with Atlantic Records. Your publishing is intact. There has been a press release concerning your first album. Publishers are calling *you*! What do you do? Let your lawyer talk to them. You will get a sense of what is available to you, and it will set up "relationships" that will facilitate future dealings.

Whether or not you do anything at this particular moment depends on how badly you need cash and how much front money is being offered. If you can afford to gamble that you will have a hit record, it is obviously better to wait, because your bargaining position will certainly be stronger after a hit record. You will have the handle on ol' Archimedes' lever. On the other hand, if your record flops, you may have lost an opportunity to pick up a sizable advance—not an altogether unpleasant dilemma.

There is an awful lot in this chapter. Let's see if we can pull it all together with some dollars-and-cents examples and a little quiz. This will be an "open book" test and you may use the Lexicon.

Your publisher has gotten your song, aptly entitled "At Long Last" (for which you wrote the words and the music), to the famous singer Kvetchan Grone. Kvetchan records "At Long Last" for what proves to be her first crossover album. "At Long Last" is released as the "A" side of the first single out of the album. The single goes platinum, selling one million copies. Larynx Records, Kvetchan's record company, insists on a "rate" with respect to all songs. Your publisher agrees.

When the album is released, you are pleasantly surprised to find that Kvetchan recorded another of your songs, "Better Late Than Never," which you wrote in collaboration with another writer. "Better Late Than Never" was the "B" side of the next single out of the album. It enjoyed exactly the same 1,000,000 sale as the first single. The album ultimately sold 500,000 copies, just winning a gold record. Sheet music of "At Long Last" sold 15,000 copies, and the album's matching folio sold 30,000 copies. The matching folio contained the ten songs that were in the album, which included an ancient hymn and the "Star-Spangled Banner." The folio's wholesale price was $3.13. When the foreign royalties came in to the publisher, they were $40,000 with respect to "At Long Last" and $15,000 with respect to "Better Late Than Never." Both singles had the same amount of air play. "At Long Last" earned writer's performance royalties of $40,000. "Better Late Than Never" was licensed as a commercial for a computer dating service. The fee was $20,000. "At Long Last" was dramatized as a motion picture about a man who is freed after spending one hundred and two years in prison, for which use the publisher received $20,000. Your contract with respect to "Better Late Than Never" was signed by you as it was received from the publisher. You received a copy of this book before you wrote "At Long Last," and the contract for that song was negotiated with benefit of an entertainment lawyer. Your sheet-music royalty with respect to "At Long Last" was 10¢. "Better Late Than Never" was never printed in sheet-music form. Incidentally, your advance for "Better Late Than Never" was $100. Your advance for "At Long Last" was $250. See, I told you to use an entertainment lawyer! (His fee was $500.)

Responding to the sudden success in typical fashion, you have been shopping for a beach house in the Hamptons (or Malibu, if you're L.A.-oriented). You found one you liked for a mere $750,000. The real estate agent asked you how much cash you were prepared to pay. You excused yourself, and, with a stick, you projected in the wet sand of "your beach" your earnings to date from "At Long Last" and "Better Late Than Never." Your response to the real estate agent will be $ —————.

Don't rush! It's a typically unfair law school question! If you get a "C" we will both have done very well. Organization is the key. Let's track each income source.

Enjoy the house! While "Better Late Than Never" will probably bring you little future income, "At Long Last," by virtue of its extensive air play and success as an "A" side single, is probably now an established copyright and should take care of your maintenance problems for many years to come.

Incidentally, if you worked your way through the problem and the solution, give yourself an "A."

Sir Isaac Newton may not have known beans about songwriting, but he sure knew about writers—and people too. His first law of motion, at least the half of it that states that bodies at rest tend to stay at rest, is one that every writer has to wrestle with from time to time; we call it writer's block. Although I had intuited the need for a book such as this, I couldn't overcome Sir Isaac's postulate until I perceived something unique to offer the reader. If this were to be my song, I was desperately in need of a "hook." Well, I could offer experience. Just the thought evoked a cloud of Zs. Then I realized there was something I had that you wanted and couldn't readily obtain: access! I could speak to the people in the music business that you would want to speak to and ask them the questions you would want to ask them and pass on the answers to you. That, I thought, should be worth the price of admission. What questions? The ones that newcomers have been asking me for years seemed appropriate, and some that I've been wondering about myself. In addition to slaking your thirst for knowledge, I'd find out if I had been giving the right answers. I hope they are among the questions you wanted to ask. Marvin Hamlisch's interview, which is contained in Chapter 8, is very perti-

TABLE 2.2

Source of Income	"At Long Last"	"Better Late Than Never"
Sheet Music	15,000 copies × 10¢ royalty rate $ 1,500.00 your royalty Note: The 10¢ royalty was raised from the original 6¢ by your attorney.	Having never been an "A" side hit, no print license was sought or issued.
Matching Folio	$ 3.13 wholesale price × 10% royalty rate $ .313 unit royalty × 30,000 copies sold $ 9,390.00 total writer's royalties × .125* your song's pro-rata share (⅛) $ 1,173.75 your royalty * Your attorney, in negotiating the contract, caused your royalty to be a pro-rata share of the copyrighted songs in the folio, hence the hymn and the "Star-Spangled Banner" were eliminated, reducing the number of songs to eight rather than ten.	$ 3.13 wholesale price × 10% royalty rate $ .313 unit royalty × 30,000 copies sold $ 9,390.00 total writer's royalties × .10* your song's pro-rata share (1/10) $ 939.00 your song's royalty × ½ ** $ 469.50 your royalty * You signed the contract with regard to this song as it was submitted by its publisher, hence your royalty was a pro-rata share of all ten songs, including the hymn and the "Star-Spangled Banner," both of which were in the public domain. ** You wrote this song as a collaborator, hence you receive only one-half of the royalty.
Mechanical Royalties Single	1,000,000 copies × $.0428 *royalty rate $42,800.00 total mechanical royalty × ½ writer's share $21,400.00 your royalty * Remember Larynx insisted on a "rate" and your publisher agreed, hence the 4.28¢ royalty as opposed to the statutory 5.7¢	1,000,000 copies × $.0428 royalty rate $42,800.00 total mechanical royalty × ¼* writer's share $10,700.00 your royalty * The ¼ represents the usual writer's ½ share, halved again by the fact that you had a collaborator. He will receive the other ¼.

TABLE 2.3

Source of Income	"At Long Last"		"Better Late Than Never"	
Mechanical Royalties Album	500,000 × $.0428 $21,400.00 × ½ $ 10,700	copies royalty rate total royalty writer's share your royalty	500,000 × $.0428 $21,400.00 × ¼ $ 5,350.00	copies royalty rate total royalty your ½ of ½ writer's share your royalty
Performance Royalties	$40,000.00 Note: Since ASCAP and BMI pay writers and publishers directly, there is no division of this sum. It was stated as the writer's share, and you keep it all.		$ 00.00 *I hope you fell for the trap and assumed that since the facts stated both singles had the same air play the performance royalties of the two songs would be the same. You didn't? Then you remembered that "Better Late Than Never" was the "B" side of the second single. As such, it received little or no air play (although the "A" side, which was not your song, received the same air play as "At Long Last") and hence no performance royalties.*	
Foreign Royalties	$40,000.00 × ½ $20,000.00	total foreign royalties writer's share your foreign royalties	$15,000.00 × ½ $ 7,500.00 × ½ $ 3,250.00	total foreign royalties writer's share (that damn collaborator again!) your foreign royalties

TABLE 2.3 (Continued)

Source of Income	"At Long Last"	"Better Late Than Never"
Other	$10,000.00 $10,000.00, which represents one-half (writer's share) of the fee for the motion-picture use. This bit of income came under the catchall clause your sagacious attorney had added to your contract.	*None! You signed the form contract submitted by the publisher, which omitted a catchall clause, hence the publisher needn't share with you his fee of $20,000 from the computer dating service. Paradoxically, if your collaborator signed a separate contract with a catchall clause, he would receive $5,000.00*
Total	$104,773.75	$19,769.50
Less advance	$250.00	$100.00
Net income	$104,523.75	$19,669.50
Grand total	$124,193.25	

nent here, and I urge you to skip to it. I just couldn't bring myself to separate Marvin from the stars, where he clearly belongs.

Each of the gentlemen interviewed is a successful writer or music publisher and each is a substantial human being. In their interviews they were not always consistent with each other, or, indeed, with themselves, but they were always sincere and desirous of helping you. Read the interviews included in this chapter and in other chapters for pleasure, enlightenment, and a sense of the flavor of your industry.

INTERVIEW WITH
ROBERT FEAD

Robert Fead, throughout his career, has enjoyed key positions in major record and music-publishing companies. He is now president and chief executive officer of Famous Music.

AHS: You've had a fascinating career, and I would like you to tell our readers, who are really young people aspiring to careers in the music business, your path to the presidency of Famous Music.

FEAD: I initially came to California to work for Liberty Records, which was a small independent record company. After five years at Liberty I joined Jerry Moss and Herb Alpert as the fifth employee of a new upstart record company called A&M Records. I spent about fifteen years with A&M Records, attaining the position of senior vice president and general manager of the company. I then went to work for RCA Records in a new position called division vice president, RCA Records, USA and Canada, basically running the North American record company for RCA. After two and a half years with RCA I moved back to Los Angeles to start a small independent record company called Alfa Records, which was funded at that time by the Yanase Corporation of Japan. It was a brief stint. The timing was off and the economics for independent record companies were inhospitable. The Japanese withdrew before Alfa could be properly launched. At that point I decided that it was time to do some things with my life that I felt comfortable with and became a consultant to various new labels, publishers, and artists. Three years ago I joined Famous Music as its president and chief operating officer.

AHS: I don't want you to be overly modest in response to the next question. Since your tenure began, Famous Music has enjoyed a marked resurgence, winning awards and attaining chart positions unheard of in its long history. Fill us in a little bit on that.

FEAD: Famous is an interesting company. It is an old-line music publishing company, started in 1927 as a spin-off of Paramount Pictures. Famous had been a somewhat inactive company for quite a period of time. It was decided either to reactivate the company to a full-fledged publishing company or to explore the possibility of selling it. Publishing companies were then, as now, selling at premium prices. In the three years that I have been here, we have accomplished several things. Famous Music had never earned a number-one single record that did not come out of a motion picture. In the three years that I have been here, we have had four number-one records that had no motion pictures attached to them. We have won Grammys for an artist called Living Colour. We have increased our visibility in terms of chart and potential chart positions by probably 400 percent. For the first time in the history of the company, we are enjoying success with albums, where we control 90 percent of the copyrights. In the past Famous never had an album that sold in excess of a million records, where it controlled most of the compositions on the album. We have been successful in signing new and developing artists and placing them with labels such as Motown, PolyGram, MCA, CBS, and Giant Records, Irving Azoff's new label.

AHS: What you are saying, if I'm hearing correctly, is that you are signing singer/songwriters to publishing contracts and then placing them with record companies. Is that accurate?

FEAD: It's correct. We are signing either singer/songwriters or artists, Alan, and I think that the role of a music publisher today is to be the A&R face of the future. I think that we must be in the street earlier than the record companies, and we've got to be the first to find the new talent.

AHS: When you say "singer/songwriters or artists," are you signing artists for record deals?

FEAD: Absolutely.

AHS: Ah, so I'm not only interviewing the president of a music publishing company, I am interviewing a record executive.

FEAD: Well, we have been successful in signing three young girls by the name of Triplets to PolyGram Records. They completed their first album. The company was so pleased, they asked them to stay and rerecord it in Spanish. Both of those albums will be released between now and January of 1991. We signed a band called Nixon Pupils out of North Dakota. We placed them also with PolyGram Records. We signed a young group out of New York called Carboy and signed them to MCA Records. They have completed and delivered their first album.

AHS: When you said "we signed them to . . . ," are you the independent producer? Do you stay in the picture, or do you just sign them directly?

FEAD: At this point we have not been in the production business. We just sign the artist, do the publishing arrangement, and then shop the artist to the record labels.

AHS: What a terrific advantage for an aspiring writer/artist!

FEAD: It's an obvious extension of what a publisher should be doing. Probably the most significant signing which we were involved in in placing at the record labels was Martika, who we signed to a songwriting arrangement and then signed to SONY Records. Her second record, "Toy Soldiers," was the number-one record for two weeks. She's enjoyed top-ten records in probably fourteen offshore markets, and she's had four of those. Her next album is being recorded right now to be released in January by SONY.

AHS: Congratulations.

FEAD: We signed a young singer by the name of Demitrius Harvey to Motown Records, and one of our writer/producers, Tena Clark, is producing and writing that album for Motown. We've signed three young girls to Irving Azoff's record label, Giant. The group is called Simply Precious.

AHS: My next question is a little more difficult, a little more loaded, and is in no way a denigration of the service you're performing for the people you do sign. In the book, I sometimes allude to writers who are not also artists as "naked" songwriters, and I make the point in the book that they have a much tougher row to hoe than the artist/songwriter. Do you ever sign writers who don't have potential as artists?

FEAD: Well, you're absolutely right in your assessment, and it's a travesty of this industry that the pure songwriter today is much like a cobbler or a tailor; it's something of a lost art. As you know, most artists are self-contained, and if they're not writing or producing the records, the producer is writing the songs, so to sign a pure songwriter, per se, is probably the most difficult task a publisher faces. We have signed pure songwriters. We've had successes with them and we have also failed miserably. One of the pure writers that we're enjoying a nice degree of success with is a young writer by the name of Thomas Moralda, who we signed in New York City. Thomas is currently represented on the *Days of Thunder* album. He will be represented in the new Cher album for Geffen Records. He will also be represented in Richie Sambora's album with PolyGram, and he is currently writing for the new Stallone film.

AHS: How'd you find him, Bob? How did he get to be signed to your company?

FEAD: I guess we're just one of the few publishers that try to listen to every tape that's sent in to us. He submitted the tape to our New York office, and as a result of that submission we spent some time with Thomas. We listened to more songs and decided that he was someone that we could work with and whose career we hopefully could expand.

AHS: So it is possible for a naked songwriter to make a connection with Famous?

FEAD: It is.

AHS: Let me ask you this, Bob. You say you try to listen to almost every tape that's submitted. I know how difficult it is because just as a lawyer who wrote a book, I am inundated with tapes. I can imagine what comes through your door. Of the tapes that you listen to, I assume some of them are referred to you by attorneys such as myself, managers, accountants, and other people in the business. Do you listen to tapes that really come in "raw," "over the transom," as they used to say in the book industry?

FEAD: Sure.

AHS: You do?

FEAD: We do. It's probably not a normal circumstance in the business as you well know . . .

AHS: I know that.

FEAD: Scripts that come in to film companies are returned because of the potential for legal complications. We're cautious with how we listen, but we generally listen to every tape that comes in. If we find a tape we are particularly enthusiastic about, I make sure that other creative directors and other A&R personnel at Famous Music listen to it also so that everybody generally feels that it's someone we want to involve ourselves with.

AHS: One of the down sides of giving me this interview is that your mail is going to increase.

FEAD: Probably.

AHS: Well, who knows, I may be responsible for your getting a great writer. I'd like to think so.

FEAD: The only thing I can say is that if the mail increases, the cost of repairing the playing equipment will go up too, because we will listen.

AHS: Okay, I think that's the most encouraging language that is going to be contained in this edition of *Breaking In to the Music Business*.

FEAD: Good.

AHS: Do you think it's easier for a naked songwriter today than it was say five years ago?

FEAD: Not at all. There are publishers today who will not consider signing a pure songwriter.

AHS: I know you're right. I wanted to get the answer on the record. Assuming you find a naked songwriter that you're absolutely enamored of, or a singer/songwriter that you have great faith in, and it comes time to cut a deal . . . as you know there are deals and there are DEALS. Lately I've seen new singer/songwriters obtain contracts that years ago only would have been procured by writers with great track records. I see a lot of co-publishing deals where the copyrights revert to the songwriter after ten years, twenty years, or the term of the U.S. copyright. In other words, almost like an administration deal, with no permanent vesting of the copyright. When I first heard of these deals I was in a state of shock, and I'm wondering whether they have become more common in the industry than I'm aware of.

FEAD: Well, I think that every publisher in the negotiation process strives for life of copyright or for perpetuity, and I think that historically that is something that has just been a given. After all, the writer still controls the writer's percent of the publishing income, and under a co-publishing deal he owns half of the copyright and receives half of the publisher's share of income, so it's the publisher who's putting up the money who really ends up with a small portion of ownership and income. What is happening in today's marketplace is simply that some of the people who are negotiating for the writer are insisting upon a reversion of the copyright after a period of time. In today's marketplace, we talk in terms of "renting songs" as opposed to "owning them." The English marketplace in particular is one where the copyrights return in under five years. The solicitors in the U.K. maintain a very hard line on this.

AHS: Well, that's really an administration deal, isn't it, Bob?

FEAD: It is basically becoming an administration deal.

AHS: You know, Max and Louie Dreyfus would turn over in their graves.

FEAD: Of course.

AHS: Do you recognize any trends that are apt to affect young people today?

FEAD: My sense is that we're going to see African rhythms, African beats become more important than they have been. The rap musicians of today are really the street poets of the sixties. I don't know whether this could be considered a trend, but I think that we must find new ways of exposing our art form. Radio is being highly selective in terms of what they play. MTV I think is being more selective in terms of the format of what they're doing. The concert business has been rather soft this year. It's very expensive to put artists on the road, and if you don't have a hit record and if you don't have radio and you don't have MTV supporting you, it's very difficult to find a way to break an artist. A lot of record companies are underwriting a lot of short falls for small tours that work in smaller markets. The cost of doing business has gone up so I think publishers and record companies need to find ways to break records at a different level. That's not a trend, so I got off of that path for a moment.

AHS: But it's interesting anyway.

FEAD: I think that there are a couple of markets that are out there that are not being adequately addressed. I don't think that people are really looking at the baby market, and I don't think people are really addressing the market of thirty-five- to fifty-year-olds. I see this in my own circle. If you're fifty years old today, you grew up on music and it's been a thirty-year experience for you.

AHS: You grew up on melody and lyrics.

FEAD: Right. I think the fifty-year-old of today is a much younger person than the fifty-year-old person of twenty-five or thirty years ago. Music is still a very important part of their lives, and they want to buy music. I don't know what it's like in the rest of the country, but I know that you can go to Tower Records on Sunset Boulevard—and this is a plus for Russ Solomon [president of Tower Records]—and you can't buy Nat Cole CDs on the weekend because they're gone. They're simply sold out.

AHS: You know, I watch what my wife plays on the car cassette player and I see the Tony Bennett records and the Sinatra records and Glenn Miller records and all of the records that we grew up with—and now she's listening to the young guys who are singing the same kind of music.

FEAD: You look at a Harry Connick, Jr., tape . . .

AHS: Exactly. She was playing a Harry Connick tape the other day and some other young performers who were singing melody and lyrics.

FEAD: You look at a Michael Feinstein, you look at a K.D. Lang . . . this young lady has sold a million records without a great deal of airplay and she makes wonderful music! I think of that audience as a trend. I believe the end users, the consumers, want melody today. They want to hear good songs.

AHS: When you said "baby music," what did you mean?

FEAD: I think there's a whole new audience of babies. There's a baby boom going on.

AHS: What age group would you . . . ?

FEAD: Young, very young.

AHS: In years . . . ?

FEAD: I had people here last week with what I thought was a brilliant idea, children's music. They were signed to MCA Records. They're building cassette players into pillows with children's music in them, so that the children go to sleep listening to music. I think it's a brilliant marketing concept. You look at the artists today that record companies are signing, whether it's New Kids on the Block, or Simply Precious, you are looking at kids that are twelve to fifteen years old.

AHS: I have some pictures of my daughter, at age six or seven, standing on her seat at Madison Square Garden, screaming at David Cassidy . . .

FEAD: Sure.

AHS: We used to call that "bubble gum" music.

FEAD: Right. New Kids on the Block have just played to fifty thousand people at Dodger Stadium.

AHS: Okay.

FEAD: The market is from two years to seventy years of age, and music is a very important part of our life.

AHS: Bob, if you could write the specs, since you listen to every demo that comes in, for a songwriter's demo, or a singer/songwriter's demo, what would they be? I am giving you a unique opportunity to perhaps save yourself a lot of listening and a lot of disappointment. Why don't you tell our audience how they stand the best chance of getting your interest?

FEAD: Well, I think the first thing is to use professional equipment, and if the opportunity presents itself, to use a professional recording studio. As far as I'm concerned, as a music publisher, I don't think I need to hear more than four songs. I think that if you send me a tape with twelve songs on it, I'm gonna get bored. If you give me three to four songs, you had better hook me on the first song! That means that you have to come out of the box with your guns loaded and give me the best thing you have with the first cut because if it doesn't get me at the first blush I may not get to two, three, or four. Don't give me different styles of music. We already have Madonna. We have Michael Bolton and we have Joe Cocker, so I don't need to be listening to people who want to be a sound-alike. Originality is terribly important in this business.

AHS: I would swear that you read the book! It's reassuring to have verification. You sound to me like a man who enjoys what he is doing.

FEAD: I do.

INTERVIEW WITH
MAURY YESTON

Maury Yeston is a Tony Award–winning author and composer. Among his credits are *Nine: The Musical* and *Grand Hotel*. He is also the director of the prestigious BMI Music Theater Workshop.

AHS: Maury, begin at the beginning.

YESTON: I began playing and writing music when I was about six years old. Even then I was always writing songs and when I was taking classical piano lessons I was always making up my own compositions as well. I very soon fell in love with jazz and started picking up jazz improvisation. Because I was born in 1945 I lived through the early growth of not only the mainstream jazz of the fifties and sixties, but also the ascent of rock 'n' roll and rhythm and blues. So, when you combine classical music, rhythm and blues, the classical period of rock 'n' roll, and the great period of American jazz, you have virtually every stream of music represented, including the great period of folk music in the late fifties and early sixties. I was into all of that as well. I loved picking up music by ear so much that when I was taking my classical music lessons, starting at about six years old, the teacher used to assign the next Mozart sonata for the following week and I would say, "Play it for me." So he'd play it and I'd play it back for him the next week by ear. Because of that I was a lousy sight reader. I hardly ever looked at the music. I used my ear and I know a lot of young musicians who work with their gifted ears. That's an example of your talent getting in your way, because then you never confront and master reading.

AHS: What you've just said really smacks somewhat of prodigy. Do I sense prodigy here?

YESTON: I don't think so. Well, I don't know. When I was seven I won a local composition award. Maybe people thought I was—I didn't think I was—a prodigy. I used to play the piano a lot and I guess my technique was pretty good for my age. At the age of twelve or thirteen something happened to me that changed all that. My parents took me to see *My Fair Lady* and I immediately knew that I wanted to write Broadway shows. That show knocked my socks off. Just the theatricality, the people singing on the stage, everything about it, convinced me that that's what I wanted to do. I abandoned classical music training at that point.

AHS: ... with opposition from the family?

YESTON: No, they understood completely ... I had their blessing. I started playing what was called pop music at the time. I learned the fake book by heart and I used to go out and play club dates.

AHS: How old were you when you started playing club dates?

YESTON: Oh, I started playing club dates when I was fifteen. My time was divided between club dates and rock and continued interest in classical music. I was from Jersey City and I used to play jam sessions in the basements of black churches where I met a lot of very superb black musicians from what might be called the "inner city." I even bought myself a set of vibes at that time and played the vibraphone for a while.

AHS: A Jewish Lionel Hampton?

YESTON: Yes, that's exactly who I thought I was. I was hardly tall enough to play it. I had to kind of stand on my toes to play the vibes. But all of those early experiences created a very catholic kind of music taste and palette in me, and they also eliminated any possibility that I can ever be a musical snob. To me, good music is good music. Great music is great music, no matter where it comes from. I think that early experience of having a catholic interest in all of the styles of music conditioned my current career, because I live in many different musical worlds at once and I am kind of a communicator between worlds of music that ordinarily have had walls between them. I've been in a situation where I've been a Yale professor teaching very high-level graduate courses in music theory ...

AHS: Let me interrupt for a moment. We have you through puberty and now you're a Yale professor ... Let's discuss the interim, because that's where most of my readers are.

YESTON: Well, finally it was time to apply to college and one of the places I thought I might be interested in going to was Juilliard, because I was very interested in becoming a composer. So I went for a Juilliard interview and the interviewer asked me what I wanted to do. I told him, "Well, I want to write music," and he said, "Are there any special kinds of compositions that you are interested in?" I said, "I want to write all kinds of music, but I have a problem in that I am not a very good sight reader." Well, he got furious at me. He said, "How dare you apply to Juilliard and say that you are not a very good sight reader! If we were a school teaching playwriting and you were William Shakespeare and you came in here and said, 'I don't know the alphabet very well,' do you think we should accept you?" And of course I said, "Well, Shakespeare was a really great writer. Yeah, you should definitely do it."

AHS: [laughing] Don't blow it.

YESTON: [also laughing] Yeah. So I didn't apply to Juilliard. I applied to various colleges and one of the places I got into was Yale. When I got into Yale my advisor was the head of the music department. I told him, "Gee, I want to compose music but I'm not a very good sight reader." I remember what he told me because I have told the same things to so many of my own students at Yale. He said, "Well, if you want to be a composer, all you have to do is write music and you are one. If you don't write music you're not one."

AHS: Writers write.

YESTON: Yes, writers write. He said, "That's the first thing. The second thing is that if you are not a very good sight reader, learn. There are only five lines."

AHS: [appreciative laugh]

YESTON: . . . and that's exactly what I did. I went and learned immediately. I thrived at Yale. I wrote musicals and I studied composition and I studied everything else under the sun, because I believe that you have to develop yourself as a person in order to be a writer. You are always writing about people and you're writing about human experience and you're writing about life and you're reflecting your own life in your work, even if it's abstract work like music. You're accessing your emotions. Any writer who has had any experience knows the difference between busy work, or what might be called "work thoroughly for craft," and work that has a personal meaning to you. Richard Rodgers, before he died, explained to me that you have to try to cut straight down into your bone. It has to matter to you in some way when you write. I find that it's a terribly important component of writing. Since the best things that you write reflect your life and reflect your experiences and reflect your perception and experience of other people, you have to be aware in order to have something to say.

AHS: I'm going to interrupt you for one second because this will be of interest to the young people who are going to read this. I would gather from what you've said that you consider a formal education, if it's available, of benefit.

YESTON: It's essential. It's absolutely essential. You have to have a formal education because there comes a time when you get your first, wonderful, inspirational idea, and the song that you're writing, or the piece that you are writing, is 65 percent accomplished, but there are problems with it. You have to have another side of you that can look at your own work, as a critic, and say, "What's wrong and how do I fix it?" You have to be able to understand that the art of writing is the art of rewriting. It's formal education that will enable you to stand back from your work and understand what you are doing, so that your work isn't writing you, but you're controlling it. What you have to do is find a way of learning the elements of music. If that means finding an experienced piano player who will sit down and show you what the names of the chords are, fine. If that means going to your local library and taking out a couple of books, elementary books, on the elements of music, which are available everywhere, fine. Anybody can do that and this kind of knowledge is available to everybody. We can't speak to each other unless we can communicate and speak a language, and music, like everything else in the world, has a technical language. It's not complicated and it can be learned. You just have to go out and get a couple of books and find a couple of experienced people who will show you. What's great about the world of music is that you can always find musicians who are willing to explain things to young people. As a general principle, as a general rule, the musical world is made up of people who do share their knowledge and who do share their talent and who love to show other people how to do things.

AHS: And of course if you can get a college education and go to Juilliard, so much the better.

YESTON: If you can get a college education and go to Juilliard that's fine, but let me tell you something. Most of the great writers in the world who have written the greatest things that were written in the world, who have made more money than most other people in the world writing music, and have brought more happiness and pleasure through music to more people in the world—most of those people didn't go to Juilliard.

AHS: Now, you're at Yale and you're studying . . .

YESTON: Now, I'm at Yale as an undergraduate and I'm studying and I'm writing every kind of music in the world. I'm writing songs. I'm writing musicals and I'm writing orchestral music. I wrote a very big cello concerto for a huge orchestra and it won a big prize at Yale and that, combined with other things, enabled me to win a fellowship that sent me to England for two years. I should say that that cello concerto was written in 1967. Its first performance was in 1977. It was premiered by Yo-Yo Ma, who is, I guess, our greatest living cellist, with a big orchestra, but it took ten years to get a performance, so one of the things that you have to learn is . . . patience. Another thing you have to learn is: it's one thing to want to write music and it's another thing to make a living. Any reasonable person who wants to have a career in the music business had better understand that you have to have a day gig. You have to find a way of paying the rent, buying the food and putting it on the table, while you are busy occupying yourself, developing your musical career. Very few people get lucky enough to have a hit song the first time out and live on it until they have another one. In my case, my day job was teaching, because I reasoned, and I planned it very carefully, that teaching is a profession in which they don't pay you a tremendous amount of money, but they do pay you a tremendous amount of time. There's no school in the summertime, you have Christmas and Easter off, you have the weekends, and if you're teaching in a university situation, or something like that, you have even more extra time. If you're a teacher you have some spare time to pursue another career. You have time to write. That's not to say that you don't have time to write doing other things, but teaching is a particularly good way.

AHS: We have many good writers who are musicians, who wait on tables, drive cabs.

YESTON: Absolutely.

AHS: I don't think there's any vocation that I haven't heard of as an interim source of income.

YESTON: But in my case that was my plan. I wanted to teach at a university level, so I got a Ph.D. in music theory and I was very fortunate that my Ph.D. dissertation was immediately published as a textbook by Yale University Press, and I was appointed to the Yale faculty. Very soon I was basically in charge of the whole undergraduate program. I was supervising music majors and supervising composers.

AHS: How old were you?

YESTON: I was at that time twenty-eight.

AHS: Very young.

YESTON: I was very young. While I was doing that I was writing a new project called *Nine: The Musical,* based on Fellini's movie *8½,* and within a few years the Eugene O'Neill Foundation awarded it a stage reading at their summer conference. When *Nine* was given its staged reading it attracted a tremendous amount of attention. I really should go backwards, because something happened in the late sixties that really did change my life. I was in Cambridge, England, at Clare College, squirreled away from the whole world behind the walls of a school that was built in 1350. I opened up a copy of *Newsweek* and read that there was a Broadway producer by the name of David Black who was producing a new musical based on *Alice in Wonderland.* Now I had written a musical version of *Alice in Wonderland* in college, and I very much wanted my score to be considered by this man. I didn't know whether he had writers. So I wrote to him and said that I had read about his project in *Newsweek* and that I had written the score for *Alice in Wonderland*, and if he was ever in England, I'd like to come to London and play it for him. He wrote me back and said that he would be coming to London in about a month and that he already had some writers, but that he would like to hear my work. I met him in London. I played him my songs. He was very helpful. He said, "I like your material very much. Unfortunately, I already have two writers who are writing my score, but I think you have talent and when you get back to America, in New York there is a workshop for people who write musicals called the BMI Music Theater Workshop. It's run by a man named Lehman Engel. You write to Lehman Engel and tell him I recommended that you go there." That changed my life. I applied to the BMI Music Theater Workshop and I was accepted, and Lehman Engel taught me how to write musicals in that workshop. He also taught Ed Kleban, who wrote *A Chorus Line*, how to write musicals. He taught Alan Menken and Howard Ashman how to write musicals. They wrote *Little Shop of Horrors* and *Little Mermaid*. In many cases he suggested that people who, prior to their entrance in the workshop, worked with lyricists to write their own lyrics. He convinced me to write my own lyrics. He convinced Ed to write his own lyrics. Kleban ultimately wrote the lyrics to *A Chorus Line*. He started out as a composer. Every year BMI showcases the best material written in the workshop at the Edison Theater. That's how my work first was exposed to the whole entertainment industry in 1975–1976. While I was still a graduate student, my songs were shown to all the producers and the agents and writers . . .

AHS: And what goes around comes around because you are now . . .

YESTON: I am now head of the Advanced BMI Music Theater Workshop. Lehman died, and I took over teaching. I have very, very gifted people in that workshop who are now writing shows that are about to appear on Broadway.

AHS: And I think that if this book enjoys success, you'll get a lot more applications. You told me at a cocktail party, many months ago, how Alan Jay Lerner was a factor in your career . . .

YESTON: Oh, he certainly was. He certainly was.

AHS: I'm jumping the gun again. We have you as a Ph.D. aspirant. You were writing *Nine* and . . .

YESTON: Writing *Nine* and it was being showcased. I had written another show based on the first five books of the Bible. The working title of it was "One, Two, Three, Four, Five." It was showcased and it got the attention of Herman Levin, who was the producer of *My*

Fair Lady. He called me and said he wanted to produce my show. Of course, I met with him and I began to work with him. He was very close to Alan Jay Lerner, naturally, and one day he said to me, "Alan Jay Lerner really should hear this score," and he picked up the phone. Lerner had an office downstairs from him in the same building and he came up and heard my work. As a result he said to me, "I would like you to come to me from time to time and play me your things, and I will give you criticism." He said that in his own case Oscar Hammerstein said that to him and used to give him criticism. I was very honored that almost a kind of baton was being passed from lyricist to lyricist and it never has ceased to amaze me how professional writers, particularly in the world of theater, nurture each other and nurture the young writers. So, I would say to any writer who aspires to write Broadway music and Broadway shows, that if you get yourself noticed and if you get your work up to a certain quality, you can really be assured of the interest and the help of the professional theatrical community. Sheldon Harnick has also given me a tremendous amount of advice and encouragement. Ed Kleban really functioned as my big brother in this business, and I'd like to think that I do that for young writers as well.

AHS: You wrote *Nine.* Music and lyrics?

YESTON: Music and lyrics. And created the show.

AHS: It was very successful.

YESTON: It won the Tony Award as Best Musical of 1982, and I won the Tony Award for Best Music and Lyrics.

AHS: And now you are an established Broadway writer. What do you do after that?

YESTON: Well, you write your next show. Right now as we speak, my work in *Grand Hotel* has been nominated. I was nominated for another Tony and two Drama Desk Awards for my contributions to that score.

AHS: That's one where you were called in more or less as a collaborator.

YESTON: As a play doctor, but I ended up writing and rewriting about half the score. It was a fantasy come true. I was sitting in my home one day and my telephone rang. It was Tommy Tune on the phone from Boston. *Grand Hotel* had just received not very good reviews in its previews in Boston. He said, "This is Tune. I've got a room for you at the Ritz-Carlton Hotel with a piano. Come to Boston and save the show."

AHS: Which you promptly did.

YESTON: Well, I promptly went to help. It was a very exciting experience, and I guess what I would say to young writers reading this is: one of the primary rules for opportunity is that you have to be ready when the opportunity strikes. You can't say: "Oh, when I get that opportunity I'll tend to my craft." You have to be ready with the goods when you get the call. That's terribly important. You don't write one song and spend your life trying to get it published. You write your next song.

AHS: There is something that you haven't mentioned and that was *Goya* . . . and CBS . . .

YESTON: Well, actually what happens is, once you establish yourself as a theatrical writer people think of you in those terms, but I have had numerous other experiences. For example, earlier in my career, in the mid-seventies, when the George Lucas organization and RSO Records wanted to cause to be created a *Star Wars* Christmas record, the producer of the record was having a great deal of difficulty collecting material. He had polled a lot of writers, who wrote songs that thematically mentioned *Star Wars* in one way or another, but he did not have a record that made sense as a whole, because it had characters and it needed a story. I was very fortunate in that when he came to me I suggested that the record really be treated like a musical, and I ended up writing about three-quarters of the record. One of the songs from it, "What Can You Get a Wookie for Christmas When He Already Owns a Comb?", turned out to be a moderate radio hit. That was really my first hit on the radio. It's a good example of . . .

AHS: What is a "wookie"?

YESTON: A "wookie" is a big furry beast from the *Star Wars* movie. The wookie was a favorite character, big and covered with hair.

AHS: Just for the benefit of those who may not be familiar with the wookie, such as myself.

YESTON: A whole generation, I guess, knows what a wookie is. But, in the case of that particular recording, when we did the demo, I wrote a song for the robots to sing and when we did the demo I kind of made my voice like a bunch of robots. When we went to do the recording the producers of the record couldn't find anybody who could make quite that sound, so I actually ended up beginning my recording career at that time. I am those robots! But, there's a good example of the cross-fertilization of the music. Here I was a Yale professor at the time. I was supervisor to all of the undergraduate majors. I was on the one hand working in what might be called a very high-level artistic classical world of music, and on the weekends I was driving down to New York and singing like a robot on a pop record about a popular movie. It's always been my function in the world of music to be in a lot of different worlds at once and to modulate between them. That's why I have enjoyed my career so much, and I would advise anybody else to be very flexible and to hang very loose, too. So that really was my first experience breaking into recording technology and recording technique, and

as a result, the producers of a new musical based on the life of
Goya approached me to write a musical based on the life of the
great Spanish painter Francisco Goya, starring Placido Domingo.
When we realized it would be some time before Mr. Domingo
might be available for the theater, that's when I readily suggested
that we consider doing a recording first. Because I had had a very
good experience, not only in the *Star Wars* recording, but also with
recording *Nine: The Musical*. So I was very fortunate that a project
came my way which played directly to my strong suits. I first went
to the Yale library and as scholar learned everything I could about
the great Spanish painter, Goya. I was working with the greatest
living opera singer of our time, probably the greatest male voice on
the planet, Placido Domingo, so I had an opportunity to marshal
everything I had learned from the world of classical music, from
the world of opera, from the world of bel canto and apply it to
another world that I knew and loved deeply, which was the world
of musical theater. Here was my chance to find a way for millions
of young people to hear for the first time Placido Domingo in a
new context, in a popular context. As that project developed, we
eventually brought in Dionne Warwick, Gloria Estefan, Richie
Havens, and the talents of Phil Ramone as a record producer, and
ended up creating an initial introduction of the score in a way that
had never been done before in an intrinsically popular way. Subsequent to that, one of the love duets from *Goya* actually became
a big radio hit.

AHS: " 'Til I Loved You" with Barbra Streisand and Don Johnson.

YESTON: " 'Til I Loved You." Absolutely. It became a big hit. So when we
ultimately present this show it will have a song in it that's already
been a hit on the radio, which is a very big plus. Even as we speak,
I believe that record is about to be released in Spanish. One of the
things I would also advise young people who want to break into
the various aspects of writing in the music business is to understand that each area of the music business is different. For example, my work in scoring film has been very interesting. I have
worked a lot with young filmmakers. My first job was with a man
who came to me and said, "I'm making my first experimental film
and would like you to do the score." Now, I had never done the
score to a movie before. And I thought, no matter how much he's
paying I can learn from this and get some experience. I scored the
film for flute, harp, double bass, cello, and classical guitar. It was
a little film about fifteen minutes long called *Ripe Strawberries*. In
the film was a young actor who was very talented by the name of
Raul Julia. I think I probably made about fifty dollars from this
movie, but as it turned out the film won a few awards and it began
to be played in theaters. Then it was picked up by HBO and

Showtime, and it still appears from time to time on cable network. It's being played for millions of people and it's a very nice credit for me. I'm very proud that it was my first film score. But the lesson there is sometimes you work to learn and you never really know what's going to see the light of day. Good work always has a way of seeing the light of day. In the case of recordings, I was very fortunate when I began writing *Goya* that I had very talented producers, but I didn't know when I started writing a Broadway show that I was going to have recording artists like Richie Havens and Gloria Estefan and Dionne Warwick appear on the record in addition to Placido Domingo. When that happened I was there, ready to make changes and ready to change the nature of the material to suit the people who were in it. In the case of Broadway shows you have to understand that no one person can do it by themselves. It's always a collaboration. No matter how talented a music or lyric writer you are, you still need a playwright, you still need a director, you still need a lighting designer, you still need producers. Broadway shows now cost upwards of 4, 5, 6 million dollars and they're very risky. You are constantly in a situation where even if you do your best work, you rely on other people and their abilities. I started writing *Nine* in 1973. It finally appeared on Broadway in 1982. I started writing the other show I told you about . . .

AHS: You had a day job?

YESTON: Yeah, I had a day job. I started writing *1-2-3-4-5* in 1976. Larry Gelbart joined the project as a book writer in the mid 1980s, and we still haven't seen our first official New York production, but we look forward to it. Here's a story that may have a very interesting ending that we don't know yet. Several years ago I was approached, together with Arthur Kopit, the famous American playwright, by a Broadway producer, who had an idea of creating a musical based on the *Phantom of the Opera*. He paid us a reasonable sum of money, and we wrote a book and a score to the *Phantom of the Opera* which we were very proud of. Geoffrey Holder, the noted director, was engaged to direct the show, and we began to do backers auditions in an attempt to raise money to produce the show. Just before we began to do our backers auditions, Andrew Lloyd Webber, the noted English composer, announced that he had an interest in writing a score based on the *Phantom of the Opera*. Since the *Phantom of the Opera* was in the public domain, that is to say, nobody had exclusive rights to it, anybody could do it. He proceeded with his project. The mere rumor that that very powerful and influential and important composer Andrew Lloyd Webber was going to write a *Phantom of the Opera* was enough to dry up sources of support for the American version that had already been written. I was of course disappointed, but that is part of the business—and it's a very important part of the business.

AHS: That's an interesting story.

YESTON: Now, curiously enough, a group of theaters is very interested in putting on my version of the *Phantom of the Opera*. So in the final analysis I may see a presentation of my work.

AHS: You may have a few more complications from a legal point of view.

YESTON: No, I don't think so. But, you never know. I also have the option of taking a lot of the music that I wrote for this project and putting it in another project. Alan Jay Lerner told me once that *Gigi* was based on three songs that were left over from *My Fair Lady*, and when I looked quite surprised at that, he looked back at me and said, "Well, they're both Cinderella stories," which is true. There are numerous cases of songs that appear in musicals which had actually been written for other functions in prior musicals. One of the nice things about music is that it's a very malleable commodity. With different words and with a different treatment it can have different effects. A very famous story is the story of "Somewhere Over the Rainbow." When Harold Arlen and Yip Harburg first wrote "Over the Rainbow" they played it for their film producer in Hollywood, and he rejected the song because Arlen played a very ornate, over-embellished version on the piano. A lot of very fast-moving accompaniment notes. After the producer said, "I'm not sure I like this song," they said, "Wait a minute, perhaps we haven't presented it right." Then Arlen presented it with a very simple, spare accompaniment, and of course everybody fell in love with the song at that point and the rest is history.

AHS: A few questions. Do you ever feel resentful of singer/songwriters who have a platform for the song they write . . .

YESTON: No, not at all.

AHS: . . . including their own record?

YESTON: No, you can't do that. I don't feel resentful of singer/songwriters in the same way that I don't feel resentful of the ocean that makes waves that flow in and out on the beach. It's the nature of the world. The world changes. You have to accept reality and work with it. It used to be that songwriters wrote songs and music publishers took these songs and placed them with recording artists who did not write songs and who needed songs. That situation started changing in the 1950s through the 1970s, and as a result you find a minority of artists who don't write their own material, although it goes in cycles. These days there are many artists who are looking for songs all the time. And even some singer/songwriters who have awakened to the idea that if they record other people's good work as well as their own good work they may have a better batting average. I don't resent them at all.

AHS: Do you think you might be less gracious if you didn't have a talent for conceiving and writing shows and if all that was left to you was . . .

YESTON: I might not be in this business if all that were left to me was writing songs for the recording industry alone. I don't think I would ever put all of my eggs in one basket like that. I would probably spend a good deal of my time being a record producer.

AHS: Trying to get cut-ins on the songs.

YESTON: Exactly. I think young writers ought to understand that it's a very, very difficult undertaking to make a career *only* as a songwriter aiming for AM radio. That is a very difficult career. How often can you have a hit, really and truly?

AHS: I'm kind of glad you said that because it's one of the premises of this book that a naked songwriter starts off with a disadvantage.

YESTON: Yes, you have a tremendous disadvantage if that's what you are doing. You really have to branch out, either perform your own work as a recording artist or have an opportunity to do a lot of different things. For example, one of my students at BMI is a very gifted theater writer, and we were visited by a representative of the Disney organization who hired her as a staff writer, writing for the Disney Channel and writing for various Walt Disney projects. There's an example of a writer who worked at her craft assiduously and whose talent was recognized.

AHS: That's very unusual today because very rarely do you have staff writers. In the old days, when I broke into the business, staff writers were very common.

YESTON: That's right. They were everywhere, with publishers all the time. We may return to that world, but I think that anybody wanting to break into the business ought to understand the following: the world will have its music with you or without you. It's been my experience that cream rises to the top. If you work hard, if you keep an open mind, if you keep learning all the time, and if you have access to places where people who are looking for music can hear your work, then you have a fighting chance at pursuing a career as a writer in the music business. It could be that the song that you think is going to be a hit never gets recorded and something else that you think less of catches somebody's attention and just happens to fit . . . events that you have no control over. Let's look at a song like "Tie a Yellow Ribbon," which I believe had already been a hit. During the Iran hostage crisis, people began to tie yellow ribbons around trees and as a result the song came back on the radio as a monster hit. It made a great deal of money for the authors.

Perhaps this is a good place to talk about why it's not a good idea simply to imitate what was just successful. If you write a song, it's going to take a while before somebody else hears it. It's going to take a while before it's recorded, and it's going to take a while to be distributed. If you imitate something that you just heard on the radio, by the time your imitation sees the light of day, it may be a year later. You cannot predict the future. You can't chase the market. All you can do is do your best work and hope that your best work attracts attention. To put it another way, there is a school of thought that says you cannot write a popular song. You can write a wonderful song and if you're fortunate it becomes a popular song.

AHS: You're a Ph.D. You're obviously terribly articulate, very very bright. How hip are you with regard to the business aspects of your work?

YESTON: Oh, you have to be very. I keep up with it all the time and I read every publication, not only *BMI* magazine, but *Dramatists Guild Quarterly, Billboard, Variety.* This is, after all, your business and you must understand that if you are writing music you are in show business and show business is two words. There's the "show" and there's also the "business," and business carries with it all the trappings and all of the elements—the good ones and the bad ones—of capitalism. You'd better familiarize yourself with what those trappings are. Let me put it another way: when you create a song, as the writer, you own it, lock, stock, and barrel . . . you own all of the publisher's rights, you own every penny that will accrue to that song from mechanical sales, every penny that will accrue to that song from play on the radio, every penny that will accrue to that song from some grand right through its performance in the theater. If you're not prepared however in some way to share part of that money with other people, who for a share of that money will enhance the value of that song, then you're not thinking practically and you're not thinking clearly. Everybody is trying to make a living and so you have to understand that if somebody is willing to take that song and represent it and work it, and try to get other people to record it and protect it and make sure that the copyright is not infringed, and print it and distribute it, they're not doing that for their health. They're doing that for something.

AHS: You've just lead me to my next question. You've gone down almost my whole list and I haven't had to ask you a question What is your perception of the role of the music publisher today? A lot of writers today consider it an anachronism. They think, Well, I can get my performance income directly from BMI, the record company will pay me my mechanical income. Why do I have to give a publisher a share of the copyright or a share of the income? What are they going to do for me?

YESTON: It depends. There are many people and organizations that call themselves music publishers. We live in a very big world, which is now becoming bigger. It used to be that the Soviet Union and the Eastern Bloc countries did not recognize the international copyright conference. It used to be that people could go and perform your work in those areas of the world and you would never get paid. People think, mistakenly, that music is free because it's in the air. Music is not free and it should not be free. One of the fundamental functions of a music publisher is to give you arms and legs in places of the world that you couldn't dream of. Let me give you an example. A version of my show, *Nine: The Musical* was produced in Australia. It toured Sydney, Melbourne, Adelaide, and Perth. It did extremely well. I was invited to Australia by the company to the Sydney premiere and when I got there they showed me with great pride the Australian cast album, which they had produced and distributed illegally, without any permission. It was ultimately the job of my music publisher to correct that inequity. A music publisher today who can represent you and collect your money and see to your interests in Tokyo, Rio de Janeiro, Amsterdam, London, Paris, Sydney, is absolutely essential to what has now become the international character of the music business. To call yourself a publisher and simply say "I'm going to collect my BMIs" is to misunderstand the ability that a good publisher has to collect money that you never knew existed and enhance the value of your copyright over the long run. Now mind you I am talking about a publisher who actually will work with you by making good deals with foreign subpublishers, disseminating your music, and continually getting more cover records for you.

AHS: When I met you today you were absolutely bubbling over with enthusiasm over a folio that you had just received.

YESTON: Yes, that's right. The folio for *Grand Hotel*, the musical, which is just extraordinary. It is not only a book that carries my music from the show, it's also got photographs in full color of the original Broadway show so that people who have never seen the show will have a sense of what it looks like. Here's an example of the music publisher doing a favor for the producers of the show who really don't even have an interest in the music publishing. But this will send people to buy tickets to see this show.

AHS: . . . and then they'll buy the record . . .

YESTON: And they'll buy the record, etc., and the process never stops. Somebody once told me that a piece of music copyright is the only thing in the universe that keeps getting more valuable the more it's used.

AHS: Do you own your own copyrights? Do you share them?

YESTON: I own my own copyrights and I pay a fee to a publisher to administrate those copyrights. I have been very fortunate in that my negotiating strength has been such that I have been able to do that. Were it not such, I would quite readily make any reasonable deal that would stimulate and give an incentive to an organization to profit by selling my music.

AHS: I know you have an attorney because I banged heads with him in an adversarial sense when you were one of the parties and I represented your adversary. Are there other professionals involved in your career? Manager? Producer?

YESTON: No, there's an agent. It's terribly important. I am very fortunate that my agent is one of the most prominent theatrical agents in the world.

AHS: Give her a plug.

YESTON: Her name is Flora Roberts. She represents Stephen Sondheim. She represents Alfred Uhry, who has just won a Pulitzer Prize. She represents numerous wonderful clients. She is a terribly important person in my career. But, there again, I never regarded that it was her job to get me work. I always regarded that it's my job to be a self-starter; that just as my old professor told me, "If you want to be a composer, you have to write." I don't wait to see if she gets somebody who wants me to write something. I wake up every morning in a disciplined way and say: "What will I write today?" I am invariably working on more than one thing.

AHS: You work every day?

YESTON: I work everyday.

AHS: If something does come your way, what does stimulate you to write?

YESTON: Something has just recently happened to me that I am very proud of. Carnegie Hall is going to be 100 years old next year. Carnegie Hall has commissioned me to write a series of songs in honor of its centennial. They've also commissioned from other people a symphony, a piece of chamber music, and an opera, but in the area of cabaret song, they have given me this commission. I am working very assiduously.

AHS: What a wonderful opportunity.

YESTON: Thank you. What I am writing for it is a song cycle. I'm writing a series of songs that are linked, not only by musical style, but also by the story that the lyrics tell. This is a form created by Franz Schubert, and yet I am writing it in a modern style . . . another opportunity to combine various worlds of music that I love so much. I am writing kind of a classical song cycle, but I am writing it in a Broadway cabaret style.

AHS: You sound like you're having a wonderful time doing what you're doing.

YESTON: I am having a wonderful time. There is, as I've pointed out elsewhere in this interview, always heartache involved in any profession, but the heartache will only be a large percentage if the work that you've written hasn't yet been performed. Yes, that's hard and that's frustrating, but compared to the hard frustrations of other kinds of careers—doctors who lose patients—I think that the frustrations of being a creative writer can be lived with.

AHS: You have children, don't you?

YESTON: Oh, yes.

AHS: How many?

YESTON: Two sons.

AHS: Do they show talent?

YESTON: They're both very, very gifted musically. Yes, very.

AHS: And you would recommend to them the pursuit of the music profession?

YESTON: I would neither encourage nor discourage them. I think anybody who wants to pursue a career in music has to be told the grim realities: a very small percentage who try actually succeed in supporting themselves full-time with revenues from music. You have to understand that. In fact, there was a time when my family tried to talk me out of this. They marshaled an uncle of mine, who was very well-spoken, to have a talk with me about it. He said to me, "If you want to succeed as a writer of music you have to be one of a very few number of people." Then he said, "But I would like to point out to you that business is still one of the only professions where you can be perfectly mediocre and make a very good living."

AHS: [laughing] On that note I think that we'll conclude this. Thank you so much.

YESTON: You're welcome.

INTERVIEW WITH
MILTON OKUN

Milton Okun, producer of, among other artists, Peter, Paul and Mary, John Denver, and Placido Domingo, is also the founder of the Cherry Lane group of music publishing companies.

AHS: Milt, what criteria do you take into account in evaluating a writer's merit or worth?

OKUN: Just talent. In the case of the music, I look to see whether writers show individuality and creativity in composition or whether they merely use formula melodies and formula chords. I look for original ideas and for a sense of structure in both the lyrics and the music. If a writer can structure a song so that it has a beginning, a development, and an end, even if I don't like that particular song or the idea of the song, I know that it is written by a good writer. I am interested in good ideas and interesting development.

AHS: I remember once, a long time ago, I played an artist for you and you asked me how old he was. When I told you I thought he was twenty-seven or twenty-eight, you said, "If he can't tune his guitar by now, forget it." That always stuck in my mind.

OKUN: Right. I think for a singer or a musician there are certain elementary musical qualities that are needed to be a professional, and it would be hopeless for someone who doesn't have an ear for tuning an instrument to become a singer or an instrumentalist.

AHS: But I think perhaps you and two other people in the world would have noticed that the guitar was a little bit out of tune.

OKUN: Wrong.

AHS: Wrong?

OKUN: Most professionals are not perfectly in tune, and while I have a good ear, I would not have made that comment if the guitar was not grossly out of tune.

AHS: How relatively important is it to you that a writer also be an artist or a potential artist?

OKUN: Well, from my point of view as a record producer, obviously it would be much better to find a writer who is potentially a strong performer. I think, however, that people who have real writing and composing ability shouldn't be discouraged if they are not performers. It makes it a little tougher in the current musical scene to be a writer only, but if a writer has talent, that's the important thing.

AHS: How many of the writers who submit cassettes to you, or whom you have come across in your day-to-day business, are trained in music? How many of them actually know music notation?

OKUN: I don't think that knowing music is a prerequisite for being a good writer or performer, because I don't think that there is a much higher representation of trained musicians than nontrained musicians among songwriters. I get many cassettes from people who are good musicians, but most come from people who have no musical training. Training doesn't help if there is no talent or creativity. It is just that a person who can write good songs will be able to do more with his talent if he has a knowledge of sight reading, notation, and harmony. It makes the job easier if one has a sound basis in musical skills.

AHS: Does Cherry Lane ever hire staff writers on a salary basis, and what is your attitude in general towards the economics of dealing with fledgling writers?

OKUN: Cherry Lane is basically a company that works in tandem with my production activities. I do enough production, and we have enough writers without hiring staff writers, to have all that we can handle as far as promotion and development of material is concerned. We don't want to get into the mass business of signing writers and developing more copyrights than we can efficiently work, because we believe we have a big responsibility to our writers that must be fulfilled. However, since we're so strongly oriented towards record production, our situation may be unusual. Probably most other publishing companies are looking for talented new writers.

AHS: It seems to me that what you just indicated was that you would be much more disposed towards a writer who is also an artist at this stage than you would if he were not an artist.

OKUN: Yes, I guess for us that is the case.

AHS: To what extent is the source of material that is submitted to you a factor? In other words, if something comes in unsolicited, what is the likelihood of its being carefully listened to, assessed, and evaluated, as opposed to material that is sent to you by producers or lawyers or people in the business? Do you actually listen to all the stuff that comes in?

OKUN: No, I can't. I don't think I have ever found a viable piece of material that was submitted by an amateur writer. In recent years, I haven't gone through unsolicited tapes, but in my early years, when I started working with Harry Belafonte, one of my responsibilities was to go through all the songs submitted to him. I went through thousands and not one song ever got far enough to be recorded. Then, after Belafonte, while working with folk groups like The Brothers Four, The Chad Mitchell Trio, and Peter, Paul and Mary, I listened to hundreds and hundreds of submissions, and while I liked a number of the songs and presented some of them to the artists, somehow they were dropped along the way. As far as I can remember, no unsolicited song has ever been recorded through my efforts. However, when I came across a writer who I believed had talent, even though I didn't like the particular song he may have sent me, I encouraged him to write more and send me other work. Sometimes, that would pay off and I would get some songs that I liked.

AHS: What is the policy now at Cherry Lane with respect to unsolicited material? A lot of people are afraid of infringement claims and rather than run the risk of . . .

OKUN: We're not afraid of infringement claims. I don't think we have ever had one. But that's not the reason for discouraging writers from sending unsolicited material. We know from years of experience how little chance there is of receiving anything usable that way. Our policy at Cherry Lane is to return all tapes from unknown sources without opening them. If we know the writer or recognize the source, we certainly consider the material.

AHS: Milt, in an era where young writers are aware of the value of publishing and are being advised to retain it, what incentive does a publisher offer writers to part with all or part of their copyrights?

OKUN: We prefer to have all of the copyright but will accept whatever part is available. If I have to have a song or have to use it, I think we are fortunate to get whatever part we can. I would never refuse a song because we cannot have all of it, although it makes much more sense to work on the songs that we own entirely or almost entirely, rather than on the others. However, I really don't think there is a difference in our work on partially or on wholly owned songs. As a practical matter, I don't see the benefit to a songwriter of making an issue of keeping part or all of his copyrights at the beginning of his career. I think he loses as much or more than he gains, unless he is such an immense talent that people have to have his material. It strikes me that any publisher would be less interested in a writer who withholds part of the copyright. I believe that from an economic point of view, the publisher serves an important function and it is to the writer's benefit that the publisher prosper if he's going to be associated with it. I think, for example, the writers who have been with Cherry Lane through the years and who have assigned their copyrights to Cherry Lane have benefited by Cherry Lane's success as much as Cherry Lane has benefited.

AHS: What do you mean by that?

OKUN: If a company is successful and has a strong, well-paid staff, many more records go out to artists and many more records go to the radio stations for air play. More songs are printed, and more books are sent to foreign countries. The publishing company benefits and the writers benefit through the performance income.

AHS: Sort of circular; having the copyright gives you the incentive, and having the success gives you the wherewithal to perpetuate the success.

OKUN: That's true. Because we are a successful publishing company, we have been able to go very strongly into print music, so that our writers benefit by having their songs extensively reproduced in chorals, and in piano and guitar books for school and other use. It strikes me that the long-term economic and artistic welfare of the songwriter is better served by increased use of his songs than by his getting part of the publisher's share of the income.

AHS: Interesting. The question of demonstration records always comes up. Writers and artists want to know how to do a demo. If you could prescribe the ideal demo that you'd like to listen to, what would it be? Would it be different for Milt Okun/Publisher than it would be for Milt Okun/Producer?

OKUN: It strikes me that a well-done demo that sounds almost like a master would be very attractive to most publishers because when they send the demo out to record producers, there would be a better chance to get a record on it. Also, for producers who think the success of a record is based on production qualities, the more you can indicate on the demo, the better. However, in my case as either a publisher or a producer, I prefer a simple demo with one instrument, either guitar or piano, as accompaniment, and a clear, pleasant voice singing the song. I want to hear the song. I want to hear the melody, the chords, the words, and I want to make my own judgment as to whether it will make a record. For those producers who think success is based on the quality of a song, and I think the majority of producers do, a simple, very clear demo is best. As a matter of fact, I am often just as happy to see a lead sheet if it's properly done. There you have the melody, the chords, and the words in front of you and you can hear it in your own mind and decide whether you can make a record of it with the artists you have.

AHS: I think there are a lot of people in publishing houses and record companies who couldn't read a lead sheet if it came in.

OKUN: That's true. I think that what I said is only applicable to producers or publishers who are musicians, and since there aren't many, maybe it isn't the best advice to give to writers.

AHS: Okay. Please give me a little of your background. It's a rather interesting career and I think our readers would enjoy reading about it. You've been trained, haven't you?

OKUN: I always assumed that I would be a musician. I studied piano as a young child, then guitar, then majored in music education at New York University. I received a master's degree from Oberlin Conservatory. My main interests were in folk and classical music.

When I was young, folk music was esoteric, out of the mainstream. I didn't care for the popular music of the period, and it is ironic to me that today I am a supposed expert in popular music only because the music I did like, folk music, has evolved into today's popular music.

After receiving my degree, I became a music teacher and taught choral and vocal music in junior high school. There was so little curricular material applicable to the twentieth century for that age group that I did a lot of my own arrangements. Then, while I was still teaching, I began to work commercially as an arranger and a singer. I quit teaching and started my full-time professional music career as a pianist for Harry Belafonte and then joined the Belafonte Singers. Eventually I became his conductor and arranger, and would still be working for him today if he hadn't fired me. Actually, it was a blessing because it forced me out into the field, where I went on to full-time arranging, directing, and producing other folk artists and folk groups.

While working for Belafonte, I started a small publishing company to copyright my arrangements of traditional songs. Later on, when I was very active as a producer and arranger, I started finding original songs and signing writers. As a matter of fact, I signed my first important writer not because I was looking for a writer to sign, but as an act of compassion. While trying to find a replacement for a member of The Chad Mitchell Trio, one of the people I auditioned was a young Oklahoma songwriter, Tom Paxton. I really hired Tom for the Trio because of a song called "The Marvelous Toy" which he had written. I was so intrigued with the song and he performed it so well that I mistakenly thought he belonged in the Trio. After a week or two of rehearsals, it was clear that his future wasn't as a member of a commercial group, and I had to tell him so. He was very unhappy and upset, because the job with the Trio was his first break after coming to New York, and to have it taken away from him so quickly was a terrible blow. I remember sitting with him in my apartment and promising to help him if I could. I signed him as a writer and started trying to get records for his songs. From Tom's point of view it was the best thing that could have happened, because he sat down and started writing with ferocity and passion, and I think he has become one of the most important writers in his field. It might not have happened if he had gone with a successful group, where all his energies would have been directed towards performing.

AHS: You were his Belafonte?

OKUN: I was his Belafonte. But the difference was that Belafonte didn't offer to spend time helping me. He just fired me.

Over the years, my work as an arranger, conductor, and then producer of folk artists has been a natural development and a continuation of my work as a music teacher. I was really hired because of my training in music. The young people I worked with loved to sing and loved folk music, but didn't have enough training to do a professional job. I was the only professional musician, or the only trained musician, at that time who had a real interest in the folk-song movement and understood its roots. There were a lot of arrangers around, many of them much better than I, but they had no concept of the tradition out of which the songs came. When they did arrangements, they used sixths and ninths, and added embellishments to the chords which were marvelous and very beautiful but had no place in "Down in the Valley" or "On Top of Old Smoky" or in any folk-based melody. I had always loved folk songs. They were an obsession with me. I knew all the chords and I had a particular combination of abilities that were needed by performers and creators who didn't have musical training. I was lucky to be in the right place at the right time. I was a teacher to them. I gave them a sense of structure and a sense of music, the better to use their talents.

AHS: When you were firing Paxton from The Chad Mitchell Trio, was there another young fellow in the group that you ultimately teamed up with?

OKUN: You mean John Denver.

AHS: Yes, I was leading you.

OKUN: About four years later, when Chad Mitchell quit the Trio, I auditioned hundreds of people and picked John Denver to replace him. It was a good choice. John had a sense of rhythm and vitality that transformed the group. They were very successful and effective in performance, but they never made it on records. When the group disbanded, and it was the most gracious disbanding of a group that I have ever witnessed, John decided to start out on his own. Thanks to the fact that you and I were able to get him a four-record deal instead of the usual one record with options, he was able to have enough time for one of his records to take off. "Country Roads" was his first hit and it was on his fourth record. Think of how many talented young people who have only a one-record deal never get that chance.

AHS: It doesn't happen any more. Those deals don't happen any more.

OKUN: I know.

AHS: You produced Peter, Paul and Mary also, didn't you?

OKUN: Yes. At the same time that I was working with the Mitchell Trio, I was asked to work with Peter, Paul and Mary by their manager, Al Grossman. When I heard them sing, I didn't think much of their musical ability. I liked each of them individually as singers, but I figured it would be very difficult to get them singing together, and the only reason I agreed to work with them was that I hoped that if I did Al a favor, he might give me work for some of his more important artists, like Bob Gibson or Odetta. That shows how much I knew.

AHS: That was before John Denver, wasn't it?

OKUN: That was before John. I had ten years with Peter, Paul and Mary, from 1960 to 1970 approximately, and during those years I worked with other folk groups at the same time. At one point I felt as if I was the General Motors of the folk-song industry. There were days when I would rehearse with the Mitchell Trio in the morning, Peter, Paul and Mary in the afternoon, and The Brothers Four in the evening, with time in between for The Phoenix Singers or Leon Bibb. The three major groups all had a significant success in different degrees and all disliked knowing that I worked with the others, so there were many difficult moments during entrances and exits, especially when rehearsals ran overtime. They were all talented, creative singers and performers who were not well trained musically, so they needed me.

I served a purpose and had many good years with them, but if they had been as well trained as they were talented, there would have been no place for me. When that era was over, I worked with Peter and Paul and Mary individually on their first solo albums and then went with John out of the Mitchell Trio.

AHS: What do you have cooking now, Milt?

OKUN: I've been extremely lucky over the years. Not only was I in the right place at the right time, but my career seems to have changed with the artists I have worked with, and the changes have always been to my liking. I was able to sing and arrange folk songs for Belafonte. Then the protest movement, really a folk movement, took hold and there were the folk singers and groups to work with. Then John, because of his sensibilities, became a part of the seventies' awakening to conservation and appreciation for the natural beauty in our country. It was a softening of the protest movement, a kind of a cry for a constructive point of view. It's part of John's great success that his songs speak to so many people. It's the reason why his songs, like Tom Paxton's, will be sung long after people will have forgotten the exact time that they were written, or even the contemporary events that led to their writing.

As to what I'm doing now. Well, I am still working with John as producer and publisher. And I am also working with Placido Domingo. Placido is a supremely talented musician, a gifted actor, and, I believe, the finest singer of our time, so this is a pretty stimulating experience for me. For a change, I'm the one who is being taught. He is already a giant star with a world-wide following in the field of opera. And what is unusual for an opera singer, and is apparent on his recently recorded tango, folk, and popular records, is that he sings ordinary songs with love and without condescension.

AHS: You know, there are an awful lot of talented people who don't make it.

OKUN: That's true. But I don't know of any great talents who don't make a mark or don't move people.

AHS: Perhaps you haven't heard of them because they never had the initial success or the break?

OKUN: In many years in music as a listener and as a professional, you hear many people. And it seems to me eventually the talented ones make it.

AHS: I don't know. . . . All the masterpieces I've given you to listen to over the years . . . none of them have reached you.

OKUN: True. But if I'm as bright as you say, you should have dropped them immediately.

AHS: I did. Most of them.

OKUN: Good. But you once played me something of someone who I really thought was talented. And I bet eventually he'll make a big mark.

AHS: Who?
OKUN: Peter Ivers.
AHS: It's funny you should say that, because he's still trying.
OKUN: Maybe the drive that keeps him trying is the most important ingredient, aside from talent, that makes a successful writer. Any really talented writer will eventually be heard if he just keeps working at it, developing his talent, if he just forgets about the "big break."
AHS: I thank you very much.

INTERVIEW WITH
IRWIN ROBINSON

Irwin Robinson has been engaged in the music publishing business for over thirty years, as an attorney and in various executive capacities. He is presently the president and chief operating officer of EMI Music Publishing worldwide.

AHS: Irwin, I know that you are an attorney. How did you get from "Esquire" to president and chief operating officer of EMI Music Publishing worldwide?

ROBINSON: I have been in the business about thirty-three years. I started out working for a very small publisher. I went to law school at night and in 1963 became house counsel for Columbia Pictures Music Division. I was house counsel for a number of years and became business affairs manager, then general manager, then vice president and general manager. In 1976, the music division was sold to EMI. Shortly thereafter I was invited by Chappell to be president of its United States operations, which I thought was wonderful. I accepted the position and I remained president and chief executive officer for eleven years. In 1987 Chappell was sold to Warner Bros. I accepted EMI's offer to be president of its worldwide music publishing organization.

AHS: Which explains why you travel so much.

ROBINSON: Which explains why I travel. That's a brief history.

AHS: I was just looking at EMI's professional roster and was surprised at the large number of catalogues and publishing companies it has acquired. There seems to be a consolidation of the music industry into fewer and fewer hands . . .

ROBINSON: Yes.

AHS: . . . and this I think also means fewer and fewer ears. How do you think this impacts on young writers who are trying to make their mark? Does it narrow the opportunities, broaden their opportunities, or leave them just as they were years ago?

ROBINSON: I think the answer to that question depends on whether the young writer is both an artist and a writer or is just a writer.

AHS: I think what you're leading to is a point of view that I share to the effect that the singer/songwriter who automatically creates a market for his own music, should he become successful as a recording artist, has a distinct advantage over what I call the "naked" songwriter.

ROBINSON: I think that's true and has been true for a long time. I think the consolidation obviously has its negatives. It's very difficult to become a new independent music publisher today. If, however, you're an artist and you get a record deal, you can keep your music publishing rights. Of course, it doesn't put you in the same league as a publisher that has a staff with which to exploit the compositions. Your exploitation is going to be your own recordings, and it's doubtful that you're going to have the time or the opportunity to show songs to other artists who might be interested in performing them, or to send them to advertising agencies who might be interested in using them in commercials. You're going to be a self-contained publisher/collection agent, in effect.

I think the consolidation that has taken place and which continues has its negative side, in that the publishers that are buying up the smaller companies accumulate large portfolios of music, and there's less "personality" involved in the direct relationship between the people who are acquiring and the songs and the writers. If, on the other hand, the acquirers decide that they're willing to make the investment in the acquisition costs as well as to invest in increasing their staffs to properly relate to the writers and exploit the newly acquired music, then I think the negative can turn out to be a positive.

AHS: In practice is it a positive or a negative?

ROBINSON: Well, I can't answer for all the acquirers. I can only answer for the companies with which I'm familiar. At Chappell we didn't do much in the way of major acquisitions. We acquired one company during my tenure. It was Interworld Music and it had a lot of good catalogues in it, including Jimi Hendrix and Hall and Oates, as well as the Sunbury Dunbar catalogue and *Hair* and Abby Schroeder's catalogue. It was fairly substantial and wide-ranging.

AHS: What staff additions did you make?

ROBINSON: We added one or two people to take care of that catalogue. We couldn't afford to add a lot more than that. The big acquisition that we've done here since I came to EMI was SBK. In that instance we really did put our money where our mouth was, because we added fifty people worldwide and that has greatly benefited us. We think that we're very adequately staffed in the exploitation area. We've improved our relationship with writers and the estates of writers of older songs. We have people who contact them on a regular basis, who go to lunch with them. We pay attention to their songs. If all those things will happen in major acquisitions, I think it's not much of a negative. But I do feel that people who are acquiring for the sake of acquiring portfolios and acquiring revenue, top line, and are not going to make the additional investment to exploit that which they've acquired, really are not doing the best thing in the world for music publishing.

AHS: I see that you are surrounded by listening equipment . . .

ROBINSON: Yes.

AHS: . . . speakers, amplifiers, whatever. As president and chief operating officer, do you listen to the acts that are being signed before they're signed? Are you active in the decision-making process as far as talent goes?

ROBINSON: Well, I do listen to some of them. The first line of defense is our creative department. They do all the listening, initially. They screen out, obviously, the good from the bad, that which they're interested in from that which they're not interested in. To the extent the deal that they would like to make exceeds their authority in dollars, it would then be referred to me and then I have to make a decision based on what I hear.

AHS: Does your creative department listen to all of the demos that come in, the ones that come "over the transom"? By that I mean demos not solicited by EMI and not sent by professional people in the business. What is your listening policy? Do you send them back without listening to them?

ROBINSON: Primarily our listening time and attention is given to the writers that we have signed and the songs coming into the catalogue. I would say that our policy now is, though it may not have been previously, that unsolicited demos are returned.

AHS: They are returned.

ROBINSON: Yes.

AHS: That makes it tough on our readers.

ROBINSON: It does make it tough on the readers; however, there's a way around that.

AHS: Ah!

ROBINSON: I say "a way around it" because if someone gets through to someone in the creative department—and I don't think people have had difficulty in doing that—or to me, and says, "Look,

I'm such and such a writer. I have a demo of three songs that I would like somebody to listen to," and they give a name and what to expect, then I usually make a note as do our creative people, and those tapes are listened to.

AHS: In other words, if they show enterprise and professionalism . . .

ROBINSON: Right.

AHS: . . . to do it in a professional manner . . .

ROBINSON: Right, to do it in a professional way. I mean, a lot of writers—and I don't know where they get their information from—will go through a phone book, and they'll just list all the names of publishing companies . . .

AHS: There are a lot of books that have lists.

ROBINSON: Right.

AHS: Half of these "publishers" are file cabinets in accountants' offices, and the writers are sending demos to file cabinets.

ROBINSON: Usually we can recognize professionalism simply from the package. If it just says "Creative Department, EMI Music Publishing," we know that they haven't taken the time or had the enterprise to call.

AHS: And if they come from lawyers and managers, I assume they get preferred treatment?

ROBINSON: They do get preferred treatment, usually because we've dealt with those lawyers and managers before. We've made deals with them and we feel they've done some prescreening.

AHS: You were with Chappell. I was at Chappell years before you. I was there when Max Dreyfus was still around.

ROBINSON: Yes.

AHS: It was old-time publishing. Publishers owned 100 percent of the copyright, and the writers received only their writers' royalties. I've done some deals with you fairly recently and I see a tremendous liberalization now. As a matter of fact, I was discussing this with another publisher, and he said to me, "Alan, you're in the era of 'rent a copyright.' " In the "old days," you gave the publisher the copyright for the life of the copyright. You got your writer's royalties. He exploited the song, hopefully, and that was it.

ROBINSON: Correct.

AHS: Now I see all kinds of deals: co-publishing deals. Co-publishing deals which really look more like administration deals than co-publishing deals, in that the copyrights come back eventually after a period of years or after the term of U.S. Copyright. With your background, don't you bridle at such deals? What tempts you and permits you to do those deals?

ROBINSON: I don't bridle because I think the deals reflect the marketplace and one's position in the marketplace. When the deals that you were talking about were being made in the Louie Dreyfus days and the Max Dreyfus days, you had very few artists who were also writers and the first exponent of their own material. So the writers who were notoriously poor businessmen, really creative people, wrote the songs and depended on other people to do the work of getting the songs performed and recorded. I think that's a different business than the business that arose years later when the writers decided to sing their own songs. They had an added string to their bow. They had added leverage. They could come to a publisher and say, "We're going to help you. We're going to get another party, a third party that's not related to you, a record company, to invest in our career, and we're going to have records out, and you're not going to have to necessarily do the job that you used to have to do in the past." So for that we deserve something more than just a royalty. I don't really bridle at that. I think . . .

AHS: But the word "bridle" did get your attention . . .

ROBINSON: Yes, it got my attention and certainly in some instances I do resist, or try to resist, especially where we're being asked to help make the record deal—which is often. We're being asked to go out and do the work, the same work we used to do as a publisher in getting songs recorded. Now we are charged with getting a deal for the writer/artist with a record company, and that's the same kind of effort and contribution really.

AHS: So what you're really saying is that if a writer comes to you and he already has a record deal, most of the work is done. You know those songs are going to be heard over the radio. You don't have a crystal ball, which will increase success, but you know they're going to get a shot and you're much more inclined to make a favorable deal than if you had to go out and first make a record deal or cause other artists to record the songs.

ROBINSON: Absolutely. That's the marketplace. Even going back to the days when the writers gave 100 percent to the companies, once a writer became established and his songs got recorded by a lot of different people, as with the Sammy Cahns and the Jule Stynes of the world, the situation changed. Once they established the relationship with Sinatra and other major artists who recorded a lot of their songs, they didn't always go through the people who were the professional managers at their publishing companies. They made direct contact and they knew when Frank was recording and when Tony Bennett was recording, and they were able to send in the songs signed "Sammy" and "Jule," and when that began to happen a lot of those writers got their own publishing firms . . . which either were partnerships with their old publishers or were administered by those publishers. What

I'm saying is when a writer got stature, even in those days, he cut a better deal. The leverage changed. This is not really a new phenomenon.

AHS: The balance of terror shifts.

ROBINSON: That's right, terror and leverage, that's what it's all about.

AHS: Do you see any trends? Do you see the industry moving in any particular directions?

ROBINSON: Well, the things that I do see may not necessarily have to do with the relationship between the writers and the publisher . . . at least directly. What I do see is an attempt on the user's part more than ever before to diminish the value of copyrights and to diminish their financial worth by virtue of a controlled compositions clause and by virtue of the fact that now, with new technologies coming, there is an opportunity for the record companies to come back once again and try to diminish mechanical royalties. I'll give you an example. CDs are taking the place of vinyl records, and the CD has a capacity of twenty songs, whereas the vinyl record, unless you made a double album, was limited to maybe twelve songs. Now you've got a situation where in order to be competitive right now the record companies are putting one or two extra songs on each CD. The record companies are taking the position that the artist has a controlled composition clause whereby he's only entitled to receive a maximum of ten times the statutory rate and at a minimum; ten times 75 percent of the statutory rate. Now when they put fifteen songs on the CD they don't call it a double package and wish to pay mechanical royalties only for ten songs!

AHS: Same max. It's a real problem. That's why it's so hard to negotiate a record contract and a publishing contract. It's very difficult. It's a series of compromises. We should point out, though, that since the new copyright act came into effect in what, 1976?

ROBINSON: It was effective in 1978, yes.

AHS: The mechanical rate was 2 cents and now it's up to 5.7 cents.

ROBINSON: Absolutely.

AHS: So that's a positive from the writer's point of view and from the publisher's point of view.

ROBINSON: It is except that if you look at the industry overall, what is the rate that mechanicals are mostly being paid at? It's way below 5.7 cents.

AHS: Three quarters.

ROBINSON: It's certainly somewhere between 75 percent of that and the max.

AHS: When it was 2 cents they were paying at 90 percent of records sold. They always took an edge.

ROBINSON: And they always seem to be finding another way to take an edge. That controlled compositions clause is the most insidious thing, and nobody can seem to do anything about it.

AHS: The funny thing is that companies such as yours, where you're allied with a record company, if you make a publishing deal with one of your sister company's artists . . .

ROBINSON: Right. I can approach my affiliated record company and ask them to agree to a statutory mechanical rate, and sometimes they will agree.

AHS: . . . you can get the full rate.

ROBINSON: Right. Correct.

AHS: So that is an incentive and an advantage.

ROBINSON: And SBK Records, which just started, came out with an announcement that they are not insisting on controlled composition clauses in their contracts with artists. They're not going to do it. They're "a publisher label." They're a publisher-oriented label.

AHS: Charles [Charles Koppelman] was always on the cutting edge.

ROBINSON: He is on the cutting edge.

AHS: I'm going to ask you a rather mundane question. I ask it of everyone because it's a question I think my readers are most interested in. They want guidance from people such as you as to how to prepare a demonstration record that's going to give them the optimum shot. What criteria would you set for the ideal demo for a music publisher?

ROBINSON: I'm going to have to ask you whether the writer is an artist.

AHS: Let's assume he's a "naked" writer.

ROBINSON: If he's a naked writer, I'd want the simplest demo that shows the song to the best advantage. I think a writer knows, if he has some professionalism, that the song he's writing is meant for a particular kind of artist. He's not going to write a song for Alice Cooper and do a piano/voice demo. If he's written a song that has a beautiful melody, if it's a ballad, with a wonderful lyric, the writer should do the simplest demo that shows that off . . . perhaps piano and voice with rhythm. On the other hand, if he's writing a song that's directed toward either his own performance medium or the performance medium of somebody who uses electronic instruments and the usual accoutrements, the demo should be done in a similar fashion.

AHS: I agree. Years ago when I broke into the business, most of your A&R people were musicians. They were people who were retired from active musicianship. They had the ability to listen to a very simple demo and hear the orchestrations and the arrangements in their heads as if it were fully orchestrated. I think the problem today with publishing companies and probably more so with record companies is that a demo had better be of pretty professional quality because the A&R people aren't sufficiently experienced to "hear" what is not there.

ROBINSON: Right, nor that imaginative.

AHS: So you'd better make the demo the way you think it should be heard.

ROBINSON: Well, the A&R people of the early days went in to the studios and actually produced records, whereas today most records are produced by independent producers and they're brought finished to an A&R department. The A&R department will then make an initial decision based on demos. If it is positive they will go to see the artist perform (the visual is almost as important as what they hear on the tape), and they'll make a decision: "Based on what we saw and based on what we heard, we want to sign this group and we'll give the project a budget." But then what do they do? They turn around and they hire a third party who is not connected with their company, who they think will do the best production job, and say, "You go in." Then they don't hear anything until the damn thing is finished. A lot of times, when the producer brings the tape in, the A&R guy says, "This is different from what I imagined you were going to do . . . we don't like this album." They then have another and perhaps still another producer do more sides, and it's a waste of the artist's money, obviously. This happens because the A&R people have wrongfully separated themselves from the creative process.

AHS: I think you're right. Do you hold your writers' hands?

ROBINSON: How do you mean that?

AHS: Well, if you sign a writer, and he comes here and he says, "Irwin," or whoever your creative person happens to be, "I wrote these three songs. What do you think?" Are there people here who will say, "Hey, song number one is terrific, song number two needs a different bass line," or "This or that doesn't sound right . . ." Are there people here who can nurture a writer?

ROBINSON: Yes. Today, however, it's a bit different. When I first started at Screen Gems the writers were physically in the office, almost on a daily basis, writing songs. It was a whole different ball of wax. They would actually come in excited because they had just finished the chorus and the verse. I remember Barry Mann running into my office saying, "I don't have the lyric, but this is the way it goes. I have the title line," and he would do "da da da" for the lyrics he was missing. But you got an idea of what he was doing, and you would say, "That sounds great. Finish it." Today, you're getting most of the stuff in the mail. The writers are not in the office. They all have home demo studios and they do a great job. They're very professional and they do these fairly elaborate demos and send them in. Because we don't have the contact with them when they walk in with it, we have a listening meeting once a week and, though I won't show you the sheet, we arrive at a consensus, which is then communicated to the writers.

AHS: You don't have staff writers, like you used to in the old days?

ROBINSON: Yes, we do . . . and we don't. We pay them as we did staff writers . . . but they work at home.

AHS: I'm talking about the old days, when you literally gave a writer an office and a chair and a typewriter or a piano, and he came in from nine to five and wrote songs.

ROBINSON: We don't do that for two reasons, really. Very often the writer doesn't want that atmosphere. He's got his little studio at home and he wants to be alone creating. He wants to bring in other writers that may not be signed to our company. We allow free collaborations between writers.

AHS: I need to take that clause out of my songwriter contracts.

ROBINSON: Right. And a lot of the writers feel much more comfortable that way. They don't want to be on the premises. And of course the second reason is that space is at a premium. We're paying probably $40 or $50 per square foot here, and we would prefer the writers work at home because to rent another floor in this building for writers would not be cost efficient.

AHS: Cheaper to buy the equipment for the home?

ROBINSON: It is.

AHS: Irwin, I thank you so much.

ROBINSON: I hope it was what you wanted.

INTERVIEW WITH
MICHAEL LEFFERTS

After a long career in the music publishing industry, Michael Lefferts is now president of Cherry Lane Music Company, Inc., the print division of the Cherry Lane group of music companies.

AHS: Michael, are you aware of the fact that you're a pariah in the music publishing industry?

LEFFERTS: No, actually, I'm one of the more benevolent and enlightened people in the music industry, bringing truth and beauty to an industry otherwise populated by people with respect to whom the word pariah would be a kindness.

AHS: Do you know what I am referring to?

LEFFERTS: No.

AHS: There is word about in the industry that publishers, music publishers, do not take kindly to you because you've been urging acts to carve out their print publishing rights from their music publishing deals. Is that accurate?

LEFFERTS: That is very accurate, and I think the people who might consider me a pariah or any like term are, for all intents and purposes, envious because they have not thought of or had the courage to do something like this.

AHS: To do something like what?

LEFFERTS: Aggressively treat print publishing rights as a separate entity.

AHS: Michael, for many, many years very few people in this industry had any idea of the importance or the significance of "print rights," and I think it's important that before we go any further you indicate briefly what we are talking about.

LEFFERTS: Print rights are a part of publishing rights . . . a small part of the publishing rights, but nevertheless a part of the publishing.

AHS: You mean ordinarily if a writer made a publishing deal, the publisher would receive the rights to exercise all of the rights attendant upon the copyright, including print, issuing mechanical licenses, collecting performance income . . .

LEFFERTS: Correct.

AHS: . . . making foreign licensing deals, etc.

LEFFERTS: Correct.

AHS: Print would be one of the small aspects of it.

LEFFERTS: Yes, and historically it has generated relatively smaller income than any of the other parts of the publishing rights that you mentioned. However, for a popular group—if the print is done properly—it can generate considerable revenues.

AHS: Let me draw a distinction, if I may. How many publishing companies today have the ability to take a song, create print product, and put it out in the market place?

LEFFERTS: Directly?

AHS: Yes, directly.

LEFFERTS: The only ones I know of that are both a record company/publishing company and a print company . . .

AHS: Forget record company. I am not asking about record companies.

LEFFERTS: . . . publishing company and a print company are Warner Bros., Cherry Lane Music, and Music Sales Corp.

AHS: And you are of course associated with Cherry Lane.

LEFFERTS: I am president of Cherry Lane Music Print Division.

AHS: What happens with all of the other publishers in the world that artists sign up with? What do they do about the print rights?

LEFFERTS: One of two things can happen. Either they have a preexisting deal with a separate print publisher, someone who's strictly in the print publishing business, such as Hal Leonard or CPP/Belwin or . . .

AHS: Or you?

LEFFERTS: Or Cherry Lane or Warner Bros. or Music Sales, although we have our own publishing companies, we are still on a par with them as far as going after independent publishers to acquire their print rights.

AHS: Have these other print publishing companies been seducing young writers and artists to carve out the print rights from their publishing deals, or is this something you initiated?

LEFFERTS: It's something that we initiated at Cherry Lane. However, the truth is that the other print companies have gone to many of the publishers and already have existing deals covering their catalogues. In other words, say Hal Leonard has paid SBK "X" amount of dollars for exclusive print rights for a period of time.

AHS: Is this an example, or are we speaking of fact now?

LEFFERTS: It's a factual example. They have a deal with SBK as a result of which the print rights to any song published by SBK would automatically go to Hal Leonard, and they would produce print product, pay the royalties to SBK, who then in turn would filter it down to its clients.

AHS: But that's essentially what you try to do also, isn't it?

LEFFERTS: It's essentially what we also try to do, but our feeling is that a lot of people, before they sign away their publishing to an entity such as SBK or BMG or Warner Bros. or Cherry Lane or anybody else, should consider the advantages of separating the print rights and dealing for them outside of the basic publishing deal. We have gone to the people who are in touch with the groups, or in control of the groups, such as the attorneys and the managers, and we have said, "Before you make a publishing deal and assign away all of your publishing rights for, say, a hundred thousand dollars, which would include your mechanicals and your performance rights and your print rights, we, the best print publisher in the world, will, for example, give you ten thousand dollars for your print rights alone. We believe you can then go to SBK or BMG or Warner Bros. or Cherry Lane or whoever and still get that hundred thousand dollars for those other publishing rights. We strongly believe that. We believe that most people don't even think about the print rights. It is strictly an afterthought that people think of as gravy. We can make it more than gravy. We can make it a significant part of your income and create a total separate profit center for the artist."

AHS: Okay, this book is intended for people attempting to get into the music business. Now, if I come to you and say, "I represent this very worthy group and they are terrific kids and they write nice songs. They don't have a record deal. Would you please give me twenty-five thousand dollars for their print rights?" What would you say to me?

LEFFERTS: I would say, "No." I would also say, "However, if you get a record deal, way before the record is coming out, way before we know whether this is going to be successful or not, let's talk again." That gives me a shot. That gives me the possibility of recouping an investment that I'm going to make in the group. I also don't believe that it should be my ears alone that determine whether we invest in this group or not. Although what I think of the group is a factor. More important is what you think of the group.

AHS: Who is "you"? Wait a minute.

LEFFERTS: You, Alan Siegel, who's coming to me saying that you represent this group. Do you really believe in this group? Do you really think that they're going to do well? That's important to me.

AHS: But my obligation is to my client, not to you, and if I think by saying that this group has a shot, I'm going to get an advance for them that'll pay the rent, I'm not going to defer to you. A lawyer can only have one client.

LEFFERTS: That's true. However, you have an obligation, I believe, to be truthful, and you have an obligation to give . . .

AHS: No, my obligation is to present the cassette to you and say, "Hey, you want to give us some money for these rights?" You have to make that decision. Besides, anybody who relied on my ears would have to have their head examined anyway.

LEFFERTS: That's exactly right and what I do is I say to you, "Do you believe—what is your opinion—do you believe in this group?" I'll give you my opinion and if we both feel that there's a shot for this group and there is a record deal, I will make you an offer for the print rights. If you keep coming to me and you keep hyping these groups to me and I keep paying you money and everyone goes down the tubes, there's going to be a point . . .

AHS: I'm going to lose my credibility with you.

LEFFERTS: That's exactly right. It is more important for me to have a relationship with you, the attorney, or the manager of the representative of the group, than the group itself. There will be a hundred groups that you will represent, but there will only be one you. If I have a good relationship with you, and you come to me and present me with the opportunity to acquire the print rights to this group, and if you're right—one out of two, one out of five— as long as there is some reasonable success, I am more than willing to enter into these arrangements with you and give you a reasonable advance in front of a record coming out. You can have what I refer to basically as "rent money." Although that may not be a totally accurate description, most of the time you're not going to get money from the record company for three months or six months down the road, but for me, if we make a deal, you're going to get anywhere from $1,000 to $25,000 up front when we sign the deal. It pays the rent. It buys the groceries. It makes the car payment. I have the print rights. If they make it big, I'm going to recoup my advance, and all of us will make a lot of money on the earnings.

AHS: That's the American way.

LEFFERTS: Absolutely that's the American way.

AHS: Let me ask you this, Michael. For years and years and years, very few people in this industry were aware of print. I've been in this industry for a long time and I remember as a kid lawyer at Chappell seeing print and being made aware of the fact that this was a very important staple of this industry. It seems that a lot of people lost sight of it, but now you don't seem to be alone in appreciating its worth. I think you have a lot of competition.

LEFFERTS: On the pop end, there are basically five companies involved in print publishing, that is Cherry Lane, Warner Bros., Hal Leonard, CPP, and Music Sales.

AHS: So, if I was a smart lawyer and I had something going, I'd set up an auction, as they do in the book industry, between you guys.

LEFFERTS: Well, you could. It depends on how hot a group you had and whether you could get a competition going and people bidding against each other. Most of us, at least Cherry Lane, are not interested in getting into a bidding situation. We have set certain criteria for ourselves. We would listen to a group, or have an established group offered to us, and we will make a determination as to what we feel would be a fair advance to be paid. On new groups that are untested, who are coming out with their first album, we have a basic standard deal depending on our relationship with the attorney, or manager, and our opinion of the music—anywhere from $1,000 to $12,500, or $15,000, as an advance, depending on a lot of different factors. Also, our deals are almost always for at least three albums. So what we are willing to do is make this investment with you and then, even if the first record is not a success, we may have a big success with the second record or the third record. I believe the record companies feel that when they sign a new act, they're figuring on having a big success by the second or third album. I don't think most of them even figure on having a big success with the very first album. So that's our philosophy, too.

AHS: When you get a new group, Michael, what do you print, usually? What would you put out in the marketplace? I know groups and writers really do get turned on by seeing their songs in print, especially when it's as beautifully presented as your print product usually is.

LEFFERTS: I appreciate that and that is true. I think there's a certain ego factor with anybody having their works in print. It's a tangible manifestation of what they do. I think that we are responsible, at least to a certain extent, for the resurgence of print music. You alluded to the fact that print was very popular and one of the driving forces in music publishing quite a number of years ago, and then it seemed to go into a period of relative decline and now it is popular again. I'll digress for a moment and give you a thumbnail history of it. Originally, music publishing was the print business. It was one of the most important things for a writer . . . having your music in print in the twenties and thirties and even into the forties. Print started to take a back seat once records emerged and the mechanical and performance royalties grew. The record business blossomed and became this fantastic industry, and print took a back seat. Historically, print music meant piano/vocal arrangements. So, as long as you had people, whether it was Frank Sinatra or . . .

AHS: Tony Bennett.

LEFFERTS: Tony Bennett, I mean all print publishers basically did piano/ vocal arrangements and people took them home and played them on the piano. Don't forget, this was in a time when a big part of entertainment still was the piano in the home.

AHS: I remember song pluggers literally playing the pianos in Woolworth's . . .

LEFFERTS: Exactly right.

AHS: . . . playing sheet music.

LEFFERTS: That's exactly right, and then people would buy the sheet music and take it home. That was a big part of entertainment. Television wasn't around and playing music was a major source of entertainment. Well, now you have television, and movies are bigger and better than ever, and there are music shows and performances all over the place. Print is not as important. However, what we realized was—and this occurred about four or five years ago—that people continued to produce basically piano/ vocal arrangements for music of today's stars, most of whom were now guitar heroes, rock stars. Piano was sometimes not even existent in the band. There was no piano. There was a lead guitar or a bass guitar, a lead singer, and a drummer. A good example is a group like Van Halen, which was the original heavy-metal, hard-rock guitar group. The publishing was controlled by Warner Bros., and they did all of the albums. In fact, they weren't even excited about the first album that Van Halen did.

They didn't even get involved in the print until the second album, so that the first publication they came out with, a folio, was a combination of the first and second album. They called it *Van Halen I and II*. After that they realized the potential of it and they came out with a matching album for 1984 and so on, *Women and Children First* and *Diver Down*, I think were the other ones. But these were all piano/vocal. There was a market. They sold lots of folios, but in truth . . .

AHS: What's a folio, Michael?

LEFFERTS: A folio is what we call a "music book." It is a collection of songs arranged for print, bound in a book, usually with pictures and some bio material.

AHS: Aren't there different kinds of folios?

LEFFERTS: Yes. For instance you might have a folio containing all of the songs on a particular album with the cover having the same art as the album jacket.

AHS: That would be a matching folio.

LEFFERTS: Right. A personality folio would be all of the songs of one group, not necessarily from one album. A mixed folio, which is a third general type of folio, contains songs from different artists grouped under one usually general banner, such as "love songs" or "rock songs," or some common thread. In any event, Warner Bros. did piano/vocal folios for all of the Van Halen albums and they sold very well. But in truth, not as well as they possibly could have because this is a guitar-driven group, and the majority of fans of this group play the guitar or want to play the guitar, or would love to learn to play the guitar as well as Eddie Van Halen or learn to play the bass guitar as well as Michael Anthony. So about five years ago, we realized that there was a great void in the print industry. We took all of these rock groups, these guitar groups, and produced guitar folios. Then we produced as a secondary folio for the same album a bass guitar folio. Then we would do an "easy guitar" folio, for the beginner, and then maybe, just maybe, we might also produce a piano/vocal folio for someone who only played the piano and wanted to play the tunes. But the main thrust was producing folios arranged for the instrument for which the band was noted and which their fans would be more inclined to buy.

AHS: And the rest was history.

LEFFERTS: Well, not history, but truthfully it was a resurgence, and now most of our competitors are following our lead. We are not the only ones, obviously, who are doing this. I mean, all the other publishers are trying to find—and the key here is to try and find—the best transcribers. The real hero is, sometimes for print purposes, not the artist so much, but the transcriber.

AHS: Now that's something that's interesting to me. You mentioned transcriber. I don't think most of our readers are going to understand what you mean. What you attempt to do and what's unique about your product, from what I understand, is that you'll take an Eddie Van Halen recording and reproduce in print exactly the notes that he played. That's the skill of the transcriber.

LEFFERTS: Absolutely correct. That is the key to the whole business. I believe we have the best transcribers in the business, and that is why we have been so successful. We have people who will sit—and love to do it, by the way—put on the earphones and play the record. They will slow it down. They will get every nuance, every sound, every riff. Every plucked string on the guitar is represented in our book and someone who is a fan of Skid Row or Van Halen or Metallica or Guns n' Roses can buy our book, can put the book on a music stand in front of him, sit there with his guitar, and play along with the album on his tape recorder, or turntable, or compact disc player. Our book will reflect exactly what is on that album, and so the student or the fan or the player will know that if he can duplicate what's in that book he will sound like Eddie Van Halen. Obviously this is almost an impossibility, but at least he has in print an exact reproduction of what Eddie is playing. . . .

AHS: He has a way of keeping score.

LEFFERTS: Absolutely. Absolutely and he knows it. If he doesn't play it that way, it's not the way Eddie played it. It really was revolutionary in our business. In guitar folios there was an occasional "easy guitar" folio, but it was never done on the scale that it is done now.

AHS: So what's your message to all of these aspiring young artists and writers?

LEFFERTS: I really believe that groups should inform their managers and attorneys, if they don't know it already, that they should make the best possible deal with the best possible publisher that they can. I think people should not be as concerned with the amount of up front money and advance money they can get. I can understand that that is very important and sometimes very necessary, even to the survival of a group, but the most important thing, whether it's the record company or the publisher, is to find people who are the best qualified to reproduce their sound, whether it is on a record or in publishing. They should make sure that their attorneys and managers understand that print is a separate entity. It's a separate item for which they can get a separate advance. They should separate it out from their publishing, go to the print publisher they feel will do the best job, represent them the best, and in effect sell the most folios and make them the most money.

AHS: Michael, I have some advice. Don't start your own car. Thank you.

LEFFERTS: Thank you.

Of course everything is listened to!

three

(SI SI) JE SUIS UN ROCK STAR

Music and lyrics by Bill Wyman
© 1981 by Ripple Music Ltd./
ITC Filmscores Ltd.

Stop! If, as I suspect is the case, your prime interest and major concern is the acquisition of a recording contract, you may have consulted the table of contents and turned directly to this chapter. If you have, it was a mistake . . . but an easily corrected one. Turn back to page 15 and start reading! This chapter will have infinitely more meaning and will be of significantly more benefit to you if you have read that which precedes it. Too many of the principles set forth in "I Write the Songs" are equally applicable to this chapter to be ignored and yet are too long to bear repetition. Similarly, the background information in the chapters that precede this one is needed to place this chapter properly in context. If you haven't yet read those two chapters, you will not have an adequate frame of reference in which to read what follows. Take my word for it, I planned it that way. Are you now thoroughly familiar with the Lexicon? If not, read it again—you will profit more from this chapter if you do.

If you knew nothing about the music business before starting this book, you probably have an edge. If you are possessed of a smattering of ignorance, I would beseech you to degauss that part of your mind as you would your tape heads.

Years ago, when I was into fishing, there were ads in the sporting magazines featuring a fisherman's "deliar." It was a little scale with a built-in tape measure. It shrank many a whopper (no, the word wasn't invented to describe a hamburger) to frying-pan size.

I used to think fishermen, golfers, and teenage males had cornered the market on hyperbole in describing their "scores." They pale by comparison with rock-'n'-roll bands describing the phantom record deals they turned down or the real record deal they finally landed. A while ago I was told by a disc jockey in whom I had great faith with respect to all things musical (but not business) that a certain new group had received a million dollars for signing a recording contract with one of the major record companies. I told him that I didn't believe it. I would have bet a Ferrari that a new band couldn't get $1,000,000 from that record company with an Uzi submachine gun. My friend was so insistent, however, that I made a note to check it out. When I was able to buttonhole an executive of the company in question and confront him with the story, his response was as I had predicted. I think it was something like "What are you smoking?" The deejay called me a few days later and acknowledged that the group had been engaging in creative arithmetic in valuing their deal. They had received a $20,000 advance on signing ($5,000 a man). The remaining $980,000 was arrived at by adding up the advances they would receive *if* they were successful and *if* the record company exercised all of its options, and by including all of the recording costs that would be spent *if* the record company recorded all of the albums it was entitled to record *if* it exercised all of its options. Well, if you figure the recording costs for from seven to ten albums at about $750,000, and if you assume, as you should, that the remaining $230,000 is advances spread out over the four remaining option pickups, with the larger portions allocated to the third and fourth option pickups (when success is assured and when the advances are in all likelihood earned before they are paid), it places the deal in perspective.

I would suggest therefore that, for the time being at least, you erase from your conscious mind all tales of sugarplum fairies you may have clung to in the past and be very skeptical of the scuttlebutt you hear in the streets. To do otherwise is very counterproductive. It's psychologically demoralizing; it renders you incapable of appreciating an otherwise satisfactory offer; it enhances the chances of "turning off" advisers who may feel they could never satisfy your expectations.

What are your chances of making it as a recording artist? If you are an awesomely talented performer *and* a great songwriter, your chances are excellent. If you are either of the above (and merely terrific at the other), your chances are good. If you are neither of the above, your chances are remote unless you are pretty damn close to being in both of those categories and, in addition, possess some unique qualities that will move a record company to believe you are salable. A surefire hit single never hurt.

What about all the successful recording artists you can name that are "none of the above"? Your assessment of their merit and talent is probably in error, or they possess some unique quality with which they are reaching, touching, and charming their audience.

I have been fortunate in that whenever I have difficulty with introductory material for a chapter, a suitable introduction seems to walk into my office. In this particular instance, it walked in on very good legs. A young man had sought an appointment to discuss my representing his band. At the appointed time he arrived, not alone, but with an exceptionally attractive young woman, who, it emerged, was the band's co-leader and lead singer. Their story, though unique to me, is probably not atypical. In fact, it is probably typical of many would-be recording artists who take their shot in the only manner they perceive available to them, fail, give up, and become assimilated into "normal" walks of life.

My visitors told me that they had mailed out seventy-five demo cassettes. They received responses from only a tiny fraction of those record companies and producers to whom their demos were sent. Only two of the responses were "encouraging"—inviting them to send more material. A&R people at two major record companies they approached in person told them that their demo would not be considered unless submitted under the aegis of an entertainment attorney, accountant, or manager. Hence their call to me.

They indicated that they had written some new songs that were better than the ones on the demo (an artist always perceives his new songs as "better") and would have a new demo in a few weeks. They gave me the "package" they had sent out, which included a picture. The picture was reminiscent of group club pictures found in high-school yearbooks. The lighting was harsh and the print was dark. The very attractive blond lead singer was all but lost in the picture. The consensus upon subsequent listening to the tape was "not bad." The songs were "not bad," the vocals were "not bad," and the production was "not bad." In the sixties or seventies I imagine the seventy-five cassettes sent out would have borne more fruit. But in the nineties, "not bad" ain't good enough!

To break in as a recording artist today, you must have outstanding new material coupled with outstanding performances. Record companies have always searched for the elusive hit single. At one time, when the industry was more musical and romantic, and less corporate, companies would gamble on records that might have a shot. Today they must feel certain.

As you will learn from the interviews accompanying this chapter and the chapter entitled "I Write the Songs," many publishers and record companies profess to listen to all material sent to them. A careful reading of the interviews will indicate that some of the executives waffle a bit on this subject. Some indicate that they "try" to listen to all material thus submitted. Others indicate that material submitted "cold" receives a more cursory listening than material received from professional sources. A really careful reading of the interviews, with few exceptions, discloses that the publishers and record companies have found the mails to be a uniquely barren source of income-producing songs and records. Apparently it is considered un-American or undemocratic not to listen to unsolicited material, or at least bad public relations. With all due respect to the publishers and record companies, it is my impression that material submitted directly through the mails by writers and artists receives cursory attention at best. After all, who is apt to continue panning for gold in a stream that doesn't produce?

Why do record companies give preferential listening treatment to demos submitted by entertainment lawyers, accountants, and managers? Because they have great "ears" and know what is and what isn't a hit? Hell, no! If they had that capacity, they would have their own record companies or be on their yachts. The answer is twofold.

First, it's good business. The same lawyers, accountants, and managers who are hustling deals for unknowns are the lawyers, accountants, and managers who represent the stars now providing the record companies with their sustenance; the same stars whose current contracts will expire and who will be seeking new affiliations or renewals of existing affiliations. They therefore have a power base, and power begets "courtesy" and preference. It's just good business to keep such lines of communication open. Most reputable lawyers, accountants, and managers will candidly advise new acts that they don't hold out the promise of a deal—only the likelihood of a considerate "listen."

Second, the lawyers, accountants, and managers provide the record companies with an automatic screening process. Ninety-nine percent of the cassettes in the record companies' bulging mailbags are not of professional quality and hence of no interest at all to them. Usually an act whose tape is submitted by a lawyer, accountant, or manager has gone through a process of "natural selection" and paid some dues. The vast majority of the acts who have found an entertainment attorney, accountant, or manager have endured rejection at one level or another, and persisted. They have usually formed and reformed or been part of several bands, and, in general, have "been around." In all likelihood, they have become or are on the verge of becoming professionals. The easily discouraged, the dilettantes, the high-school bands, the hobbyists with delusions, and those bereft of any talent at all fall by the wayside before finding and investing in professional help. The record companies know that when a tape comes from a lawyer, accountant, or manager at least some screening has taken place. None of such sources are apt to risk their credibility with the record companies by submitting junk preordained for rejection.

With knowledge born of experience, most of us (at least those of us past professional pubescence) cast in this screening role have come to realize that we don't know what is or isn't a hit. By the same process, we have acquired a sense of what is "in the ballpark" of acceptability, or at least a sense of what isn't embarrassing. Of course we are all fallible and have politely discarded acts who subsequently "made it." They love to encounter us at cocktail parties and cast disdainful "I told you so" glances at us . . . and who wouldn't relish such an opportunity?

Is it tougher to break in as a recording artist than as a songwriter? Of course it is. The economics of the business dictate that it must be. For a music publisher to accept a song from you represents a minimal monetary investment. A very modest advance and the cost of a demo usually represent the maximum financial exposure of the music publisher. Very often there is no advance and your demo becomes the publisher's demo. Hence the publisher's financial exposure is limited to the costs of the form contract you have signed.

When a record company prepares to take the plunge, it is at considerably greater risk. You then represent an investment that can be modestly estimated at a quarter of a million dollars. No, I'm not out of my mind. Artists tend to think only in terms of what crosses their palms. What about the other palms involved? Besides an advance to the artist, which may very well be modest, there are recording costs for an album, the costs of pressing records, artwork, manufacturing jackets, shipping, distribution, and promotion. "Promotion" alone could add an additional $250,000 to a record company's exposure. Between the first and current edition of this book I hosted a luncheon for the A&R department of a major record company. During the course of the lunch my colleagues and I gently chided our guests about the paucity of "signings" and their reluctance to gamble on new acts. The full impact of their response was lost on me at the time. At this point it is probably appropriate for me to confess some naiveté which has a much nicer ring than "stupidity," especially when applied to one's self. We were told that for a record to get airplay, which of course is key to its success, it must have "independent promotion" . . . that is the "help" of persons (with dubious "connections") outside the record company. They went on to state that the cost of such independent promotion was $250,000 per record. How many $250,000 shots did we think a record company can afford to take!? What was the sense in signing a host of new acts when you knew that only a small fraction of them would receive the independent promotion and that the remainder, when released, absent a small miracle, would be consigned to oblivion?

I remember leaving the luncheon feeling somewhat like a child who had just learned that there was no Santa Claus! In 1986 there were Senate hearings relative to the record industry which were focused specifically upon the practice described above. The result of the hearings was that the record companies abandoned, at least while the heat was on, independent promotion. Ironically, the record companies had relied so heavily upon independent promotion that their own promotion departments had to a large extent atrophied (if not in size, at least in effectiveness) to the point of being vestigial. There was therefore a flurry of activity in the industry as the record companies strove to bring their own promotion departments up to snuff. In the interim a lot of records released during the transition died for lack of promotion.

What did this portend for you? Good things, I thought. Record companies would be able to gamble more often because the stakes would be lower. Your music would have a better chance of finding its audience since Darwin's theory of "natural selection" would have an opportunity to work in the music marketplace.

Ironically, and unfortunately, the situation is the same today as it was in 1986. If you have followed the record industry scandals in your newspaper, or on TV, or if you have read the recent book *Hit Men,* you will realize that the record industry profited not at all from its 1986 "experiences," nor probably from any of its prior scan—oops, "experiences." Who said "Those who do not learn from history are doomed to repeat it"?

Accept the fact, therefore, that there are a lot of dollars' worth of "belief" in any record deal . . . and a lot of artists competing for that belief. How do you go about securing your share? Well, all the things said above about getting into the business, getting close to people in the business, and paying dues, as true as they were with respect to songwriters, are even more applicable to the recording artist.

If the quest for a record deal can be analogized to basketball, sending tapes cold through the mail would be the equivalent of a shot from midcourt at the final buzzer with Michael Jordan guarding you—a low percentage shot. If you have entrée to the record company through a third party who is championing your talent, the percentage rating of your shots is directly proportional to the clout of your sponsor. A supermanager with a heavy act already on the label may provide you with a lay-up; a hot producer, a shot from the foul line. On the other hand, it can be tougher to procure a supermanager or a heavy producer than it is to procure a record deal. Is there a slam dunk? Only if you can create a situation where the record company comes to you!

How do you do that? Ah, were there an easy or glib answer to that question. Unfortunately, you know the answer. You've got to create a "buzz" in the industry, and the only way to accomplish that is to work at your trade and to excel. You do this by performing and by keeping on performing and creating a following. The buzz follows and so will the record deal if you have "the right stuff." The right stuff in this context means hit songs and a quality that in the eyes of a record company is sufficiently unique to translate into that much-abused word "charisma."

The message here is not to abandon all other avenues, but, on the contrary, to pursue all avenues; don't get so caught up in shortcuts, "edges," and "contacts" that you lose sight of the fact that to be a recording artist you must first be a performing artist. So, follow up on all your "contacts," court the powers that may be able to help you, play cassette roulette if you must, but never lose sight of the fact that you are first and foremost a musician, a singer, and a performer. If you work at your art or craft or whatever else you call it, and if the talent is there, it will emerge and the pieces will fall into place and the record deal will happen, and the stardom . . . and the headaches.

At this point it would be appropriate for you to reflect on why you are reading this book. If you are anticipating a career as a performing artist as a means to an end—fame, fortune, and the good life—I would urge you better to invest your time, money, and energy in securing an education. Although fame may not follow, the chances of attaining a fortune and the good life are far greater. The entertainment road to those life goals is a low-percentage shot. If, on the other hand, a career as a performing artist is for you the end itself, then go for it! You can't lose.

You have probably heard the expression "record deal" so often and in so many contexts that you may even think you know what it means. You probably don't. Record deals come in so many shapes, sizes, disguises, and configurations that the term no longer has a definable meaning. There was a time in the not too distant past when the term had a very definite meaning. It was an exclusive recording agreement between a recording artist and a record label. The newest newcomer and the veteran star had essentially the same record deal. Oh, the royalties were different (but not that different) and the advances (if any) were different, but essentially their contracts were the same. You could track the paragraphs from contract to contract and, with a few minor variants, they were comfortingly or disquietingly similar (depending upon whether you were the newcomer or the veteran).

With the burgeoning of the record business in the sixties and seventies, huge profits were being made by the record companies. The cataract of cash stimulated the creative juices of the managers and attorneys, who proceeded to structure deals designed to alleviate the cash burden suffered by the record companies and to protect the recording artists from their resulting tax burdens. As the profits continued to flow, the arrogance and inventiveness of the artists' team kept pace. The record companies matched the artists' arrogance with their own greed and imprudence, and the fratricidal bidding wars for top artists (and even new artists) that characterized the record industry in the seventies ensued. Mopping-up operations were led by the bootleggers and the equipment manufacturers, who placed tape-copying ability in the hands of every sixth grader in America. Pac-Man and his electronic hordes roamed the carnage administering the *coup de grace* to the wounded.

As the record companies folded one by one or were absorbed by the majors, new administrations pledged to conservatism grasped the reins of the survivors, and even where the hands on the reins were the same, they became tightly clenched. The net result is a reversion to the old days and ways, diminished opportunity for you, and, consequently, a greater need for you to excel in your art and to understand the business you are trying to break into. The deal structures invented during the boom years have persisted even though the boom hasn't. When you get your record deal, you will need an entertainment attorney to negotiate it for you. The contract will run from forty to sixty single-spaced pages and is not written in English. The language is jargon and it will be cast in a style I have just christened "fail-safe convolution." The style is born of paranoia (not necessarily undeserved) and provides for each unpalatable provision to appear twice, usually widely separated in the text, once in wolf's clothing and once in sheep's clothing. The theory is simple: if the artist's attorney knocks it out once, there is a chance he won't pick it up the second time and at least there will be an ambiguity that can be played with later on. If you want to leave this to your cousin with the real-estate practice in Mineola, that's up to you, but you've been warned. In running through the deals, I will not analyze each type of contract beyond what I think you should know to avoid "giving away the store" and to enable you to maintain intelligent discussions with record people, producers, and prospective managers before your attorney is retained. This is not a "do-it-yourself" course in negotiating a record deal!

Before dealing with reality, there is one fantasy that should be discussed and disposed of. If you follow a familiar pattern, you will begin your quest for a record deal confident that if you are just heard, you will be signed. When acceptance by record companies does not follow and your disappointment and frustration mount, your thoughts, as those of many before you, will turn to making your own record, having it distributed, and "showing them all." This is a way to go if you firmly believe that poverty is the fountainhead of creativity. It doesn't work, for many reasons. First, it is very expensive; second, at this stage in your career, although you are capable of making a demo adequate to demonstrate your potential to a record company, you do not possess the skill to capture the production qualities required for a commercially competitive record; third, you won't be able to get national distribution worthy of the name; fourth, if you are able to get the record played on the air, you will not have the resources or expertise to exploit your brief success; finally, the resulting cartons of records will jam up your closet and will provide you with a "bummer" each time you open the door.

Let's now look at the basic record deals you *will* (a positive attitude is a prerequisite to success) be confronted with. We need not, and shall not, explore the exotic arrangements your attorney may conjure up when you are a proven platinum artist.

There is nothing wrong with a record company trying to give the most minimal deal possible to a new artist, especially during the early career stages when the risk is high and the chances of profit low. On the other hand, there is nothing wrong with the artist seeking the best deal he can possibly obtain. The point is that the words "right" and "wrong," "fair" and "unfair," have little place in the structuring of a record deal. The negotiation of a record deal is a balancing act. Both sides are constantly adding and subtracting from their side of the scale. The amazing thing is how often, when the artist is adequately represented, a balance is struck with which both sides feel comfortable. The process is a long one. Often months pass between the first draft and the traditional signing picture in *Cash Box* or *Billboard*.

Curiously, the consummation of a deal for an established artist usually takes much less time than a deal for a new artist. The reasons are threefold:

1. The deal for an established artist will be thoroughly discussed before it emerges as a contract, and the contract will pretty closely resemble the deal.
2. The contract will not be a form and will not contain any of the more offensive pro-record-company provisions that the attorney for a new artist has to struggle to have deleted or modified.
3. The deal will not be put on the back burner by the record company's attorney while more important things are taken care of. There will be nothing more important! No record-company employee will look forward to Christmas if he knows he is thought of as being responsible for losing a major artist because of negligence or procrastination.

There are two basic ways by which you will find yourself signed to a record label, directly or through an independent producer. In the first instance, the governing contract will be between you and the label. In the second instance, your contract will be with the independent producer, which will in turn enter into a contract with the label whereby it agrees to provide your exclusive services as a recording artist to the label. Let us consider the direct route as the basic situation, become familiar with it, and use it as a point of departure in comprehending the independent-producer situation. In either situation your accountant may recommend for tax purposes that you operate through the vehicle of your own corporation, but for our present purposes we can safely ignore that, and the term "you" as it is used in the following material can be interpreted as you or your corporation—which you will undoubtedly vest with a name of great symbolic or sentimental significance appreciated only by you or your closest confidants. In choosing such a name, please remember that it will stare back at you from your early record albums, made when you were young, impertinent, and improvident; hence try to pick a name that won't embarrass you later on. Back in the early seventies I had the pleasure of representing a group named The Fugs, which was at the time a daring and pioneering group known for the "underground" nature of their lyrics. Their corporation was named G.T.M. Inc. After seeing the name literally hundreds of times, curiosity impelled me to ask what the initials stood for. "Get the Money" was the response.

With that in mind, let's ramble through the first draft (there may be three or four) of your first record contract, which we will assume to be between you and a major record label. Let's presume, lest this be too simple, that "you" are a rock-'n'-roll group comprised of four members and that the name of the group is "Us" (which is a lot easier for me to write than "Four Musicians in Search of Fame and Fortune").

Having read Chapter 6 entitled "You've Got a Friend," Us found a suitable entertainment lawyer. As you make yourselves comfortable in his office, one member of the group hands the attorney a copy of the contract Us has been given by the record company. It is the one with the group's notations. The attorney asks for a clean copy so that his own notes will be clear. This does not present a problem, since the record company has provided you with six copies. A clean copy is found. The attorney lays both your notated copy and the clean copy aside.

"Before getting into these, we have to take care of something that is very important . . ."

"Oh, oh, here it comes; he's gonna want a check."

". . . and that is the relationship among the four of you. Are you equal members of, and participants in, Us, or are some of you 'more equal' than others?"

A hush falls over the lawyer's office as eye contact is sought (and sometimes avoided) between the various members of Us.

The attorney is trying to get Us's house in order before taking on the record company. He is concerned about two distinct areas, and his experience has taught him that it is best to resolve them at the very inception of the relationship. The first is the division of record royalties among the various members of Us. The second is the manner in which the income from the songs written by the members of Us is to be handled. Let's explore the possibilities.

Usually the members of the group consider themselves equal as recording artists, and the question is disposed of simply by agreeing to split the record royalties equally. Not infrequently, however, an entertainment group evolves in a curious fashion. There may be a nucleus of a few members who have starved together for five years and who have been the driving force behind the band, another member who has only starved with the band for one year, and a new drummer who was brought in only two weeks before the offer of a record deal came down and whose performance wasn't even on the demo that led to the deal. The veteran members of the group may well feel that the newer members should participate in royalties on a reduced level, or indeed should not participate in royalties at all but should merely receive a salary. Of course, the resolution of these questions depends on the dynamics at work within the group. If the new kid on the block is the lead singer rather than the drummer, there are certain realities that can't be overlooked. Often the group has come to grips with this question before contracts are received and the question is quickly, if not always wisely, disposed of. If it is obvious that the question has not been previously thought of, much less resolved, a veteran attorney will suggest that it be the subject of discussion among the group alone and tabled until they can give it the time and consideration it deserves. The lawyer who intrudes in this area is guaranteed to lose the trust and confidence of some members of the group and thus diminish his effectiveness overall. For our purposes, and for the sake of simplicity, let's assume that Us decides to split record royalties equally among all members of the group.

Now for the sticky question of the music income! You will recall (if you didn't skip directly to this chapter) that music publishing income is traditionally divided into two parts: the writer's share and the publisher's share, which are roughly equal. Note that when we set up this hypothetical situation, it was stipulated that the recording contract we were to examine was between Us and a major record company. We can therefore assume with relative safety that the granting of the music-publishing rights to Us songs is not a precondition to the record deal. Thus, all the music-publishing rights, including the copyrights, reside in the writers of the songs. If Us is a typical rock-'n'-roll group, in all likelihood one or two members of the group will be the writers of all or nearly all of the songs to be recorded by Us.

"So what?" you ask.

So plenty! By simple subtraction, if two members of Us write the songs and own the music-publishing rights, the remaining two members don't own any music-publishing rights. It doesn't pose a problem right now because Us hasn't even recorded yet, much less had success. Let's, through the crystal ball of experience, take a peek into the future. Us's first LP has gone gold and is still selling, and you can't turn on a radio without hearing its single, which is number five with a bullet on the pop charts, destined for number one. Is everybody happy? Sort of. Well, two members of Us are happier than two other members of Us. Relatively speaking, therefore, two members of Us are unhappy. Alas, you just can't avoid human nature! How unhappy are they and why? They are at least $300,000-worth of unhappy, and the reason is that they are not receiving that $300,000—and the two members of Us who write the songs *are* receiving it. By now I'm sure you figured it out . . . but just in case:

500,000	albums sold (gold)
× 10	songs in the album
5,000,000	
× 5.7¢	mechanical royalty per song
$285,000	mechanical income

In addition to the mechanical income, one can estimate the performance-income value of a number-one single at approximately $100,000 ($50,000 writer share and $50,000 publisher share). There's $385,000 right there. Add to this the ancillary income from print and foreign licenses and residual future income, and you can safely assume over half a million dollars' worth of unhappiness.

Is this apt to create problems for Us? If it is not recognized, confronted, and resolved early on, it most assuredly will. You don't think you'll mind driving a Porsche while the writing members of your group are driving Rolls-Royces? The hell you won't! Not only does this situation lead to friction, dissension, and jealousy, but it also has a more direct and insidious effect on Us's future product and success. When the disparity between the income of the writing and the nonwriting members of a group becomes obvious, and when the long-term value of having a continuously earning catalogue of songs in one's portfolio is realized, there is a natural tendency for nonwriters to try to become writers. In those rare instances when the talent is there, the result is a positive one. In most cases, however, the talent is not there and the result is a fierce competition to have inferior songs included as "B" sides or as "album cuts," thereby diminishing the quality, integrity, and homogeneity of future albums. When such efforts are resisted, as well they should be, the result is predictably quite negative, and ofttimes disastrous. Sure, there are times when there are no ill effects. When the egos of the group members and their maturity permit a realistic appraisal of their relative contributions to the group's success, gratitude can overcome greed and harmony may reign. But often this is not the case. The arguments on both sides can be persuasive.

A nonwriting lead singer argues: "I may not write, but I certainly am an essential element in the songs becoming valuable commercial properties. Our fans in no small part come to see and hear me. I am a very substantial part of the reason they buy our records and a primary source of the group's success. The songs are written if not for me to sing, at least with me in mind. Without me, the songs may not even be created, much less heard and economically valuable. It's not morally correct or economically viable for me not to participate in the tremendous economic benefits they throw off."

A less prominent nonwriting member offers: "The songs are written with all of us in mind. In some indefinable way we all contribute to their creation. The song as recorded by the group is not the same as when we first hear it. As in the case of good wine, something happens in the aging process. Good grapes don't necessarily produce a great wine. The evolution of the song as we play it demonstrates subtle but significant nuances that contribute to its success and value. Even if musicologically it's the same song, it's not commercially the same song. I feel I am entitled to share in the money the song earns."

On the other hand, the writer argues, with some emotion: "I've never considered myself greedy and I certainly don't want to cause pain to the other members of the group, but, frankly, the songs are the key to the group's success. There are lots of bands that can play rock-'n'-roll as well as we do who don't even have record deals, much less the economic success we do. The differences between them and us is the songs I write. That is my gift, talent, or whatever that is responsible for our success, and although I am not diminishing anybody else's contribution, I am not about to denigrate my own. I think I am entitled to additional compensation for my unique contribution. The other members are benefiting indirectly but very substantially from my songs through their huge earnings as recording artists. It's not only the money; a part of me would feel outraged at the thought of adding the name of someone who didn't contribute to its creation to one of my songs. The idea offends me and I would feel ripped off economically. I think it would adversely affect my ability to write."

What is the solution to this dilemma? There are many, and they vary with the forces at play within the group, the personalities involved, the closeness of the members, their affection (or lack thereof) for each other, their egos, and their perceptions of each other, themselves, and the group—and of course the role the songs play in the group's success. I have seen resolutions ranging from one in which all members of the group share equally as writers and publishers of all songs recorded by the group regardless of which member or members did the actual writing, to the other extreme, where the writing and publishing are held only by those members who actually write the songs. Both extremes work—and fail—sometimes. Actually, it's a difficult subject for members of a group to discuss candidly and without rancor. I usually try to ease the way by presenting the above arguments in a hypothetical manner, thus making sure the various positions are on the table without any one of the members having to expose his innermost thoughts and risk incurring the displeasure of the co-members. If the situation seems appropriate, I may offer for consideration the following as a possible Solomonlike solution:

The actual writers of songs recorded by the group receive sole writer credit and full writer royalties. The copyrights and the publisher's share of income with respect to songs recorded by the group are assigned to a publishing company owned equally by the members of the group. How would this work out for our mythical four-man group, Us? Assume two members co-write all the songs and a given song earns $10,000. Then $5,000 would be writers' royalties and $5,000 would be the publisher's share. The members of Us would receive the following shares of income derived from the music rights:

	Writer Income	Publisher Income	Total
TABLE 3.1			
Writer Member A	$2,500.00	$1,250.00	$ 3,750.00
Writer Member B	2,500.00	1,250.00	3,750.00
Nonwriter Member C	-0-	1,250.00	1,250.00
Nonwriter Member D	-0-	1,250.00	1,250.00
	$5,000.00	$5,000.00	$10,000.00

Thus the special contributions of the writers are recognized. The contributions of the nonwriters are recognized, albeit to a lesser degree, their jealousy abated, and their inclination to write, perhaps poorly, is stilled. Harmony is maintained, and all members of the group are participating in the creation of a valuable asset which will stand all of them in good stead when their days as performers have passed. Notice that the writers remain total owners of all rights to songs not recorded by the group and are free to develop that aspect of their talent unencumbered and unhindered.

How you ultimately work this problem out depends on facts peculiar to your group, but work it out you should. Good luck!

With that out of the way, you can get back to the business at hand: the recording-artist contract. Us's contract is the latest form of contract being used by one of the major record companies. If Us ran true to form, the notes and comments made by the members of the group may not focus on key negotiable areas. By this I mean that the average neophyte recording artist often expresses shock and dismay at the clauses in the contract that are by custom and usage immutable and acceptable. By the same token, there are no notations adjacent to the most outrageous and negotiable paragraphs. The contract received by Us consists of sixty single-spaced pages . . . twenty-seven pages more than the thirty-three page contract referred to in the first edition! It is a ponderous insomnia-fighter, unintelligible to all but experienced entertainment lawyers. It is not "fair." It was created by very competent, well-remunerated lawyers whose job it was to create a document highly favorable to their client, the record company. It was not their job to make it "fair." It is the job of the artist's attorney to cause changes that will render the contract more equitable.

To analyze a sixty-page record contract word by word, line by line, even paragraph by paragraph, is beyond the scope of this book and the limits of your patience. It is not, however, beyond your lawyer's ability to perform such an analysis; indeed, it is his obligation. When he does so, as he must, he is exercising professional diligence even though the record company will characterize it to you as "nit-picking." When you hear from the record company's people that your lawyer is a pain in the (expletive deleted), smile pridefully and tell them that's what you pay him for. It means you probably have a good one! When the sixty-page contract is dissected, forty of the sixty pages consist of boilerplate clauses found in all record contracts, which are not usually the subject of discussions between the artist and his attorney unless specific questions with respect thereto are asked by the artist. Do not lament over this . . . it keeps your fees down. Also, don't be misled. Although the boilerplate clauses are not discussed between you and your attorney, they must be discussed and negotiated between your attorney and the record company's attorney because, although universal in subject matter, boilerplate clauses do vary in their effect on your life and future income, depending upon the malevolence of their creator.

The remaining twenty pages of the recording contract cover the "deal points." When the deal is struck between the record company's representative and your representative, whether your manager or your attorney, a transcript of the conversation would probably be less than a page. It is just such a page that the business affairs representative of the record company sends to the record company's lawyer in the form of a deal memo with instructions to prepare your sixty-page contract.

So, lest this chapter have the same soporific effect that a full-length record contract has, I shall limit the scope of our discussion to the deal points and to those items that I have learned come as a shock or surprise to artists. Now is a good time to get a cup of coffee and take a deep breath—you will need both.

Exclusivity

All contracts between record companies and pop artists are exclusive. This means that for the duration of the term of your contract with the record company, you may not record for any other record company. The record company is not, of course, exclusive to you. It can record and release records by as many artists as it chooses. Unfair? Not really. The record company, with justification, feels that if it invests the time and money to "break" you and if it takes the initial gamble on your talent, it is entitled to enjoy the fruits of its investment and not have you depart with your enhanced stature to a rival label. If you find this intolerable, your only solution is to become a classical musician or an opera singer. These are the only recording artists who enjoy the ability to flit from label to label. This, however, is not a solution available to many.

Remember, exclusive *means* exclusive. No exceptions are apt to be tolerated. If you wish to carve out exceptions, now is the time to do it. Two exceptions to exclusivity that can usually be won in the initial negotiation of a record contract are an exception to permit you to record jingles and an exception to permit you to record as a sideman on other artists' sessions.

Note also that if "you" are a group, your exclusivity extends to you as a group and to each member of the group as individual artists. Therefore, abandon any thought of avoiding your contract by leaving the original group and becoming a single artist or forming a new group.

The Term

Now that we know that your services are to be exclusive to your record company, the next logical question is: For how long? This is negotiable within limits. I assure you it's not going to be for twenty minutes. For many years the standard term for a record contract was one year, with the record company having the right to extend the term for four additional one-year terms. These are the "options" you have heard about. When your records are successful, the record company "exercises its option" to extend the agreement. When the record company thinks you've had it as an artist, it does not exercise its option for the next year and the contract ends at the end of the year for which the last option was exercised. Democracy does not reign here; the option to continue the relationship belongs to the record company, not to the artist. Don't waste energy fretting about this; accept it. No lawyer can change it—not even yours!

Before this, I explained to you that contracts evolve like insurance policies, in that whenever the insurance company gets burned, a rider to cover the situation is added to the policy. In record-company contracts, the same principle applies, although the Band-Aid is applied in the form of a language change or a new paragraph, rather than a rider. A while back, Olivia Newton-John effected a crucial change in the contract you will receive from your record company. I know, you never even met her! Ms. Newton-John and her record company, MCA Records, sued each other at a time when she had not completed the number of albums she was obligated to deliver to MCA. Lest she decide to bless a new record company with her not insignificant services, MCA sought a court injunction to prevent her from recording for another record company until such time as she completed the number of albums she was obligated to deliver under her MCA contract. MCA, most experts thought, had been quite correct in its position that Ms. Newton-John's contract was suspended each time she failed to deliver an album by the deadline prescribed in the contract, and that therefore she would remain the exclusive recording artist of MCA until such time as she fulfilled her obligations to MCA even if that time went beyond the expiration of the contract's five-year maximum term. The court, however, was of a different mind and expressed its doubt that Ms. Newton-John's failure to perform her obligations under the contract could extend the contract beyond its specified five-year maximum term. In other words, a five-year exclusive recording contract could not be converted into a seven- or eight-year exclusive recording contract by virtue of the artist's failure to perform the services required of her (or him) during the term of the contract. Consequently, the record companies were threatened with the loss of their ability to compel the delivery of valuable product and with the loss of their most valued artists.

The court's decision acted to throw the switch on thousands of word processors throughout the entertainment world as record companies and their attorneys rushed to "correct" the court's "mistake," at least with regard to their future signings.

Thus, Us's contract, and no doubt yours, will have a term not defined in numbers of years, but, rather, in numbers of albums delivered, with options for additional numbers of albums to be delivered in the future. Accordingly, "contract years" becomes "contract periods," and the exact duration of your exclusive recording artist contract becomes quite conjectural and elusive. At this stage of your career, you are in all likelihood so preoccupied with *getting* a record contract that it is of little concern to you what its duration may be. That is understandable—but short-sighted. So much of the aura of record deals is associated with advances, royalty points, recording costs, and the like that the duration of the contract sometimes takes a back seat. It should not. A year saved at the end of a record contract can translate into the dollar value of several royalty points over the entire previous term of the contract.

It is in the artist's interest to have the maximum duration of the contract be as short as possible. The record company, on the other hand, strives to have a term of as long duration as possible. Why? The bargaining position of a recording artist is weakest at the beginning of his career, and his initial recording contract will, in all likelihood, be the most favorable for the record company that it will ever be able to negotiate with that artist. Once stardom is reached, the balance of power shifts to the artist, and his next record contract is apt to be a "monster." The record company cannot lose by a long-duration contract. If the artist fails to become successful, the record company bails out of the association by not exercising its option for the next contract period. If the artist becomes successful, the longer the record company enjoys the advantage of the relatively low royalties and advances it was able to negotiate with the "new" artist, and the longer it is able to keep the artist out of its competitors' clutches. Even if a new contract is to be negotiated with the successful artist before the expiration of the full term of the original contract, the remaining years provide the record company with increased leverage during the renegotiation.

A look at the applicable language of the Us contract, which is a rather insidious example of the term language that has come into use, will illustrate this point:

1. *Term*

    1.01

    The term of this agreement will begin on January 15, 1990, and will continue for a first Contract Period ending nine months after the date of completion of the masters to be used in manufacturing the disc Phonograph Record units to be derived from the last Master Recordings made in fulfillment of your Recording Commitment for that Contract Period under paragraph 3.01 below.

    1.02

    You grant Company four separate options to extend that term for additional Contract Periods ("Option Periods") on the same terms and conditions, except as provided herein. Company may exercise each of those options by sending you a notice at any time before the expiration date of the Contract Period which is then in effect (the "current Contract Period"). If Company exercises such an option, the Option Period concerned will begin immediately after the end of the current Contract Period.

(Paragraph 2 omitted for our purposes.)

3. *Recording Commitment*

    3.01

    During the Contract Period indicated below, you will perform for the recording of Master Recordings as indicated, cause those Master Recordings to be produced and delivered to Company (the "Minimum Recording Commitment"). During each Contract Period, you will perform for the recording of Master Recordings sufficient to constitute one Album.

    3.02

    You will fulfill the Minimum Recording Commitment for each Contract Period within the first three months of the Period.

    3.03

    (a) During each Contract Period indicated below, Company will have the option to increase the Recording Commitment for that Period as provided below ("Overcall Recordings"). Company may exercise that option by sending you a notice at any time before the end of the Contract Period concerned.

    1. With respect to each Contract Period, Company will have the option to increase the Recording Commitment by Mas-

ter Recordings sufficient to constitute one (1) additional Album.

(b) Each time Company exercises an option referred to in subparagraph 3.03 (a):

1. You will deliver the Overcall Recordings to Company within three months; and

2. the current Contract Period will continue for nine months after the date of completion of the masters to be used in manufacturing the disc Phonograph Record units of the Album comprising the Overcall Recordings.

I ask you, how would you like to have to read that stuff for a living?

Now for a bit of arithmetic. The term begins on January 15, 1990. Us must complete its first album within three months thereafter (a somewhat unrealistic time period). Nine months later, the company exercises its right to receive an additional recording (the company is in no rush to exercise this option). A full year has now expired! Add three more months (again highly unrealistic) for delivery of the additional recording. Us is now fifteen months into the first contract period. Add nine more months for the first contract period to end pursuant to Paragraph 3.03 (b) (2), and if my addition is correct, the first contract period will take a full two years.

Using similar arithmetic with respect to each of the option periods, Us is staring at a minimum of ten years with its first record company—in all likelihood, its entire career. The Olivia Newton-John case has resulted in a recasting of record contracts in such a way as to diminish your opportunity to enjoy a second bite of the apple of success. Incidentally, you might as well add approximately two years to the total term, because none of the albums is apt to be completed within the three-month periods provided in the Us contract. Remember you will be on the road touring to promote each album, and you will also have to write the songs for each new album!

Had this book been written in the seventies, one short paragraph would have sufficed for our discussion of the term. Developments in the industry, including the Newton-John case, and the increased conservatism of the record companies, have elevated the importance of the term as it is now constituted in record contracts to a prime subject for negotiation.

An understanding by you of the foregoing is important, because the term provision as integrated into the Us contract is kind of subtle—it doesn't present a red flag to alert you to its ramifications. So even if your contract is worded somewhat differently, make sure someone on your side does the arithmetic. If your record contract is of modest duration, you may be content to pay your dues and look forward to your second bite of the apple in your next contract. If it is of inordinately long duration, you must try to write your second bite into it in the form of royalties and advances in subsequent contract periods which are consonant with the success you may assume you will have attained by virtue of the record company's having exercised its options for so many successive contract periods and albums.

Okay, enough for the problem. What is the solution? Your attorney will try several gambits. The success of each or all of them will depend, as usual, on your leverage (how anxious the record company is to sign you) and your attorney's ability to read the signals he receives in the course of the negotiation. Obviously, any solution, in order to work, has to be acceptable to both sides. Thus the record company must avoid the Newton-John case and have the right to your services for a long enough period to justify its investment in you. On the other hand, the artist cannot feel he is signing away his entire professional life for a too-modest remuneration.

The basic structure of the Us contract term can be maintained and the duration of the term shortened in three ways. First, the total number of albums can and should be reduced. Second, the time period (nine months in this case) between the delivery of the first album in each contract period and the company's exercise of its right to an overcall recording can and should be reduced. Third, the nine-month period between delivery of the overcall recording and the expiration of that particular contract period can and should be reduced. How much can these periods be reduced? It depends upon how long they are to begin with, the record company involved, and the usual intangible factors inherent in your bargaining position. A reduction from nine months to six months would not deprive the record company of any of the protection it needs (six months being adequate in most cases for them to assess the desirability of exercising their options for overcall recordings and additional contract periods) and would shorten the term by a full two and one-half years, leaving a still too-long term from the artist's point of view. An additional cut in the term can be accomplished only by reducing the maximum number of albums available to the record company. From the artist's point of view, ten albums is too much. A reduction to seven or eight albums, which should be considered reasonable by most record companies, would bring the total term down to a duration that both sides could live with.

There is a much simpler approach which may meet with acceptance by the record companies, especially if negotiated as part of the deal while the deal is still in its talking stage. Once a draft contract is received, changes in its structure are harder to make because of the bureaucracy involved in the process. Generally, the larger the record company, the larger the bureaucracy and the more permissions are needed to make a change in the company's contract form.

Representing the artist, I would ideally like to see a seven-album deal with one album delivered during each nine-month period. Albums two and three would be elected by the record company on the basis of individual options, whereas the options for albums four and five and albums six and seven would be exercised as two-album "packages."

The total duration under this package comes to sixty-three months, or a little over what was the traditional five-year term, and the two-album "sets" lend some stability to the deal for the artist after the record company has had sufficient experience with him/her to make an intelligent decision as to whether it wants more product.

Perhaps you can do better, perhaps you will do worse; at least you will, I hope, understand what you did and be better able to conduct yourself in a manner that will enable you to make the best of your situation.

Product

Although we pretty much covered this subject in the section covering the term, there are a few additional comments that are in order. During the sixties and early seventies it was more the rule than the exception for a record contract to provide for the initial recording obligation to be in terms of sides rather than albums. The record company would cause the artist to record two or four sides. A single would then be released, and, depending upon how it did, perhaps another single. If the single did well enough to justify a further investment, the record company would cause the artist to record "sufficient additional sides" for an album. Later on in the seventies, when the record industry was booming and money was plentiful and there was little resistance by the consumer to the purchase of albums, it was thought to be more efficient, once the artist was in the studio, just to do the album and pick the singles from the album. Accordingly, virtually all the record deals made during the mid and late seventies were album deals. In the eighties, there was a reversion to "singles deals." The theory behind the singles deal is simple. If the record company is to take a shot on a new artist, and if it is to make a mistake, it is better to make a $20,000 or $50,000 mistake than a $100,000 mistake. If the single looked good, the record company could always exercise its option for sufficient additional sides for an LP.

Although the Us contract discussed in the preceding pages calls for albums, your deal may start with a single. Don't be overly distressed if you don't receive an album deal. There is a theory that the record companies have a tendency to be more generous with future royalties and advances when their initial investment is relatively small.

On the bright side, it seems incontestable that where there is a limited amount of money for investment in new artists, the smaller the initial investment, the more new artists are going to be given an opportunity. One of the artists who may profit as a result could be you!

As we enter the nineties, the current industry practice seems to be to start artists with album deals, except in the dance and rap fields where singles deals are still very much in evidence.

Recording Costs

Perhaps after reading this, you will prepare your material and rehearse your songs *before* going into the studio. It is in your interest to do so since all recording costs are ultimately borne by you. Although the record company will pay the recording costs initially, it will charge them to you as advances against your royalties as and when earned. The only exception that comes to mind is in the case of classical artists, who are paid from the first record sold and who are not charged with recording costs. Why? "Tradition" is the best answer I can find. But don't be jealous; the same tradition acts to make their royalty rates significantly lower than those paid pop artists.

The definition of recording costs contained in the Lexicon will suffice for your purposes at this time. The actual language in the Us contract is three single-spaced paragraphs long, and its inclusion will serve little purpose other than to confuse you. Your lawyer can chip away at it, but the chips will be little ones at best.

In the basic beginner situation, the record company quite understandably seeks to maintain as much control as possible. Their experience has shown them that too often when they have relinquished control, disaster results. Record company executives become prematurely gray when the entire re-cording budget for an album has been expended and all they have to show for it are four or five sides. The best protection the record company has is to sign the producer directly, make him submit a budget for approval, make him live within its limits, and pay the bills itself upon receipt of vouchers. All record-company contracts have a clause whereby the record company has the right to have a representative present at all recording sessions; too rarely do they avail themselves of this right. Too often do record companies abdicate their responsibilities once the contract is signed. Indications are that they have learned (or are learning) this lesson. Most pop artists are young and have not yet attained the maturity that should accompany the responsibility they are so happy to assume. There are two major causes of excessive recording costs. The first is a failure to prepare adequately before going into the studio. Thus, the artist learns his material while paying astronomical studio rates when he could have done so in a loft or a house rented for the purpose at a fraction of the cost. The other is an obsessive quest for unattainable perfection—not knowing when a song is captured well enough to move along to the next number. The result is half an album that is overrefined and half an album that is rushed and inadequately rendered. How does this happen? It's a fact of life that often the producer loses, or never acquires, control over the artist . . . and, unfortunately, the record company usually ain't minding the store. Re-member that ultimately it's *your* money that's being wasted and *your* record that's going to suffer from a shortage of money!

Although the foregoing reflects the most common recording-cost structure and illustrates the principles you should be aware of, there are an infinite number of variations on the theme. Sometimes, because of their manager, their attorney, leverage, or other factors, new groups receive more sophisti-cated and "favorable" deal structures. One of these—much coveted by new artists and their representatives—is the recording-fund structure. Its basic premise is that the record company will set aside a specified sum for each album to be delivered by the artist. Usually the amount of the recording fund escalates from the first album to the last album. That portion of the fund not used for recording costs is to be kept or received by the artist as an advance. Sometimes the recording company pays the recording costs as they are incurred and pays the "balance" to the artist upon delivery of the album. Sometimes the artist or its corporate alter ego receives the entire fund and assumes the responsibility for paying recording costs. In the last case, the record company, in order to insure its receipt of an album, will spread the payment of the fund out over the course of the album's production. For example, one-third upon commencement, one-third at the halfway point, and one-third upon completion.

New artists greet this scheme with enthusiasm because they invariably underestimate what the album will cost and therefore anticipate a big payday when it is completed. Often, to their dismay, there is nothing left over.

Beware of inflation. What may seem to be a generous recording fund when you start your first album in 1990 may be grossly inadequate when you start your sixth album in 1995 or 1996. You must try to make sure now that the escalations in the fund are sufficiently large, or that there is a provision for a "cost-of-living multiplier" so that rising recording costs do not all but absorb the pocketable portion of the fund that will be available to you in 1996.

Advances

As you have already learned from the foregoing, there are advances and ADVANCES. In this section we shall be concerned with the real advances that you actually can put in your pocket and use as you see fit, as opposed to mythical advances such as recording costs, which, although charged against your future royalties, are not received by you for your own use.

Like most things today, advances ain't what they used to be. In general, they are considerably less in their dollar amount than they were in the past, and are further shrunken by the diminished value of the dollar. So be warned: you are not going to become instantly rich merely by virtue of landing a record deal. Considering the effect that grotesquely large advances had on some new artists who were ill-prepared to receive them and who were misguided or poorly managed, I am not at all sure that this is a totally negative development. Nevertheless, notwithstanding their diminished size, advances are very much on the minds of aspiring recording artists, and on those who derive their income from serving them.

Advances usually escalate, rising from album to album as the term progresses. Initial advances can be very modest. "None" is very modest indeed, yet not unheard of in today's marketplace. Quite often the initial advance is measured by the artist's needs in order to commence recording. For example, the initial advance may be based on how many dollars are needed to rent a rehearsal loft for a few months, or the costs of essential equipment needed to enable the artist to proceed. After the initial advance, it is really just a question of bargaining. The artist's representative tries to get as much as possible, and the record company tries to give as little as possible. The record company's generosity is usually directly proportional to its estimate of its risk of recoupment. Hence advances are kept low for the early albums, when the artist's success is totally conjectural, and rises dramatically with the artist's longevity. The theory is simple: if the artist doesn't make it after the first few albums, the record company won't pick up its options for future albums and won't have to pay the higher advances called for with respect to those albums. On the other hand, if the options are picked up, it probably means that the artist's success has been established, or is at least predictable and the advances will be recouped out of the artist's earned royalties. The dilemma for the record company arises when, after a few albums, the artist is hovering in the gray area between success and failure. If the advance for the next album is too high, it is a deterrent to the record company picking up the option. Most of the haggling over advances therefore takes place with respect to these middle albums. Large advances for albums which occur late in the term are often not as much of a problem; they have a cosmetic effect in making the contract appear attractive, and by the time they must be paid, the artist is established and recoupment of the advance is pretty well assured. In fact, the advances for albums late in the term are often earned when the record is shipped. So, to some extent, the large advances granted late in a contract term are illusory . . . or so argues the attorney for the artist. The record company, of course, argues the other side of the coin: "Why worry about the advance for the albums late in the term, especially if it's an illusion? The artist, at that stage of his career, will be recouping anyway. We'll only be giving him his own money, so why make a fuss?"

Well, it's nice to know that on a certain date, or with a certain event, a large chunk of money is going to be coming in; it helps in planning. Besides, who knows when a career is going to crest?

Advances vary in amount depending on so many variables that it is impossible to suggest a rule of thumb. Factors that enter into the ultimate result range from the enthusiasm the record company has for the artist (or its fear of losing him to a competitor) to the financial shape of the record company, the manager involved, the chemistry between the negotiators for the respective parties, whether the artist is a singer-songwriter or a multi-member group, astrological signs, the record company's previous bad experience, whether publishing is or is not involved, the royalties payable, who had a good lunch that particular day, and many other factors.

The following schedules of advances (Table 3.2) are derived from two contracts that were chosen for their illustrative value. They have been simplified for our purpose. They are a bit dated, and hence shouldn't be looked to as indicative of current deals. For their intended illustrative purposes, they remain valid. You will see that they vary considerably. Schedule I is derived from a contract between a singer-songwriter with no track record and a

TABLE 3.2

Advances

	Schedule I			Schedule II
	Record Advance		Co-Pub Advance	Record Advance
	Minimum	Maximum (Note 1)	(Note 2)	
Initial Term				
Album 1	$ 6,000	$ 6,000	$ 4,000	$ 70,000 +7,500 (Note 3)
Album 2	6,000	15,000	4,000	70,000
1st-Option Term				
Album 3	10,000	25,000	6,000	100,000
Album 4	15,000	35,000	8,000	125,000
2nd-Option Term				
Album 5	20,000	40,000	10,000	125,000
Album 6	25,000	60,000	12,500	150,000
3rd-Option Term				
Album 7	30,000	80,000	12,500	150,000
Album 8	30,000	80,000	12,500	250,000
4th-Option Term				
Album 9	(Note 4)	(Note 4)	(Note 4)	250,000
Album 10	(Note 4)	(Note 4)	(Note 4)	300,000

Notes:

1. In the original draft of this contract, the advances provided were lower than the minimums seen above. In the course of negotiation, they were raised to what you see. When the deal was about to "blow" and the only open point remaining was the advance, a "kicker" was devised whereby the advances set forth would be raised by the difference between 66 ⅔% of the artist's royalty earnings on the previous album and the recording costs of that album, not to exceed the total advance set forth in the column labeled "Maximum." When both sides want a deal to "make," they find a way!

2. As a concession for granting co-publishing rights (without which grant the deal would not have been made), the record company agreed to waive an administration fee and agreed to delete the "controlled composition" clause (about which you will learn more shortly).

3. The $7,500 sum represented the cost of some equipment Us desperately needed. I don't think Us will be able to complete the albums required during the initial term for the $70,000 recording fund provided, much less pocket any real advance. The group thinks it can. The record company merely took the position: "Then you'll ask us for more money and we'll listen to what you did with the $70,000 . . . and we'll see."

4. The original draft provided for another option term. As part of the negotiating process, the fourth option term was traded in exchange for the modest advances and the publishing interest. Thus, after the eighth album, the Schedule I artist is into his second record deal. If he has become a superstar, he is now looking at $1,000,000 plus per album while poor Us is looking at $250,000 and $300,000 less recording costs. In addition, if the record company has exercised its option for the fourth option term, you can bet that Us will have earned its advance before it receives it. That's what I meant by "illusory."

newly established record company. This artist also signed a co-publishing agreement with the record company's publishing affiliate. The advances under the co-publishing agreement are listed separately. The two are independent, and the royalties and advances under each are not cross-collateralized against the other. Schedule II is from the Us contract, which, you will recall, is between a four-member rock-'n'-roll group with no track record and a major record company. The advances in Schedule I are in addition to recording costs. The Schedule II advances are inclusive of recording costs. Hence, to compare the two, you must deduct $75,000 to $100,000 (perhaps even more if the inflationary spiral continues) from the advances in Schedule II in order to compare the two.

Which deal is better? You're pretty knowledgeable by now—you figure it out. The answer is not really important. They were the best deals that could be negotiated for the artists with their respective record companies by their respective attorneys.

The important lesson to be learned is that each deal has its own dynamics and tempo. Entire deals can't be compared, much less isolated individual aspects of deals. An artist who is worth X to one record company may be worth much more to a company that has a gap in its roster which that artist fills. How can you tell if the advances in one deal are better than the advances in another deal without knowing the royalties being paid? Speaking of which . . .

Royalties

The Scriptures rarely come to mind in the course of negotiating or reading a record contract. Nevertheless, upon the conclusion of the royalty clause, I rarely fail to be reminded of Job 1:21: ". . . the Lord gave, and the Lord hath taken away. . . ."

Every royalty clause starts with the royalty rate the record company will pay the artist with respect to "net sales of albums sold in the form of disc records through normal retail channels in the United States." The royalty rate stated is usually referred to as the "base royalty" or some similar phrase. The remaining five or six pages of the royalty provision are devoted to debasing the base royalty. It is your attorney's job to resist the encroachments on the base royalty to the extent possible.

The base royalty is invariably a percentage of the record's selling price. Some record companies structure their royalties on the wholesale selling price, some on the retail selling price. The rule of thumb is that a wholesale royalty rate is roughly double that of a retail royalty rate. For example, if MCA, which operates on a retail system, were to offer you a royalty of 8 percent, SONY, which operates on a wholesale system, would, in order to match MCA's offer, have to pay you 16 percent. In terms of dollars, the two offers would be roughly the same. Why? Because the wholesale price of a record is approximately one-half of its retail price.

What is an adequate royalty rate? Simple. The most you can get. How is it determined? By the law of the marketplace—the law of supply and demand. The smaller the royalty the artist is paid, the larger the record company's profit. Thus the struggle begins. All of the references to leverage and bargaining position and other variables that I have referred to in connection with advances and elsewhere apply equally to royalties. What is an adequate or acceptable royalty for a new artist? In the last year I have seen contracts proposing base royalties ranging from 7 percent of retail to 12 percent of retail (14 percent of wholesale to 24 percent of wholesale). What is adequate or acceptable to the artist is usually a function of how often he has felt the sting of rejection and how desperate he is to have his chance. Whether the royalty is for a singer-songwriter or must be divided among a five-member group is also a factor in determining "acceptability" or "reasonableness." I usually feel that if the initial royalty offered is 7 percent of retail or more, the record company is serious and wants to do business. I also feel that no offer should be rejected out of hand merely because of a royalty rate that falls short of a preconceived minimum. There are too many ways to play this game.

Before proceeding further, a word of warning. A quick glance at a base royalty may not tell the whole story. Sometimes a deal is structured in such a way that it is the artist's responsibility to procure *and pay* for the services of its producer. Hence the base royalty in such a contract includes the royalty the artist will have to pay the producer, and that royalty (3 percent–4 percent of retail) must be deducted from the base royalty to arrive at the actual artist's royalty.

Royalty rates, like advances, are usually subject to escalation or increase. Royalty escalations take two forms. The first is an increase in the base royalty from album to album, or from option period to option period as the deal ages. The second is predicated upon sales, with the royalty rate being increased or "bumped" as sales of an album rise above certain agreed upon plateaus. This form of escalation usually works on an album-by-album basis, and the bump only operates with respect to sales that occur after the plateau has been reached that gave birth to the bump. Record companies, when contemplating plateaus, think in terms of the Himalayas or the Rockies. Artists' attorneys think in terms of gentle hills. Finding the right altitude is part of the negotiating game. Record companies like to make the first plateau gold and the second platinum. Artists' attorneys consider these somewhat illusory for any artist who is less than a superstar, and try for 150,000 or 200,000 units as the first plateau. The sales contemplated in calculating these plateaus are usually the combined U.S. and Canadian sales.

Sometimes the artist can obtain the best of all possible worlds and can negotiate escalations combining both methods. The sizes of the increments are subject to negotiation, and logically are to some extent dictated by the initial base royalty. The smaller the base royalty, the more generous the bumps are apt to be. More of this later on when we again compare the royalty provisions of the two deals we compared in the advance section.

You have already learned from the Lexicon and the chapter entitled "Pennies from Heaven" that you can't multiply the base royalty times the selling price times sales and come up with your royalty in pennies. You've learned that packaging costs, free goods allowances, and the like must be factored in to that calculation. To go beyond those basics I think would be counterproductive and would result in a loss of the forest for the trees. Let's leave the rest of the calculations to the accountants and concentrate for the remainder of this section on how your base royalty can and will be whittled away, and the extent to which the erosion can be, if not prevented, at least diminished. Some record companies have more outrageous form contracts than others. Although custom and usage have, over the years, operated in the artist's favor, many record companies cling to form contracts that do not recognize such custom and usage. Although they will change the offending and outdated provisions if they are asked to, they will not do so voluntarily. Let's assume we are dealing with one of those contracts. Better safe than sorry.

Before the advent of the vinyl disc in 1948, records were pressed from a brittle and breakable composition. To avoid the expense of receiving and crediting returned broken records, the record companies gave their customers an automatic 10 percent credit and told them to throw out the broken records. This magnanimous gesture was passed on to the artist, who was quite logically paid a royalty on 90 percent of the records sold. Fair is fair! Although no record has broken in transit since 1948, and the breakage credit soon disappeared from record-company invoices to their customers, payment "on 90 percent of records sold" curiously still persists, albeit rarely, in some artists' contracts. If the record company is requested to change this to payment "on 100 percent of records sold," it will do so. If the request is not made, you will receive payment on 90 percent. If you have a base royalty of 10 percent, your failure to catch this has the net result of reducing your base royalty to 9 percent!

Similarly, when tape cassettes and 8-track cartridges were born, the record companies, perhaps with justification, took the position that because of low sales volume, their high price, their experimental nature, or whatever, they could only pay a half royalty rate with respect to sales of "records in the form of tape." Well, today record companies pay the same royalty rate with respect to tape as they do with respect to discs.

For many years it was the custom for the royalty rate on sales made outside the U.S. to be one-half the royalty rate on domestic sales. Artists' representatives started whittling away at this, and it became clear that a better royalty rate than one-half the domestic rate was available. How much better varies with the size of the base royalty rate and the royalty your record company receives from its foreign licensees. It appears that even international record companies adhere to rather rigid licensing arrangements between their domestic and international divisions. The higher the royalty the record company receives and the lower the base royalty it has to pay you, the easier it is for it to pay you a royalty on foreign sales approximating your base royalty on domestic sales. Very often, as you will see in the chart at the end of this section, the foreign royalty rate varies from country to country, depending upon the deal your record company has made for itself with respect to each country.

The royalty rate for 45-rpm single records is usually less than that for other formats. Singles are looked upon primarily as promotional devices with a low profit yield for the record company. It is in the artist's best interest to have the record company promote singles, and hence a reduced royalty to make such promotion practical for the record company is not without justification.

Had someone told me that compact discs were not mentioned in either the Lexicon or text of the first edition I would have quite frankly told them that they were crazy. Imagine my shock therefore when in the course of making the last revision I made this discovery! No, I don't think that I was careless the first time around. CDs just weren't a factor worthy of mention back in 1982 or 1983 . . . nor was it anticipated that they would become a factor in the foreseeable future. In the years since, compact discs have grown in popularity beyond the wildest expectations of even their most enthusiastic proponents. They have entirely supplanted vinyl discs.

When compact discs first hit the market their suggested retail price was in the thirty-dollar range. Because there was little hardware with which to use them, and because of their cost, it was anticipated that they would not be a profit center for the record companies for many years to come . . . perhaps never. Accordingly, the record companies determined (not without some justification) that they could not pay a full royalty based on the CDs' suggested retail price. To make a long story short, they took the position that they would pay the same royalty (in cents) on CDs that they paid on the comparable vinyl LP . . . notwithstanding the discrepancy in their respective suggested retail selling prices. If the artist's attorney balked at this, the record company's rejoinder was, "Okay, we won't issue CDs of your artist." This of course was not acceptable to the artist. Nevertheless, no attorney worth his salt could agree to lock his client into an "experimental" royalty for the seven or eight years the contract might endure. Accordingly, various accommodations were developed, all of which are now obsolete.

As we have already noted, as we enter the nineties, vinyl LPs are history. Therefore any CD rate predicated upon LPs must leave something to be desired. Accordingly, the industry developed another cockamamie formula. The royalty on CDs would be 130 percent of their wholesale price. "Whoa," cried the artists' lawyers, "with CD prices getting lower and lower, soon we'll be getting less for a CD than we did for a vinyl LP." Thus was born the phrase, ". . . but in no event less than the royalty payable with respect to a comparable analog cassette." Another chapter *temporarily* closed in the never-ending dramatic struggle between the artist and the record company!

It would be ideal if your CD clause had a provision whereby if the general policy of your record company changes so that CD royalties become more favorable to artists than the "same pennies" deal you have, your contract is automatically deemed changed to reflect such more favorable royalty. Without this you can find yourself to be an established artist who is receiving a less favorable CD royalty than a brand-new artist just signed to the label. This will make you very unhappy! I just tried to obtain this clause for a major artist . . . and failed!

In addition to the aforementioned major areas, your base royalty rate will suffer shrinkage with respect to a slew of other special areas, including sales through record clubs, sales of budget records, licensed uses of your records, K-Tel–type sales, and premium sales. All of these are grist for your attorney's mill. To pursue them in detail here would be to go beyond the scope of this book and overly burden and confuse you.

Are you still pondering the advances received by our two sample artists? After preparing Table 3.3, I have concluded that it is "dated" and too detailed and complicated to be required reading. If you skip it, your comprehension of the chapter will not be adversely affected. Neither will your career. But, on the other hand, for those of you who are into it, it might be fun to romp through the chart. Consider it reference material that you can refer to as and when you choose. Besides, it required too damn much work to tear up!

Currently royalties with respect to foreign territories still vary hugely. If you insist on a rule of thumb you may ponder the following which are all percentages of the U.S. royalty rate: Canada, 85–90 percent; "major" foreign territories, 66⅔–75 percent; rest of the world, 50 percent. Helpful? Not at all. The rub lies in what is major. When I am negotiating for an artist, even Afghanistan and Thailand are major, major. When I represent the record company I try to draw the line at the United Kingdom and Germany! The truth is of course someplace in between. I don't know why but in my experience Australia has always been a great music country. I always try to have it counted as a major territory . . . Japan, too.

It is important to realize that both Table 3.3 contracts started off less advantageously for the artist than what you see. Each contract element is the product of give-and-take and compromise. Probing by both sides to find the limits of the other takes a long time, and it is only after this process is completed that the real trading can take place and the contract be concluded. The legal fees charged the artist whose contract is the subject of Schedule I consumed almost all of his initial advances. If he were successful, the changes won in the negotiation would have resulted in hundreds of thousands, if not millions, of dollars in increased earnings. Alas, he was not successful, but has the satisfaction of having contributed to the college education of two fine young people . . . my son and daughter.

Video (Audio-Visual Records)

For many years the record industry has been vaguely aware, almost subliminally so, of the potential of audio-visual recordings. Since they had no conception of how the monster might surface, they sought a hedge in their

Table 3.3
Royalties

Schedule I

	Base Royalty Rate (Retail)	Foreign Royalties (Retail)
Initial Term		
Album 1	8% (Note 1)	Group A:
Album 2	8% (Note 2)	Japan and Canada - 7%
1st-Option Term		Group B:
Album 3	8%	United Kingdom, France,
Album 4	8%	Holland, Belgium,
2nd-Option Term		Luxembourg, Australia,
Album 5	9%	New Zealand, Canada,
Album 6	9%	Germany - 6%
3rd-Option Term		Group C:
Album 7	10%	Elsewhere - 4.5%
Album 8	10%	Foreign royalties remain
4th-Option Term		constant throughout the term and do
Album 9	—	not escalate at all.
Album 10	—	Audiovisual records:
		The same royalty rates apply
		to audiovisual records as
		apply to sound-only
		recordings.

Schedule II

Base Royalty Rate (Wholesale)	Foreign Royalty Rates (Wholesale)
22% (Note 1) throughout the term inclusive of a royalty to the producer which can be estimated at approximately 6% of wholesale, leaving an artist royalty of 16% of wholesale (roughly 8% of retail)	Group A: United Kingdom and Canada - 16.5% Group B: European Economic Community, Japan, Australia, and New Zealand - 14.7% Group C: Elsewhere - 11% These royalty rates remain constant throughout the term (Notes 2 & 3) and include the producer's royalty.

Audio-visual records: (Note 4)

	U.S.	Foreign
Videodisc units	10%	7.5%
Videocassettes and other audio-visual records	7.5%	5%

Notes (Schedule I)

1. In addition to the escalations shown, there are "bumps" of ½% at plateaus of 250,000 units up to 1,000,000 units. For example, if Album 1 sold 780,000 units, the royalty rates payable to the artist would be as follows:
   On sales up to 250,000 units - 8%
   On sales from 250,000 to 500,000 units - 8½%
   On sales from 500,000 to 750,000 units - 9%
   On sales from 750,000 to 780,000 units - 9½%
   The base royalty rate on singles and EPs is a flat 7%.
2. This contract also has a feature whereby the highest royalty rate reached on the preceding LP becomes the base royalty rate for the next LP. For example, the starting base royalty rate on Album 2 would be 9½%. The maximum royalty attainable, by agreement is 11%.

Notes (Schedule II)

1. The base royalty rate escalates to 24% on sales between 500,000 units (gold) and 1,000,000 units (platinum) and to 26% on sales in excess of 1,000,000 units (platinum).
   The base royalty rate on singles is 16%; on EPs it is 18% with a bump to 20% on sales over 250,000 units.
2. Foreign royalty rates are reduced as follows with respect to singles and EPs:
   Group A: Singles - 12%; EPs - 13.5%
   Group B: Singles - 10.7%; EPs - 12%
   Group C: Singles - 8%; EPs - 9%
3. Foreign royalty rates are escalated, with respect to albums only, on foreign sales in excess of 1,000,000 units as follows:
   Group A: - 19.5%
   Group B: - 17.3%
   Group C: - 13% plus an egg roll
4. Audio-visual royalty rates are based on wholesale. Please see the discussion in the next section.

contract definitions of "phonograph record" and "masters." A typical definition reads as follows: ". . . any device, whether now known or unknown,
on which sound alone *or sound accompanied by visual images* may be recorded. . . ."

The attorneys for the artists asked, "What does that mean?" The record
companies said, "Don't worry about it," whereupon the artists' attorneys
started to really worry! Thus the "stand-off" compromise evolved whereby
both sides agreed not to exercise audio-visual rights without the consent of
the other. Then one day everyone woke up to find that the future was present
and that the age of audio-visual recordings had dawned—not yet exploded,
but very definitely with us. Therefore, the first edition of this book had the
following passages:

> You are breaking into the business at the very threshold of the audio-
> visual revolution. No one yet knows how it will be manifested. Two
> things are now apparent. First, a stand-off is no longer acceptable to the
> record companies, which are insisting on a present right to take you into
> the audio-visual arena. Second, no one is sure of what the appropriate
> royalty or other compensation for the artist should be. Two solutions to
> the problem are illustrated in the royalty schedules shown in Table 3.3.
> Neither of the solutions, payment at the same royalty rate as sound re-
> cordings (Schedule I) or at a greatly reduced rate (Schedule II), seems
> viable in the long run.
>
> A standard will evolve in the not too distant future. For the time being,
> it is sufficient for you to be cognizant of the problem.

Well, here we are two editions further into the not too distant future, and
no real standard has evolved. MTV prospered, and the record company's
lawyer's word processors hummed, and the already flatulently overburdened
record company contracts swelled another ten to twenty pages! Not only
were there more pages, but save for the poor bastards who spent weeks
drafting and redrafting them, they were for the most part unintelligible . . .
and to no small degree still are. I had planned to make video a separate
chapter in this edition but upon reviewing my materials I decided that to
justify an entire chapter I would have to really concentrate on the contractual
provisions relative to audio-visual rights, and to do so would depress me and
confuse you, neither of which possibilities were terribly attractive.

Video clips (the short one-song promotional videos you see on MTV and
similar shows) and videocassettes are not yet consistent money-makers for
either record companies or artists. It is still the case, although it will probably
change in the not-too-distant future, that relatively few video clips or video
cassettes recover their costs, much less provide the artist with a royalty. There
are, of course, exceptions; Michael Jackson's "Thriller" sold over 800,000
copies, The Stones' sold over 200,000 copies of "Video Rewind," and of
course, Madonna videos sell well. Some heavy metal artists also make money

from video. The success of Madonna's "Justify My Love" video single (400,000 copies) may be an anomaly or it may be the start of a trend; it is too soon to tell. Acting on the success of the Madonna video single, Capitol Records is now about to release a new MC Hammer video for "Here Comes the Hammer" which will contain the clip and some miscellaneous footage. According to *Billboard* magazine, the MC Hammer clip alone cost in excess of one million dollars to make. How do the record companies hope to recoup the formidable expenses of video production? Why is the risk taken?

Last things first. The risk is taken because the record companies believe they need the videos to promote their new audio records. There are few honest record executives who would deny that video clips are, at least thusfar, primarily promotional tools of the record company. They attempt to hedge their bets in ways that are very expensive and painful to you. Until the advent of video, the record companies always justified charging recording costs against the artist's royalties by balancing it against their risk in advancing it, and their costs of manufacturing and promoting the resulting records. Promotion was traditionally a cost borne by the record company . . . until video, that is. If any standard has evolved out of the video revolution it is the standard position taken by the record companies that all costs of videos are charged as advances against the artist's royalty account . . . notwithstanding the fact that they are primarily promotional devices. To make matters worse, the video costs are charged against any and all of the artist's royalties, audio as well as video (i.e. cross-collateralized). What can you do about it? Very little. Your attorney will try several gambits, in addition to cajoling, begging, muttering, and crying.

First he may try the "promotion" argument I made above and request that the costs be totally absorbed by the record company. He has about as much chance as a snowball in hell. The next and more fruitful position to take is that video costs should be split between the artist and the record company. This suggestion sometimes meets with acceptance. If you are successful in engineering a split you can be assured that the record company will insist that your share of video costs be fully recoupable from your audio as well as your video income.

If a sharing of costs is not greeted with enthusiasm, logic then dictates the argument that if all the costs of video are going to be charged against the artist, they should only be charged against video income . . . especially since they are primarily promotional costs, traditionally within the record company's ambit. Good luck! What you may end up with, after a struggle, is a compromise whereby half the video costs may be recouped from audio income while still being fully recoupable from video income.

What control can you have over video costs? You can ask for the following rights of approval:

1. Whether or not to do a video. This is of course tantamount to the old standoff provision of the pre-video days. Chances are that it won't fly.

2. Approval of the production budget, including the fees and royalties

payable to the video producer. After all, it is your money. This is recognized as another way for the artist to bring leverage to bear. Record companies don't enjoy your having leverage. Chances are you won't get it. But, it's certainly worth a shot.

3. Approval of the song that is the subject of the video. Chances are this will be dictated by which song seems to "take off" and "deserve" the video. Possible. But there seems to be little choice, or difference of opinion here.

Any approvals granted will be subject to the tag, "not to be unreasonably withheld." You ask for everything and hope the record company becomes sufficiently uncomfortable about saying no, to ultimately yield on something. When it comes down to the bottom line, nobody can make you perform on a video (or on a record for that matter), and if you're hot enough and persistent enough you can force some things to go your way. On the other hand, you need your record company behind you, and if you make enough of a pain of yourself you can turn them off . . . oblivion follows. Be patient, if you are successful your turn to be unreasonable will come. Remember, if you make it, the balance of terror shifts.

Do you get paid for videos? Of course, at least theoretically. You must, however, keep in mind the fact that up till now only a handful of artists have recouped their video costs and actually realized income. A survey of video royalty provisions can leave you numb. There is no standard, and the provisions in many instances are so equivocal, ambiguous, and convoluted as to leave you scratching your head. Basically you receive 7½ percent to 10 percent of the wholesale price on sales, and a percentage varying from 10 percent to 50 percent of "net receipts" on licensed uses. The number of deductions and subtractions taken in arriving at your royalty on sales and your "net" share of receipts from licenses are limited only by the imaginations of the record company's royalty manager and the lawyer drafting the contract. Right now they tax my comprehension, are certainly beyond yours, and consequently beyond the scope of this book. Incidentally, the situation with respect to the use of controlled compositions in connection with video is just as muddled. When income from video becomes a real factor, the contract provisions will standardize and become comprehensible. They'll have to. Perhaps this will all be ripe for the fourth edition!

Now listen up! Don't forget that although a record contract is long and broken up into many sections and topics, it is still a unified document. You must never get so embroiled in one topic that you permit yourself to forget what is buried somewhere else in the boilerplate. Record contracts (and contracts in general) are quite often constructed with that in mind. One thing you must be ever mindful of are the exclusivity provisions of your contract. Your contract makes you exclusive to the record company in connection with phonograph records. "Phonograph records" is defined in your contract to be inclusive of any device by which sound alone or sound accompanied by visual images may be recorded. Suppose you have an opportunity to be in a motion picture, or on a TV special, either as the star or as a guest. There will in the case of a theatrical motion picture, and quite likely in the case of a cable TV special, be offered for sale a videocassette of the production. Unless you carve out an exception in your record contract you will have to go hat in hand to your record company for permission to do the project. Will they grant permission? Probably, if they think it is a good move for your record career. They may, however, try to exact tribute from the producer in the form of points or in the form of acquiring rights to the video package. This type of complication can be just enough to queer the gig for you. It can also cost you dearly if you are the packager of the project. When you make your record deal, when these possibilities are remote, is the time to try for the concession. Some reasonable compromise is possible. I am particularly fond of one company's way of dealing with this:

> Artist may perform in theatrical and/or television motion pictures and in other television productions, provided that the agreement pursuant to which such performances are rendered expressly prohibits the release by any person of so-called soundtrack Albums or Records of such performance by Artist. For the purpose of this paragraph *"Records" shall not include audio-visual devices embodying all or substantially all of the motion picture or television production embodying the performance of Artist.*

Controlled Compositions

From 1909 to 1976 the mechanical copyright royalty record companies were required to pay the copyright owners of songs was two cents per record. From 1976 to 1985 that mechanical copyright royalty rose in steps to five cents. Unfortunately, the rise in the mechanical royalty took place at a time when record sales were ebbing and the record companies were beginning to hurt. Consequently, the controlled-composition clause in record-company contracts assumed new importance. A controlled-composition clause provides that with respect to songs owned or controlled by the artist, a mechanical license for the use of such songs will be issued for a royalty less than that required by the Copyright Act. When the statutory mechanical license rate was two cents, the usual controlled-composition clause called for a rate of one and one-half cents. It was really quite academic, because when a knowledgeable entertainment attorney resisted the reduction, the record company invariably folded on the point.

Alas, such is no longer the case. The record companies are now unyielding in the retention of their controlled-composition clauses and insisting upon a three-quarter of "statutory" rate in lieu of the statutory 5.7 cent rate.

In the first edition I said that deletion of the controlled-composition clause was a tough but sometimes winnable battle. It is no longer winnable! Greed is boundless and the record companies are not immune to its siren song. Once they consolidated the controlled-composition clause, their natural tendency was to embellish it. Your contract may therefore contain language not only granting the record company a three-quarter rate on your songs but also making you responsible for the difference between the statutory 5.7 cent and the 4.275 cent controlled-composition rate with respect to non-controlled compositions! How does this work? Devastatingly! Watch. Suppose you have a ten-song album, five of which were written by you and five of which are owned and controlled by strangers who are disinclined to grant your record company a "rate." Ordinarily the record company would pay you or your publishing company 5×4.275 cents or 21.375 cents per album plus another 28.5 cents to the other publishers ($5.7\textcent \times 5 = 28.5\textcent$). Under the insidious clause I have just referred to the difference between the 28.5 cents the record company must pay to the unrelated publishers and the 21.375 cents they would have paid with respect to controlled compositions, 7.125 cents is simply deducted from the mechanical royalties that would otherwise have been payable to you. So instead of receiving 21.375 cents per album, you now receive only 14¼ cents per album ($21.375\textcent - 7.125\textcent = 14.25\textcent$) Neat, huh? This is certainly a battle worth fighting, and it is winnable ... sometimes.

Merchandising

"What goes around comes around!" When I first started in this business every record contract included a merchandising clause. This clause gave the record company the right to use and exploit your name and likeness in connection with the advertising, exploitation, and sale of products and services, and to share the income therefrom with you. What kinds of products and services? Any kind your lawyer didn't bar! Usually, if you asked the record company to delete the merchandising clause they did so, or at least modified it so that they couldn't exercise the right without the artist's consent. It was a freebie, something they didn't exploit or care too much about; a concession they could make graciously ... something for the lawyers to show their clients "they got!" Eventually, merchandising was just dropped from most recording contracts, and therefore was not an issue worth mentioning in the first edition of this book.

Well, here it is 1991 and guess what's crept back into the record company contracts? You guessed it, merchandising. To make matters worse, the record companies are tending to jealously guard the right. A number of the major record companies acquired interests in merchandising ventures and naturally began to pursue merchandising rights in their record contracts. Well, once one company adds a clause, it doesn't take long for the others to get on the bandwagon. Not unlike sharks in a feeding frenzy ... they eat whether hungry or not.

In a contract I am currently reviewing, "merchandising" is not accorded a separate heading or even defined in the definition section. The subject is buried in the "rights" section where it takes a sharp eye to find it. Remember, as I said elsewhere, never read a record contract when you're tired! What do you do when you find it? First you try to have it deleted. Failing that, you try to limit it to the extent you can.

You may wonder at my concern in this area. After all, you may think, the record company is doing the "work," and they are sharing the revenues 50/50, so what's so terrible? The major concern you and your advisers must have in this area is that the merchandising rights retained by the record company are not of such scope that they interfere with your ability to exploit your success as a personality in the very lucrative field of advertising . . . your ability to appear in, or use your name and likeness in connection with, radio, television, and print advertisements endorsing or extolling the virtues of everything from toothpaste to tires, or as in the case of one of my dearest friends, sausages to shoes. It isn't enough that the record company's merchandising rights are nonexclusive. Every lucrative advertising deal involves exclusivity. Colgate isn't going to pay you a fortune to smile for its toothpaste unless you can guarantee that you won't be simultaneously smiling for Crest. That is a guarantee you can't give if somebody else (your record company) can grant the right to use your name or likeness to Crest. Many of the merchandising clauses are so broad as to encompass just about anything, and so vague as to give you or your advisers little ability to steer a safe course. Just about the last thing you want to have to do is to go back to your record company to ask permission to do anything! Every favor asked is a favor owed. If that last sentence sounds like it came out of a fortune cookie, I apologize, but it's true. You've been warned!

Approvals

A first draft of a recording contract rarely gives the artist much of a voice in the creative decisions attendant upon the production of his records. Indeed, some contracts initially provide that the record company will choose the songs to be recorded. This is especially vexing to a writer-artist, and is in fact more honored in the breach than the observance. Nevertheless, there has evolved through the years a list of factors over which the artist may secure control, or at least a right of approval. Some of these are:

Producer
Musical compositions to be recorded
Times and places of recording (and video filming)
Pictures and biographical material pertaining to the artist
Final sound mix
Album covers, including the artwork
Liner notes
Joint recordings
Use of the artist's recordings in connection with premiums
Coupling of the artist's recordings with recordings by other artists

Recording budgets
Cuts to be used as singles
Video songs and scripts

Independent Producers

Suppose, rather than signing directly with a major label, you are discovered by and signed to an independent producer. Is this better or worse than signing directly with a major label? Well, it's certainly a lot better than not being discovered at all. How much better depends on the independent producer involved. If it's a legitimate independent producer with a demonstrable track record who is respected in the industry—congratulations. If it's someone who is unknown, untried, and untalented—good luck and beware . . . he's gonna scare the hell out of the record companies.

If the independent producer who is interested in you is of the first kind, you have to be flattered by his interest and consider any offer he may make very seriously. If the independent producer who exhibits interest in you has no track record, is generally unknown and without clout, I would be inclined to place him on the back burner until all other avenues have been exhausted.

Logic dictates that if you deal with an independent producer, the economics of your deal are not apt to be quite as favorable as they would be if you were dealing directly with a major label (of course, without the clout of the independent producer, you might never attract the interest of a major label). A record company is prepared to pay a certain maximum for each act it records. When the artist is signed through an independent producer, that maximum has to be shared by the artist and the independent producer. In addition, almost universally, the independent producer will seek all, or at least a substantial part, of your publishing. It is the publishing interest that makes the deal viable for, and attractive to, the independent producer. There just isn't enough there to justify the effort, responsibility, and risk without it. To illustrate: suppose the independent production company receives a royalty of 12 percent of retail from the label. If the artist is a group, it's going to ask for a royalty in the 7 percent to 10 percent range. If the power behind the independent production company is also the line producer, he would be entitled to 3 percent to 4 percent without the headaches attendant upon operating what amounts to a record company. If the independent production company has to lure an outside line producer, there is very little (if anything) left indeed. Thus you can see why giving some or all of your publishing in a deal such as this is really not optional.

There are a few basic independent-producer deal structures. In the first deal structure, if you didn't know better, you would think you were dealing with SONY, MCA, Capitol, Warner Bros., or some other major record company. It's a contract identical to the sixty-page monster we just discussed, and it is negotiated with the same fervor and at the same expense. In turn, after signing you, the independent producer (assuming it's found a deal for your services) negotiates its own sixty-page contract with a major label. Wherever the independent producer does better with the label than you did with the independent producer, it benefits. For instance, if the independent producer is paying you a 6 percent royalty and getting 12 percent, that's better for the independent producer than if it pays you 8 percent and it gets 12 percent. Similarly, if under your contract with the independent producer, you receive a "one-half rate" on foreign sales, and in the independent producer's contract with the record label, it gets a "three-fourths rate," it can pocket the difference as profit. Incidentally, this is a perfectly legitimate way of doing business; it's called free enterprise. It is also very expensive and conducive to dissension. Guess who's paying for recording costs in this situation? Right, you are! So the independent producer starts with that edge—plus, in all likelihood, the publishing.

Well, after a while, some wiser heads concluded that it was to neither the independent producer's nor the artist's benefit to have them beat each other up, especially in view of the fact that they would have to live together for a long time. Thus evolved the short-form "pass-through" independent-production deal. This saves about forty-five pages of legal fees and usually has both sides feeling better about each other than the format set forth above. It works like this:

First, the artist's royalty is set. It can be a percentage of either the retail or the wholesale selling price, or a fraction of the royalty the independent producer receives from the record company, or a combination. For instance, the contract may state that ". . . the artist shall receive a royalty rate equal to one-half of the royalty rate received by the independent producer, but *in no event* less than 6 percent of the retail selling price . . ." Thus, there is a floor to the artist's royalty and a built-in escalation in the event the independent producer has significant "bumps" based on the artist's success.

Next, advance language is provided, which could be a fixed number of dollars, or a share of what remains after recording costs are paid. Who bears recording costs? The artist or the independent producer? You can bet that the first draft will have you paying—so may the final draft—but taking recording costs off the top has been tried successfully in the past. That's why you have an entertainment lawyer.

Next, the "pass-through" contract earns its name by stating that essentially all of the fiscal provisions of the independent producer's contract with the record label are "passed through" automatically to the artist. By way of example, if the independent producer receives a "three-fourths foreign rate," the benefit is automatically passed on to the artist. Similarly, the artist receives the same free-goods limitation as the independent producer, etc.

The "pass through" is a format that is a simpler, cheaper, and more harmonious way to go . . . and everybody probably ends up the same way in the long run. But don't try to do it on your own just because it looks relatively short and simple. Let's put together a little independent-production-deal checklist so we'll be sure you have an awareness of the major issues:

1. "Pass through" vs. long form.
2. Recording costs "off the top"? Worth a try!
3. Advances. Do the best you can.
4. Royalties. Do the best you can . . . you need a floor and an escalator for the high end.
5. Publishing. Try to salvage at least half with a co-publishing deal *and make sure your obligations as a songwriter terminate when the record deal does.*
6. Make sure the publishing and record deals are not cross-collateralized against each other! Please!
7. Make sure you have the right to approve the line producer . . . and the right to replace him if success eludes you. Record labels will shy away from deals where they are locked in forever to a certain producer; it scares the hell out of them, for good reason.
8. Make sure there is a provision—discuss it up front—whereby if a record is not recorded and released by a major label within a certain period of time (six months to one year), the production contract *and* the publishing contract automatically end.
9. The ultimate right to approve the label deal, thus giving your attorney an opportunity to review and have input with respect to the agreement you're being "passed through" to.

A review of the Lexicon will act as a checklist of other items you may wish to consult your attorney about and ultimately toss into the negotiation hopper.

I hope that the foregoing will arm you with the essentials you need to approach your record deal realistically and intelligently. There are myriad other issues over which your attorney will do battle with the record company. With respect to some, he will prevail; with respect to others, he will not. But an informed and interested client will be of inestimable help to him.

INTERVIEW WITH
CLIVE DAVIS

Clive Davis is the founder and president of Arista Records, a former president of Columbia Records, and an entertainment attorney. Renowned as a discoverer and molder of talent, he is also a successful songwriter and producer.

AHS: Of course, we could refer the readers to your autobiography, *Clive*, but, instead, perhaps we could have a brief synopsis of the route one takes from Harvard Law School to the presidencies of two major record companies?

DAVIS: Those things really happen, I think, or at least partly happen, through coincidence. I had been an attorney in a private law firm which happened to represent CBS, an account for which I did no work. One of the lawyers who had previously left the firm to go to Columbia Records as general counsel was being promoted, and he was unhappy with his then assistant, who would be in line to succeed him as general counsel. So, about two and a half years out of law school, I got a great offer, unsolicited, purely by luck really, to become assistant counsel at Columbia Records. Then, within six months, when the general counsel's promotion took effect, I became general counsel. Five years later, as is wont to happen in a large company, there was a political reorganization, and Goddard Lieberson, then president of Columbia Records, I think saw in me an underlying enthusiasm for the business, and it just was the right time and the right place to afford me an opportunity to become head of a company without any prior experience. From there it was all really learning the business, plunging in, and out of necessity relying on my creative instincts, which were totally untested. Although there was no indication of any prior creative credentials whatsoever, the existing situation at Columbia Records put me to the test. Columbia Records was steeped in what we call "Middle of the Road" music and classics and Broadway shows, and we had to move into the rock era. I had nobody to do it for me, because all the A&R men had grown up with Doris Day or Mitch Miller or Johnny Mathis or Andy Williams and Barbra Streisand, so I had to rely on myself. I did just that at the Monterey Pop Festival by signing Janis Joplin, and, thereafter, Blood Sweat and Tears, Chicago, and Santana. Buttressed by the confidence that came out of making the right decisions and fortified with really unexpected good luck and success, I've continued on in the creative arena, so that it's become second nature to me and now I spend probably 75 percent of my time just doing A&R work.

AHS: You're very modest. You of course know you are regarded as one of the most talented record executives in the business today. That's talent . . . not intuition and not good luck. Clive, it's very hard to make a record deal today. A lot of young artists appear to be beating their heads against a stone wall. The first look a record company gets at a new artist is usually his demonstration record. I know many of them are done in an absolutely wrong manner. If you could set them, what would your guidelines be for a demo? The number of songs? The duration of the song? The sequence, etc.?

DAVIS: I think, most often, an artist falls into the category of a singer-songwriter, where his focus is on trying to write a hit song. Let's distinguish that kind of artist from a progressive FM rock-oriented group. You can't have the same rules for every artist, because what is appropriate depends on the category of music. For the singer-songwriter, those that are coming up in the tradition of Paul Simon and Carole King and James Taylor, I think that diversity isn't that significant. I think the important thing is really how many hit songs you're capable of writing! I would limit the tape to no more than six songs. Rather than try to show that you could write a jazz song and a hard-rock song and a soft song, or a ballad and an up-tempo, the only criteria should really be the strength of the material and whether or not it qualifies to be a hit record or a hit song in your own mind. That is what we are looking for to break through new artists today in this category . . . not how introspective the artist can be. Occasionally, there is the unusual, the unique artist who stands apart from those who are writing material in the genre of hit material or general singer-songwriter material. The best example of that currently is Rickie Lee Jones. Again, I would not submit more than six or seven songs, but in that category, you would try to demonstrate the uniqueness and originality. Clearly she has, in her phraseology and her words and her imagery, like Springsteen in the early days, made it on the uniqueness of the material. In the singer-songwriter category, I myself can listen to a piano and voice demo because you are listening primarily to the song, and not so much to the artist's voice. If you like the songs and feel they're hits, you're going to see the artist in person after that anyway. Obviously, if you have the money, it is possible to enhance it, perhaps with a rhythm section, in a local recording studio for $15 to $20 an hour, as distinguished from the $100 to $150 an hour it costs to record masters. I would say you should keep it simple and keep the number of songs limited to around six.

In the AOR category, where you're talking of a group usually, clearly everything applies that I said before, but you just can't, you cannot, do a piano-and-voice thing. You would have to do the group in a demo studio. Here again, do only the strongest material. Usually it's a good idea to keep in mind the fact that companies are going to look for different criteria in assuming whether or not you can break through. One is whether there is an AOR classic, that kind of cut that cannot be a hit single but which is akin to those classics that broke Bob Dylan and those classics that you look for in a Bruce Springsteen, or if it's harder rock, you're looking for the strength of the material and the playing. Your demos have to be a little bit more carefully planned out. But again, I would do no more than six tunes and just the strongest, strongest material which will show what makes you distinctive; either a unique sound or your ability to create classics or hits.

AHS: Do you appreciate receiving pictures or lyric sheets with demos?

DAVIS: I think lyric sheets are helpful. It takes the strain out of trying to listen for every word. Pictures are useful. Sure, I think it's nice to see what the artist looks like. Not essential. But certainly useful.

AHS: What is the selection process at Arista? Do you use the committee system? Is it your A&R staff? Ultimately, I'm sure you pass on each act that's signed to Arista, but, ordinarily, does it go through the lower echelons first?

DAVIS: Yes. All demos are reviewed by the A&R staff. If I received a demo in the mail, I would immediately send it to my A&R staff for reviewing. During that process, if anybody is felt to be that talented, the cassettes, as you can see, reach me and I listen. But the early selectivity is at the A&R staff level.

AHS: I would gather from what you've already said that an artist who creates his own songs is looked upon with more favor?

DAVIS: It really is much easier, because if you don't create your own songs, the standard of performance is extraordinarily high for that new Streisand, that new Aretha Franklin. Clearly, in the AOR category, you've got to do your own material. If you're just a performer, you've got to be awesome in talent today, I think, to depend on other people's material and to have a company willing to take on the burden, either itself or through the producer, of finding hit songs for you.

AHS: An instinct question: what's the most common turnoff . . . the most common mistake that makes you think . . . "Ah, that's not for me"?

DAVIS: Usually, when it comes unsolicited from the outside, most of the material is, frankly, not of professional caliber. I think the common mistake of those that have talent is to describe or showcase versatility, rather than strength. So if someone is a great ballad writer, instead of submitting six great ballads, he'll submit two ballads and put all his eggs in those baskets and then do several up-tempos and other things.

AHS: What chance does an unsolicited demo have of being listened to, as opposed to demos brought in by various attorneys, accountants, and managers? What is your policy?

DAVIS: At Arista, it is 100 percent. Everything is listened to. I mean, unsolicited demos take longer to get listened to than a demo submitted by an established attorney or a manager with a track record. Not that I've had any good luck with unsolicited tapes, but there is something about my background or training which requires me to have everything answered. So we answer all mail. I guess I grew up in that tradition. So, not to puff about it, it's just something that we do. We listen to everything.

AHS: I got the impression that you indicated you've had very little success with unsolicited tapes?

DAVIS: Yes . . . very little success.

AHS: Any at all?

DAVIS: "Unsolicited" means not solicited from attorneys and managers, but, rather, through the mails from unknown people. I've recorded through Columbia and Arista maybe two, but I can't recall anything coming from an unsolicited private person that has proven significant.

AHS: It's a very small percentage considering the number of tapes you've listened to?

DAVIS: Oh, very. Now on the other hand, obviously, through managers or producers or attorneys, you expect more.

AHS: You must receive an awesome number of cassettes a year. Do you have any idea of how many?

DAVIS: No, because I don't know what comes into the A&R department. They keep track of it; there is a log. I guess I personally get—it varies—somewhere about sixty a week. My A&R staff might get many more.

AHS: Would you venture a guess as to what percentage of artists that submit themselves to Arista sign deals?

DAVIS: I could put a percentage, but it is a low percentage, because we have prided ourselves on being a lean company and becoming the alternative to CBS and Warner's. We do not sign ten to get one and throw them up against the wall to see if they stick. We've tried to be very selective. We have only forty-eight to fifty artists on the roster, thirty-five of whose last albums sold in excess of 200,000 units. We have enjoyed great depth and diversity, which stood us in good stead during the previous two flat-growth periods in the record industry. Although I think it's a healthy industry, we are really among the few survivors. Of all the new companies that were started, there are really only two that have survived the last ten years. Among Casablanca, RSO, Arista, Chrysalis, and others, Chrysalis and Arista are the only survivors. The others really have fallen by the wayside because they had only one or two artists, whether it be the BeeGees and Clapton, or whether it be Donna Summer and The Village People. Once those artists peak, the company is dead. Although we had our Manilow at the same time, we broadened into R&B and we broadened into AOR and to jazz progressives, so that we have thirty-five artists whose last albums sold in excess of 200,000 copies. That gives us, with The Kinks and The Grateful Dead and Melissa Manchester and Air Supply—you can just go up and down the line; Aretha Franklin, Dionne Warwick, and just a whole host and variety of artists—good depth. We sign selectively; we focus the spotlight for artists such as Dionne and Gino Vannelli and The Kinks and Aretha. We've been able to bring them back after others had sort of not done their jobs. So we listen carefully, sign selectively.

AHS: Do you prefer a prospective act to be affiliated with a line producer when they come in?

DAVIS: It really depends on the artist, and of course the producer. I mean there is nothing better than to get an artist with a great producer. It makes your life so much easier. That combination is terrific if it's there. If it's with a lousy producer, you sort of cringe because you realize that although the artist might be talented, you know it can't be of long-lasting value because the producer is not that heavy . . . he was just there first. So you've got to be careful. When it's there, where it is a good combination, it's ideal.

AHS: Last question! Do you prefer your artists to come equipped with managers, or do you prefer to mix and match?

DAVIS: Truthfully, there are so few really good managers that it creates a great burden when an artist comes to you and asks you to recommend a manager. It's tough. I prefer the manager to be experienced, whether he is a son of a bitch or a nice guy. The worst thing is to come with an amateur manager who really doesn't know what the hell he or she is doing . . . and it's chaos. They think they're never getting enough, or they're unsure whether or not they are, so they're just totally unrealistic. On the other hand, you don't want someone to be just a lamb. I'm all in favor of a good, strong professional manager that you can relate to and work in harmony with. We all have the same mission, so it makes it that much easier than if we have to pick up all the pieces and fill the void as sometimes we do through produce managers or A&R or myself. I certainly prefer an artist to have a strong professional manager, but I have never *not* signed an artist because the manager is inexperienced. . . . It's the artist that you are concerned about. There are times, during everyone's career, where you just have a terrible relationship with a manager or even with an artist, but you can never give the artist up if the talent is there. Even if the artist is a pain in the ass or if the manager is, if the talent is good or extraordinary, you must be willing to put up with a lot of personality extremes and sometimes pettiness, sometimes greed, sometimes intolerance. . . . You just have to do it.

AHS: Any advice or words of wisdom you'd like to pass on to the young people out there who are trying to get started in this industry?

DAVIS: Well, that it is tough; it is highly competitive; it's got to be in your blood; you've got to live it and breathe it. It's an exciting area to work in. It's not easy to get into, because the points of entry are somewhat specialized. If it is in your blood and you do love it, and that love coincides with a real ability, it's a most challenging field of career endeavor and opportunity. I have found it never dull and always challenging and exciting.

AHS: Thank you very much.

INTERVIEW WITH
DOUG MORRIS

Formerly a singer, songwriter, producer, and entrepreneur, Doug Morris is now president of Atlantic Records.

AHS: Doug, first I'm going to ask you for a little bit of your background. I know a *little* bit of it, having been around as long as I have, but I'd appreciate a synopsis of the route you took to where you are at present.

MORRIS: I started as a songwriter and singer.

AHS: I never knew that!

MORRIS: Oh, yes. I spent hours hacking out my own songs on the piano and singing them. I had a record out with ABC and one with Epic—very checkered records, no success. They were basically influenced by the people who were popular then—I think that was the time of Neil Sedaka. My first connection was with a publishing company. I think it was Leeds Music—Lou Levy—but there was another guy there whose name I think was Dave Brown. He was the chief song-plugger then, and he brought me over to Epic Records; that's how I got my contact with Epic. I made a record with Jim Fogelsong & the Jordanaires, and failed, and I did another record with Bert Burns for ABC and failed. I did a bunch of records, went into the Army, and kept writing and recording. When I came back, because of my songs, I got sort of a job with Bert Burns and Bobby Mellon writing. They took the publishing of the songs and gave me $35 a week as an advance. I also did the filing and a lot of other stuff. After the Army, I got a job at about $125 a week working for Bobby Mellon as a "professional man," which means taking songs around to record companies and artists. After about a year and a half there, I got an offer from Laurie Records to be an A&R person. Laurie invited me because they liked the demos that I made of my own stuff. At Laurie I started producing some material I wrote and some other records. I had a little success with "Sweet

Talking Guy" by The Chiffons, which I wrote and produced, and a couple of other things, like "Are You a Boy or Are You a Girl?" It was interesting. . . . I learned promotion because in those days it was different from today—the promotion was more natural. You'd ship a record and the radio stations seemed to *need* the product, and if you had a hit, you found it out quickly. Learning promotion naturally followed producing my own records, because I wanted them promoted. I found I wasn't as good a producer and writer as some other people, so I went into the administrative part of the business, particularly A&R, which is looking for other talent. After about four or five years there, after becoming general manager and vice president, I decided to go into my own business. I realized that the record business is much more simple than people make it out to be. If you have a great piece of product and you get it on the radio, people will come and buy it. I opened Big Tree Records, and after ten years sold it to Warner Communications, whereupon I became the president of Atco Records, and ultimately the president of Atlantic Records.

AHS: Doug, you mentioned that it was a simple business back then. You were talking in a time frame of about ten years ago. Now, as president of Atlantic Records, do you still find it a simple business?

MORRIS: It's a simple business in the respect that if you get something people want, they're going to buy it. That's the simple part of it. Getting that piece of product is not that simple.

AHS: I couldn't have asked for a better lead-in. I've noticed many fine things about your company, but one thing has really impressed me: it's the only major record company whose A&R people periodically call me and my partners to ask: "Hi, how are you? Do you have anything new that we haven't heard?" I noticed that we don't do too many deals; that you're extraordinarily selective, as you must be, which leads me to the core of this interview. There are thousands of artists out there who are aspiring to record deals. What are your prime criteria in selecting talent?

MORRIS: It's a combination of several things. The musical ability, which comes first, performing ability and magnetism of the artist . . . the ability to project a certain image; and third, the management. If you get all three pieces together, you have a very good chance of success.

AHS: When you talk about musicianship . . .

MORRIS: By musicianship, I really mean talent. Greatness as a writer, greatness as a singer . . .

AHS: You're including the quality of the songs in that. . . .

MORRIS: Oh, sure! The talent comes first. It's not exactly the songs, but it's the combination of the songs, and how the artist renders the song. Some people write great songs, but they're not artists. Their songs become hits by other artists. We prefer, given the choice, an artist who is also a writer, because then we know we are always going to get the benefit of his best songs. Talent is the first consideration. The second most important factor is the artist's—I hate to use the word "magic" or "charisma"—ability to offer something special onstage. The third consideration is that they are well managed by someone who is reasonable, open-minded, and intelligent.

AHS: Do you prefer them to come to you *with* a manager or would you like to find the talented artist and perhaps make a match?

MORRIS: Ummm . . .

AHS: What if you get a wonderful artist and you can't stand the manager?

MORRIS: Well, that's a problem, but if he's a good manager, I'm *going* to stand him. I'm not going to not stand him. If he doesn't understand the business, then we won't get along, because it's a very logical business and most of the real professionals understand it. It's pretty common knowledge what a deal is for a beginning artist, what a deal is for a middle artist, and what a deal is for an established artist, so if you get a manager who is knowledgeable, normally there is no problem. If you get someone who's nuts, it doesn't work.

AHS: My point is this: if an artist came to you and you were enthusiastic about him as an artist . . .

MORRIS: I would try to suggest someone or make sure that he meets a lot of managers and finds someone with whom the chemistry is correct.

AHS: One of the big puzzles and problems for young artists is the demo record, which is their calling card to the record company. If you could set the criteria for a demo, what would your criteria be?

MORRIS: Criteria? Technically? Do you mean state of the art? No, just as long as it's clear and you can get the melody and you can get the lyric of the song. You can make a very good demo on a home tape machine; just playing the guitar or piano, that could be perfectly adequate. If you have the financing and you want to go further, it's very easy to go into a small studio and it's really not that expensive.

AHS: How many songs would like to see on a demo?

MORRIS: I'd like to hear at least three songs by an artist before I get interested, but if someone brought me in one phenomenal thing, I would certainly be very receptive to hearing more.

AHS: What about the kid who sends you in a tape with ten cuts on it or eleven cuts? Does that turn you off?

MORRIS: Ummmm . . . I don't know. I really can't answer that because what I would normally do is give it to one of the A&R people and they would listen. I don't know how they would feel about it. I don't think I would take the time to listen to ten cuts.

AHS: What's the ideal number? If you had your choice . . . three, four, five?

MORRIS: I normally can tell with three cuts if I'm dealing with something that I'm interested in, and if I really like it and we want to go further, then I'd ask them to start preparing more songs. Once artists know that they're on the way to being signed, they suddenly get very creative and it's very interesting to observe that phenomenon.

AHS: I always recommend to artists that they place their best song first on the tape. A lot of artists are inclined to build up to the best song. . . .

MORRIS: I don't believe you should be subtle—best shot first. You're 100 percent correct.

AHS: What kind of selection process do you use here, Doug? I know, for instance, that Paul Cooper will call me and I'll send him some tapes and then he'll call me back and thank me very much and tell me he passes, but what happens in between the two calls? Do you go through a committee, or . . .

MORRIS: A demo will normally go through our A&R department, which is composed of about seven people. They have listening sessions and they basically decide whether it's in the ball game or not in the ball game. Ultimately, it will come to me or to Ahmet and we'll make the decision. Ahmet Ertegun is the chairman of the board of the company.

AHS: You've already told me how important the song is. Are there any particular things that turn you off instantly?

MORRIS: No.

AHS: You've very open-minded. . . .

MORRIS: Oh, yes.

AHS: How important is the source of a demo?

MORRIS: What do you mean "the source of a demo"?

AHS: I know, for instance, that when we entertainment lawyers send in a demo, it's usually listened to. We usually get a response. I imagine it's the same with accountants and managers and other people that you're going to have a long-term relationship with. As a matter of courtesy, I imagine they get listened to. What about all the stuff that comes in over the transom from Oshkosh or Duluth?

MORRIS: We try and listen to it, but, in truth, I would suspect that if someone we know or have a rapport with submits something, it gets a quicker "listen to."

AHS: A more thorough "listen to"?

MORRIS: I'm not sure about "more thorough," but it certainly would get precedence. If you hear something that comes through the mail and it's great, you're going to chase that though, too.

AHS: But is everything that comes in through the mail listened to?

MORRIS: We try to; sometimes it's difficult, but we try to, we try very diligently to.

AHS: Have you ever gotten lucky on something coming through the mail?

MORRIS: Not as a record, but I believe we found songs through the mail which we have used for other artists.

AHS: But never a record?

MORRIS: I really can't think of any at this moment, but I wouldn't want to say no because I'm not sure. . . . It certainly is an advantage if a demo comes from someone we know.

AHS: Do you have any idea, do you keep any track, of how many tapes you get a year?

MORRIS: No. I have no idea, but we get *many*. I have no idea of the numbers.

AHS: Can you give me an idea of how many signings of new artists you did this year?

MORRIS: In truth, I don't know. I don't have it at my fingertips, but not many . . . not many. We're signing more than most labels, I believe, because our business hasn't been declining—it's been increasing—and when an act comes along that philosophically meshes with what we're doing, we will sign it.

AHS: Do you have any preference with regard to whether or not an act comes in associated with a line producer? Do you like to pick the producer?

MORRIS: It doesn't matter to me. If an artist comes in with a line producer and the product is very good, we'll go with it; if the artist comes in without an attachment, we'll try to guide the selection of a producer.

AHS: Do you have any feelings about independent production companies versus signing the artist directly?

MORRIS: No. The end result is the only thing I'm interested in.

AHS: A hit?

MORRIS: Yes, the music, that it's great, and that they're good in person and that they're well managed.

AHS: I thank you very much. Is there any word of advice you'd like to give to the stars of the future?

MORRIS: Well, for people who are truly serious, the only thing I would advise is to be true to what they are as an artist, and not to try to cover a broad spectrum. Don't try and do a disco record and a rock record and a middle-of-the-road record. If you're a rock-'n'-roll artist, be a rock-'n'-roll artist—that's really the truth. Very often we get demos that are designed to demonstrate diversification. You'll have a couple of good rock cuts, then a jazz cut, and then a ballad, and that really *does* turn me off, because the really great artists *are* what they are, and they can't be anything else.

AHS: Do you think some of them don't know what they are at that stage of their career?

MORRIS: No. I really believe that they know what they are. For the ones that are destined to be great rock-'n'-roll artists, rock-'n'-roll should be all that they care about. They may *like* other kinds of music, but rock-'n'-roll should be what they want to perform. The dance artists are going to end up dance artists and rhythm-and-blues artists are going to be rhythm-and-blues artists. Jazz artists are jazz artists. There can be fusions, but when I hear a potpourri of music by one artist, it's not interesting to me, not interesting at all. I like to know what they are and that *they* know what they are, because that image factor is, second to the music, the most important thing as far as I'm concerned.

AHS: Do you like lyric sheets with your demos?

MORRIS: Not particularly.

AHS: Do you like pictures submitted?

MORRIS: It doesn't matter. The music is the first thing. If the music interests me, then I or whoever else is involved with it, will search out everything else. It really doesn't matter what people look like in today's idiom. Some of the biggest artists aren't the most handsome people in the world. They're just talented.

AHS: Some of them can't even sing very well.

MORRIS: Well, I don't agree with you there. I do think that the ones who are successful have something, although it may not be what we think of as good singing in the classical sense. Bob Dylan certainly wouldn't have been thought of as a good singer, but he had something that touched his audience—in his moment, he had something in his voice, in his performance, that touched people. As a matter of fact, most of the singers that do commercials are fine singers; they're technically excellent and they have great intonation, but very rarely do they make successful records.

AHS: I didn't want any of my readers to be turned off by the fact that they didn't have classically good voices. . . . I asked the question with that in mind.

MORRIS: No. It doesn't matter. Just that they can "touch." There are a lot of artists who, though not technically great singers, had the ability to reach an audience. They sold millions of albums. It *is* good that they be distinctive, whether it be a Stevie Nicks, who is identifiable as soon as she comes on the radio, or the Rolling Stones . . . when they come on, you know it's them. Being identifiable, having an identifiable vocal sound, is very, very important.

AHS: Doug, I thank you very much.

MORRIS: I enjoyed it very much.

INTERVIEW WITH
DONALD GRIERSON

Don Grierson, after an extensive career in all aspects of the record industry, is now senior vice president, A&R, for Epic Records.

AHS: Don, readers are for the most part young people who are eager to get into the music business. So that they can relate to the things you are about to tell them, a thumbnail sketch of your career to date might be helpful.

GRIERSON: Born in England, immigrated to Australia when I was seven with my family. I got into radio when I was eighteen at the local hometown radio station which had an audience of I think ten. I did everything from filing the records to eventually becoming music director of the station and playing (I was on the air every night) various kinds of music; we had to cater to everybody. Most of the pop music that I was playing came from either England or America, but primarily America, and I just had to come to where the music was. So in 1963 I came to America with basically no money—it was a little easier to live in those days—landed in L.A. and went to work for a California Music One-Stop, Pico Boulevard, for a buck-sixty an hour. I had to work a lot of hours overtime to survive. They gave me a raise to a buck seventy-five, and I thought things were looking up, you know? A year after that I was introduced to Gary Owens, who is a very famous disc jockey in Los Angeles. He took a liking to me and introduced me to Jerry Moss at A&M, who helped me get a job with the local distributor for A&M in Southern California. I worked there for two years, was drafted during the process, even though I was not a citizen. After the service, I went to work for Capitol as West Coast singles promotion. That was in '66. Worked there till almost the end of 1969. Left, did a couple of different things with small labels that just didn't work out. Then I worked for MGM doing promotion. In 1970 I went to RCA West Coast doing A&R administration, coordinating all the independent labels that they had, which was a chance for me to really see the other side. I had done promotion, but this gave me my first taste of A&R in the "inside" sense. They went through about three presidents during the period of time that I was there, and the fourth one decided the West Coast group wasn't necessary and eliminated most of us. That disillusioned me, but after that I got a chance to go back to Capitol. Jim Mazza, who had been in sales when I did promotion, had moved up to head of International and asked me to come in and do

international promotion and to A&R the incoming EMI product to Capitol. So I had the best of both worlds. Did that for two
years, and was promoted to head of Merchandising and Advertising which was out of the blue, but it was a chance to learn
another end of the business. I did that for two years, and then in
'78 they created EMI America. Massa became president and I
became VP of A&R for the new company. I stayed there for four
years, then they brought me back to Capitol as head of A&R. I
held that position for three and a half years, when I came to CBS
as senior VP, A&R, for Epic.

AHS: And the rest is?

GRIERSON: And the rest is current history, yes.

AHS: Did you ever aspire to a career as an artist or songwriter?

GRIERSON: No. I was always a listener and when I listen today, I always
listen as a member of the public, as a Joe Public. I always listen
as though I was in my car driving and listening to the radio and
asking myself if it is making me respond. So I always listened. I
never played, never had any aspirations to be a star or attempt
to do any of that. I can't sing a note, I can't write a lyric, I can't
hum and really hold a melody . . .

AHS: But you did have a passion for the business.

GRIERSON: Yeah, but the business came later. I had a passion for music. I
had a passion for records first of all. I mean when I walked in
that One-Stop and got my first job in California, and there were
just tables and tables full of singles and albums, I was literally in
heaven. Because every label I'd ever heard of, every record was
there physically. It was like, this is it, this is the only place I
wanted to be in life because I was in love with records.

AHS: How much of your salary did you take home in records as
opposed to cash?

GRIERSON: Well, labels did send their promo copies. I used to take those
copies. I'd play them, and I'd talk to customers about them,
trying to sell them.

AHS: So you were promotion man already!

GRIERSON: Absolutely, I was the promoter.

AHS: As a result of previous editions of this book, I have been accused
of being too negative about the prospects of a neophyte making
it in the music business as a recording artist. I have maintained
to this day that you can't be too negative about the average
person's prospects. Would you take exception to that?

GRIERSON: No, not in general. I don't think so. It is *really* tough. There are
a lot of acts signed, but in comparison to those who would love
to be a recording artist, it's minor.

AHS: And out of the acts signed, how many of them become a success?

GRIERSON: Very small. It's the nature of the game, you know. There is no finite way of doing this. No matter how good a singer you are or whatever, there is no guarantee of anything because you can't compute it. It all comes down to opinion. Everything I do is based upon my opinion. The public's opinion is the final one. But how do you compute that? You learn from lessons and you learn what doesn't work, but you still can't be sure of what works.

AHS: You can't be sure, but to maintain a position such as you have, you have to be right more often than you're wrong—otherwise you're not here anymore.

GRIERSON: That's what they tell me.

AHS: You must be able to predict the public's acceptance—not perfectly, we all know that—but with some fair degree of accuracy. You know what's in the ball park and what's not.

GRIERSON: You do. And I think doing what I do as the head of the department, you have to have a staff of people who have various tastes so that you don't miss anything.

AHS: But even if a member of your staff likes something, he still brings it to you. You still listen to it. And you have to make the decision.

GRIERSON: Somebody has to play devil's advocate, right? If it's not me it's somebody above me.

AHS: What is your favorite kind of music?

GRIERSON: Personally?

AHS: You personally, yes.

GRIERSON: Well, in general I love music. I mean I can go home and listen to jazz some nights. I can go home and listen to reggae and love it. And the next night I'll play Van Morrison, you know, and then I'll play the Living Colour album. I'm a very versatile music person.

AHS: As an A&R man, which genre of music would you say you can pick as well as anybody?

GRIERSON: I would simplify that by saying that I always kind of orient myself to the singer, the voice, and the song. I think the mass market, history, will tell you that's the singer, a great singer, a singer who has style. Ray Charles, Joe Cocker—they're singers. Then Frank Sinatra's a singer. There are various kinds of singers, but they all have a distinctive quality. When you hear such a voice, and it's married to a great song, and of course well-produced . . . then I think you're going to be competitive time after time after time.

AHS: When you go for a job interview, you make sure your hair is combed and your suit's pressed and your shoes are shined . . .

GRIERSON: Not some of the guys I've interviewed.

AHS: Well, that's why they didn't get the gig.

GRIERSON: Not necessarily. A&R is not based upon looks. It's based on instincts.

AHS: When you present a demonstration record, this is the first impression an A&R man has of the artist. And one of the things I try to impart to neophytes in this book is how do you present that demonstration record so that when it is put on for just a second, the A&R person doesn't say, "Oh my God, not this." I know you are inundated with demonstration records. When you do listen, there have to be things that turn you on, or turn you off. What would prompt you to say, "This isn't for me, I'm not wasting my time on this, this is amateur hour"? So, if you were to advise your daughter in twelve years or so . . .

GRIERSON: She's picking the hits already.

AHS: . . . how to do a terrific demonstration record for a hip A&R man, what would you say?

GRIERSON: Well, there are some basic guidelines I think that are always fair to fall back on. One is never overload a tape. I mean three, four songs is absolutely enough. I know, for me, and other people say the same thing, when you get a tape with ten, fifteen, twenty songs, you put that at the back because it's like "Oh God, I don't have the time for that right now, I'll get to it later." I think three or four songs is right. If you listen to any album, with the exception of the classic albums, most albums have the two or three hits, and then really the balance of the album doesn't do much for you. The great albums have more hits and they have more character and they become the great ones. They're the ones that sell the millions. Most albums don't . . . because they're not good enough to sell millions; they're not deep enough. The same thing applies when you bring in a demo tape. Give the meat to the A&R person. Give the meat because what you're trying to do is intrigue us. What we're looking for is something that catches our attention. You don't have to have five or six or eight songs to do that. If you've got something really worthwhile to offer, it should come out in the first two or three songs. It should be in the first song. And then again we have to listen in the context of the kind of act that is being presented. If it's an alternative kind of act, you have to listen to that within a different set of parameters then you would if you're listening to a singer who may or may not write the songs, but has a voice.

AHS: What do you mean by an alternative act? I'm not familiar with that expression.

GRIERSON: Okay, there are established marketplaces . . . such as rap or country. They call a certain kind of music alternative—

postmodern. It's more the college-oriented music. The music that the college stations would feature first, that the college audience would be attuned to. R.E.M. is a very big act. They came out of the alternative circle. Their first albums were the kind of albums that never got played on mainstream radio because their style of music, their type of song, is not formularized. I have no problem with that, but it's not mainstream. Certain acts don't come from the main, they start out on the periphery, capture an audience . . . have some quality that intrigues a minority, and they then through time and experience and growth grow into the middle. And some of the biggest acts in music didn't automatically go on pop radio because they weren't formula enough for pop radio. Epic has a very big act now called Living Colour. When we signed that act, we never expected that act to be a mainstream act immediately. We hoped it would grow to that. Well, we got lucky, and the first album did sell about 2 million around the world and we got a hit single out of it. But it wasn't anticipated on our part. We were surprised, very pleasantly. We hoped to sell 150,000 albums the first time out. We thought that would have been a really good first statement for this black band that plays rock and roll with a real edge and social-conscious lyrics . . . not something that would go on Top 40 radio immediately.

AHS: Not only am I getting a terrific interview, but I have a new word for my glossary, "alternative music."

GRIERSON: Use the term "postmodern" as well.

AHS: Postmodern as well, okay.

GRIERSON: So, going back—if you know up front the genre of music you are about to listen to, then you can kind of orient yourself. If it's totally cold, then you have to have an open mind, and you have to hear something that makes you go "There's something here I want to go back and listen to again." Either a voice, a sound—if it's vocal harmonies, that could be it—or it could be a guitar player that has incredible sound, or it could be the kind of song you hear, a song that just really makes you go, "Ooh, I have to hear that again, that's really a great song." It could be one of many things, that's why it's so hard to answer that kind of a question because doing what we do, we have to have a pretty open mind to music in general, since there are many, many kinds of music out there that are selling.

AHS: What about an artist who fancies himself as capable of dealing with several other genres? Other people have told me that's the kiss of death as far as they're concerned.

GRIERSON: Dangerous, yeah.

AHS: They want an artist to know who he is, what he is . . .

GRIERSON: From a starting point. You can grow once you've established some kind of acceptance and base. You can then spread out and show other sides. But initially, if you are all over the place you can confuse people, and when that happens, nothing can happen. I think you must emphasize your roots, your real strength, your real soul first, then you can grow from that.

AHS: In the past I maintained, I think now erroneously, that it was sufficient to do a guitar vocal demo or a piano vocal demo. I don't think you can any more. I'm thinking of changing that position. When I broke into this business, most of your A&R people were musicians. They had years and years of experience, and I thought then that you could do a piano vocal demo and they could supply the orchestrations and hear it the way it would ultimately sound. I'm not sure that today A&R people in general have that much musical background. Do you have to help them a little bit?

GRIERSON: In general I would agree with that. There are various kinds of A&R people, but there are a lot of young A&R people today who don't have that kind of background, that kind of sense, because they're caught up more in what's going on in the streets. And they're hanging out in the clubs and they're searching for new talent on that level. You do get a certain number of A&R people—and there's not a lot of us—who listen to and for the singer and the song. That's an old-fashioned part of A&R. I certainly, at the same time, work very hard at keeping an open mind to the alternative music of today, the music that isn't formularized, doesn't have the basics of say hearing a Joe Cocker or hearing a Whitney Houston great voice and then saying, okay, let's find the songs that those artists can feel and sing and which are commercial. That's one kind of A&R, where a piano vocal or a guitar and vocal would sell you the song for that artist. And if the artist is selling themselves, if that voice is there, I mean you can just imagine a singer like a Joe Cocker, singing with a piano, "You Are So Beautiful." If you couldn't hear that, or hear that something special was there, then you wouldn't be doing your job very well. That's one kind of A&R. But today, there's not a lot of that kind of music coming out anywhere. So it's more group-oriented, it's more street-oriented.

There is so much equipment available that's inexpensive, so you can make great-sounding little records and demos at home in your bedroom. Today, a lot of the demos are produced on various levels, and we are hearing many different kinds of presentations. Depending on the kind of act that you are, if you're trying to get a deal, you have to decide how you want to do that.

At the same time, if you are trying to sell the ability to relate to the mass audience and you are a singer, or the band is a singer of songs, then don't try and overly complicate things by a hip demo, because the strength of that demo will be the singer and the song. If it's the sound of the guitar player, then emphasize that. Most acts don't happen, because there's nothing specific about them. There is nothing great or unique about them. They're good. There is a lot of talent out there, an enormous amount of talent. But not a lot of it is distinctive. And that's why it's very hard to be successful.

AHS: But in general, you would say that today a demo ought to be produced somewhat.

GRIERSON: To some degree, yes. But it can be overproduced, and I think that's more dangerous than not. Do you want shorter answers on this?

AHS: No, no, we'll shorten them as we go along. Don't worry.

GRIERSON: That's right, you can always subtract, you can't add.

AHS: I think it's fairly clear that given your druthers, you would prefer an artist who writes great material . . . have it all self-contained. But given the average demo that comes across your desk, if the artist does not write their own material, is that a negative for you?

GRIERSON: Not necessarily, because I believe that if you have a big part of your puzzle solved and you need to add something to it to make it a total, then you can go elsewhere for that sometimes. I mean, if you hear a great voice and the material is not necessarily all together, if you hear a great voice and that person or that artist doesn't write, that's another thing that you have to look at, because that means that you have to find ten or twelve songs for every album. But if the singer is a writer, and is short a song or two, there are various ways you can remedy that. You can put them with different writers to co-write, or you can go outside to other writers—the best writers in the world are out there, trying to get people to record their songs—and try and find a song for them. I think it's much easier for an act if they write their own material, because then it is *your* soul, not only in your performance but in what you're singing about. Most of the great acts in this day and age are, if not totally, somewhat self-contained. There are the pure singers who need material or co-write.

AHS: Where do you go for that material in those instances where you have a singer who you're very enthusiastic about and you need material?

GRIERSON: It's very simple. You go to the publishers, you go to writers. I talk to publishers and writers every day of my life. Half the time I do it even though I don't need a song from them, because I want them to know that I'm always interested in what they have—because one day I'll need a song. And they may send me songs when I'm not really looking for them, because they know that I will listen. And half of the problem for writers and publishers is that no one listens to their songs. So I will always listen. This creates a work load sometimes, but the good publishers will only give you songs that they feel you would have some interest in. I've got stacks of tapes here . . . some of the songs I'll go back to time and time again, because somewhere along the line I think there's a possible use for them. I open every creative door I can to get songs so that if one of my artists has an open mind to a song, or is not a writer, then I may find something that they don't have. Then I can bring in the cherry to put on top of the cake. Example being, on the Bad English album, which we had a platinum album with last year. The number-one song from that album was a song written by an outside writer. Cheap Trick's "The Flame" was an outside song. There are a number of examples that I have been involved with and other people have been involved with where you go to the great writers and hopefully get a great song for your great artist.

AHS: That's the "R" part of A&R.

GRIERSON: Yes. And I don't think that we should ever as an industry forget that.

AHS: I think a lot of people have forgotten it.

GRIERSON: To a great degree I think so.

AHS: That "Repertoire" part of it is . . .

GRIERSON: I have noticed a trend to more interest in the outside song or outside co-writing, where an artist who is normally self-contained is willing to go out and write with others. It's changing a little bit.

AHS: This will make a lot of our readers very happy.

GRIERSON: The writers especially. Publishers are signing acts that are self-contained, and then they're still doing publishing—it's just a different kind of publishing.

AHS: I'm going to ask you a touchy question because I know you'll answer it. Unsolicited tapes. Tape comes in through the mailroom and you have cartons and cartons of tapes. What are the chances of that tape being listened to?

GRIERSON: In general, if a tape comes in totally cold, it's tough, very tough.

AHS: I'm not surprised.

GRIERSON: The primary reason is time.

AHS: I ask the question fairly well knowing the answer.

GRIERSON: It's real tough. People always have to remember one thing. I've done panels and things and this question comes up every time. They think we have nothing else to do but sit and listen to their tapes. The biggest responsibility an A&R person has is working with the artist he or she has already got signed, because when you sign that artist you make a commitment to that artist. You're putting dollars on the counter to do that. It's going to cost you money to make a record, there's no question. So that can, depending on the type of artist, take a little bit of your time or can take a lot of your time. You have to also work within your own company to help bring that artist to its attention, let them know why you signed the artist, what they're all about—again, time-consuming. Sometimes they don't live in your neighborhood, so you have to go and visit them, travel to them. That's time-consuming. You're also going out to clubs. You're also going to sales meetings, you're going to lots of different things. So the time to sit and listen to tapes that somebody out of the blue sends is sometimes just impossible.

AHS: It seems to me you'd go crazy after a while just listening to tapes all day.

GRIERSON: Yeah, if that's all you do, you'd lose your sensitivity.

AHS: How big is your staff?

GRIERSON: Epic, under my auspices, including myself, has seven full-time A&R people. But Epic also has Epic Associated and it has a Black Division under Hand Cardwell. The Black Division has, including Hand, three A&R people, and the Associated side, under Richard Griffith, has three A&R people, including Tony Martel. So Epic and Epic Associated have thirteen people.

AHS: Which tapes get the listen? I know the lawyers send in tapes, the managers send in tapes, accountants . . .

GRIERSON: The ones that will get the attention are the ones that, yes, come from people you know, obviously that's first . . . people who you know are in the business. Every now and then somebody will come up with some incredible idea and it will intrigue you and you'll listen to the tape. An artificial time bomb came in with three sticks of dynamite, wires, a little alarm clock, and a tape attached to it. And there was a cute little note on it, so we listened to that tape. It was okay, nothing special.

AHS: I once got a tape from Cleveland. It was in a box full of rocks, pebbles. It said "Cleveland Rocks." You know you go a little nuts after a while.

GRIERSON: If everybody does gimmicks, then the gimmicks go. But every now and then something will catch your attention from a weird source. But yes, with people who are in the business in some professional sense, we assume that they should have some instinct . . .

AHS: Prescreening.

GRIERSON: . . . to some degree, and that's a fine line too. But at least they are supposed to be in the business and know a little about what it's all about and have some prescreening process themselves.

AHS: So you would assume that whatever's coming is at least professional.

GRIERSON: Or if you are an artist and you really believe without reservation that you have something to offer, find somebody who can help you open a door. That could be a guy at Tower Records who knows the sales guy at a record company. It may not work a lot, but sometimes that guy will say, "You know, I heard something," because we have incentive plans for people in the field. If a salesman finds a tape for us and sends it to us and we sign it, he's going to get taken care of. There's an incentive plan for that.

AHS: When you listen to a tape, how long does it take you to know that isn't for you, that you're not interested? Seriously?

GRIERSON: Sometimes very quickly, it just doesn't do anything for me; other times you do a little spot-checking. The first song, you know it's not too bad, you move to the second, not too bad, the third—after that you start to go, "I've lost interest." But if something intrigues you, you hear a good sense of melody, then to me you should follow through a bit further because melody's a very important part of what it's all about. Again, if you hear a sound, sometimes it's even the way it's produced in the demo. It's like, "There's something happening here, let me check it again." A lot of things are just so the same and so basic and so nondescript, that it doesn't take very long for you to say, "Sorry."

AHS: Besides the ten- or twelve-cut demo, are there any other things that turn you off absolutely and instantly?

GRIERSON: Hmm. If somebody forces his way in, being obnoxious, and some people are—they think that's the way to do it—that doesn't do anything for me at all. I mean I really feel offended by that. People who call up and abuse people in the company because they didn't listen to their tape . . . those kinds of things will never work with me. Quality is important. If you have a terrible-sounding tape, and in this day and age it's not that easy to do, but still sometimes the piano is four miles over here and the voice is three miles over here. That goes in the garbage can real quick. Think professionally. If you were in this position, what would you be willing to put up with?

AHS: Do you like to receive pictures with tapes? Maybe not the first tape, but the second tape?

GRIERSON: No. If someone looks pretty or handsome or has a look, fine. But first and foremost it's the music. If it's a video, it can be a cheap home-done video, but if it's a video where there's some professionalism to it, just in the sense of lighting that shows off a part of an artist, you can get a better picture . . .

AHS: But the black-and-white glossy doesn't cut anything . . .

GRIERSON: Doesn't do much for me. I see a lot of pretty faces . . .

AHS: I once got a tape from an artist, she was absolutely gorgeous. And I sent her picture—I think I sent one to you also—and some A&R man wrote back, "Gee, if she sounded the way she looked, we'd sign her."

AHS: It is very hard for an artist to find a manager. That's worth the powder to blow him to hell with. There are a lot of managers, but there are very few good managers, and the good managers just can't manage that many people. Does it appeal to you that an artist coming up here has a manager? Or would you rather put them together with a manager who you thought was appropriate?

GRIERSON: I would say yes to both those questions, to a degree. If an artist who has something above average to offer comes in with a professional manager who really is a manager, not just somebody who coveted the name, that is helpful to us because there is somebody there who could be the buffer. We have a young artist on the West Coast who up until just a couple of weeks ago didn't have a manager, and she went into the office one day because we needed to get some photos. Something happened and she got all nervous and flustered and started to cry. It wasn't because anybody gave her a hard time—she just had to make a decision, and it was just too much for her because she's not ready for that yet. Since that time she actually has signed with a manager, and she's so much more composed now because she doesn't have to worry about that detailed day-to-day stuff. A manager is very important just to the psyche of the artist sometimes. On the other hand, if you find an artist who doesn't have a manager and who has something really special to offer, then getting them with somebody who is a real professional, who has some power in the marketplace, who has the ability to make things happen, has some foresight and a vision for that artist in the long term and who can sit with a record company and develop plans and think long-term—that's a big plus to us. A good manager working with a good record company is a big plus. It really is.

AHS: I think we've done it, Don.

GRIERSON: That's it, this is easy.

AHS: I've consumed a lot of your time. Now I feel guilty about the demos you haven't listened to during this time.

Cassette Roulette

four

GET IT RIGHT THE FIRST TIME

Music and lyrics by Billy Joel © 1979 by April Music, Inc., Impulsive Music, Inc.

Although I have forgotten all I ever knew about navigation, gunnery, the Morse code, and the like, one of my officer candidate school lectures remains vividly in mind. It was a class in naval etiquette, and most of the time was devoted to the proper form in which to have our calling cards printed and the appropriate manner in which to disseminate them. I'll bet you didn't know that in the entry hall of every commanding officer's residence there is a little silver tray upon which an officer paying his respects is expected to leave a calling card. Well, I never had the cards printed, never left one, and never suffered any dire consequence. In fact, I never again thought of that lecture until psyching myself to write this chapter.

This chapter is about your calling card—your demo record. The difference is that if you don't follow the rules, the consequences for you will be much more serious.

This is to be a short chapter because it is a redundant one. Many of the music-publishing executives and record executives whose interviews appear following the chapters on songwriting and recording have answered searching questions about demo records. Their answers are fuller and much more interesting than the distillation that follows. For those of you who have your amps plugged in and are overrehearsed, here is the short course:

How many songs should be on a demo?

In general, a minimum of three and maximum of six. The rule is not rigid, but fewer than three leaves the listener without a sense of what you are about, and a large number of songs is a definite turnoff to people who spend their days listening to demos. If they haven't heard "it" after three songs, you can bet the eject button will be pressed. Of course, if you are a songwriter submitting particular songs to a publisher or an artist, there is no minimum.

In what sequence should my songs appear?

Best song first, second-best song second, third-best song third, etc. This is an absolute, unbreakable rule. To do otherwise is the height of folly. Many inexperienced writers and artists think of "building" a demo as one would an album. Wrong! Don't be subtle. If you think you are going to build your listener up gradually and knock him out with the fourth song, you're in for a surprise—he's never going to hear the fourth song.

What is a sure way to diminish my chances of impressing a publisher or a record-company A&R person?

Submit a demo that illustrates how diversified and varied your talent is. Include a ballad, a rocker, perhaps a jazz number, and top it off with a novelty tune. Buy a box of Kleenex for the tears as the "passes" pour in. Although I didn't realize it until I started interviewing music and record executives for the preparation of this book, a varied demo seems to be the universal kiss of death. The publishers and record companies, especially the latter, want to know who you really are, and want to know that you know who you are. If you are a rock-'n'-roll writer or artist, do a rock-'n'-roll demo. If you are inherently a MOR writer or artist, do a MOR demo. Be yourself, not what you think "they" may be looking for.

Must a demo be made in a recording studio or can it be made at "home"?

The answer really depends on who is making the demo, the intended purpose of the demo, and how well equipped the "home" is.

If you are a songwriter and are "demoing" a song for submission to a publisher or an artist, in all likelihood you can do the demo without resorting to a studio. A simple piano or guitar vocal should be adequate as long as the equipment you use is capable of producing a cassette that is clear and pleasant to listen to. Most modern equipment found in the homes of music-oriented people is equal to the task. The publisher is listening for the song, not your talent as a singer, nor for your ability as a producer. In the back of his mind he is going to consider whether your demo can be used as his demo, so keep that in the back of *your* mind.

If you are a singer-songwriter preparing a demo for record companies, the criteria are a bit different. Record companies, when listening to singer-songwriter demos, listen at least initially for the hit song. Competition for record deals is so fierce, however, that one can't help but feel that the better the demo the better the chance. If you can embellish your performance with a rhythm section in an inexpensive demo studio, it probably wouldn't hurt. But, good Lord, don't throw up your hands and quit because you can't do this. It is not an essential.

If you are a group depending for recognition upon your "sound," it would seem that the closer your demo approaches master quality, the better are your chances. Thus, unless "home" is a very well-equipped loft, a demo studio is indicated.

Can I sing my songs on my demo or must I procure a "professional" singer?

Well, obviously, if you are a recording artist, you damn well better sing your songs. If, however, you are a songwriter, the question is well worth asking. The answer depends on how bad a singer you are. You don't have to be a good singer, but if you are so bad that the song can't come across, you would do well to use a friend who can sing or a professional demo singer to sing the lyric. If you sing passably well, your interpretation of the song may more than make up for your vocal deficiencies. Even if you can sing well, it would not be best for you to sing one of your songs that is clearly intended for a singer of the opposite sex with a clearly different vocal style. If you have a torch song clearly written for a sultry, sexy female voice and you happen to be a male baritone, you might well profit by having the song demoed by a female with a sultry, sexy voice.

How can I make sure that my demo lands on the little silver dish and not on the floor where it will go unnoticed?

By doing your homework. Record companies are turned off by amateurism. Even if you are not yet a professional in the technical sense, a professional attitude is appreciated and helps create a receptive attitude. Have the letter accompanying your demo typed neatly, so that it is legible. Include only relevant and pertinent information that will aid the listener. Two pages on how badly you want to become a star will, I assure you, be counterproductive.

Be professional enough to learn the name of the particular person in the record company or the music publisher who is the appropriate listener for your music and address your demo to him or her personally. Sending a MOR cassette to the head of the Black Music Division doesn't inspire respect for your professionalism. Addressing a demo to Capitol Records, Hollywood, California, is akin to consigning it to oblivion.

And, for God's sake, don't forget to put your name, address, and phone number directly on the cassette. Cassettes and boxes are soon separated.

What is the one thing every writer and artist can do to better his demos?

Be incredibly selective about the songs. If you have any doubt about the quality of a song, don't use it.

Should my demo be in the form of a video?

This has become, since the first edition, an oft-repeated question. The answer is yes . . . and no. You see, it's one of those questions that can only be answered by "It depends." I have asked the same question of several A&R and other industry people and have received answers varying from a resounding "No!" to "It's nice if. . . ." Where does this leave you? It leaves you with a problem. You're going to have to make a judgment call. The following quotes are representative of the feedback I've received:

"No way, they always pick the wrong song to do the video on."

"They don't have the money to do it right, and the results are amateurish and counter-productive."

"I'd really prefer to see the time and effort put into a really great audio demo. The songs are still the key factor. If I hear something really great, I'll manage to see them one way or another."

"If I'm impressed, it was a good idea. If it leaves me cold, it was a waste of money."

Desperate for a position to take, and to pass on to you, I called Don Grierson, then director of A&R at Capitol Records. Don is so articulate and intelligent that he has the ability to "pass" on one of your acts and have you hang up the phone with a smile on your face. He didn't disappoint me. The following is the essence of what he said to me:

> Video can help . . . it's really difficult to see an act otherwise, and video gives us another perspective. It's more difficult for us to view a video than it is for us to hear a cassette. Here in California we do a lot of listening in our cars! To some extent I guess whether it is viewed would depend on who sends it. With the exception of a Pink Floyd, or very visual acts, the songs and the singer are still the most important things. If there are limited dollars available, I'd recommend spending them on a really good eight-track demo—the key considerations for us are intriguing songs and vocal quality. It takes time and money to capture these to best advantage.
>
> Perhaps video should be the next stage. The video should have quality, but simple camera work. It should demonstrate the unique qualities of the act—show what they have to offer. If an act has great movement, uniquely good, the video should key on that. If there is a particularly charismatic lead singer you might wish to key on him or her with closeups and eye contact. Keep it simple, and plan it intelligently, and always remember the songs are the key. Don't let the tail wag the dog!

The general impression I received was that if video is not readily available to you it is no cause for discouragement, and that a video is not a substitute for a good audio demo but rather a "nice," next-stage supplement.

Assuming that you decide that, by reason of your unique qualities, video is the way for you to go. How do you finance it? Obviously you can rely on the same sources that you would rely on for your audio demo. Not very helpful! I was recently discussing this plight with Denny Somach, whose Cinema Productions had a video-intensive label deal with Capitol Records. Denny, who has been on the cutting edge of the video revolution since its inception, was more helpful. College film departments, he suggested, can be approached with a view toward making your video a class or department project. A little bartering of services might make your suggestion even more attractive. Denny also pointed out that local cable companies are very often starved for programming for their public access channels, and may very well make their facilities and staffs available to you. You end up with air exposure, and a copy of your performance to use as a video! Both of these possibilities require only a phone call to get them in motion. The price is right!

Have you seen any of the old World War II aviation movies on TV? They all had an obligatory scene in which, after clobbering the ballbearing factory in Schweinfurt, the pilot reaches for the radio: "This is Blue Leader. . . . We left our calling cards. . . ."

Make sure your calling card isn't a "bomb."

five

SHOW ME THE WAY

Music and lyrics by Peter Frampton © 1975 by
Almo Music Corp. and Fram-Dee Music Ltd.

As an aspiring recording artist, sooner or later you are going to be faced with the most important decision of your career: the choice of a manager. Note well that the decision is not whether or not to have a manager. You will have a manager. You must have a manager!

How important is it that wisdom accompany this decision? Well, if the statistics follow the current trend, they show that your relationship with your manager will probably endure for a longer period than will your relationship with your spouse! At least during the early years of your career (and probably during the not-so-early years too), you may well spend more time with your manager than with your spouse, and your emotional reliance on him may be even greater. One would hope, therefore, that the choice of a manager is made with less impetuosity than ofttimes accompanies that other choice. Rather than incur the wrath of Ann Landers, Dear Abby, or Dr. Brothers, we had best abandon this track and leave the spousal considerations to them.

Although the Lexicon offers a definition of the manager's role, it is very difficult to portray the essence of the manager-artist relationship. One could analogize a manager to a football coach or a manager of a baseball team, and in certain areas, such as strategy planning, it might be valid. Further use of this analogy fails because the nature of the relationship between the coach or baseball manager and their players is really one of employer-employee rather than the very personal and symbiotic relationship that should exist between the recording artist and his manager. Not only does the manager mastermind your career, whip your record company to have product in the cities you are touring, and coordinate the myriad people, trades, and skills involved in the pursuit of your success, but he's also the guy holding your forehead when you retch from nerves before going on.

Sufficiently impressed with the importance of the decision you must make? Okay, let's try to go about it wisely, for, as in the choice of a spouse, it is very expensive to correct a mistake.

I know I said "sooner or later" you would need a manager. If you run true to form, you're wondering which it is: sooner or later? *When* to acquire a manager is probably the most frequently asked question concerning the subject of management. In the abstract, the question is susceptible to a simple answer. Ideally, you should have a manager the moment you decide to pursue a career as a performing artist. Before you run off in search of the yellow pages, it is my unhappy task to remind you that we live in a less than ideal world, and that the world of entertainment, though probably no less ideal than the real world, certainly isn't any more so. If you are to choose a life in the fast lane, be assured that the road to perdition is well-paved. With reality in mind, let's revise our answer to "when." You should acquire a manager as soon as you find a good one who wants to manage you. There are two key words in this statement: "good" and "wants." Let's discuss the latter first. There is little sense in having reluctant management. To hound and badger a prospective manager into signing you, even if you are able to do so (which is unlikely), is counterproductive. You will remain a contract in a file cabinet until you accomplish something on your own. In the meantime, you will be without the guidance you need and, in all likelihood, you will have signed, out of misguided gratitude or anxiety, a less favorable management contract that you could have negotiated had you been sought after. When a manager wants to manage you, you will know it—he'll come a courtin'. This is not to say that you should not initiate the contact. Once he is aware of your existence, he must believe that with his guidance you (and he) can become successful, rich, and famous. If you are less than positive that any prospective manager fervently believes this, I would suggest that you not engage his services.

How do you know a manager is good?

There are three general categories of managers. The first, and smallest in number, are the supermanagers. They are the "heavy hitters" of their profession. They manage the superstars and are to no small extent responsible for their success. Record-company presidents take their telephone calls.

The second, and by far the most numerous, are those who work at their profession, gather experience and knowledge, work hard to develop their artists, but who, for one reason or another, have not yet broken a "monster" act. As the trades put it, they are "bubbling under." It is from their ranks that the supermanagers of tomorrow and, in all likelihood, your first manager will emerge.

The third general category, the soft underbelly of the management profession, is that of the would-be managers. They call themselves "managers" (anyone can do that, you know; there are no educational or licensing prerequisites) but know little or nothing about the entertainment industry other than a few buzz words they use to turn on unsuspecting and inexperienced artists. They make little effort to learn, or are perhaps incapable of learning. They usually carry with them dog-eared Xerox copies of other managers' form contracts with the original names blanked out. If, in spite of them, something should happen with regard to an artist they "represent," they run to an entertainment attorney, and the artist finds that he is being managed by a manager being managed by a lawyer. Ultimately, you will buy him out or sue him—both expensive. Such would-be managers are a blight on an honorable profession, are shunned by legitimate managers, and should be shunned by you.

Artists, especially those who have tasted of success, are very demanding of their managers, both emotionally and with respect to their time. Being all too well aware of this, supermanagers are reluctant to overextend themselves and consequently represent but a few artists at any given time. Simply stated, there just aren't enough supermanagers to go around. The demand for their services from artists who already have a "name" is so great that your chances of affiliating with one of them early in your career are remote.

Thus, if you are to enter into a management relationship sooner, rather than later, it will probably (having been warned of the third group) be with a manager in the second group. You can hope that you will be the monster act that will propel him into the ranks of the supermanagers.

Whether or not a prospective manager is good enough to be entrusted with your career is a question not susceptible of scientific determination. Sometimes it's easy, as in those instances where a supermanager perceives you to be a prospective David Bowie. It's easier too when a prospective record company endorses a manager and indicates that if he managed you, it would feel secure enough to close a deal. Most of the time, however, life conspires to make things more difficult, and the mating of an artist with a manager is somewhat more of a crap shoot for both. But even in the ancient game, the knowledgeable player exercises some control by knowing the odds. The best way to narrow the odds in your favor is to spend as much time as possible with a prospective manager. Spend that time listening and asking questions. Talk to the other artists he manages. Take a reading of their barometers of satisfaction. Does he have a game plan for your career? Does he understand what you are about? Does he have a handle on you? Check him out with your attorney and with other people in the business that you have come to know, and then make a value judgment. Unfortunately, there is no litmus paper that tests compatibility, or I'd tell you to buy some and use it.

I will now give you Siegel's Rule (modesty forbids "Law") for eliminating prospective managers (note this is not a rule for choosing managers; I am neither sufficiently stupid nor sufficiently courageous to propound that rule):

IF YOU HARBOR A SUSPICION THAT YOU ARE SMARTER, BRIGHTER, OR MORE INTELLIGENT THAN HE IS, LOOK ELSEWHERE.

Of course, this leaves some of you with a wider field to choose from than others. You must realize that your perception, as well as its accuracy, is important.

Elitism? No. Pragmatism. If the rule is ignored, the manager will be unable to manage effectively because you will be unmanageable. He will not be able to lead because you will not be able to follow. As is said in the Scriptures, "And if the blind lead the blind, both shall fall in the ditch." If the above seems a bit philosophical to you, let me leaven it by making a flat and unequivocal (albeit personal) statement. Every supermanager I have had occasion to deal with has been, if not brilliant, extraordinarily bright. There is an old adage known to all familiar with aviation lore: "There are old pilots and there are bold pilots, but there are no old bold pilots." Similarly, there are dumb managers and great managers, but there are no dumb great managers.

One other thing—there are no dumb record-company presidents. Who do you think your manager is going to spend most of his time working with, over, or on, during the most critical period of your career? You guessed it. There are few things more stimulating than witnessing a heated "discussion" between a really knowledgeable manager and a record-company president— or few things more depressing when the manager is overmatched.

Suppose you were very careful in selecting a manager who you believed was perfect for you; suppose you waited patiently till you found the one who believed in you and who you believed was good enough to manage you (this could be after your very first gig, or not until you have landed a record deal); and suppose, just suppose, you were wrong and it was a mistake. It could have been a mistake for many reasons. Conceivably you were conned by one of those so-called managers in the third group we discussed above. Perhaps the manager you chose would have been terrific for someone else but the chemistry between the two of you just wasn't right. Just possibly your nature is such that you demand inordinately much of a manager and will never be satisfied—a Flying Dutchman doomed to sail for eternity through an endless sea of managers. Maybe one of the manager's other acts made it big at the wrong time (for you), and you feel you're not getting enough of the manager's time. Could be you realize he's just a lousy manager.

In any case, the question remains: If you've made a mistake, how do you cut your losses, and how do you minimize the effect of a wrong choice in the future? The first part of the question is easy to answer. You run—do not walk—to a competent entertainment attorney (see Chapter 6). The answer to the second part is less expensive. You study the remainder of this chapter so that you understand the consequences of the contractual relationship you are contemplating.

The nature of the relationship between the manager and the artist is a unique one. It is perceived differently, of course, by managers and artists, and even by one manager and another and by one artist and another. At one end of the spectrum you have the position that it is strictly an employer-employee relationship, with the manager being merely the artist's hired hand. At the other end of the spectrum, you have the manager who acts as if his artists work for him. Somewhere in the middle, you have those who conceive of the relationship as a partnership, through which each makes a valid and valuable contribution to the success of the artist's career.

Although I have seen management contracts reflecting each variation stated above, the key word in the preceding paragraph is "perceived," because regardless of how the contract reads, the attitude of the people involved in the relationship will govern what is really important—how they treat and act toward each other.

The vast majority of management contracts are structured in a manner whereby the artist retains the services of the manager to advise the artist in connection with his career. For these services the artist pays the manager a share of the artist's gross income. Although the relationship is not in the technical sense one of "employment" (with its many legal ramifications), but, rather, one between "independent contractors," the artist is hiring the manager and is, in everyday language if not in the legal sense, the employer. The manager works for the artist—usually.

At this point I think it is appropriate to share a grotesquerie with you that is illustrative of all that a management contract and a manager-artist relationship should not be. As they used to say at the beginning of the old radio dramas: "This story is true; only the names have been changed to protect the innocent". . . and unfortunately, in this instance, the guilty too!

Several years ago, I was approached by a manager who indicated that he had just presented a new management contract to a group he represented, and that he thought they ought to have independent counsel represent them. A friend of his had heard me lecture on management contracts while attending an entertainment-law course and had recommended me. I thought the manager was being quite noble and prudent. I met with the group and was presented with a thirty-page agreement (the average management contract runs from two to five pages) and was told that their manager had instructed them to have me read it in their presence, advise them on the spot, and not to permit me to make or retain a copy of the agreement. I refused to represent them on this basis. They called the manager and received "permission" to have me make a copy and to review it in the normal course and provide them with a letter of comment setting forth the major points in contention. Another meeting with the artists was scheduled. The review of the agreement was revelatory. It was a pastiche of the most onerous clauses that could be culled from a variety of contracts, including many that were not of management origin. It was clearly unconscionable (so onerous and one-sided as to be unenforceable by a court) and to a great extent unintelligible. By its terms, the manager all but owned the artists. It was as close to being a slave contract as one is apt to come across. It had annexed to it promissory notes and confessions of judgment for many, many thousands of dollars, representing sums the manager had purportedly loaned or advanced to the artists.

At the subsequent meeting with the artists, they were advised of the nature of the agreement, and the fact that it was not susceptible of fixing. They were also advised that the agreement was such that a letter of comment would be of no purpose and would be so long and expensive as to be impractical. I advised them that the agreement was so out of tune with industry norms that

I could only recommend that an entirely new agreement be drafted. It was at this point that they forlornly advised me that other copies of the agreement and the notes as well as the confessions of judgment had been signed by them before the manager had approached me. What was going on? Perhaps belatedly, I got the message. I was being used to legitimize what amounted to a charade. My letter of comment was to be used solely for the purpose of demonstrating at some future time, if and when the agreement was challenged by the artists, that they had had counsel, indeed an "authority," advise them and that they had ratified the existing contract with full knowledge of its contents. Fade out.

Several years later I received a call from the artists. They had "fired" the manager and had, at great expense, won a lawsuit he had brought to enforce the confessions of judgment. Some record companies were now interested in them and they wished me to represent them. I indicated that I would do so, but warned them that if they had any success, the manager would surface and claim rights under the old management contract. Why, I asked them, had they gone along with the manager's scheme three years before? They thought at the time that they were on the verge of success and were threatened with abandonment and lawsuits for the monies the manager had advanced. They were concerned that either of these threats, if carried out, would have destroyed all they had striven for over the years. Well, they had modest success, and, as predicted, the manager sued them under the so-called management agreement. At great additional expense to the artists, the manager's action was defeated and the abominable agreement finally laid to rest. A happy ending? Not really. The artists' prime years were spent fending off their manager rather than building a career, and monies better spent on that career were dissipated on legal expenses that could have been avoided.

"Combination plates," though tasty and tempting when served in Chinese restaurants, lose their piquancy when they appear as a part of an entertainment package. All too often a management contract appears as the fried rice! When this happens, the sauce covering the "egg foo publishing" is usually cold and congealed, and the crust on the "production roll" is a bit soggy.

"What the hell is he talking about?" you ask. Very often new artists, when "discovered," are presented with a set of papers consisting of an exclusive recording-artist contract, an exclusive songwriting contract, and a management contract. Usually, when the combination plate is served, the waiter is an independent producer. In this event, the management contract is the dish from Column B. Sometimes the waiter is a manager, and the songwriter and recording contracts are Column B dishes.

How and why do these situations evolve? Usually they are a function of paranoia, sometimes of greed, and sometimes the result of the best business judgment of the waiter serving the lunch.

The songwriting and recording-artist courses have already been served (see Chapters 2 and 3), and you are presumably a gourmet with respect to those dishes, so, for a moment, let's devote ourselves to the management contract in the context of the combination plate.

The independent producer who signs a recording artist does so in the belief that the artist can be, indeed will be, a huge success, a real megabucks machine. He also perceives of this potentially huge success as being his creation, a product of his knowledge, prescience, guts—and money. Is it not understandable for him to be concerned that some stranger, whose natural role tends to be antagonistic to and competitive with his, will arrive upon the scene and interfere with his game plan or intrude in his dream? What better way to avoid that threat than by throwing in a management contract too?

On the other hand, managers are not immune to the failings of human nature. Often when about to invest heavily of themselves and their treasure in what they perceive as *their* creation or dream, they dwell on the frailties of the manager-artist relationship, the absence of security, the absence of an equity or ownership position, and all the zillions of dollars they are about to make for some strange music publisher, record company, or producer. The result is often an order to their attorney to ". . . sign him as a writer and artist too!"

Sometimes these combination plates work out. The lawyers prepare the contracts so that the apparent conflicts of interest are resolved (the manager waives management commissions on the artist's income from the related songwriting contract and recording-artist contract). Sometimes the producer-turned-manager demonstrates a talent for his adopted role, and the manager expanding into the production and publishing areas proves competent.

If partaking of a combination plate is the way to get your career launched, reach for the soy sauce, but be aware of where the Rolaids are, because indigestion may follow.

There are two major weaknesses in the combination-plates situation. They are equal in importance and you should understand them. One of the main functions of a manager is to drive, wrestle, and cajole others involved in your career—the record company and music publisher, among others—to act more in your interest and less in their own. If "their interests" are his interests, the checks and balances are gone, and the entire system tends to lose its equilibrium. Can your manager renegotiate your deals with his own companies? Few are sufficiently objective or saintly. The other inherent weakness should be clear. If a producer-publisher launches his management career with you, you are obviously not getting the best and most experienced manager. If a manager decides to launch a production and publishing empire with you as its nucleus, you are obviously not getting the best and most experienced production and publishing support. The dishes on a combination plate are never all from Column A. Ordering your manager à la carte is usually more satisfying.

Enough of this food analogy! Let's look over a typical management menu—oops, I mean contract. In general, management contracts are the shortest of the entertainment contracts dealt with in this book. Are they also the simplest? I think that depends on how much you know, or perhaps on how much you are disposed to fret over all the possibilities their seemingly simple clauses engender. An honest answer is "Yes—and no."

The brevity of the average management contract is perhaps what makes it the most insidious of the agreements to be thrust upon an inexperienced artist. When handed a twenty- or thirty-page exclusive songwriter or sixty-page exclusive recording-artist contract, there is built in an early warning device that triggers the brain to think: "Whoa! Maybe I'm not prepared to handle this. It looks 'heavy.' Help may be needed." The management contract, often printed on the front and back of a single page, is less apt to trigger the same response. In addition, its language is beguilingly straightforward and simple. This is a function, unfortunately, of its all-encompassing nature rather than the benevolent attitude of the manager or its creator, the manager's attorney. It is much simpler to say that the manager is to receive commission on "all gross income" rather than to dissect "gross income" and deal with its constituents. It is not until you have an inkling of what "all gross income" means that you wish you had sought help before signing the damn thing. In all fairness, many managers are as unaware of the Machiavellian nature of some of the clauses in their own contracts as you are.

You should be aware of certain universal features of management contracts and the issues that should be raised, discussed, and resolved in the course of their negotiation.

Let's start at the beginning, the very beginning. In the first few lines of the contract, you will find your name as "Artist" and next to it you may well find the name of a strange corporation as "Manager." For months now, you have been hanging out with, been romanced by, and have decided to place your trust and confidence in John Doe. Doe's name is no place in the agreement. When you ask him about it, he explains that he works through a corporation for tax reasons, that it is quite common and you don't have to worry about it. Worry about it! . . . if you don't want to find yourself managed by strangers sometime in the future! Whether Doe or his corporation is named as the manager, insist on language that states that you may terminate the agreement if, at any time during the term, Doe ceases to be in charge of and to have the primary responsibility for the day-to-day supervision of your career. This is called a "key-man" clause and protects you in the event Doe sells the corporation, retires, or seeks to assign your contract.

The word "exclusive" is invariably prominent in a management contract. As in the other entertainment contracts we have explored, it is a one-way street. You are exclusive to the manager; he is not exclusive to you. He can manage other artists but you cannot have another manager while he is managing you. You cannot change this clause, nor should you wish to do so. You can always fire your manager; the nature of the relationship is considered one of trust and so personal that a court will not force you to "live with" a manager you abhor. But—and it's a big BUT!—if you fire him without legal cause, you will be required to continue paying him, *and* his successor, compensation. A very heavy burden indeed.

Few would argue that a manager who was instrumental in the creation of a successful career was not entitled to a contract of sufficient duration to enable him to enjoy the fruits of his labor. What happens, however, if you made one of the mistakes alluded to above? In general, a performer's career is relatively short, and to be tied to what proves to be an ineffectual managerial relationship for a long term is disastrous. When you read the first draft of your management contract, it will in all likelihood provide for a term of five years. Perfectly fair and fine if the relationship works. If it doesn't, it's the precursor of a lot of trouble. Except for these rare instances in which the relationship is severed by mutual agreement, you may look forward either to buying your way out of the contract or to an expensive lawsuit (which will probably end in a negotiated settlement anyway). The solution to this dilemma, which is usually acceptable to both the artist and the manager, is to provide language in the contract whereby if certain criteria of success are not met within prescribed time frames, the artist will have the right to terminate the contract. The criteria are usually couched in terms of gross income earned during a specific period of time. The one exception to a dollar criterion is the one for the first step up the term-duration ladder. It is the thing in the forefront of each artist's mind—a record deal.

If drafted by the artist's attorney, and assuming a five-year term, the clause will probably read more or less as follows:

> Artist shall have the right to terminate this agreement by notice in writing to the manager at the following times, upon the happening of the following events:
> a. At the end of the first year of the term hereof in the event the Artist has not entered into an exclusive recording artist agreement with a major record company.
> b. At the end of the second year of the term hereof in the event the Artist has not earned gross income during the preceding year of (X) dollars.
> c. At the end of the third year of the term hereof in the event the Artist has not earned gross income during the preceding year of (Y) dollars.

Assuming that your manager is willing to accept such an arrangement (and some won't, feeling it can take two or three years to bring the artist to the point where he is ready for a record deal or to earn significant gross income), his attorney will attempt, quite properly, to dilute the burden of the success criteria. How? Watch. Take "a" above. First, he'll try to change "entered into" to "received an offer for" and, finally, he'll probably try to delete "major" or at least insist on a very broad definition of "major." Dastardly? Reprehensible? Not at all. How could it be? These changes are exactly what I would try for if I represented the manager. Both sides can make, and will make, moving and convincing arguments for their respective positions.

The result? Usually a compromise that approximates "fairness." Of course, if the record deal already existed, there would be a dollar criterion in "a."

Interested in how to dilute "b" and "c"? I'll redraft as I would if I were the manager's attorney:

> c. At the end of the third year of the term hereof in the event that the Artist has not *received offers for employment which, if accepted,* would have resulted in gross earnings during the preceding *two years totaling* (Y) dollars.

What did this little revision accomplish?

1. Although Y remained the same, it now includes dollars for gigs that should not be accepted, because to do so would be counterproductive in the building of your career—gigs that the manager would not want you to accept!
2. Y now also includes dollars for gigs that you could not accept because of a conflicting engagement.
3. Even if raised to a higher amount, say, to Z dollars, it now covers two years. If you had a great year in the second year of the contract and earned Z dollars or more, but your manager neglected you entirely during the third year and as a result your career was plummeting, you could not terminate because the criterion had already been met in the second year. Thus, the very purpose of the clause is frustrated.
4. It convinced you that you ought to have an entertainment lawyer negotiate your management contract.

Management contracts invariably contain a disclaimer, usually in bold-face type, to the effect that the manager will not act as an agent to procure employment for the artist. This disclaimer is twofold in purpose. It prevents a termination of the agreement by the artist based on a claim that the manager falsely represented that he would procure employment for the artist. In addition, most jurisdictions require employment agents to be licensed as such. Managers as a rule are not licensed agents and hence may not function in that capacity. If a manager procures employment for the artist, it may in certain jurisdictions constitute sufficient grounds for the artist to terminate the management contract. Note that in certain jurisdictions agents are referred to as "Artist's Managers" as opposed to "Personal Managers." Don't confuse the two.

I put it off for as long as I could, but now it is time to deal with the manager's compensation. I procrastinated because it presents some very complex issues which are not easily explained. I have, for many years, argued the issues about to be presented from both sides of the bargaining table, and always manage to feel I am absolutely right. If this section sounds a bit schizoid, it is because it is. Alas, there are a few rights or wrongs in connection with the issues that arise with respect to a manager's compensation.

Simply put, the traditional compensation for managers is a share of the artist's gross income from any and all sources in the entertainment field. The share varies, but anything between 15 percent and 25 percent is within the ball park. It is negotiable in some circumstances and not negotiable in others. I determined not to include sample form contracts in this book because I was confident that they would be misleading and misused. There is no definitive contract on any entertainment subject, and the one chosen for inclusion in a book intended for laymen would attain an undeservedly exalted status and implied endorsement. Contracts thus included would be misused by do-it-yourself types, who could not appreciate the subtleties wrought by clever professionals with hash marks covering their sleeves and battle stars adorning their breasts. I also felt that their inclusion would interfere with the readability (such as it may be) of the book and would act as a deterrent, rather than an aid, to comprehension. Although I am not going to break my own rule, I am going to bend it to the extent of including below the compensation language I drafted some time ago for my manager clients. It has stood the test of time and will serve to highlight the major problems we are confronted with in all management-compensation provisions. In this excerpt, "I" is the artist, and "You" is the manager:

> Instead of payment to you of a fixed compensation or fee, I agree to pay to you a commission equal to twenty (20%) percent of my "gross earnings" (as hereinafter defined) from any and all sources in the entertainment or allied fields including but not limited to, television, motion picture, radio, stage, personal appearances, the production of and performances contained on phonograph records and mechanical or electrical transcriptions, music publishing, songwriting, commercial endorsements, and from the sale, lease, license or other disposition of literary, dramatic and musical material or productions, for use in any medium of communication or entertainment, whether now known or hereafter invented, and from any and all allied, kindred or other fields of entertainment or endeavor (including but not limited to cable television, pay television, audiovisual devices, etc.) in which I may be professionally engaged.
>
> You shall be entitled to the above compensation from all gross earnings *received by me during or after the term* hereof to the extent such gross earnings result from any and all agreements and arrangements *now existing, as well as those entered into or substantially negotiated during the term hereof, and in addition, from all renewals, extensions, amendments, modifications and substitutions of any such agreements and arrangements,* notwithstanding the fact that such gross earnings may be received by me after the expiration of the term hereof.
>
> *"Gross earnings"* shall mean all monies, properties, and consider-

ations of any kind or character, including, but not limited to earnings, fees, advances, royalties, re-use payments, bonuses, gifts, profits, proceeds, allowances, shares of stock and stock options, without deductions of any kind, whether payable directly or indirectly to me, or to any person, firm, or corporation in my behalf, if such are related to my professional activities and career.

The first problem arises with regard to what items of gross earnings (note, I used gross "earnings" as opposed to gross "income," because for technical reasons I felt it was broader and more inclusive) the manager is to receive commission on. The language above is quite comprehensive (I hope) and is designed to include everything the artist receives, whether he keeps and has the use of it or not. From the artist's point of view it would appear patently unfair for the manager to receive commissions on monies the artist does not enjoy. Some examples? Okay.

Suppose your record contract is in the nature of an independent production contract and by its terms the record company pays to your independent production company $100,000 per LP. It is your obligation to produce and deliver a finished album. The recording costs are $78,000. Under the above language, assuming your manager's commission is 20 percent, he is entitled to $20,000. Let's see, $78,000 for recording costs, $20,000 for the manager, and $2,000 for you—but only temporarily, because the entire $100,000 was an advance to you which you must pay back out of your royalties.

A similar situation arises when a record company gives you money for tour support. Suppose you receive $100,000 from your record company for tour support. Assume the tour costs you $110,000 and your gross earnings from the tour are $90,000. The manager is entitled to 20 percent of $100,000 plus 20 percent of $90,000, a total of $38,000. Not bad? What did you end up with?

$100,000.00	tour support
+ 90,000.00	gross earnings
$190,000.00	total
− 110,000.00	costs
$ 80,000.00	
− 38,000.00	manager's commission
$ 42,000.00	your net?

Not quite. In all likelihood, there is a 10 percent agent's fee, another $20,000 off, reducing your "end" to $22,000. Want to add insult to injury? The $100,000 (or at least half of it) that you received from the record company was probably an advance against your future royalties.

One last example. You have presumably become successful and a TV network offers you a special, for which they will pay you $1,000,000. You hire all the talent and pay all production costs. What's left over, you keep:

$1,000,000.00 received from network
− 670,000.00 talent and production costs
$ 330,000.00
− 200,000.00 manager's commission
$ 130,000.00
− 100,000.00 agent's commission
$ 30,000.00 your net

Well, you didn't lose money!

Are the three situations set forth above possible? Yes. Were my numbers manipulated for dramatic effect? A little. Are they likely to happen? It depends on the manager and the situation. If the contract language were not modified to exclude recording costs, tour costs, and packaging costs, I would venture to say that in the early stages of your career, when money is tight, most reputable (and wise) managers who are in for the long haul would waive or at least defer commissions on those costs. How do managers respond if requested during the negotiation of the management contract to exclude such costs from commissionable gross income?

There are a relatively small number of managers who will make no concession whatsoever, feeling that they would prefer to handle each situation as it arises on an ad hoc basis. They feel they will make a proper judgment based on the relationship and the financial situation at the time in question.

Some will yield on all.

Most managers will yield on recording and packaging costs.

It appears that the toughest of the three for a manager to swallow are the tour costs. From the manager's point of view, I have heard the following arguments:

1. "Tours, early in a career, are the toughest part of the manager's job; this is where I really earn my keep and it's one of the few sources of income for me at this stage of an artist's career. I need it to cover my nut."
2. "The primary purpose of a tour is not to make money for the artist. The primary purpose is to promote the then-current album. The artist's payday is down the pike—from record sales. He's the one who will be the superstar with heavy earnings for many years. I may not be around next month, much less five years from now. What about my contract? Today it's a contract; tomorrow it may just be an expensive lawsuit."

It's easy to see where reasonable men may differ.

The next portion of the compensation language to be discussed is probably the most difficult to resolve to the artist's and the manager's satisfaction. The issue is the extent to which the manager is entitled to commissions after the end of his contract with the artist, with respect to both events during the term of his contract and certain income sources occurring after the term has expired. Study the second paragraph of the quoted compensation language. Now let's consider the following situations:

A. Your management contract expires when you have recorded three albums of a six-album record deal. You enter into a management agreement with a new manager before recording albums four, five, and six.
B. After completion of the sixth album in A above, your new manager renegotiates your record deal and you sign a new contract with the same record company for four more albums.
C. Your record deal and your management contract expire at about the same time. Your records recorded during the term of the record deal will continue to earn substantial sums for many years.

The question is, of course, to what extent is the original manager entitled to commissions?

In situation A, it is clear that he is entitled to receive commissions on the earnings from albums one, two, and three. It is also clear from the contract language that he is also entitled to commissions on albums four, five, and six. The new manager is also entitled to commissions on albums four, five and six. Therein lies the dilemma. You are going to have to pay a double management commission—unless something was done to change to the above language before you signed the contract containing it, or you have made an appropriate modification in the new manager's contract.

In situation B, given the quoted language, you will also pay double commission on the four additional albums under the new deal. To avoid this, you would have to give up a lucrative deal with your present record company, with which you feel at home, for a deal with another record company.

In situation C, it is clear, and in my opinion properly so, that the manager must continue to receive commission on those earnings for as long as you do.

There are more questions and problems in the above situations than I have raised here, but these will suffice to familiarize you with the kinds of problems that can arise. Obviously, it is in the artist's interest to negotiate language that preserves his economic integrity and ability to pursue his career in a positive manner rather than being motivated by a need to avoid double compensation. It is equally obvious that it is in a manager's best interest to preserve the language in his contract as his lawyer drafted it.

This is one of the few situations where I can feel equally comfortable on either side of the bargaining table. Managers make cogent arguments for their side of the question. If they are instrumental in creating an artist's career, why, they argue, should they be cast aside just when their labors are about to bear the ripest fruit? Why should not the subsequent manager, who is inheriting an already created situation, not waive his commissions or at least accept a diminished commission? To some extent, the justice of whatever resolution is arrived at depends on how "wonderful" the original manager was, and what part of the artist's success is rightfully attributable to the manager's skill and effort. Unfortunately, management contracts do not come with crystal balls, hence each side must negotiate the best deal possible in the blind, so to speak.

From an artist's point of view, the most felicitous resolution is for the manager to receive commission with respect to all services performed by the artist, including recordings, that are rendered during his tenure as manager, but not those that occur after he is no longer manager. The commission with respect to such events should be applicable to all income from such commissionable events so long as they earn income.

Curiously, some very fine managers also subscribe to this philosophy, as you will learn from the interviews accompanying this chapter. You will also perceive that there is little unanimity of opinion among the managers interviewed. By nature, they are a rather independent lot.

One last observation. There is language in certain management forms whereby if the artist forms a corporation for certain purposes during the term (to do packaging, for instance), the manager is to receive a share of the stock in such corporation. Be very wary. You are contracting for advice and guidance—not a "partner."

All management contracts have a paragraph devoted to the powers the artist grants to the manager to act on the artist's behalf. Invariably they are so broad and so all-encompassing as to be tantamount to a general power of attorney. I defined and commented on powers of attorney in the Lexicon. Take a minute and look it up again. Under the usual management contract as presented to the artist, the manager can sign *any* contract (including a long-term recording contract) on the artist's behalf without so much as asking the artist's opinion, much less permission. Few managers would, or do, utilize these broad powers. Then why have them in? The answer is that they shouldn't be in, and therefore it is incumbent upon you to take them out. The only power of attorney appropriate in a management contract is the limited power to sign contracts for short-term personal appearances. Often, buried in a powers clause, you will find the right granted to the manager to receive all of the artist's gross income, to deduct therefrom his commissions and other sums owed him by the artist, and then to remit the balance to the artist. One might well understand a manager's reluctance to have all income payable to a young artist inexperienced in financial matters. Artists, too, experience qualms, whether justified or not, in losing dominion over their monies. A satisfactory compromise is for the artist and the manager to agree upon a mutually satisfactory business manager or accountant to handle all income and to account to both the artist and the manager, as dictated by the management contract.

Although we have explored the major and most troubling issues in the traditional management contract, we have not discussed—nor can we—some of the more aberrant or unusual provisions that come along. The negotiation of a management contract is not for do-it-yourselfers. You're in lawyer country and you had better know the terrain. Hire a guide.

INTERVIEW WITH
SHEP GORDON

S hep Gordon is the founder of Alive Enterprises, Inc. He has been instrumental in the careers of Alice Cooper, Debbie Harry, Anne Murray, Teddy Pendergrass, and other artists.

AHS: Shep, one of the classic problems with young artists is the question of the chicken or the egg. Young artists can't get a really good manager because the really good managers aren't interested. How does a young artist get to meet a manager or get a manager interested in him?

GORDON: I'm sure there are a lot of different paths. I'm sure that given twenty different artists, there will be twenty different ways that they meet their manager, but all the paths are just . . . hard work . . . banging your head against the wall until it opens up.

AHS: How would you advise someone to go about doing that?

GORDON: Just to believe in what they are doing and find out how much they are willing to give up. What sacrifices they are willing to make. I used to always tell Alice that it was only a couple of guys who started Christianity, because they believed in it. I think if anybody believes in what they're doing, they have a chance of doing it. It's just dedication.

AHS: What are the key considerations in determining whether you or your organization will take on a new act? Do you take on new acts?

GORDON: Acts that are new to our office, yes, but rarely acts that are new to the public. My main consideration most of the time is whether an act is one of a kind. I love to deal with "one-of-a-kinds" and have the opportunity to make a history book. When I say "one of a kind," I mean unique talent, something unique within them, either in the way they look or the way they sing, some kind of unique gift that's singularly them. Usually, I would say the greatest deterrent to making it for any artist has nothing to do with their art; it has to do with their understanding of what it takes to make it. So I tend to gravitate towards artists who have been out there for a long time knocking their heads against the wall so that they know when it's better. New artists don't really know when it's better because they're just starting. So fantasy and reality become mixed. This is really a business. And a lot of new artists, when they get their first successes, expect it to be some kind of a luxurious ride through the world, and that's really not what it is about. You burn out much too fast. For me, the long haul is really important, so I usually become interested in tested people—people who have persisted.

AHS: You really didn't hit exactly what it is that they should be looking for. You indicated that new artists really don't know where it's at, but what kind of things don't they know?

GORDON: No, no, I'm not saying they don't know where it's at. In order to be a successful, commercial star, one part of the puzzle, but only one part, is talent, another part of the puzzle is personality, another part of the puzzle is being able to allow people to do things for you, another part of the puzzle is presence when you walk into a room. There's a lot of pieces to a puzzle that makes someone a star, a talent being only one. So when someone has been out there in the wars for years, usually . . . most of the pieces of the puzzle are developed. Whereas, with a new artist, his art may be as valid as anyone else's, but perhaps he may not be the kind of person who can show up for dates on time. It's not within his character. He may be the kind of person who, when asked the wrong kind of a question, gets offensive and explosive. He may be the type of person who needs a lot of time in the country and would rather dedicate himself to his personal life rather than to his career. He may be the kind of an artist who, when he has reached a certain plateau of economic reward, loses all incentive to grow professionally. He may be the kind of artist who has problems in his relationships with women and, because of it, constantly suffers depression which adversely affects his work. There are a million different possibilities, and it's not limited just to the music field . . . it's present in every other area. I'm sure in professional sports there are great quarterbacks who just couldn't adjust to the system. I like things that are straight, clean, and simple, and someone who works for his career and does it for the right reasons. I don't mean it to degrade their art at all; it's just that the art is a very small portion of it. An artist is on stage an hour and ten minutes out of twenty-four hours and works only a couple of days a week and only a couple of months a year. What he does for the rest of his time, how he conducts his other life . . . that other stuff is really important, really important.

AHS: Do you consider it a positive or negative factor if an act has a record deal, or would you rather take an act and put together your own deal?

GORDON: Ummm! Each case is different. It depends on their record company and the deal.

AHS: This is one of the dumb questions.

GORDON: No. It's valid, I have no preference.

AHS: The next question you may not want to answer, but I think most young artists are interested in managers' fee structures. I know they do vary considerably.

GORDON: I'd say they vary between 15 and 20 percent. That's a reasonable range, considering what a manager does for an artist.

AHS: I remember in the old days when certain managers were getting fifty percent.

GORDON: Yes. Well, I guess, I'm sure there are relationships where maybe it's deserved. I would say in the normal course of business, 15 to 25 percent is reasonable.

AHS: Shep, do you generally try to participate in the publishing or production of an act you manage on an equity basis?

GORDON: I try to participate in everything involved with the artist's career. I won't get involved with an artist unless I'm rewarded economically in every phase. If someone wants to eliminate a portion of income, then I would have to eliminate part of the day. . . . That would be absurd.

AHS: I want to clarify my question. I think I didn't articulate it clearly enough. I certainly understand that you expect to be commissioned on publishing, for instance, but do you require an equity interest in the publishing? For instance, ownership of a copyright?

GORDON: I don't require it. I'd like it, but I don't require it.

AHS: Do you have a fixed-fee structure or does it vary from act to act?

GORDON: It varies.

AHS: I would imagine it would.

GORDON: It varies on what their nets are. How expensive it is for them to operate. It's really all about—for me—the long haul, and everybody making what they want to make out of it. It does me no good if I make a lot and they make nothing.

AHS: What is the minimum term of years for which you'll get involved?

GORDON: I don't sign acts. I still have no contracts.

AHS: You don't have any contracts with your artists?

GORDON: I still don't. [Laughs.]

AHS: It's a handshake and when they get fed up they walk, or if you get fed up, you walk, and that's it? But not too many people walk.

GORDON: Yes, I've had some. Everybody has been really honorable. It's been really nice. No one's ever given me cause to regret not having a written contract. All of them, all of my ex-clients, are really amazing.

AHS: It is a tribute to you.

GORDON: And to them.

AHS: Well, you pick your acts.

GORDON: [Laughs.]

AHS: You find each other. . . . The next question becomes moot because I was going to ask you whether you would agree to terminate a contract under certain circumstances if various criteria weren't met. Since you have no contracts and your acts are free to walk at all times . . .

GORDON: At all times.

AHS: . . . the question becomes moot. . . . Do you feel that the new audio-visual aspects of the industry are affecting the careers of aspiring artists?

GORDON: I don't think they're affecting young artists. I think it's the future of the industry. I think it's the way that in the future musical artists will get their art to the public and be paid for it. I think it's all within that audio-visual world. But I don't see the artist having to change now because of it, necessarily.

AHS: Do you invest your own money in acts?

GORDON: I would if I had to, but I don't start with any new ones, so I really don't come up against that situation.

AHS: You haven't started with any new ones, but if somebody came in who had that particular charisma . . .

GORDON: It's possible, but it would not be a condition. You know what I mean . . . in the course of the artist's career, if investment was called for I would do it. Plenty of times I've put a fortune into artists even when they were established . . . as you well know. I do whatever it takes.

AHS: I assume your compensation is based on a percentage of gross income.

GORDON: Yes.

AHS: Do you normally commission gross income that the artist doesn't actually receive, such as recording costs?

GORDON: No.

AHS: Or cost of touring?

GORDON: Yes.

AHS: You take commission on gross touring but not on recording?

GORDON: No, on recording; yes, on touring. I work on a percentage of gross on touring.

AHS: You work very hard on tours, don't you?

GORDON: Yes.

AHS: Do most of your acts make money on tours?

GORDON: All my acts.

AHS: With new acts, that very often isn't the case.

GORDON: Difficult . . .

AHS: So it's a different situation?

GORDON: Really difficult, and it's a large part of my business, too. I have been doing a lot of other acts. We're really honing it to a science now. I did Kansas's last show. We produce the show, package it, and put it out so it makes money.

AHS: I find your handshake deals so refreshing because I hate drafting and negotiating management contracts. There are certain areas that are never properly resolved. There is just no simple resolution for some of the problems. One of the things that comes up most often is the question of the duration for which the manager is to be commissionable on something that took place while he was managing, and the problems of double compensation. Suppose the artist signs a record contract during the fourth year of a manager's five-year deal. The record deal is for five years; if you pay that manager for the full five years and you don't renew with him, where do you get the money to pay the commission to the subsequent manager? You work on a handshake, so I guess you don't come to grips with this as a practical matter.

GORDON: No. I came to grips with the problem, at least in my own mind. I want to be paid on the records I worked on for their life.

AHS: Just the records you worked on?

GORDON: And that's what we shake hands on. But if I negotiate a five-year record deal, and after the first year of the deal we separate, they can keep the next four years, but I want to be paid on the records they put out in the first year . . . for their life.

AHS: I always think of that as the equitable and proper solution.

GORDON: I think it is. I think the concept that it's the manager who gets the record deal is a little bit silly. It's the artist. The record company doesn't give up a lot, or anything more than they want to give up.

AHS: It's very tough, especially for a new artist to walk into a record company and get a deal.

GORDON: He needs a manager.

AHS: But if a Shep Gordon walks him in, at least he's going to be listened to.

GORDON: That's it.

AHS: They won't make the deal because of you . . . maybe . . .

GORDON: Exactly, so I don't know if just because you're the one who gets them to listen, you really deserve to own a piece of the artist's life.

AHS: I think you're going to be drummed out of the managers' union if you persist.

GORDON: I'm not in it. They don't even invite me. I'm not very popular.

AHS: Shep, how did you get into the business? What is your background?

GORDON: I was a sociologist. I went to the University of Buffalo, and got my master's at the New School.

AHS: Then you became a manager?

GORDON: No. I just floated around and didn't do anything. Then I ran into the Chambers Brothers one day. They were living next door to me; they came in one day and they said, "You're Jewish, aren't you? . . . You should be a manager." I said okay.

AHS: That's the way it started?

GORDON: That was it.

AHS: It's funny. I thank you very much. Any pearls of wisdom that you would pass on to an aspiring writer or artist today?

GORDON: Just not to be discouraged by anybody about anything, ever. . . .

If they really believe in what they are doing, all things are possible.

INTERVIEW WITH
DAVID SONENBERG

David Sonenberg felt himself miscast as an attorney and evolved into one of the leading managers in the music business. He has managed such artists as Meat Loaf, Southside Johnny, BeBe and CeCe Winans, Jim Steinman, and Jimmy Cliff.

AHS: I remember negotiating with you as an attorney, many, many years ago. I think my readers would be interested in knowing why you chose management over a legal career.

SONENBERG: I was originally interested in doing something in the entertainment industry myself. The only reason I applied to law school, to be totally frank, was to find an alternative to serving in Vietnam. They were granting deferments for doctors, lawyers, and engineers. I felt law was the only viable option for me. Once I graduated from law school, I decided to practice entertainment law. But it wasn't something that I felt I'd be doing for a long time. I viewed it as a means of learning about the entertainment industry. During the five years that I practiced entertainment law at a firm, I was always straining at the leash. I was representing a group of young music clients who I particularly liked, but my firm was not really interested in entertainment lawyers acting as agents for these people. That's essentially what I was doing. I was taking people who really couldn't afford to have attorneys and was spending an enormous amount of time trying to get them record contracts. When it became a point of conflict for me to do that within the context of the firm, I decided to go out and start my own law firm, and in relatively short order I realized that what I was really doing was not so much practicing law as managing people. These people did not have record contracts, and what I was doing was going down and saying, "Gee, I don't like your guitar player. I think this song is better than that song. I think you might finish it in this fashion. Why not wear a tuxedo instead of blue jeans?" I realized that these were not the kinds of things you learned in law school.

AHS: You were managing.

SONENBERG: Right. I was reluctant to take off my three-piece suit and become a manager, because a manager to me was the epitome of a parasite, and I never aspired to be a manager. Slowly I started to realize that that's in fact what I was doing. I was particularly enamored with two of my clients. One was Jim Steinman and the other was Meat Loaf. I couldn't get them a record deal for love or money. At this point I had my own firm, so no one was looking over my shoulder.

AHS: I remember when you were negotiating with Albert Grossman for a record deal, and I represented Albert.

SONENBERG: In fact that project is what turned me into a manager. RCA Records signed Meat Loaf and they wanted Jimmy Ienner to produce the record. Jimmy Ienner loved Meat Loaf, but he was not particularly thrilled with Jim Steinman's songs. Meat and I were committed to a Steinman/Meat Loaf package and so we had to find a record producer who liked Steinman. We found that in Todd Rundgren. Unfortunately RCA did not like Todd, because Todd had just delivered a Hall and Oates album that was not successful. We loved Todd particularly because he liked us. We thought he was talented, and it was a thrill to meet somebody with a big name in the industry who thought what we were doing had genuine merit. RCA wouldn't allow Todd to do the record, and as a result we had to buy our way out of RCA Records. It was going to cost $35,000.

AHS: Albert put up the money for that . . .

SONENBERG: There was an investor who was prepared to put up that money, provided that he had some reasonable insurance that Meat Loaf was being managed properly. Up until then, Meat was asking me on a regular basis to manage him. I didn't want to be a manager. The investor said he'd put up the money if I was in fact the manager, and so at that point we entered into a management agreement. So I became the manager by virtue of that third-party investment. Then we started to do the record with Todd, but we didn't have money to pay him. So Todd made an arrangement with Bearsville, which was his record company, that they would put up the studio costs. We agreed in principal to a producer's advance and royalty for Todd, which has turned out to be a very profitable deal for him, probably the most profitable of his career, but he showed us a lot of good faith and he really did the project totally on spec. Bearsville had the right to acquire the Meat Loaf project if they wanted it for a fixed fee. I think the sum was $75,000.

AHS: I think they declined . . .

SONENBERG: They did. In fact, the bottom line, with all due respect to Albert's memory, was that he just felt that Meat was too fat. As a result we had a finished record, produced and mixed by Todd Rundgren, and Bearsville was not interested. Now Bearsville had invested a fair amount of time, effort, and money, by advancing all the studio cost, plus Todd had put in a fairly significant amount of time for free, up to this point. Paul Fishkin, who was running Bearsville for Albert, loved the Meat Loaf album, and when Bearsville didn't want to sign it he sent it over to Warner Bros., who was the distribution company and was financing a lot of Bearsville activities. Warners passed on it. There was a period of almost a year in which that record was in my briefcase, finished, mixed, and not one record company was interested. It really was by a stroke of tremendous good fortune that Steve Popovich, who had passed on this record when he was the head of A&R at Epic, had started up his own company, Cleveland International, and after about nine or ten months of looking for acts, he said, "Do you have anything?" I failed to tell him that he had passed on this once, and I said, "Yeah, I got this Meat Loaf record which I think is great." I sent it to him and he loved it. That record became a gigantic success. At that point I really made the break with law completely and went into the management business.

AHS: What other acts have you managed since then?

SONENBERG: Well, I've managed Southside Johnny and the Asbury Jukes, Jimmy Cliff, Bebe and CeCe Winans, who just had a gold album on Capitol Records. I manage Keith Thomas, who produced Bebe and CeCe Winans, and the new Vanessa Williams album, Phillipe Saisse, and three new acts, The Spin Doctors on CBS, Billy Phillips on SBK, and The Joneses on Atlantic Records.

AHS: It's interesting because you're managing writers and producers, as well as artists, which probably enables you to manage more individuals than you would ordinarily if you were just managing successful artists.

SONENBERG: Truthfully, from a time point of view, it's a lot easier to manage a producer than it is to manage an act which is on the road doing three hundred dates. Also a producer's sensibilities are dramatically different. Most producers are really more business-oriented and have less need for the spotlight. To represent writers and to represent producers gives me a . . .

AHS: . . . cross-fertilization . . .

SONENBERG: In a sense. For example, I'm producing a movie right now called *Rumble in the Jungle,* which is about the Muhammad Ali/George Foreman fight in Zaire in 1974. We have 350,000 feet of feature film that was shot by the Maisell brothers. In producing that film, I need songs. I need people to produce soundtracks. It gives me an opportunity to cross-pollinate successfully.

AHS: That probably brings me to the seminal question when you talk about the manager/artist relationship. It's really a chicken-and-egg type of thing. An unknown artist will come to me and say, "I have to have a manager. Where am I going to find a manager?" And if you go to a manager, he'll say, "I'm really not terribly interested in an act that hasn't shown anything yet." How does a new act find a manager, and are you at all interested in neophyte acts?

SONENBERG: Well, truthfully, I've always had neophyte acts. I've never had the good fortune of having an established artist who I really thought was fantastic call me up.

AHS: But, now that you've arrived, I imagine the pickings are easier.

SONENBERG: Yeah, except for the fact that at this stage management is a very difficult job. If you're not truly motivated to do the work, you're not going to do a good job, and as you get more successful, it becomes increasingly difficult to stay motivated. So, even if a big artist called me, it would have to be a situation where I felt I could make a contribution, where it was exciting and dynamic. Oftentimes the big acts that call have passed their peak, are somewhat lost and disoriented or are unhappy with their careers, not necessarily so much because their manager did a particularly good or bad job, but because their careers were not in good shape, regardless of whose fault it was. If I could help to move an act in the right direction, really make a contribution and *really manage,* I would be interested. The word "manage" is such an unusual word. How many managers truly *manage* their artists? How many artists allow their managers to direct them? That's a difficult relationship to preserve. Just because you have a contract which says you are the manager doesn't mean that you are doing anything except being the custodian of the ego, fears, and emotions of your client.

AHS: . . . and income . . .

SONENBERG: And income. But for me to get involved with a big act, it would have to be because I respected the artist and the artist respected me. To just get a percentage of a big piece of pie at this stage is not worth it.

AHS: I'd like to get back to the primary question. This is for our readers. How does a young act, individual or group, find a manager? I have always given a glib answer to that—and not a very satisfying answer—which was to persevere: "You do good things and a manager will find you." It doesn't give them a whole lot of confidence. Maybe you could do a little better.

SONENBERG: Well, it's hard. I'm inundated with tapes, and the people in my office have now begun to say, "I'm sorry, we don't accept tapes." Primarily because we can't listen to the vast majority of the tapes we receive. Since there's so much competition today, I think what an act has to do is persevere. That's critical, because few managers go out on a regular basis, scouring the clubs, devouring every tape they're sent. However, from time to time, if I'm going for a drive I'll pick up a handful of tapes, I'll listen, and sometimes I have come across tapes that I have liked. Your odds, if you send a tape, are not particularly great, but on occasion the right person is going to hear a tape and be moved by it. I had a young girl who worked for us for a summer and she was a big fan of a group called The Spin Doctors. She kept talking about The Spin Doctors, and finally I promised to go see them. They were great. I signed them and now they're on CBS Records.

AHS: That young lady ought to get a point.

SONENBERG: And what about the mother that bore her? What's really critical is to realize that since it's so hard to attract people's attention, I think you have to find ways to charm people. I say charm because I think that's usually what gets to me as opposed to bludgeoning persistence. If I get a tape that comes in with a little note that has a certain, I'm calling it charm for lack of a better word . . .

AHS: Charm's a good word.

SONENBERG: You find yourself warmed by the note and you sense the humanity of that person. You feel the flesh and blood and you feel the intelligence and the vulnerability of that person and you're moved to contact him, if nothing else than to just say, "You know, I'm taking a minute out of my crazy, lunatic schedule just to tell you that you reached me and you moved me."

AHS: It's funny, because I know exactly what you're talking about because it happens to me, albeit rarely. But when it happens you know it. You respond. You go out of your way and do something. This is a question I usually reserve for music publishers and record people. I'm looking at the cabinet full of tapes behind you. Most of these young people are very interested in the demo: what to do, what not to do. Over the years I have generated certain ground rules: don't overload the tape, just three or four songs, the best song first; be true to yourself, don't try and spread yourself out, do what you do best. Are there any particular things that turn you off instantly when you see or hear a demo? Any gems you would want to pass on to these young people with regard to demos?

SONENBERG: I think I subscribe to your general parameters of not showing too many colors at once. Most artists feel that they can do a lot of different things, and I think it's very important to be focused so a manager and a record company can quickly say, "I understand what this is all about." To do a ballad followed by a dance tune, followed by a bluesy tune, followed by a rock tune, just confuses the issue. With that caveat, nothing else really turns me off. I don't need to hear a very slick demo, I can hear a piano and vocal. The most important thing, I think, is to try to avoid being generic. A lot of people come and say, "This is as good as Bon Jovi." Yeah, so what. If a record company is going to sign something new and if a manager is going to get excited about something new, it should *be* something *new*. I think a demo should be personal to the artist. The more personal the tapes, the better.

AHS: I'm gonna ask what will sound like a silly question. I'll try to justify it. Would you—assuming you've become interested in a new act—prefer that it had a record deal in its pocket, or would you prefer being able to cast that deal yourself, picking the record company, negotiating the terms? Would you consider it a terrific incentive if they already had a record deal?

SONENBERG: I have mixed emotions about that. Record companies tend to make decisions by committee, so whether you first go to the lowest A&R man on the totem pole or you go to the top, all it takes is one person in the chain to say "It ain't so great" for the whole committee to say "pass." So, in a sense the frustration and the rejection that both a manager and his artist feel in that process is difficult. However, at the end of the day, if I end up finding somebody who's interested in making a deal, I'm usually more satisfied with the nature of the record agreement, and the relationship that became bonded as a result of it. Everybody feels like they were there at the birth of it. There's an artist that I manage who came to me with a fully negotiated record contract. It doesn't have the tools that I think are necessary really to give the record a fair shot, so I'm operating from a handicapped position in that regard, but I didn't have to go through the horrible experience of finding a record company in the first place. So, it's got its good and bad points.

AHS: Recently I had to do a management contract. I have always hated management contracts. Thank God there are younger people in the firm who can do this. I was looking through a collection of management forms, because they had lost my forms file, and I saw contracts that varied from twenty-five pages down to three. I went through all of them, from top to bottom. I rejected most of them as off the wall. They just went too far and most of the things were going to be rejected in a negotiation anyway, so why bother . . . all you're doing is engendering bad will. I have found that most management contracts come down to three or four major issues. First, I'm going to ask you what your contract looks like, because managers usually proffer the first draft, and then I'm going to ask you a few specific questions, and maybe argue with you a little bit. Are your contracts of the twenty-five page variety or the three-page variety, or somewhere in between?

SONENBERG: Three.

AHS: Oh, then we are on the same wavelength. What is your compensation structure usually? Percentage of gross?

SONENBERG: Percentage of gross, with some exclusions from the gross . . .

AHS: Recording costs?

SONENBERG: Recording costs, tour support, video costs, sound and light expenses on the road. Those are the principal exclusions. Packaging costs.

AHS: An enlightened manager. I've met managers who absolutely refused to yield on tour support, saying that's the core of their income structure. Everybody will give on recording costs. Not too many people give on the lighting.

SONENBERG: Well, to be frank, I have a practical approach to this, and my approach is that if it's a marginal situation, I as a manager am not likely to be making any money. If it's not a marginal situation, there's more than enough money to go around. We don't have to nickel and dime our artists on tour support and recording costs.

AHS: Well spoken. What term do you usually insist on? How many years?

SONENBERG: Five.

AHS: Not three plus two? You're willing to make some concessions on what is commissionable, yet you're insisting on the straight five years?

SONENBERG: Yes.

AHS: Suppose you're starting your fifth year and your artist signs a new record contract, which is nowadays eight or nine years. A management contract in its original draft form provides for commissions on any contracts entered into for the full duration of that contract, any extensions thereof, etc., etc. This is something that as an artist's attorney I find anathema because I'm scared to death of double commissions. When your term ends and the artist goes on to another manager, now he's got to pay your commission and the new manager also wants a commission.

SONENBERG: Well, you know, I share your concerns. Having been an attorney representing artists, I'm well aware of all the issues. I certainly argued the other side long enough. Clearly it's a difficult issue as to when a management commission should be terminated. If I sign a nine-year record contract for an act in the last twenty minutes of my management agreement, then it would be very difficult for that act to give me a full commission for the next nine years when they have a new manager. At the same time, if I sign them to a recording contract in the first twenty minutes of my agreement, and at the end of my five years we decide to part company and there's three years to go on the record contract, it's not necessarily unfair that I should be getting either the full amount or some significant portion of my commission. The new manager has nothing to do with the original record contract, and maybe he shouldn't get a full commission on that agreement. Remember, the new manager is inheriting a successful artist who has the ability to earn big money on the road. That should be enough incentive for the manager to want to get involved.

AHS: I wish I were an artist. I would try to get you as a manager. You are a very reasonable fellow.

SONENBERG: Well, I haven't agreed to waive my commissions, but I understand the argument and it's a serious one. At the same time, from a manager's point of view, five years may seem like a long time, but in the grand scheme of things, most acts do not happen overnight and an overnight success really is five years. So, just as the act is beginning to happen, the act and the manager may be parting company. The manager agreed to waive tour support, to waive video, to waive recording costs, has made little or no money in the course of the five years, and if he doesn't continue to commission the fruits of that record contract for some significant period of time, then why did he agree to all those waivers up front?

AHS: Another question which comes to mind, and you may not wish to answer this: Do you ever pump your own funds into an artist, supporting him while he's getting going?

SONENBERG: Yes.

AHS: Not a lot of managers admit to it.

SONENBERG: Well, I do it. I will never contractually agree to it.

AHS: I don't think anybody would ask you for it.

SONENBERG: Well, some artists do and some artists feel like, "Hey, listen, man, you know, if you're really that into it then you should be prepared to commit twenty grand because what's twenty grand, it's chump change, man." I think the job of a manager is to invest his time, effort, and energy, but he's not a bank. However, if you've invested time, effort, and energies in something and now in order to get the brass ring you have to pay for a demo or have to put your artist in a rehearsal studio or

AHS: someone's being thrown out of his apartment, then more often than not you're either constrained to make a financial investment or you voluntarily do so because you think there's good reason.

AHS: Do you ever insist on an equity position?

SONENBERG: No.

AHS: Never take a publishing interest?

SONENBERG: If you're prepared to waive commissions on a large number of things, and essentially are going to be working for nothing until such time as an act really does happen, it makes good sense to acquire equity in something. That's the justification for taking an equity interest publishing as opposed to commissioning that aspect of an artist's earnings.

AHS: I would bet from listening to you that you don't insist on a power of attorney.

SONENBERG: I don't. A contract doesn't insure a good relationship with an artist. If you have a good relationship, power is not that important, and if you don't have a good relationship, even if you have the power nobody is going to accept your power if there's trouble in Tahiti. As a practical matter, I need a power to sign day-to-day booking contracts because in many instances you can't get paid unless there's a contract signed, and the artist may not be available. The other power that I do insist upon is the power to endorse checks.

AHS: I have usually traversed this one by suggesting that the artist and the manager mutually pick an accountant who handles the funds, disburses commissions to the manager, and pays the artist the rest. It keeps the manager out of an adversarial position. How do you envision the relationship between the manager and the other people on the artist's team: the attorney, the accountant? I have had some managers who've said, "I want to be in from the inception. I want to help pick the attorney that I'm going to have to work with. I want to help pick the accountant. I want to really be the general in change of the entire strategy." Sometimes that just doesn't happen. Sometimes an attorney's been with the act long before you have been, loyalties are established, and you have to come to a *modus vivendi*. So sometimes I imagine you have to accommodate.

SONENBERG: To be honest, the healthiest situation is when the manager doesn't act as the general, when the artist finds a lawyer or when the artist finds a business manager or finds people who he likes, trusts, and respects. When they say to the artist "We really like your manager," it has impact and gives the artist comfort. Let's face it, the bottom line here is for the artist to really feel "I have a fantastic manager. I like him. I respect him. I trust him. Other people like him and respect him and trust him." If I as the manager handpick the lawyer and handpick the accountant, for those people to say to the artist "Boy, your manager is great" is not going to be particularly meaningful.

AHS: Let me ask you a question I've never asked a manager before. How do you gird yourself against the inevitable perfidy?

SONENBERG: Well, explain perfidy to me so I can answer it intelligently.

AHS: I have found over the years that though I have been very blessed myself, there is a fickleness amongst artists and that as their careers change, their heads are meddled with and muddled by others, and they take on spouses in the course of the relationship. And sooner or later, these relationships tend to rupture, notwithstanding how much you've done or how good you've been. There is a great chance of being unappreciated and being cast aside, and I think that has to do things to people's heads. I've seen it with managers who've devoted their lives to artists only to have found themselves displaced for no reason that they can perceive. They didn't fool with the acts' money. They didn't steal. They didn't betray them. The relationship just kind of wore out like a marriage between a husband and wife could wear out.

SONENBERG: Well, I would say that you can't gird yourself. To say that you will not be hurt when someone no longer values your being is absurd. If you are that type of person, you probably will never be a particularly good manager in the first place because it takes a fair amount of passion and caring in order to carry the day. Now if I am passionate, and then at some point along the line the artist says "Gee, you know you just ain't cutting it anymore," or for whatever reason, it has to hurt. I don't think there's any way not to be hurt by that.

AHS: I hope it never happens to you. Thank you, David.

SONENBERG: Thank you. I enjoyed it. I'm glad you came.

INTERVIEW WITH
BUD PRAGER

Bud Prager, president of E.S.P. Management, Inc., is an outspoken and truly professional manager. Artists such as Foreigner, Bad Company, and Damn Yankees flourish under his guidance.

PRAGER: What is this interview about?

AHS: You still don't know what this is about.

PRAGER: I still don't know what this is about. My preface to you is, if this has anything to do with management . . .

AHS: It does.

PRAGER: . . . is that the attitude toward the profession depends on the time of the interview. For example, if a manager is in the midst of an act happening and has something exciting going on, he loves the world, he loves his artists, and he thinks it's a wonderful profession. Those moments are rare.

AHS: But I gotcha in one.

PRAGER: No, you don't.

AHS: No?

PRAGER: No, quite the contrary. When you're going through traumas, whether it be with artists or with the record companies, then management is a dreadful profession, so the answers depend on the time and the circumstances, not on the reality of the profession.

AHS: There are certain truths that are inalienable—that has been said before and we'll get to those—but I was under the impression that you had a lot of acts that are happening now.

PRAGER: I do.

AHS: Yeah, so . . .

PRAGER: But I'm angry at the industry, the quality or caliber of the executives who run the industry, which everybody realizes is abysmal, and the—what's the word?—the ups and downs, the vicissitudes of the artist/management relationship.

AHS: What acts are you representing now that are "happening"?

PRAGER: Bad Company, number-one AOR [Album-Oriented Rock] track for the second time, number-one album AOR and headlining a very successful tour, making money . . . positives, three positives.

AHS: Give me some more acts that are positive.

PRAGER: Damn Yankees.

AHS: Yes.

PRAGER: . . . had a number-one AOR track, successful second track, third one is out now and is going to be a huge hit. There's your prediction. This isn't going to be a hit, it's going to be a big, big hit. Now that means there's a difference, a huge difference between an AOR hit and a CHR hit, and this will be both.

AHS: CHR is . . . ?

PRAGER: Top 40.

AHS: Contemporary Hit Radio, is that what it is?

PRAGER: Yeah, one of the horrendous verbal delineations inflicted upon us by *Billboard* magazine.

AHS: You're not going to spare anybody, are you? I got you on a good day, all right!

PRAGER: I actually like the way that rolled.

AHS: Yes, you'll roll your pencil over it, I'm sure. What about Giant? Is Giant doing well?

PRAGER: Yes, Giant had a significant first album and toured the U.S. and Europe. Damn Yankees is out touring with Bad Company, so it's a really successful package that oddly enough was opposed by almost everybody—co-managers, the artists, agents, almost all opposed this match-up. One of the principals that I had to deal with said, "These two acts together looks to me like shit," and he's now told me as recently as yesterday, "I think this is the package of the year." He couldn't see what I saw, no disrespect to him, but he couldn't see the Bad Company . . .

AHS: I want to get into your vision a little bit later . . . Now what I really want to establish are your bona fides. I'm asking you who you represent.

PRAGER: I've got so many bona fides that it's . . .

AHS: Let's talk about your bona fides.

PRAGER: Well, I've been involved with performing rights organizations, production companies, publishing companies, and record labels, but I was born to be an artist's manager, and that . . .

AHS: You've got to back that one up.

PRAGER: Why?

AHS: Because the tradition, or the belief in the industry, as ill-founded as it may be, is—and this is going to offend you—that managers are people who really can't do anything else and that they fall into being managers.

PRAGER: Correct, it's not ill-founded.

AHS: Okay.

PRAGER: If you can't play guitar or sing, what do you do? Well, you become friends with someone who plays a guitar and sings, and you end up saying, "Well, I should be your manager." And if you get to be his best friend, he'll say, "You got to be my manager." Then the artist becomes successful and nine times out of ten they look for a professional manager and get rid of the friend who shouldn't have been there in the first place.

AHS: Which are you now, friend or manager?

PRAGER: Absolute professional manager.

AHS: When you verified what I said, you were talking about too many managers who really aren't equipped to be managers . . . ?

PRAGER: That's correct.

AHS: Okay.

PRAGER: . . . and the managerial profession suffers the indignity of all those people. The record companies are of two minds, they want their artists to have professional management, but a certain kind of acquiescent subservient management. They do not want a forceful manager who might have ideas that conflict with their control, so you have a real battle there. It's not healthy for a manager to be opinionated and have a sense of direction or purpose in combination with the artist. The record companies want control more than anything.

AHS: When you said you were "born to be a manager," . . .

PRAGER: Yes . . .

AHS: . . . I interrupted you. What did you mean?

PRAGER: In an earlier life I was a very inadequate musician. I played classical clarinet, was concert master of my high school symphonic orchestra. Then I went into the army, and I ended up in a fabulous band, a big band, with some great musicians from Woody Herman–type bands, Gene Krupa–type bands, fabulous musicians, and I got in (it's a long story and it would take a book). The guys in the band, I was in Korea with them. A friend of mine sent me letters that I had written him from Korea, and in one of those letters I related that one of my band members had said, "Bud, you have a great smile, but you're the worst musician I've ever played with," . . .

AHS: Meaning you?

PRAGER: Yeah, those guys said, "You're a terrible musician. It's really hard to have you in the band, but when we get back to civilization, you're the kind of guy we'd like to have be our agent." Back then there wasn't such a thing as a manager. What they meant was I had an affinity for knowing what to do, when to do it, how to do it, and how to make decisions. I don't mean this in any denigrating way towards current musicians, but musicians should be musicians, and managers should be managers. The two together should forge a destiny, but you have artists now who somehow feel that they should be making decisions they are not qualified to make, and you have managers who are not qualified to do their role, but I'm ideally cut out to be that counterpart.

AHS: This experience, this Korean experience, this was before you went to college and law school, or after, or between?

PRAGER: Before.

AHS: You told me that although you went to law school you never became a lawyer. You said that with such pride that I was offended slightly, but it's okay.

PRAGER: Pride in what, that I went to law school?

AHS: That you didn't become a lawyer.

PRAGER: Oh, no, no, I was the general manager of a performing rights organization, SESAC, and I went to law school at night, which was very difficult, and I did not get a thorough education in the law because I couldn't apply myself directly. I was working very hard, traveling extensively. I missed the first four or six weeks of law school because of an antitrust suit involving, believe it or not, gospel music in shape notes. By the time I got back I didn't know whether I was coming or going. If you think back to your first four weeks of law school . . .

AHS: The toughest four weeks of your education.

PRAGER: Yeah, that's when you get indoctrinated and brutalized into thinking in terms to enable you to survive your next three years. I missed it and it was a dreadful uphill battle. I don't know how I graduated.

AHS: Bud, I really don't want your whole law school history. You once said to me, in one of your fits of modesty, that you probably had the best ears in the rock 'n' roll industry.

PRAGER: Well, that sounds like it should be tempered. As good as . . .

AHS: Then temper it.

PRAGER: . . . as good as any ever. My indoctrination into rock music, not rock 'n' roll—I use strange delineations here—was when my first partner called me up and he was so excited he could hardly breathe . . . he was over the moon. He said, "The most exciting thing in the world happened." I remember I was in a luncheonette. My partner was Felix Pappalardi and we had started with absolutely nothing together, just two dreamers, but he was an immense talent and we complemented each other perfectly. He called me and he was just . . . ecstatic isn't even close, and I had been pushing for him to become a producer at Atlantic. He had never produced anything of too much consequence, and I had been pushing behind the scenes for him to do Sonny and Cher or Buffalo Springfield at Atlantic. He told me he's "got it," he's "got it," and it's the most "amazing thing," and "oh my God," and I wondered which one it was and I said, "Who is it?" and he said "Cream." Well, to me that was the most depressing moment . . . and he'd sensed it and he said, "Bud, this is going to be history." I thought, "Well, okay," and I remember saying to him, "How long do you think this will take?" because I couldn't wait for him to get finished with that so he could do something worthwhile. By the way, I think the album was done in about three weeks and probably cost about ten thousand dollars. The album was *Disraeli Gears,* which revolutionized our industry. You don't realize it. Nobody realizes it.

AHS: Was Cream a big-name act at the time?

PRAGER: Their first album sold about 15,000. That was hardly dramatic.

AHS: I just wanted to put it into perspective for the readers.

PRAGER: . . . 15,000 or 20,000, it was nothing, but Felix kept telling me that there was this change coming. There was this whole thing, this underground radio. There was no such thing as underground radio at the time. There was a little station in San Francisco. It was the first of the underground stations. When Felix went to San

Francisco they knew he was coming, and they started playing an hour of Felix Pappalardi productions. When we got to the station, they asked him if he had any Cream tapes with him. He did. They played them and it just started a whole thing and the underground station in Los Angeles got a copy of the tape from San Francisco. Atlantic called Felix, "How dare you? Who do you think you are?" Well, it forced the album out prematurely and it exploded. Atlantic started getting reorders. They got in a huge reorder from Detroit and the sales manager called up and said, "You got the wrong album. There's no single on this album. You got the wrong number." He said, "Which one are you reordering?" They gave him the number of the Cream album, and he said, "It can't be. We don't have a single out." It was impossible to sell those kinds of numbers in that day. If you had a single, you could sell albums. When you didn't have a single, you couldn't sell albums. Cream broke that barrier and Jimi Hendrix, those were the two. So Felix indoctrinated me. He would explain and play these things for me because he knew that I had a classical background and he would throw parallels. This is interesting for you, by the way. He sat me in front of big speakers, put on Cream, and said, "Now, listen, but listen to it this way . . ." He was wonderfully verbal. He had four years of education at the University of Michigan in music. He said, "When you listen to Cream," (which is a three-piece group), "imagine you are in Carnegie Hall and you're looking at the symphonic orchestra. Ginger Baker, the Cream drummer, is all of the percussionists in the back, the tympany, the drums, etc.—he's all of those. Jack Bruce, the bass player, is the big stand-up basses and the cellos and the violas and all of the instruments that have to do with what you're hearing from that section. Eric Clapton is the whole left side of the strings, maybe forty-fifty strings, plus your lead instruments."

Have you ever thought of this, or done this?

AHS: No, but I'm listening.

PRAGER: What happened is that talented young people, who historically went into classical music as an outlet for the natural progression of their talents, saw that they could get two or three other guys, get together and make the same music, so rock is an extension of classical music. It's just that there's a lot of garbage and crappy players doing this because they want to get girls and because it's the thing to do, but in its finest form, it's an extension of classical music. If you put on great rock groups like Cream, and certain others that I love, you have something magnificent, because they're really talented people. The grown-ups of the world have always regarded this as teenage crap. It isn't. Some of them, like Jack Bruce, are fantastically talented, classically trained musicians.

AHS: Did one of the groups happen to be Foreigner?

PRAGER: In terms of the classical evolution, no . . .

AHS: I'm being cute and introducing the fact that you have represented Foreigner, because you didn't make mention of it.

PRAGER: No, Felix was the first. Cream was a dramatic example of the explosion of rock music.

AHS: Did you manage Cream?

PRAGER: No. Cream broke up very quickly. Massive amount of problems. They wouldn't even stay on the same floor of the hotel together— three guys. When that broke up, Felix and I started Mountain with Leslie West. Became a headline group, gold albums which were big at that time. When that broke up, again massive problems and everything else, we had made a huge deal with CBS, Clive Davis, at that time. They broke up after I think two albums, and then we formed West, Bruce and Laing. Felix had become pretty non-functional from drugs.

AHS: Were you working now as a producer?

PRAGER: Me?

AHS: Yeah.

PRAGER: No, never.

AHS: Was Felix?

PRAGER: Felix was the producer and bass player and singer in Mountain.

AHS: He produced and you managed?

PRAGER: Yeah. He produced Cream, I did not manage them. But if I hadn't been there, Felix would never have gotten to produce Cream. When that broke up, Felix and I formed Mountain with Leslie West as the lead guitar player/singer, and I was co-managing and Felix was producer, writer, arranger, bass player, singer, leader.

AHS: And co-manager.

PRAGER: Co-management because of me in a reverse thing because we were partners. West, Bruce and Laing, Felix just had an interest in through Leslie but he had no other involvement with them. Felix dropped out because of his drug problems. Although we managed Leslie West and Corky Laing, Robert Stigwood had Jack Bruce of Cream. To put our deal together with CBS we had to undo all the deals that these guys had . . . ten to fifteen contracts which took me about a year and a half of sorting it out. We (the group and my partner, Gary Kurfirst) wanted the deal with CBS, but Stigwood wanted it with Atlantic because of his deal with Ahmet [Ertegun]. This would be the first group on their new label, RSO. So there was a conflict between managers and everything. Eventually, the conflicts were resolved and the band went to CBS. Anyway, when that broke up, it was the Leslie West Band, and out of the Leslie West Band came Mick Jones and Foreigner. That was the real turning point.

AHS: And you represented Foreigner for how many years?

PRAGER: Starting in 1976.

AHS: And still?

PRAGER: Yeah.

AHS: I have sent you tapes in the past.

PRAGER: Yeah.

AHS: It's fun getting back the responses because you're a very witty guy, but you're also the most vicious commentator on tapes I have ever seen. I once sent you a rock and roll group that you thought had possibilities, and you must have invested a year's time working with them and never found them to mature to the point where you wanted to sign them. So you are very, very selective in who you manage. And that kind of leads me to a question that most of my readers have on the tips of their tongues: "When the hell is he getting to this?" How does a new group get a manager? It's sort of a chicken-and-egg thing. How do you advise a new group to go about getting a manager because they need a manager, and yet the only managers they're going to get are the kind that you alluded to initially?

PRAGER: Yes.

AHS: And then they're going to ultimately have to switch to real managers. Do you have any ideas for them? Suggestions?

PRAGER: Well, there's a bigger problem. Most of the people you're talking about should be thinking in terms of what they're doing as a profession. They're not qualified to compete in the professional rock world, but they do because it looks so easy and as I said earlier it's a way to get girls.

AHS: They don't know about it at this point.

PRAGER: I know, but you're asking how some hack painter with no talent and no distinction and no future gets into a gallery on Fifty-seventh Street? He doesn't, he shouldn't; if he has to paint, fine, he should go paint. But in terms of competing with the cream of the crop and the real professionals and the ultimate professionals, he can't! The next question is, how do you know if you're an "ultimate professional"? You don't. But there's very little "talent" in blinking capital letters. Amongst all of this rubble, most are just hacks and journeymen. How does a young kid out of law school get into a good law firm?

AHS: He does extraordinarily well in law school, and then they seek him out.

PRAGER: We don't have the same criteria. You don't get grades for amateurish guitar playing. You get grades in law school so that you're measured. We have no measuring stick. So anybody can just take up a guitar and hack away at it and say, "I'm a guitar player, how do I get a manager?" Well, basically, talent should seek its own level.

AHS: I guess it does ultimately.

PRAGER: Most of the time. I know some great talent with some lackluster management, but it suited them. Are there some really talented people who would have had a career with proper management? Yes. When I was having my battles with A&M, I had lunch with Gil Frieson, then president of the label, and he said, "We're not used to dealing with somebody like you. This is a new experience. Seven out of ten of the managers that we deal with don't know anything." I thought he was charitable. There used to be a handful, so now there are probably ten or twelve competent, knowledge-able, professional managers . . . how many artists are there?

AHS: Let me cut to the chase. How does a young rock group, like the one I sent to you, that you thought had talent and were kind of interesting, how do they ordinarily find a manager such as a Bud Prager?

PRAGER: You send a tape, or you go through an attorney, the way you did it. If they had sent me a tape, nothing would have happened, but you sent it to me, so I listened to it. Most guys like me don't want to listen to a tape.

AHS: I understand that.

PRAGER: And they don't want these new bands. They're a plague. They take forever and, you see, if you're successful and you have good rela-tionships with the record companies and you play a different kind of a game, they want you to take all kinds of things. They offer you anything that has no manager or that is changing managers. I'm in a different category. I'm difficult. That goes with me. I'm difficult so those kind of things aren't offered to me as much.

A guy was in here last night and he is talented. I sat down with him and I spent some time with him. He told me last night that coming in here was different from going to see anybody else. I said, "I know that." I'm very aware now of what this experience is on both sides. The minute he played the tape, I said, "You changed your vocals." He looked at me like "Goddammit, nobody else would notice that." I had told him to do certain things and he did them, he did one right, he did one wrong. I'm underneath the tape, inside the tape, as opposed to the people he's playing for who are outside the tape.

AHS: So what you're really saying is, as a manager, or even as a potential manager, you are very much into the music.

PRAGER: Everybody says they're into the music.

AHS: I know, but I mean it literally.

PRAGER: I'm inside the music. There's another artist I'm working with who's a fascinating guy, Doug Feiger. I went through his tape, but he's working with one of the best producers in the world, a guy named Don Was. The most "in" producer in the world right now. So I said, "I'm not going to get into all this stuff with you." But I saw him at lunch, and he said, "Any comments at all?" I went through my notes and I said, "Well, what song do you consider important?" He told me and I said, "Yeah, in that one, there's this section that isn't right." He said, "Goddammit. I knew I had that in there. I knew there was something wrong with it and I could never figure out what it was." He said, "Well, what is it?" So I go back and listen. I called him up and I said, "Take it out, it doesn't belong in there." He said, "You're absolutely right. I never thought of that." Now, is that a big deal? Not really. But I can do that on every song, on every phrase, almost every note . . . does it fit? Is it right? Is it part? These guys don't have people who can do that. Who do you think can do that? The guys who they write with or play with can't do it.

AHS: A lot of people would think, or protest, that that really is not a manager's function.

PRAGER: It isn't.

AHS: They just get a tremendous bonus with you.

PRAGER: That's correct.

AHS: They're getting a producer . . .

PRAGER: It has nothing to do with management. But—and there's also another thing I thought you were going to say—wait a minute, isn't this, in a sense, corporate intrusion into art? Isn't this infringing upon the artist's domain? So shouldn't it be where he creates something . . . and you know what I say? Nonsense! In the music business, and it's the music *business,* we're not on the art side at this time. Would I do this to Bob Dylan? Absolutely. Now if you go back to when Dylan was king of the world, would I do it with him then? No. Would he ask me to do it? Maybe. Would it have made a difference? No. But what about Dylan now, who hasn't had a successful album in let's say ten years and is making records and is still doing the same mundane stuff surrounded by people who say to him, oh, Bob, this is the best thing you've done, this is great, this is terrific, and he is saying, oh yeah, because there is nobody there to challenge him. He's unchallengeable, he's God. Not to me he wouldn't be, at any stage. If he brought me his best work and said what do you think? I might say it's really great or I might say, well, what about this or what about that. And you know what he would say, damn, yeah that part in there always bothered me, what do you think?

AHS: You've heard that a lot apparently over the years.

PRAGER: It's a peculiar thing. I have a distinctive feel or appreciation for rock music. When it's right, it kills me. When it's wrong I can see or hear problems or things to improve. The magic of rock music, when everything comes together, is rare and wonderful. I have ultimate respect for talent—but most everyone can use a legitimate sounding board. I happen to be one. Capable of creative input.

AHS: We were talking about the relatively few managers before.

PRAGER: Yes.

AHS: Do you think most of them have this ability or tendency?

PRAGER: No.

AHS: So you can be a great manager without being "inside" the music.

PRAGER: I'm just a fluke. This isn't something that a manager should be, could be, will be or anything. No, the answer is no. I think it's peculiar.

AHS: But your clients get a plus.

PRAGER: Yes, the ones who know how to use it get a big plus. That's part of the reason why Bad Company is number one. On the other hand I had very little to do with Damn Yankees musically. Very little. Fortunately they got the right producer [Ron Nevison]. When you get into managerial talents—and this is more relevant to what you're doing here—one of those talents is being able to know which producer will suit the music. Mick Jones and I pick every producer for Foreigner. Terry Thomas, who is emerging as a star producer, is a major contributor to Bad Company and Giant. Most of the managers can't do that. It's shocking. Most of the record people don't know either. Most of the A&R people don't have a clue. Again, if you really want to know whether a producer is right or good or talented, it's really helpful to be able to get inside the music as opposed to looking at his credits on a sheet of paper. I have that talent. I'm really good at that. My best talent is probably managing producers. I just didn't have the time to do it in a big way.

AHS: A few moments ago you underscored the word "business." You said we're in the music *business*. Being a manager is a business, too. I would like to segue into the manager/artist or manager/producer relationship on a business level. I assume that you commission gross income as do most managers.

PRAGER: Yes.

AHS: Can I also assume the percentage varies with the talent?

PRAGER: Yes.

AHS: Give us a ball park figure in percentages.

PRAGER: They're all either 15 or 20 percent of gross.

AHS: Do you exclude from gross certain . . .

PRAGER: Yeah, I excluded actual recording costs, and on touring, the rea-

sonable net cost of sound and lights. But it's not that simple anymore, because when a band is touring they get reimbursed for
sound and light. So, I'm not sure—that's become a vagary to me.
I think basically you commission gross.

AHS: No, from you.

PRAGER: I should get much more from records and publishing in most cases
for what I do. Other managers are collecting the same percentage
and not contributing so much insight, input.

AHS: As a practical matter, when you sit down and do the contract,
nobody at that point really has the ability to appreciate what your
contribution is. So you're negotiating a more or less standard type
of contract. I know your contracts are short. You like them that
way. Do you insist on an equity interest in publishing?

PRAGER: No.

AHS: You have come to that conclusion through experience? I know at
one time you did.

PRAGER: I did, and I should. I think about it a lot but if I was starting out,
if this was, you know, ten or fifteen years ago and I was starting
with a band, I would do it. Right now I figure I don't know how
much longer I'm going to do this. It's not life or death to me. It's
not crucial to me. So I just want to do it and I hope things succeed,
but as far as an equity interest in the publishing, no. But if it was
ten or fifteen years ago I would do that.

AHS: But certainly you commission publishing income and songwriter
income.

PRAGER: Yes.

AHS: When do you think an act ought to have a manager? At what point
in their career? When they have a record deal, when there's a
record company interested, before there's a record company interested . . . ?

PRAGER: There's no answer.

AHS: I didn't think so. I thought that's what you were going to say.

PRAGER: I know. I remember speaking to one of the star A&R guys in
England [David Bates] about some group that I had heard of. He
was arrogant, conceited, egotistical, and whatever. Perhaps he
earned it. He signed some big groups. I called him up about the
group . . . I can't think of the name right now and so far they've
achieved little or nothing. He said, "I'm working with the group.
I'm putting the music together. I'm putting the record together and
when we're finished with the record, then we'll interview managers." I said, "Well, you won't be interviewing me." These A&R
people, the guys and girls who are doing these A&R functions,
want to find the talent, control the talent, support the talent, and
become important. That's how they want to make their careers.
They don't want some managers—whether powerful like my

group, or some amateur—getting in the way of their dominance.
I'm serious.

AHS: I know you are.

PRAGER: The number-one A&R guy in America is John Kalodner. John is,
I consider, a protégé of mine. He tells me how much I taught him,
then when he does interviews he thanks chairmen of the boards.

AHS: What label is John with?

PRAGER: Well, he was with Atlantic when we worked on Foreigner together
and he's been with Geffen. He has signed some big acts. For Geffen
he signed Aerosmith and Whitesnake. I'm sure I'm omitting a
couple of others. He's number one. And I always tell him, he's a
pseudo-manager. He can complain about terrible managers and
how much he misses me and how people don't help him and
everything, but he wants it that way. He's got a terrible conflict.

AHS: The argument I would make on the other side is that their success
depends on their batting average. And their batting average is
going to be higher if the groups that they've chosen are managed
by people who know the business. That would increase their success ratio.

PRAGER: They want to do everything so that they can establish dominance
and control . . . then bring it to the Tony Smiths of the world. That
would be their fantasy. The artist is forever indebted to them, as
the person who made their career possible . . . and then you hand
it off to someone important who won't screw you.

AHS: Who won't drop the ball at that time.

PRAGER: Yeah, who will help you take it to a higher level and be professional. But if Tony Smith is going to suddenly assert control (I
don't mean him personally), and the A&R person is going to be
shunted aside, then the fantasy falls apart. So the artist has to go
to a friendly manager. Someone who will respect the territory of
the A&R person.

AHS: Do you ever invest your own money in acts?

PRAGER: Yes.

AHS: With reluctance or do you expect to do it?

PRAGER: To me, it's having the courage of my convictions. I did it with
Mountain, a lot of money. I did it with some other people at that
time. I did it with Foreigner, Tommy Shaw, who's in Damn Yankees. I do it as part of my work. I don't like it.

AHS: That's a surprising answer. Not an answer I get very often, I must
say.

PRAGER: No. There are very few managers that put their money where their
mouth is.

AHS: How long a term . . .

PRAGER: Oh, by the way, I figured out once that every signing, on average,
costs me $75,000 to $100,000.

AHS: You mean the lawyers' expenses and . . .

PRAGER: Travel, supporting the group, loans, advances, demos, and then expenses when they're starting because they don't make money, and just getting things to a point where they either make money or not make money. I'm in for $75,000 to $100,000 at that point.

AHS: That's interesting. How long do you like to sign a group for in years?

PRAGER: My usual contract is three years with a two-year option based on them achieving a certain degree of success.

AHS: Which is kind of illusory because if they don't achieve that success, you're not going to want to continue with them anyway after three years, right?

PRAGER: No, it depends.

AHS: So it's something that makes the lawyers feel happy, that they have something to show their client?

PRAGER: Well, you've just touched on another bane of the industry, which is lawyers in our business. We're in a tremendous time period of lawyer dominance. How about that, now that we've got through with artists screwing up the industry, A&R people screwing up the industry . . .

AHS: Let me get through . . .

PRAGER: . . . managers being incompetent and lawyers being predators.

AHS: Ooh. I take exception to that.

PRAGER: I want that edited out that you take exception to that.

AHS: There is one clause in every management contract that drives everybody crazy. I think what happens in these damn contracts is that something gets in and is perpetuated because people are afraid to take it out. This is that all too familiar clause where the manager is entitled to commission, for so long as an agreement negotiated during the term and any substitutions therefore exists, etc., etc., etc.

PRAGER: Yeah.

AHS: I can give you a hypothetical case which underscores the point. Suppose you're in your last year of a contract with an artist, and they then sign a five-year record contract. At the end of your term they decide that it took you four years to get them a record contract and you weren't the greatest manager in the world. Now that they have a record contract they want a real manager. This is the story we were talking about before. So they get a real manager. Now if the contract is taken literally, there is no money left to commission the new manager. You've got a double-commission situation because theoretically they have to pay you a commission, and the new manager, because he's going to be working with them, certainly wants to get a commission. Do you ever waver on that clause when it's being negotiated, compromise it?

PRAGER: Yes, absolutely.

AHS: How do you do that?

PRAGER: I'm more philosophical about all this now. The first manager should have a declining commission on future work, and the second one should come in and have less and go up. All these things are so minor.

AHS: I sit here in your office and we're surrounded by gold and platinum records and hundreds of cassettes. Whose cassettes are these? Where do they all come from and what's their purpose? They're not commercial cassettes, so they're obviously demos.

PRAGER: One of the downfalls of our industry—and this is said with a smile—is that in the sixties, for a new band to present their music they had to get a big—I forget what they're called—2 inch or ¾ inch tapes, and you had to have one of these big machines. You had to go over and thread the tape and it was difficult for them to make those tapes. So somehow there was a higher quality and a higher ethic, a higher integrity from the talent level. Today, any kid can get himself some kind of a machine and get a few guys and go in and make a tape for no money. So this place is inundated with tapes of people of no distinction, and this is nothing compared to record companies.

AHS: And do you listen to them to find out that they're of no distinction?

PRAGER: I try, but less and less.

AHS: Because your experience is such that they are of less distinction?

PRAGER: People don't sign bands from kids sending in tapes. If you went to all the record companies and you did a survey . . .

AHS: I did.

PRAGER: And it's probably down around one percent.

AHS: Not even.

PRAGER: I mean if you took the whole world, it would be under one percent. But there are some who get signed off tape.

AHS: Very, very rarely. I haven't found a record company . . . Clive Davis at Arista said he found a song *once* on an unsolicited tape.

PRAGER: So the kids making tapes and sending them to record companies and managers is a waste of time. What should they do? They should go through attorneys to get to managers, or attorneys to get to record companies.

AHS: That's because of the predators who are around. I didn't forget that, I'm going to get to that in a minute. I happen to be your predator.

PRAGER: By the way, I found out that attorneys—I didn't know this—they charge to send these tapes to record companies.

AHS: I do not.

PRAGER: Okay, but some of them do. They have a fee. They take the tape

and they sign some kind of an agreement. Then they mail it out
and they collect a fee from these kids. And that's okay, they're
earning it, they're spending time and effort.

AHS: I don't do that. I send a tape to you first, and have you tell me
whether I should waste my time on it.

PRAGER: So far, your batting average is very low.

AHS: That's true.

PRAGER: Every so often an attorney does send me a tape that I find interesting or worth considering or talking about. One good example . . .

AHS: We spent a lot of time talking about the group I sent you.

PRAGER: Yeah, they were close, but they couldn't get it right. And what they
had, by the way—and this is of value to a young band—the lead
singer looked good and he had a terrific personality. The guitar
player was talented, and I felt that he would become something
valuable musically. But they never got it and they were being
seduced by people around them telling them how good they were
and not to listen to me. And so you get into a contest, which is
always a test.

AHS: I should point out that was around four or five years ago, and we
haven't heard from them since.

PRAGER: No, they got themselves allied with someone who used to be very
successful in the music business and is now totally passé, and he
must have told them how great they are and what he was going to
do for them. I could tell you who it is . . .

AHS: We know who it is but we're not going to mention it.

PRAGER: . . . it's a myth, but it's illusory, because the person they're dealing
with has no credibility in the field that they wanted to be in. But
in my case, I tell these guys what's missing. I tell them what they
have to do. I point it out. I show it to them. I help them. If they can
get it, they become real talent.

AHS: What did you mean when you referred to attorneys in our industry
as being predators and dominating? Obviously it was a pejorative;
you weren't pleased with the situation.

PRAGER: Right.

AHS: Can you elaborate on this a little bit?

PRAGER: It's again a contest for who has control of the artist. A manager, I
think, will usually come out second to the attorney because the
manager is susceptible . . . I haven't had this happen to me. I've
avoided it by avoiding what I call the L.A. lawyer syndrome.
They're the power brokers.

AHS: So at least you let us East Coast guys off the hook.

PRAGER: Right. Historically, the L.A. syndrome is much different from the
East Coast. They were the ones who I believe originated percentages. Am I wrong? You're looking at me blankly . . .

AHS: I don't know. We don't charge percentages.

PRAGER: Well, they certainly do out there. I recently met with a new band that I liked, and I had a separate meeting with the attorney, who scrutinized me because he helped the band. He's the adviser to the band and he has a percentage of the band, so he doesn't want a manager whose percentage and influence could interfere with or upset the balance. You're dealing with another pseudo-manager. The meetings became academic because the band's music didn't develop enough to meet my standards. My ideal picture of the industry is where managers are managers and attorneys are attorneys. But because of the ineptitude of managers, they make it possible for or invite the attorney to play a more powerful role.

AHS: Are you really talking about a breed of attorneys or attorney/ managers? They're functioning in a dual role.

PRAGER: Attorney/power brokers. They want the power over the situation. This is all a battle for power among all of the different interests, and the artist in the early stages—you have to understand this, too—is standing there with his hands out. He's done a tape and he has his hands out, saying please help me. I'll do anything, I'll sign anything, but please help me. Now, you have an entirely different entity looking at you when his record is number 12 with a bullet. Suddenly *he's* the world, *he's* the universe, and you're the person who is lucky enough to be part of his orbit and you didn't really do that much and anything you did could have been done by anybody else. So all of the contributors are now fortunate to be a part of his trip. The attorneys are the ones who come in to get rid of all these people and to clean up everything and tell the guy how nothing was done right before and how wonderful it is that they're there to make everything right. Is there anything wrong with that? No.

AHS: Well, the way you present it, it sounds terribly cynical . . .

PRAGER: It is. It is the state of our industry. By the way, this is a commentary on these wonderful young people that you're talking about, who are sending out tapes, who are saying please help me, can you please get somebody to listen to my tape. The classic story of the music industry—and I tell this to the people I work with—is the movie *The Treasure of the Sierra Madre*. Are you familiar with the movie?

AHS: John Huston, Humphrey Bogart . . .

PRAGER: Yeah. But Walter Huston, I think.

AHS: Walter Huston, right. John's father.

PRAGER: Anyway, going up the mountain they're all for one, one for all, you help anybody, you give anything, you do it because it's the pursuit of mythical gold. But when they actually find real gold, those very few fortunate ones, then you find out the true character of the people that you're working with. In these little neophyte baby-band situations that you're talking about, there's no problem . . . the gold is still mythical. What should they do? They should try and find somebody who'll get their tape into the hands of a record company or a manager or an attorney—anything at all. Sending tapes through the mail to managers and record companies I think is a tremendous waste of time and effort.

AHS: Everything I've discovered in my interviews indicates you're absolutely right on that.

PRAGER: So what do you do? You try and go to a concert, meet somebody, become friends with somebody, use any connection you can to get it in the hands of somebody valid who will take the time to listen to it, and hope that there is something of consequence on the tape. What kind of a contract should they sign with a manager? If it's a neophyte group and a neophyte manager, you sign a piece of paper, year by year, mutual approvals, and you hope for the best on behalf of the manager and on behalf of the artist. Protecting one or the other? There's nothing to protect at that point, except it's disadvantageous to have a long-term overreaching contract if the manager isn't going to be a bona fide contributor to the trip. The artists—if they are talented and become successful, and are saddled with an inadequate manager—somehow find a way to get rid of him. Correct?

AHS: Always.

PRAGER: For better or worse, it will end.

AHS: All of these relationships are fragile.

PRAGER: Yes. Now, even if you have a really good manager who does a really good job for an artist and they become successful and the artist doesn't think the manager is up to the standards they require, they will get rid of him. There are plenty of situations I've known where guys felt that they did a good job, did a lot, and got thrown out. That's life, you can't help it. By the way, there's another factor, which is the corruption of the artist by the record company. This is part of the performer pattern of our industry, and I tell this to every artist that I work with . . . because when they come in, they think they're going to be different. They have values, they're going to be good people, they're going to be loyal people! They don't realize that when they sign with a record company, they're one of 80 or 100, 120 artists—they don't mean anything. But if the record starts to happen, the people at the record companies are the ones who most directly contribute to the corruption of whatever values that artist has. Are you aware of that?

AHS: I'm listening.

PRAGER: How does it work? You have a bunch of guys who come from, at best, middle-class backgrounds, but usually less, who suddenly are being catered to. Oh, can I get you a cup of coffee? Oh, you know, let's have champagne. Oh, we're going to take you, we're going to get you, we're going to do you. The people they're talking about are young guys who took up guitars at twelve years old, neglected their education, neglected a lot of their values, and are suddenly being treated like royalty. They are getting a distorted picture of not only the world, but of themselves. But that's wonderful. Who wouldn't want to be treated like royalty? Who wouldn't want to have people falling all over them? Interviews, what do you think of Iraq's attack on Kuwait? Or whatever. So they lose all their perspective, and the record company you can count on as the principal contributor because the guys at the record company who are surrounding the artist want to be able to say he's my friend. I hung out with him, we did this together or we did that together, and he's my friend.

AHS: Wouldn't that corruption be a normal outcome of the huge bucks that accrue to a successful artist? Wouldn't it be very difficult not to be corrupted if you're nineteen, twenty, twenty-one years old, and all of a sudden you're making a million dollars?

PRAGER: Can't be avoided. You hope that there are some real values. The corruption is part of the game. And it's okay, it's part of our business. It's really nice if someone has some values and background. It's better to have an artist who's becoming successful at twenty-seven or twenty-eight than twenty-one or twenty-two.

AHS: They've already been through it all.

PRAGER: Failure is a wonderful character-builder. Doug Fieger of The Knack—I didn't like The Knack, I didn't like what they stood for, I thought they were a horrendous happening in our industry when they *were* successful, and now they're trying to make a comeback. I don't know what will happen, but anyway I was asked to have lunch with Doug Fieger before I passed. I had lunch with the guy and it was a wonderful experience, because he went from nothing to stardom and screwed it up so badly—I tell you, it's a classic example of the seventies' debauchery. He told me that it's a miracle that he's still alive. I found that most of the people who survive that type of excess aren't really all there. They've lost something along the way. The brain can only take so much assault. This guy is totally together—he's been clean and he's in the programs, you know, whatever the programs are, and he's been in them for about ten years. He's a counselor, but he doesn't preach, he's not holier than thou. He's just a delight. He said, "If I can come back and achieve some success, do you realize how much appreciation I'll have now for the things I didn't even see then?"

AHS: Why did you pass?

PRAGER: I didn't.

AHS: I thought you said you passed.

PRAGER: No, I was going to until I met him. Now I'm rooting so hard for him.

AHS: Are you going with him?

PRAGER: Yeah.

AHS: Great, congratulations.

PRAGER: If my attorney ever gets the contracts together, I'll be his manager.

AHS: Didn't those contracts go out?

PRAGER: My attorneys are not exactly the speediest in the world. I'm giving them the benefit of the doubt, that it's just summer doldrums.

AHS: I think that's a good note to quit on.

INTERVIEW WITH JERRY WEINTRAUB

Jerry Weintraub is the founder of Management III and has managed such performers as John Denver, Bob Dylan, and Neil Diamond, among others.

AHS: The first question is one that seems to come up a great deal: What comes first, Jerry, the chicken or the egg, insofar as managers for unproven artists go? Usually they can't attract a good manager, because good managers aren't interested in people who haven't accomplished something.

WEINTRAUB: I don't think that that's necessarily true.

AHS: Do you think it's imperative that a young artist start off with management? And, if so, how does he go about attracting a good manager?

WEINTRAUB: I don't think it's imperative that a young artist start off with management at all. I think it's imperative that a young artist finds a . . . if he's a singer, finds his way to a record company . . . somehow, that believes in him. All the record companies are interested in new talent, and they do listen to music. The major companies have hundreds of employees, and they have people who are always listening to new tapes. I don't think it's imperative they have a manager. I think it's great for a young artist if he has a manager with a reputation who can help him, who could pick up a telephone and get him a record deal or at least have people listen to him and take notice of him early on in his career. How do they get a manager? You know, we're the biggest management company in the world and we have some new artists here, and they found their way here.

AHS: That's my next question.

WEINTRAUB: How? I don't know how.

AHS: How do they find their way to you? What attracted you to the new artists you represent?

WEINTRAUB: To be honest, initially they're attracted to me, personally. Very few new artists can attract my attention unless they attract somebody's attention in my company first. We have a couple of new artists that we're working on right now, and they attracted somebody's attention around here. And somebody attracted my attention. They said, "Come down and listen to this."

AHS: What are some of the key considerations that would turn you on to a new act?

WEINTRAUB: Me, personally?

AHS: From a business point of view.

WEINTRAUB: The only thing that turns me on to an act is how many seats they sell, how many records they sell. I'm a businessman, you know.

AHS: Is it important to you that an act also be a writer, for instance, a singer who writes his own material?

WEINTRAUB: No.

AHS: It doesn't matter to you?

WEINTRAUB: Not necessarily. I mean I have a history of working with those people. . . . Diamond and Dylan and Denver, you know. I work with such artists, but it isn't a necessity. [Jerry declined to address a series of questions relative to his fee structure, indicating that he considered the subject to be confidential.]

AHS: What is the minimum term of years for which you would get involved with an act?

WEINTRAUB: A new act? It takes years to get a new act launched. Over the years, I've noticed that two things accompany the success of an act. First, a certain fickleness develops, and there seems to be a diminished appreciation of what the manager accomplished in aiding the artist to attain his success. In addition, a lot of people who are not by profession managers feel that once an artist is established, they are then capable of handling his career from that point forward. Thus, a manager has to contend with a natural tendency on the part of the successful artist to experiment with change, and a growing pool of "experts" who are not reluctant to take advantage of that tendency. Thus far, because of my success and reputation, I have been the beneficiary of that tendency towards fickleness. Nevertheless, I would not enjoy having the fruits of my labors, in connection with an artist's career, enjoyed by another manager, or would-be manager, who comes upon the scene after the initial gamble

in time and effort has been taken by me. I think the only
protection that a manager has, in that situation, is his contract
with the artist, and I would therefore like that to be for as long
a period of time as possible . . . at least five years.

AHS: One last question because I can see you're very busy. Have you
contemplated the effect that the new technology and the audio/
visual exploitation are going to have on the industry, and how
it will affect new artists?

WEINTRAUB: New artists? It doesn't affect new artists initially. It will affect
them later on, depending on how their lawyers negotiate their
contract with the record company, television company, and so
on.

AHS: With the audio-visual thing being so important, will acts have
to have more than just good voices . . . and good songs to
attract a record deal?

WEINTRAUB: I don't think the record companies are too concerned yet. I
think they're still selling a lot of records, so if a guy can write
and sing songs . . . a deal can be made. I know that there are
a number of artists that I don't think will be worth anything in
the audio-visual field, but still sell a lot of records. Look, the
audio-visual field is the coming thing, there's no question about
it, and so is cable. I am very, very cognizant of this and I have
been for years, and I have been very, very careful in all my
contract negotiations with everybody, to protect those areas
for my artists. I can say that my artists are protected in those
areas. I don't think everybody has done that. I think a lot of
people are going to wake up one morning and find out that
they don't own and control a lot of stuff they thought they
owned and controlled. We have protected these things and I
think they're going to be the most valuable things that we
have.

AHS: Give me a little of your personal background. I think the readers would be interested in that.

WEINTRAUB: Ah, I don't know how I got into show business, you know,
I found my way into it somehow. I came from New York,
and you either became a doctor or a lawyer or a CPA or
went into the garment center or show business. I found my
way into show business. I started as a page boy at NBC,
went from there to the mailroom at William Morris, and
from there to MCA. From MCA I went into my own business. And the rest is pretty much history. I was in the right
place at the right time.

AHS: And had a great deal of talent.

WEINTRAUB: No. . . . I've been involved with a lot of artists with a great deal
of talent. . . . I have a talent for what I do, sure, but I've been

lucky with the artists I've represented . . . they have been great for me.

AHS: And they have been very lucky to have you.

WEINTRAUB: Well, I appreciate it.

AHS: And I thank you.

WEINTRAUB: Thank you, Alan.

The execution of a contract

six

YOU'VE GOT A FRIEND

Music and lyrics by Carole King
© 1971, Colgems-EMI Music, Inc.

Getting a little bored reading about you? Okay, let's talk about entertainment lawyers for a while.

Whether or not you greet the idea with enthusiasm, I must advise you that an essential part of your success kit will be the services of a *qualified entertainment lawyer*. Note that the italics are not an accident: no, a lawyer will not do; he really should be a *qualified entertainment lawyer*.

To become a lawyer today is very difficult. Once that goal is attained, however, it is easy to become an entertainment lawyer. All it requires is the declaration, "I'm an entertainment lawyer." It's kind of like the old joke: "Make me a malted," and the genie responds, "Okay, pfft, you're a malted!" Well, pfft, you're an entertainment lawyer. "Just like that?" you ask. Yes . . . and no. Puzzled?

A person aspiring to become a lawyer, not unlike the person aspiring to become a singer or a songwriter, must also pay dues. After graduating from college, he must succeed in being accepted into a law school. Once accepted into a law school, he will spend the next three years studying, among other things, contracts, torts, evidence, civil procedure, federal practice, international law, constitutional law, conflicts of laws, trusts and estates, commercial law, criminal law, taxes, labor law, corporate law, family law, comparative law . . . and squash. Notice anything missing?

Graduation day finally arrives. Does our hero emerge as a lawyer? No. To be a lawyer and practice law, he must first pass the bar exam of the state in which he hopes to practice. After three years of law school, shouldn't the bar exam be a snap? Perhaps it should be . . . but it ain't. The law school graduate has no idea of what the law is in his state. In law school he learned that with respect to each issue in each course he took, there were four points of view—"the best one" and three others—none of which was wrong. What will our would-be lawyer do? He does the same as every other law school graduate does. He enrolls in a cram course, where for six or eight weeks he attends classes for eight hours a day, absorbs fifty-five pounds of photo-offset material, and learns the real "best view"—the view he had better learn if he is to pass the bar exam.

So, he studies all the questions and answers of the last twenty-three state bar exams, and passes, and ultimately is granted his license to practice law.

Just think, a sovereign state has just licensed our friend to defend you on a murder-one rap, co-op your apartment house, merge your father's railroads, represent you in your divorce, and negotiate your record and songwriting contracts (if you beat the murder-one rap). While at law school he took a course in criminal law and a course in evidence, and the fifty-five pounds of material that came with the cram course contained three pounds of criminal law. You're right; you didn't see entertainment law listed in the law school curriculum, and there wasn't an ounce of it in the entire fifty-five pounds of cram material. Obviously, it makes more sense to hire our graduate for your murder problems than for your entertainment problems.

Why no training in entertainment law? Of the four hundred students entering a particular law school in any given year, only 2.3 of them are going to practice entertainment law. Forty-seven of the fifty states do not boast a New York City, Los Angeles, or Nashville; hence no body of law relative to entertainment ever evolved. Even in New York, California, and Tennessee, where the entertainment industry thrives, there are few laws directly pertaining to it, and relatively few lawyers practicing it.

Inspired by his part in his high-school production of *Guys and Dolls,* or by his experience as a member of a teenage rock band, or by his thirst for the glamour of "the business," our neophyte subscribes to *Billboard,* and pfft . . . you guessed it . . . declares himself to be an entertainment lawyer.

I don't know if it would be legal for a newly licensed physician to perform a triple bypass operation on you, but he would sure have a hell of a time finding a hospital in which to do it. All a self-proclaimed entertainment lawyer needs is a yellow pad! Sunglasses are optional equipment. If there are no special degrees for entertainment lawyers, no uniforms with insignia, no certificate to hang on a wall, how does an artist or songwriter distinguish an entertainment lawyer from all the other breeds?

An entertainment lawyer is a lawyer who, by design or accident, has evolved a practice consisting primarily of clients whose business interests are in the ambit of the entertainment industry. There are various subspecialties within this category—for example, motion pictures, television, music and records, and theater. They have, through mistakes made at the expense of your predecessors, garnered the experience necessary to guide you through the business and legal maze associated with your profession. In choosing one, it behooves you to make sure you're not a "predecessor."

Ah, but you're a cynic. "He's drumming up business. My family lawyer has been practicing for thirty years; he can handle any contract." Wrong! If he deserves your faith in him, he'll do one of two things: he'll find a good entertainment lawyer to act as his "colleague" on your matters, or he'll find a good entertainment lawyer and refer you to him. If your faith is misplaced, he'll represent you himself. He's licensed to do it. But regardless of what the bar examiners said thirty years ago, he's *not* qualified. It's a test of character. After all, if a local boy is going to be another Elvis, is it not human nature to want to board the glory train? If you read the papers, you will note that the "top" murderers, the real professionals, are always represented by well-known criminal lawyers. This is probably the only instance where using the "family" attorney is appropriate. Your life is on the line, too, at least your professional life. If someone accused of murder were to hire an entertainment lawyer to represent him, he would deserve the chair, and would probably be so rewarded. If you intend to be a professional in the entertainment industry, treat yourself no less kindly than a murderer does.

The Anglo-American system of jurisprudence is known as the "adversary system." Every attorney practicing under it is trained and obligated to act as an advocate of his client's cause—a hired gun, if you will. It is not his function to be "fair" or "impartial"; it is his obligation to do as well for his client as is possible within the bounds of professional ethics. Your "adversaries," the record companies and music publishers, retain some of the best entertainment lawyers in the business. It is incumbent upon you to do no less.

When is the appropriate time to engage an entertainment attorney? The facile answer is, "Before it's too late." Actually, that answer is not very helpful, for two reasons: first, the uninitiated don't really know when "too late" is approaching, and, second, it varies from situation to situation.

If you are a songwriter but not an artist, you can in most instances wait until there is some "action"—until some publisher indicates a desire to contract with you with respect to your exclusive services as a songwriter or with respect to one or more of your songs. At that point it is incumbent upon you to demonstrate enthusiasm without committing yourself to any specifics. The easiest way is to be honest: "Sounds great, but I just stick to the music part; my lawyer handles the business end." Then, find "my lawyer" damn quick.

As an artist or singer-songwriter, you may profit more from an early association with an attorney than would the "naked" songwriter. There is more diffusion in the songwriter's career—he will enjoy relationships with and have his songs published by many publishers. The songwriter's dealings with publishers reflect more of a nurturing or evolutionary process. Exclusivity is not endemic to the songwriter-publisher relationship. It *is* to the artist-record company relationship. A writer can place a song with one publisher in the morning and another with that publisher's competitor in the afternoon. The artist-record company relationship is more of a "big bang" relationship. The monetary and career stakes are high. The record company has a large investment at risk, and the artist has failure at risk. The industry knows only of a writer's successes. Have a flop record as an artist, and the whole world knows and remembers it. The record industry is more frenetic, and access to it is more elusive.

One way to acquire access to the record companies is through an attorney who has some clout. While a songwriter can make the rounds, a neophyte artist finds it much more difficult to be heard. An entertainment lawyer usually can get you heard. So, as an artist or singer-songwriter, it is wise to seek a relationship with an entertainment lawyer when you have a demo you consider representative of your talent and upon which you are willing to stake your career.

When you make a major investment or purchase, it is usually after much rumination, soul-searching, comparison, and shopping. The search for the attorney who will guide you through the most important decisions of your professional life should be made with no less care than you would exercise in purchasing an amp. The process is really not mysterious; in fact, it's quite simple. As you make your way through the industry, you will meet other artists and writers as well as producers, publishers, managers, and the myriad people associated with them. When you deem the time is right to seek the services of an attorney, ask the people you've met whom they use, whom they recommend, whom they have heard about. Amass a list of several who seem promising and call them. Explain who you are and that you would like to meet with them to discuss possible representation. Entertainment attorneys come in all sizes, shapes, and forms. Some look like bankers and some look like freaks. In Los Angeles, entertainment lawyers are not permitted to purchase or wear neckties. In New York, ties are permitted but not mandatory. You will visit posh offices with general practices spanning all specialties, of which entertainment will be only one. You will visit smaller offices housing only a few attorneys whose practice is devoted entirely to entertainment law. Each has advantages and disadvantages, and the trappings are not dispositive of the issue. You can find warmth, understanding, and compassion on Park Avenue, and, conversely, an elegance of manner and style at less pricey addresses.

There are only two elements upon which your choice should be based: competence and compatibility. The only way you will be able to secure a handle on these qualities is by meeting and talking with several prospective counselors, and asking a lot of questions—tough questions. The dynamics of a first meeting between a prospective attorney and a prospective client are interesting. You should realize that while you are appraising him, he is also trying to determine whether or not you are a good gamble upon which he should bet his time. If you have nothing going for you *yet*, no record company offers, no songs on the charts, in short, no track record, the established entertainment attorney has to assess the likelihood of your developing into a profitable, fee-producing client. Once your success is secured, you can be sure of being treated in princely fashion. The trick is to find the entertainment attorney who will treat you that way before your coronation.

Lawyer stories circulate among artists and writers much the same way as client stories circulate among members of the entertainment bar. The concerns shown in these stories are evident in the following questions asked by your brethren, all of which found their genesis in the experiences (mostly bad) of others, and deserve to be asked—and answered:

"Will you take my telephone calls, and will you get back to me promptly if you can't?"

This is one of the greatest sources of frustration and dissatisfaction among artists and writers who are not yet established. Stars always have their calls responded to rapidly—for obvious reasons. This question, even if not answered honestly at the time it is asked, may have a salutory effect when you call in the future.

"Will you [assuming you are talking to a prominent attorney with a large supporting cast] actually work on my matters or will they be delegated to someone else?"

An honest answer should be, "Yes and yes." Where his prestige and experience are needed, he should be personally involved. For example, he should "talk" your deal with a record company. But for him to fill out your copyright registration certificates would be a waste of his time and your money and that chore should be delegated to a less senior attorney with a less senior billing rate.

"Who are some of your clients?"

A good question if you are trying to establish whether you have truly found a bona fide entertainment lawyer. Ethical considerations aside, he will probably supply you with a litany of names that will knock your socks off. Don't ask for their phone numbers—he won't give them to you. In most instances he'll probably drop enough names and war stories so that you won't have to ask the question. What the hell, lawyers are human, too.

"How much will you charge me? I don't have much money, you know."

You won't surprise him with this question. He has been evaluating the economics of representing you all the time you have been sitting in his office. Everybody seems to feel uncomfortable when it comes to discussing fees, especially young lawyers and inexperienced clients. The young lawyer's discomfort stems from an innate insecurity over his worth (often well founded) and a fear of scaring off a real, live client. The inexperienced client's discomfort stems from a fear that he won't be able to pay the bill (also often well founded). An old wardog of a lawyer and an experienced businessman have no such problems; they deal with it openly, like any other business factor, and both fare better for it.

To leave the question of fees undiscussed, especially with an inexperienced client, can only lead to bitterness and unhappiness. Lawyer's fees have, of necessity, kept pace with the soaring inflation and concomitant increases in overhead. An unprepared client is apt to need mouth-to-mouth resuscitation and heart massage when he opens his first bill. His lawyer should feel chagrined and sheepish if the client's faltering words "I . . . I . . . I had no idea . . ." are spoken with justification. If your lawyer does not raise the issue of fees, you should. It will be the only time till you attain stardom that you will have him on the defensive—and it may convince him that you intend to pay your bills.

There are many ways to skin a cat, but only three basic fee structures utilized by entertainment attorneys. There are, however, an almost infinite number of variations and combinations of the three. In looking at them, let's keep your present stature and status (or relative absence thereof) in mind.

The annual retainer is a neat and most satisfactory fee arrangement, and one that you should be cognizant of for the future, though not one that you should consider at this stage of your career. It entails a fixed annual fee, usually divided into twelve equal monthly payments. After it is agreed upon, the client is presumably entitled to call upon the services of the attorney in more or less unlimited fashion without the payment of additional sums, with certain exceptions. For an annual retainer to work, it must be fair to both sides. To arrive at a fair annual retainer, there has to be a history between the attorney and the client, and a degree of stability in the client's career. As in most areas of commerce, the annual retainer involves a trade-off. The attorney receives the security of knowing that he has a fixed source of income that he can rely upon for the duration of the retainer term. In exchange for his obligation to make the fixed payments, the client should receive a financial reward; thus the annual retainer should be significantly (but not excessively) less than his straight-time charges would have been. Hence the need for a history, or track record, in the relationship before a fair and mutually satisfactory annual retainer can be arrived at. If things get out of balance, one party or the other will feel ripped off, and the relationship will break down. Annual retainers only work when there is mutual trust and respect and an understanding that the retainer is subject to review and reevaluation by both parties at regular intervals. Most new attorney-client relationships involve fervid activity by the attorney in the initial stages, when he must review and sort out existing contracts and relationships, unscrew things previously screwed up, and, in general, get the client's house in order. This period is usually followed by a period of general calm. You can't have it both ways—have the benefit of the retainer while the attorney is battling a hurricane of paper and then switch to time charges when the storm has passed and your legal affairs are drifting through the horse latitudes. You would be surprised at how often this is suggested, with insouciance, by clients.

There are three items that are never included in a retainer and for which you will be billed separately and additionally. They are litigation, services rendered at your behest in a distant geographic location ("travel"), and disbursements. These should be mentioned and discussed. If your attorney fails to mention these, it is not because he is laying a snare for you. He just presumes (incorrectly) that you couldn't possibly think otherwise. Although I do not subscribe to the practice of reducing retainer agreements to writing, other attorneys may do so. There is no right or wrong on this point. I have just never found it necessary; nor do I feel the practice compatible with the kind of relationship I hope to nurture with a client.

The most usual fee arrangement, and the one that in all likelihood will be suggested to you, is that of paying for services on a time basis. Under this arrangement you pay your attorney (as you would a plumber) for the time he spends on your matters. All attorneys do, or at least should, keep precise records of their time. It is their inventory control. It is their only way of knowing the economic viability of their various client relationships. Therefore, time is kept even in a retainer relationship, and it is the tool used by the attorney in reevaluating a retainer from time to time. You can be sure that whenever you leave your attorney's office, the first thing he does is make a notation in his diary of the time spent with you. He also does this when he finishes a phone conversation with you. It matters little to him whether his time is expended in meetings or over the phone. You might also find it useful to know that there are usually minimum time units. There are no three-minute diary entries. Minimum units vary from "tenths" to "quarters of hours." So, if you wish to minimize your legal bills, call only with respect to matters of substance, and call (except in emergencies) when you have collected enough queries to make the most economical use of a minimum unit.

Hourly rates vary from location to location, from law firm to law firm, and, within a particular firm, from lawyer to lawyer, depending on seniority. You will enjoy the dubious distinction of paying fees that are well into the high end of the spectrum. The industry the entertainment bar serves requires that its practitioners maintain offices in the highest-rent districts of the most expensive cities in the country. The nature of the clientele requires surroundings and trappings consonant with its attainments, status, and, alas, sometimes only dreams. And this elitist bar faces competition for the best and brightest of the current law school graduates, who are now being offered about $85,000 per annum to start by the Wall Street firms. You're going to pay for a lot of overhead. But take comfort in the fact that your legal fees are tax deductible. The trick is to earn the income from which to deduct them.

Hourly rates vary from about $75 per hour for the new associate to about $300 per hour for the firm's senior partner. Invariably your time charges are a blend of various rates. No new associate is permitted to work without supervision and review of his work by a more senior lawyer. The disparity in hourly billing rates has been rationalized by the observation that the more experienced lawyer works faster and hence it all evens out. To some extent this is true, but in fact, when you are dealing with the more stratospheric hourly rates, there is no doubt that there is a prestige or clout factor built in. It would be absurd to use a $300-an-hour senior partner to plug names and titles into a form songwriter agreement, and few clients would countenance it. The clout factor has real economic significance in those instances where, because of it, a record company's first draft incorporates what its lawyers know will be demanded by an experienced attorney with whom they have previously dealt. If five or six billable hours of negotiation can thus be avoided, the economic benefits accruing from the judicious use of a more senior attorney can easily be realized. Often an experienced attorney can predicate a new deal upon a contract he negotiated with that same company for another client. Thus the weeks that were spent forging the original deal, which were paid for by another client, are reduced to a few brief meetings. A not inconsiderable savings to you! Besides, when you become a star, you will expect your price to rise. So does the entertainment attorney.

There are two more factors that should be discussed between you and your lawyer, whether you are on a retainer or time basis. Both will be reflected in your bills and should be talked about either in your initial meeting or when they are likely to occur. Woe to the lawyer who doesn't at least mention them.

An entertainment lawyer is likely to do a certain amount of agenting or hustling of tapes in an effort to obtain a record or publishing deal for his clients. He does this, and indeed is sought after to do this, because over many years he has acquired access to the industry's deal makers. It is unrealistic to think that he will charge you only for the tenth or quarter of an hour it took him to make the contact that resulted in the deal. He fully expects, and is entitled to, a reward consonant with his accomplishment. It is incumbent upon him, however, to warn you of this up front.

Occasionally an event arises in an artist's career that is so important and time-consuming for his attorney that an extraordinary fee arrangement is dictated by circumstances. Once again this is justified and perfectly accept-able if discussed openly and thoroughly before the work is undertaken. To present an unsuspecting client with a whopping bill without first setting a proper predicate is uncomfortable for both the attorney and the client. Even if the bill is paid without a hassle, the relationship invariably suffers.

Another form of fee structure that is sometimes (though not often) agreed upon between lawyers and novice artists is a percentage of the artist's gross income. In theory, it seems fine. While the artist is earning little, he is not saddled with disproportionately large legal fees. On the other hand, if the artist makes it, the attorney is rewarded for his faith, loyalty, and willingness to gamble on the artist's talent. Fair, you say? In theory, perhaps. But human nature, unfortunately, has a way of interfering. On the one occasion when my firm tried this, all went well up to a point. That point was reached when the artist, after several years of being carried by the firm, finally made it. His success was sudden and big. As the artist's accountant related the story, when he presented a six-figure check to our order for the artist's signature, it was promptly torn up with the observation that "No [expletive deleted] lawyer deserves that much!" You might want to try this fee structure if you can find someone with a great deal of faith in your talent and honor.

There is a good possibility that, regardless of the fee structure arrived at, your attorney will ask you for a "retainer in advance." This is a payment in an-ticipation of the services to be rendered, and it will be applied against your bill. It is not a negative reflection on you or on him. It is merely a reflection of his experience and the number of times he has gotten burned in the past. There is an uncanny correlation between unfulfilled dreams and unpaid bills. If a deal doesn't reach completion, regardless of how hard the attorney has worked, and notwithstanding the prodigious hours he has poured into it, he knows the like-lihood of receiving compensation for his time is relatively small. Groups are par-ticularly prone to such conduct. The members seem to draw upon and reinforce each other's baser instincts. So, if you're serious, bite the bullet; it hurts for only a minute. Besides, the modest advance will probably buy thousands in credit.

Every successful entertainment attorney works at 150 percent of capacity. No matter how clean the top of his desk may be, in it, or near it, is a pile of work that is overdue for completion. Each pile has a top and a bottom. The guar-anteed method of having your work occupy the bottom is not to pay your bill. Even if you can't pay it all at once, part payments are welcome and will assure a continuing interest in your matters. Ignoring bills courts disaster on another level. Eventually, you will become too embarrassed to call for advice or for an appointment. You will either seek another attorney, in which case you will pay again for his education with respect to your matters, or act without the aid of an attorney, in which case you will pay dearly to have your self-inflicted disasters rectified. Attorneys, contrary to popular belief, are human, and will respond to a demonstration of a sincere effort to honor an obligation.

Using your attorney to say "no" for you or otherwise take care of unpleasantness is not an act of cowardice. It is an invaluable use of his time. No attorney worth his salt will shrink from the role of heavy. One of the most useful functions attorneys can serve is as an insulator between their respective clients. While they are "leveling," their clients can be having a pleasant lunch and their future creative endeavors can proceed unmarred by all the exchanges that begin with "Frankly . . ."

Some artists and songwriters fear that the introduction of an attorney into their relationship with a record company or music publisher will poison the relationship, demonstrate a lack of trust, or otherwise jeopardize their chances of closing a deal. Quite to the contrary, most legitimate record companies and music publishers welcome the introduction of an experienced entertainment attorney into a negotiation. (Of course, they may welcome some more than others.) Their reasons have nothing to do with altruism. They have all had contracts challenged, after an artist or writer has attained success, on the grounds that the artist or writer was not represented by counsel at the time the contract was signed and that the contract was "unconscionable" and lacked "mutuality." Translated, this means that the contract was so one-sided or unfair that the artist or writer couldn't have understood it, and hence the court should not enforce it. The presence of an experienced entertainment attorney on the artist's or writer's behalf effectively nullifies such a challenge. In addition, the presence of an entertainment lawyer expedites the conclusion of the negotiation in that endless hours are not wasted discussing points that the nature of the business dictates can't be changed. The entertainment attorney has a perception of which points these are. As a result, a reservoir of acrimony is avoided that might otherwise carry forward into the relationship.

Sometimes instinct or some factor other than logic determines the pairing of entertainment lawyers and their clients. As a young lawyer, I was very flattered to be chosen by a prestigious client of our firm to accompany him and his staff to an industry convention in the south of France. The purpose of the trip was to negotiate foreign publishing and record deals with substantial advances. I had heard that the client had a strong belief in astrology. During a lull in our rounds of meetings, I casually asked him whether he really believed in "that stuff." His reply was simple. "You're here, aren't you?" He had had his astrologer work up charts on all of the attorneys in the office. He chose the best chart to accompany him. Well, who is to say? We came home with a lot of money!

Sooner or later, you're going to need a good entertainment lawyer, and sooner is probably better.

Home taping—when it's YOUR royalty!

seven

I'VE HEARD THAT SONG
BEFORE

Music and lyrics by Sammy Cahn and Jule Styne © 1942 by
Cahn Music Company and Morley Music Company

With perhaps the exception of sex, few subjects hold more mystery or engender more unfounded anxiety for the uninitiated than the subject of copyright. Both abound in misconceptions (no pun intended), misinformation, and misapprehensions.

I was shocked to learn recently of a group that declined a wonderful opportunity to do a showcase performance simply because they had not yet registered their songs for copyright. What foolishness! What motivated them to act this way? I wondered. Was it fear that they would lose the copyrights in their songs? Was it fear that their songs could be ripped off with impunity if they were not registered?

In any case, read the following, accept it blindly, casting all old misconceptions and superstitions aside, heave a sigh of relief, and relax.

You *automatically* acquire a copyright in your song the *instant* you create it.

In general, copyright registration does not provide you with copyright protection. You acquired that when you created your song. Copyright registration merely bestows upon copyright owners certain advantages in the enforcement of the rights they already possess. Although copyright registration is desirable and to be encouraged, it is not invested with the urgency you may have previously attributed to it.

You may perform your songs to your heart's content, even on network television, without fear of losing your copyrights—whether or not they are registered.

Similarly, you may record your songs, without registering them, without fear of losing your copyrights.

On March 1, 1989, the United States finally joined the Berne Convention. As a result, a copyright notice need not be affixed to works first published after that date. The inclusion of a copyright notice on such works, though desirable, is strictly optional. With respect to works first published prior to that date the requirement of notice persists, but even then the Copyright Act permits you to correct an omission or mistake should you have failed to provide a copyright notice or perhaps used an erroneous one. As a practical matter, in most instances "publication" will not take place until there is a commercially released recording of your song. There is little chance of printed "published" copies until after a successful record, because no print market will exist. You can also be fairly well assured that neither a record company nor a music publisher will permit "publication" of your songs without an appropriate copyright notice.

The general subject of copyright basics has been so well handled by the United States Copyright Office in its Circular r1 that, rather than rewrite it, as learned as that may have me appear, I have asked the publisher to reprint it in its entirety in this chapter—thereby saving you a stamp. Read it. It will clarify many things that may have puzzled you up until now. It may also convince some of you skeptics that what I wrote above is true. You may think I have dealt cavalierly with copyright, and in fact I may have, but I did so because I have perceived an untoward preoccupation with the subject by inexperienced artists and songwriters. An acceptance and comprehension of what is contained in this chapter and in Circular r1 is all you really need in your arsenal at this stage of your career. Later on you will have "experts" to handle such mundane matters for you.

Your concern should not be about copyright, but, rather, about creating copyrights worth worrying about.

Considering the number of copyrighted songs that are recorded and broadcast each year, the number of infringement claims of any substance at all is infinitesimally small. Of that small number, I would venture that most of them involve unconscious or unintentional copying. Most arise because a writer's subconscious has captured a musical phrase, stored it, and reprocessed it as its own. Considering that both you and Beethoven had only twelve notes to play with, it is truly amazing that infringement isn't rife. But it isn't. Oh, well, Shakespeare and I fooled around with the same twenty-six letters, and we haven't run afoul of each other either.

There are two Ripleyesque facets of copyright I want to pass on to you before moving on. Believe it or not, if two writers independently create the same song, they can enjoy independent and separate copyrights in that song. And, believe it or not, it doesn't matter who wrote the song first. Unlike patents, where the first to register wins all, there is no seniority or priority accorded the first to create a copyright. No infringement can take place without a copying.

If you read Circular r1, you will perceive that before you can bring an infringement action you will have to register your copyright. You will also realize that certain other advantages (such as establishing prima facie validity of your copyright) will follow early, rather than later, registration.

Should you fret about the possibility of someone stealing your song? Hardly. Most writers share your belief that the songs that *they write* are the best; therefore, why steal an inferior song? Besides, if an infringer makes your song a hit, it's a way of breaking in!

Incidentally, the Copyright Act provides that copyright protection is not available for any work of the United States Government, so here, for your pleasure and enlightenment, is Circular r1.

Copyright Basics

WHAT COPYRIGHT IS

Copyright is a form of protection provided by the laws of the United States (title 17, U.S. Code) to the authors of "original works of authorship" including literary, dramatic, musical, artistic, and certain other intellectual works. This protection is available to both published and unpublished works. Section 106 of the Copyright Act generally gives the owner of copyright the exclusive right to do and to authorize others to do the following:

- *To reproduce* the copyrighted work in copies or phonorecords;
- To prepare *derivative works* based upon the copyright work;
- *To distribute copies or phonorecords* of the copyrighted work to the public by sale or other transfer of ownership, or by rental, lease, or lending;
- *To perform the copyrighted work publicly,* in the case of literary, musical, dramatic, and choreographic works, pantomimes, and motion pictures and other audiovisual works; and
- *To display the copyrighted work publicly,* in the case of literary, musical, dramatic, and choreographic works, pantomimes, and pictorial, graphic, or sculptural works, including the individual images of a motion picture or other audiovisual work.

It is illegal for anyone to violate any of the rights provided by the Act to the owner of copyright. These rights, however, are not unlimited in scope. Sections 107 through 118 of the Copyright Act establish limitations on these rights. In some cases, these limitations are specified exemptions from copyright liability. One major limitation is the doctrine of "fair use," which is given a statutory basis by section 107 of the Act. In other instances, the limitation takes the form of a "compulsory license" under which certain limited uses of copyrighted works are permitted upon payment of specified royalties and compliance with statutory conditions. For further information about the limitations of any of these rights, consult the Copyright Act or write to the Copyright Office.

WHO CAN CLAIM COPYRIGHT

Copyright protection subsists from the time the work is created in fixed form; that is, it is an incident of the process of authorship. The copyright in the work of authorship *immediately* becomes the property of the author who created it. Only the author or those deriving their rights through the author can rightfully claim copyright.

In the case of works made for hire, the employer and not the employee is presumptively considered the author. Section 101 of the copyright statute defines a "work made for hire" as:

(1) a work prepared by an employee within the scope of his or her employment; or

(2) a work specially ordered or commissioned for use as a contribution to a collective work, as a part of a motion picture or other audiovisual work, as a translation, as a supplementary work, as a compilation, as an instructional text, as a test, as answer material for a test, or as an atlas, if the parties expressly agree in a written instrument signed by them that the

work shall be considered a work made for hire. . . .

The authors of a joint work are co-owners of the copyright in the work, unless there is an agreement to the contrary.

Copyright in each separate contribution to a periodical or other collective work is distinct from copyright in the collective work as a whole and vests initially with the author of the contribution.

Two General Principles

- Mere ownership of a book, manuscript, painting, or any other copy or phonorecord does not give the possessor the copyright. The law provides that transfer of ownership of any material object that embodies a protected work does not of itself convey any rights in the copyright.
- Minors may claim copyright, but state laws may regulate the business dealings involving copyrights owned by minors. For information on relevant state laws, consult an attorney.

COPYRIGHT AND NATIONAL ORIGIN OF THE WORK

Copyright protection is available for all unpublished works, regardless of the nationality or domicile of the author.

Published works are eligible for copyright protection in the United States if *any* one of the following conditions is met:

- On the date of first publication, one or more of the authors is a national or domiciliary of the United States or is a national, domiciliary, or sovereign authority of a foreign nation that is a party to a copyright treaty to which the United States is also a party, or is a stateless person wherever that person may be domiciled; or
- The work is first published in the United States or in a foreign nation that, on the date of first publication, is a party to the Universal Copyright Convention; or the work comes within the scope of a Presidential proclamation; or
- The work is first published on or after March 1, 1989, in a foreign nation that on the date of first publication, is a party to the Berne Convention; or, if the work is *not* first published in a country party to the Berne Convention, it is published (on or after March 1, 1989) within 30 days of first publication in a country that is party to the Berne Convention; or the work, first published on or after March 1, 1989, is a pictorial, graphic, or sculptural work that is incorporated in a permanent structure located in the United States; or, if the work, first published on or after March 1, 1989, is a published audiovisual work, all the authors are legal entities with headquarters in the United States.

WHAT WORKS ARE PROTECTED

Copyright protects "original works of authorship" that are fixed in a tangible form of expression. The fixation need not be directly perceptible, so long as it may be communicated with the aid of a machine or device. Copyrightable works include the following categories:

(1) literary works;
(2) musical works, including any accompanying words;
(3) dramatic works, including any accompanying music;
(4) pantomimes and choreographic works;

(5) pictorial, graphic, and sculptural works;
(6) motion pictures and other audio-visual works; and
(7) sound recordings.

These categories should be viewed quite broadly: for example, computer programs and most "compilations" are registrable as "literary works"; maps and architectural plans are registrable as "pictorial, graphic, and sculptural works."

WHAT IS NOT PROTECTED BY COPYRIGHT

Several categories of material are generally not eligible for statutory copyright protection. These include among others:

- Works that have **not** been fixed in a tangible form of expression. For example: choreographic works that have not been notated or recorded, or improvisational speeches or performances that have not been written or recorded.
- Titles, names, short phrases, and slogans; familiar symbols or designs; mere variations of typographic ornamentation, lettering, or coloring; mere listings of ingredients or contents.
- Ideas, procedures, methods, systems, processes, concepts, principles, discoveries, or devices, as distinguished from a description, explanation, or illustration.
- Works consisting **entirely** of information that is common property and containing no original authorship. For example: standard calendars, height and weight charts, tape measures and rulers, and lists or tables taken from public documents or other common sources.

HOW TO SECURE A COPYRIGHT

Copyright Secured Automatically Upon Creation

The way in which copyright protection is secured under the present law is frequently misunderstood. No publication or registration or other action in the Copyright Office is required to secure copyright (see following NOTE). There are, however, certain definite advantages to registration. (See page 238.)

Copyright is secured **automatically** when the work is created, and a work is "created" when it is fixed in a copy or phonorecord for the first time. "Copies" are material objects from which a work can be read or visually perceived either directly or with the aid of a machine or device, such as books, manuscripts, sheet music, film, videotape, or microfilm. "Phonorecords" are material objects embodying fixations of sounds (excluding, by statutory definition, motion picture soundtracks), such as audio tapes and phonograph disks. Thus, for example, a song (the "work") can be fixed in sheet music ("copies") or in phonograph disks ("phonorecords"), or both.

If a work is prepared over a period of time, the part of the work that is fixed on a particular date constitutes the created work as of that date.

PUBLICATION

Publication is no longer the key to obtaining statutory copyright as it was under the Copyright Act of 1909. However, publication remains important to copyright owners.

The Copyright Act defines publication as follows:

"Publication" is the distribution of copies or phonorecords of a work to the public by sale or other transfer of ownership, or by rental, lease, or lending. The offering to distribute copies or phonorecords to a group of persons for purposes of further distribution, public performance, or public display, constitutes publication. A public performance or display of a work does not of itself constitute publication.

> **NOTE:** Before 1978, statutory copyright was generally secured by the act of publication with notice of copyright, assuming compliance with all other relevant statutory conditions. Works in the public domain on January 1, 1978 (for example, works published without satisfying all conditions for securing statutory copyright under the Copyright Act of 1909) remain in the public domain under the current Act.
>
> Statutory copyright could also be secured before 1978 by the act of registration in the case of certain unpublished works and works eligible for ad interim copyright. The current Act automatically extends to full term (section 304 sets the term) copyright for all works in which ad interim copyright was subsisting or was capable of being secured on December 31, 1977.

A further discussion of the definition of "publication" can be found in the legislative history of the Act. The legislative reports define "to the public" as distribution to persons under no explicit or implicit restrictions with respect to disclosure of the contents. The reports state that the definition makes it clear that the sale of phonorecords constitutes publication of the underlying work, for example, the musical, dramatic, or literary work embodied in a phonorecord. The reports also state that it is clear that any form of dissemination in which the material object does not change hands, for example, performances or displays on television, is *not* a publication no matter how many people are exposed to the work. However, when copies or phonorecords are offered for sale or lease to a group of wholesalers, broadcasters, or motion picture theaters, publication does take place if the purpose is further distribution, public performance, or public display.

Publication is an important concept in the copyright law for several reasons:

- When a work is published, it may bear a notice of copyright to identify the year of publication and the name of the copyright owner and to inform the public that the work is protected by copyright. Works published before March 1, 1989, *must* bear the notice or risk loss of copyright protection. (See discussion "notice of copyright" below.)
- Works that are published in the United States are subject to mandatory deposit with the Library of Congress. (See discussion on page 241 on "mandatory deposit.")
- Publication of a work can affect the limitations on the exclusive rights of the copyright owner that are set forth in sections 107 through 118 of the law.
- The year of publication may determine the duration of copyright protection for anonymous and pseudonymous works (when the author's identity is not revealed in the records of the Copyright Office) and for works made for hire.
- Deposit requirements for registration of published works differ from those for registration of unpublished works. (See discussion on page 238 of "copyright registration" procedures.)

NOTICE OF COPYRIGHT

For works first published on and after March 1, 1989, use of the copyright notice is optional, though highly recommended. Before March 1, 1989, the use of the notice was mandatory on all published works, and any work first published before that date must bear a notice or risk loss of copyright protection. (The Copyright Office does not take a position on whether works first published with notice before March 1, 1989, and reprinted and distributed on and after March 1, 1989, must bear the copyright notice.)

Use of the notice is recommended because it informs the public that the work is protected by copyright, identifies the copyright owner, and shows the year of first publication. Furthermore, in the event that a work is infringed, if the work carries a proper notice, the court will not allow a defendant to claim "innocent infringement"—that is, that he or she did not realize that the work is protected. (A successful innocent infringement claim may result in a reduction in damages that the copyright owner would otherwise receive.)

The use of the copyright notice is the responsibility of the copyright owner and does not require advance permission from, or registration with, the Copyright Office.

Form of Notice for Visually Perceptible Copies

The notice for visually perceptible copies should contain all of the the following three elements:

1. *The symbol* © (the letter C in a circle), or the word "Copyright," or the abbreviation "Copr."; and
2. *The year of first publication* of the work. In the case of compilations or derivative works incorporating previously published material, the year date of first publication of the compilation or derivative work is sufficient. The year date may be omitted where a pictorial, graphic, or sculptural work, with accompanying textual matter, if any, is reproduced in or on greeting cards, postcards, stationery, jewelry, dolls, toys, or any useful article; and
3. *The name of the owner of copyright* in the work, or an abbreviation by which the name can be recognized, or a generally known alternative designation of the owner.

Example: © 1989 John Doe

The "C in a circle" notice is used only on "visually perceptible copies." Certain kinds of works—for example, musical, dramatic, and literary works—may be fixed not in "copies" but by means of sound in an audio recording. Since audio recordings such as audio tapes and phonograph disks are "phonorecords" and not "copies," the "C in a circle" notice is not used to indicate protection of the underlying musical, dramatic, or literary work that is recorded.

Form of Notice for Phonorecords of Sound Recordings

The copyright notice for phonorecords of sound recordings* has somewhat different requirements. The notice appearing on phonorecords should contain the following three elements:

*Sound recordings are defined as "works that result from the fixation of a series of musical, spoken, or other sounds, but not including the sounds accompanying a motion picture or other audiovisual work, regardless of the nature of the material objects, such as disks, tapes, or other phonorecords, in which they are embodied.

1. *The symbol* ℗ (the letter P in a circle); and
2. *The year of first publication* of the sound recording; and
3. *The name of the owner of copyright* in the sound recording, or an abbreviation by which the name can be recognized, or a generally known alternative designation of the owner. If the producer of the sound recording is named on the phonorecord labels or containers, and if no other name appears in conjunction with the notice, the producer's name shall be considered a part of the notice.

Example: ℗ 1989 A.B.C., Inc.

> **NOTE:** Because of some questions that could result from the use of variant forms of the notice, any form of the notice other than these given here should not be used without first seeking legal advice.

Position of Notice

The notice should be affixed to copies or phonorecords of the work in such a manner and location as to "give reasonable notice of the claim of copyright." The notice on phonorecords may appear on the surface of the phonorecord or on the phonorecord label or container, provided the manner of placement and location give reasonable notice of the claim. The three elements of the notice should ordinarily appear together on the copies or phonorecords. The Copyright Office has issued regulations concerning the form and position of the copyright notice in the *Code of Federal Regulations* (37 CFR Part 201). For more information, request Circular 3.

Publications Incorporating United States Government Works

Works by the U.S. Government are not eligible for copyright protection. For works published on and after March 1, 1989, the previous notice requirement for works consisting primarily of one or more U.S. Government works has been eliminated. However, use of the copyright notice for these works is still strongly recommended. Use of a notice on such a work will defeat a claim of innocent infringement as previously described *provided* the notice also includes a statement that identifies one of the following: those portions of the work in which copyright is claimed or those portions that constitute U.S. Governmental material. An example is:

© 1989 Jane Brown. Copyright claimed in Chapters 7–10, exclusive of U.S. Government maps.

Works published before March 1, 1989, that consist primarily of one or more works of the U.S. Government *must* bear a notice and the identifying statement.

Unpublished Works

To avoid an inadvertent publication without notice, the author or other owner of copyright may wish to place a copyright notice on any copies or phonorecords that leave his or her control. An appropriate notice for an unpublished work is: Unpublished work © 1989 Jane Doe.

Effect of Omission of the Notice or of Error in the Name or Date

The Copyright Act, in sections 405 and 406, provides procedures for correcting errors and omissions of the copyright notice on works published on or after January 1, 1978, and before March 1, 1989.

In general, if a notice was omitted or an error was made on copies distributed between January 1, 1978, and March 1, 1989, the copyright was not automatically lost. Copyright protection may be maintained if registration for the work has been made before or is made within 5 years after the publication without notice, and a reasonable effort is made to add the notice of all copies or phonorecords that are distributed to the public in the United States after the omission has been discovered. For more information request Circular 3.

HOW LONG COPYRIGHT PROTECTION ENDURES

Works Originally Copyrighted on or After January 1, 1978

A work that is created (fixed in tangible form for the first time) on or after January 1, 1978, is automatically protected from the moment of its creation, and is ordinarily given a term enduring for the author's life, plus an additional 50 years after the author's death. In the case of "a joint work prepared by two or more authors who did not work for hire," the term lasts for 50 years after the last surviving author's death. For works made for hire, and for anonymous and psuedonymous works (unless the author's identity is revealed in Copyright Office records), the duration of copyright will be 75 years from publication or 100 years from creation, whichever is shorter.

Works that were created but not published or registered for copyright before January 1, 1978, have been automatically brought under the stat-ute and are now given Federal copyright protection. The duration of copyright in these works will generally be computed in the same way as for works created on or after January 1, 1978: the life-plus-50 or 75/100-year terms will apply to them as well. The law provides that in no case will the term of copyright for works in this category expire before December 31, 2002, and for works published on or before December 31, 2002, the term of copyright will not expire before December 31, 2027.

Works Copyrighted Before January 1, 1978

Under the law in effect before 1978, copyright was secured either on the date a work was published or on the date of registration if the work was registered in unpublished form. In either case, the copyright endured for a first term of 28 years from the date it was secured. During the last (28th) year of the first term, the copyright was eligible for renewal. The current copyright law has extended the renewal term from 28 to 47 years for copyrights that were subsisting on January 1, 1978, making these works eligible for a total term of protection of 75 years. However, the copyright *must* be renewed to receive the 47-year period of added protection. This is accomplished by filing a properly completed Form RE accompanied by a $6 filing fee in the Copyright Office before the end of the 28th calendar year of the original term.

For more detailed information on the copyright term, write to the Copyright Office and request Circulars 15a and 15t. For information on how to search the Copyright Office records concerning the copyright status of a work, ask for Circular 22.

TRANSFER OF COPYRIGHT

Any or all of the exclusive rights, or any subdivision of those rights, of the copyright owner may be transferred, but the transfer of *exclusive* rights is not valid unless that transfer is in writing and signed by the owner of the rights conveyed (or such owner's duly authorized agent). Transfer of a right on a nonexclusive basis does not require a written agreement.

A copyright may also be conveyed by operation of law and may be bequeathed by will or passed as personal property by the applicable laws of intestate succession.

Copyright is a personal property right, and it is subject to the various state laws and regulations that govern the ownership, inheritance, or transfer of personal property as well as terms of contracts or conduct of business. For information about relevant state laws, consult an attorney.

Transfers of copyright are normally made by contract. The Copyright Office does not have or supply any forms for such transfers. However, the law does provide for the recordation in the Copyright Office of transfers of copyright ownership. Although recordation is not required to make a valid transfer between the parties, it does provide certain legal advantages and may be required to validate the transfer as against third parties. For information on recordation of transfers and other documents related to copyright, write to the Copyright Office for Circular 12.

Termination of Transfers

Under the previous law, the copyright in a work reverted to the author, if living, or if the author was not living, to other specified beneficiaries, provided a renewal claim was registered in the 28th year of the original term. The present law drops the renewal feature except for works already in the first term of statutory protection when the present law took effect. Instead, the present law permits termination of a grant of rights after 35 years under certain conditions by serving written notice on the transferee within specified time limits.

For works already under statutory copyright protection before 1978, the present law provides a similar right of termination covering the newly added years that extended the former maximum term of the copyright from 56 to 75 years. For further information, write to the Copyright Office for Circulars 15a and 15t.

INTERNATIONAL COPYRIGHT PROTECTION

There is no such thing as an "international copyright" that will automatically protect an author's writings throughout the entire world. Protection against unauthorized use in a particular country depends, basically, on the national laws of that country. However, most countries do offer protection to foreign works under certain conditions, and these conditions have been greatly simplified by international copyright treaties and conventions. For a list of countries which maintain copyright relations with the United States, write to the Copyright Office and ask for Circular 38a.

The United States belongs to both global, multilateral copyright treaties—the Universal Copyright Convention (UCC) and the Berne Convention for the Protection of Literary and Artistic Works. The United States was a founding member of the UCC, which came into force on September 16, 1955. Generally, a work by a national or domiciliary of a country that is a member of the UCC or a work first published in a UCC country may claim protection under the UCC. If the work bears the notice of copyright in the form and position specified by the UCC, this notice will satisfy and substitute for any other formalities a UCC member country would otherwise impose as a condition of copyright. A UCC notice should consist of the symbol © accompanied by the name of the copyright proprietor and the year of first publication of the work.

By joining the Berne Convention, an act that took effect on March 1, 1989, the United States gained a protection for its authors in all member nations of the Berne Union, including an additional 25 countries (as of September 1988) with which the United States formerly either had no copyright relations or had bilateral treaty arrangements. Members of the Berne Union agree to a certain minimum level of copyright protection and agree to treat nationals of other member countries like their own nationals for purposes of copyright. A work first published in the United States or another Berne Union country (or first published in a non-Berne country, followed by publication within 30 days in a Berne Union country) is eligible for protection in all Berne member countries. There are no special requirements. For information on the legislation implementing the Berne Convention, request Circular 93 from the Copyright Office.

An author who wishes protection for his or her work in a particular country should first find out the extent of protection of foreign works in that country. If possible, this should be done before the work is published

anywhere, since protection may often depend on the facts existing at the time of *first* publication.

If the country in which protection is sought is a party to one of the international copyright conventions, the work may generally be protected by complying with the conditions of the convention. Even if the work cannot be brought under an international convention, protection under the specific provisions of the country's national laws may still be possible. Some countries, however, offer little or no copyright protection for foreign works.

COPYRIGHT REGISTRATION

In general, copyright registration is a legal formality intended to make a public record of the basic facts of a particular copyright. However, except in two specific situations,* registration is not a condition of copyright protection. Even though registration is not generally a requirement for protection, the copyright law provides several inducements or advantages to encourage copyright owners to make registration. Among these advantages are the following:

• Registration establishes a public record of the copyright claim;
• Before an infringement suit may be filed in court, registration is neces-

*Works published with notice of copyright before January 1, 1978, must be registered and renewed during the first 28-year term of the copyright to maintain protection.
Under sections 405 and 406 of the Copyright Act, copyright registration may be required to preserve a copyright on a work first published before March 1, 1989, that would otherwise be invalidated because the copyright notice was omitted from the published copies or phonorecords, or the name or year date was omitted, or certain errors were made in the year date.

sary for works of U.S. origin and for foreign works not originating in a Berne Union country. (For more information on when a work is of U.S. origin, request Circular 93);
- If made before or within 5 years of publication, registration will establish prima facie evidence in court of the validity of the copyright and of the facts stated in the certificate; and
- If registration is made within 3 months after publication of the work or prior to an infringement of the work, statutory damages and attorney's fees will be available to the copyright owner in court actions. Otherwise, only an award of actual damages and profits is available to the copyright owner.

Registration may be made at any time within the life of the copyright. Unlike the law before 1978, when a work has been registered in unpublished form, it is not necessary to make another registration when the work becomes published (although the copyright owner may register the published edition, if desired).

REGISTRATION PROCEDURES

In General

A. To register a work, send the following three elements **in the same envelope or package** to the Register of Copyrights, Copyright Office, Library of Congress, Washington, D.C. 20559: (see page 243 for what happens if the elements are sent separately).

1. A properly completed application form;
2. A nonrefundable filing fee of $20 for each application;

3. A nonreturnable deposit of the work being registered. The deposit requirements vary in particular situations. The *general* requirements follow. Also note the information under "Special Deposit Requirements" immediately following this section.

- If the work is unpublished, one complete copy or phonorecord.
- If the work was first published in the United States on or after January 1, 1978, two complete copies or phonorecords of the best edition.
- If the work was first published in the United States before January 1, 1978, two complete copies or phonorecords of the work as first published.
- If the work was first published outside the United States, whenever published, one complete copy or phonorecord of the work as first published.

B. To register a renewal, send:

1. A properly completed RE application form; and
2. A nonrefundable filing fee of $6 for each work.

NOTE: COMPLETE THE APPLICATION FORM USING BLACK INK PEN OR TYPEWRITER. You may photocopy the application forms if the forms you submit to the Office are clear, legible, on a good grade of white paper, and printed head-to-head (so that when you turn the sheet over, the top of page 2 is directly behind the top of page 1). Because the certificates of registration are reproduced directly from the application forms, it is vital the forms meet the stated requirements. Forms not meeting these requirements will be returned.

Special Deposit Requirements

Special deposit requirements exist for many types of work. In some instances, only one copy is required for published works, in other instances only identifying material is required, and in still other instances, the deposit requirement may be unique. The following are three prominent examples of exceptions to the general deposit requirements:

- If the work is a motion picture, the deposit requirement is one complete copy of the unpublished or published motion picture **and** a separate written description of its contents, such as continuity, press book, or synopsis.
- If the work is a literary, dramatic or musical work **published only on phonorecord,** the deposit requirement is one complete copy of the phonorecord.
- If the work is an unpublished or published computer program, the deposit requirement is one visually perceptible copy in source code of the **first and last 25 pages** of the program. For a program of less than 50 pages, the deposit is a copy of the entire program. (For more information on computer program registration, including deposits for revised programs and special relief for trade secrets, request Circular 61.)

In the case of works reproduced in three-dimensional copies, identifying material such as photographs or drawings is ordinarily required. Other examples of special deposit requirements (but by no means an exhaustive list) include many works of the visual arts, such as greeting cards, toys, fabric, oversized material (request Circular 40a); video games and other machine-readable audiovisual works (request Circular 49); automated databases (request Circular 65); and contributions to collective works.

If you are unsure of the deposit requirement for your work, write or call the Copyright Office and describe the work you wish to register.

Unpublished Collections

A work may be registered in unpublished form as a "collection," with one application and one fee, under the following conditions:

- The elements of the collection are assembled in an orderly form;
- The combined elements bear a single title identifying the collection as a whole;
- The copyright claimant in all the elements and in the collection as a whole is the same; and
- All of the elements are by the same author, or, if they are by different authors, at least one of the authors has contributed copyrightable authorship to each element.

Unpublished collections are indexed in the *Catalog of Copyright Entries* only under the collection titles.

CORRECTIONS AND AMPLIFICATIONS OF EXISTING REGISTRATIONS

To correct an error in a copyright registration or to amplify the information given in a registration, file a supplementary registration form—Form CA—with the Copyright Office. The information in a supplementary registration augments but does not supersede that contained in the earlier registration. Note also that a supplementary registration is not a substitute for an original registration, for a renewal registration, or for recording a transfer of ownership. For further information about supplementary registration, request Circular 8.

MANDATORY DEPOSIT FOR WORKS PUBLISHED IN THE UNITED STATES

Although a copyright registration is not required, the Copyright Act establishes a mandatory deposit requirement for works published in the United States under copyright protection (see definition of "publication" on page 233). In general, the owner of copyright, or the owner of the exclusive right of publication in the work, has a legal obligation to deposit in the Copyright Office, within 3 months of publication in the United States, 2 copies (or, in the case of sound recordings, 2 phonorecords) for the use of the Library of Congress. Failure to make the deposit can result in fines and other penalties, but does not affect the copyright protection.

Certain categories of works are **exempt entirely** from the mandatory deposit requirements, and the obligation is reduced for certain other categories. For further information about mandatory deposit, request Circular 7d.

NOTE: LIBRARY OF CONGRESS CATALOG CARD NUMBERS.

A Library of Congress Catalog Number is different from a copyright registration number. The Cataloging in Publication (CIP) Division of the Library of Congress is responsible for assigning LC Catalog Card Numbers and is operationally separate from the Copyright Office. A book may be registered in or deposited with the Copyright Office but not necessarily cataloged and added to the Library's collections. For information about obtaining an LC Catalog Card Number, contact the CIP Division, Library of Congress, Washington, D.C. 20540. For information on International Standard Book Numbering (ISBN), write to: ISBN Agency, R.R. Bowker Company, 205 East 42nd Street, New York, NY 10017. For information on International Standard Serial Numbering (ISSN), write to: Library of Congress, National Series Data Program, Washington, D.C. 20540.

USE OF MANDATORY DEPOSIT TO SATISFY REGISTRATION REQUIREMENTS

For works published in the United States the Copyright Act contains a provision under which a single deposit can be made to satisfy both the deposit requirements for the Library and the registration requirements. In order to have this dual effect, the copies or phonorecords must be accompanied by the prescribed application and fee for registration.

WHO MAY FILE AN APPLICATION FORM

The following persons are legally entitled to submit an application form:

- The author. This is either the person who actually created the work, or, if the work was made for hire, the employer or other person for whom the work was prepared.
- The copyright claimant. The copyright claimant is defined in Copyright Office regulations as either the author of the work or a person or organization that has obtained ownership of all the rights under the copyright initially belonging to the author. This category includes a person or organization who has obtained by contract the right to claim legal title to the copyright in an application for copyright registration.
- The owner of exclusive right(s). Under the law, any of the exclusive rights that go to make up a copyright and any subdivision of them can be transferred and owned separately, even though the transfer may be limited in time or place of effect. The term "copyright owner" with respect to any one of the exclusive rights contained in a copyright refers to the owner of that particular right. Any owner of an exclusive right may apply for registration of a claim in the work.
- The duly authorized agent of such author, other copyright claimant, or owner or exclusive right(s). Any person authorized to act on behalf of the author, other copyright claimant, or owner of exclusive rights may apply for registration.

There is no requirement that applications be prepared or filed by an attorney.

APPLICATION FORMS

For Original Registration

Form TX: for published and unpublished nondramatic literary works

Form SE: for serials, works issued or intended to be issued in successive parts bearing numerical or chronological designations and intended to be continued indefinitely (periodicals, newspapers, magazines, newsletters, annuals, journals, etc.)

Form PA: for published and unpublished works of the performing arts (musical and dramatic works, pantomimes and choreographic works, motion pictures and other audiovisual works)

Form VA: for published and unpublished works of the visual arts (pictorial, graphic, and sculptural works)

Form SR: for published and unpublished sound recordings

For Renewal Registration

Form RE: for claims to renewal copyright in works copyrighted under the law in effect through December 31, 1977 (1909 Copyright Act)

For Corrections and Amplifications

Form CA: for supplementary registration to correct or amplify information given in the Copyright Office record of an earlier registration

For a Group of Contributions to Periodicals

Form an adjunct application to be
GR/CP: used for registration of a group of contributions to periodicals in addition to an application Form TX, PA, or VA

Application forms are supplied by the Copyright Office free.

**COPYRIGHT OFFICE HOTLINE
NOTE:** Requestors may order application forms and circulars at any time by telephoning (202) 707-9100. Orders will be recorded automatically and filled as quickly as possible.

MAILING INSTRUCTIONS

All applications and materials related to copyright registration should be addressed to the Register of Copyrights, Copyright Office, Library of Congress, Washington, D.C. 20559.
The application, nonreturnable deposit (copies, phonorecords, or identifying material), and nonrefundable filing fee should be mailed in the same package.

WHAT HAPPENS IF THE THREE ELEMENTS ARE NOT RECEIVED TOGETHER

Applications and fees received without appropriate copies, phonorecords, or identifying material will **not** be processed and will ordinarily be returned. Unpublished deposits without applications or fees will ordinarily be returned, also. In most cases, published deposits received without application and fees can be

immediately transferred to the collection of the Library of Congress. This practice is in accordance with section 408 of the law, which provides that the published deposit required for the collections of the Library of Congress may be used for registration only if the deposit is "accompanied by the prescribed application and fee . . ."

After the deposit is received and transferred to another department of the Library for its collections or other deposition, it is no longer available o the Copyright Office. If you wish to register the work, you must deposit additional copies or phonorecords with your application and fee.

FEES

Do not send cash. A fee sent to the Copyright Office should be in the form of a money order, check, or bank draft payable to the Register of Copyrights; it should be securely attached to the application. A remittance from outside the United States should be payable in U.S. dollars and should be in the form of an international money order or a draft drawn on a U.S. bank. Do not send a check drawn on a foreign bank.

EFFECTIVE DATE OF REGISTRATION

A copyright registration is effective on the date the Copyright Office receives all of the required elements in acceptable form, regardless of how long it then takes to process the application and mail the certificate of registration. The time the Copyright Office requires to process an application varies, depending on the amount of material the Office is receiving and the personnel available. It must also be kept in mind that it may take a number of days for mailed material to reach the Copyright Office and for the certificate of registration to reach the recipient after being mailed by the Copyright Office.

If you are filing an application for copyright registration in the Copyright Office, you **will not** receive an acknowledgement that your application has been received, but you can expect:

- a letter or telephone call from a copyright examiner if further information is needed;
- A certificate of registration to indicate the work has been registered; or
- If registration cannot be made, a letter explaining why it has been refused.

Please allow 120 days to receive a letter or certificate of registration.

If you want to know when the Copyright Office receives your material, you should send it by registered or certified mail and request a return receipt from the post office. Allow at least 3 weeks for the return of your receipt.

SEARCH OF COPYRIGHT OFFICE RECORDS

The records of the Copyright Office are open for inspection and searching by the public. Moreover, on request, the Copyright Office will search its records at the statutory rate of $10 for each hour or fraction of an hour. For information on searching the Office records concerning the copyright status or ownership of a work, write for Circulars 22 and 23.

AVAILABLE INFORMATION

This circular attempts to answer some of the questions that are frequently asked about copyright. For a list of other material published by the Copyright Office, write for Circular 2, "Publications on Copyright." Any requests for Copyright Office publications or special questions relating to copyright problems not mentioned in this circular should be addressed to the Copyright Office, LM 455, Library of Congress, Washington, D.C. 20559. To speak to a Copyright Information Specialist, call (202) 479-0700.

The Copyright Office is not permitted to give legal advice. If you need information or guidance on matters such as disputes over the ownership of a copyright, suits against possible infringers, the procedure for getting a work published, or the method of obtaining royalty payments, it may be necessary to consult an attorney.

Copyright Office
Library of Congress
Washington, D.C. 20559

eight

MY WAY

From the moment this book was conceived, this was to be the last chapter. Perhaps it was just a case of saving the best for last or providing the obligatory pot of gold at the end of the rainbow, or perhaps I wanted to be sure of a solid ending (how could you not be interested in what these people had to say about their careers and yours?), but whatever is the case, I don't think this chapter will disappoint you . . . even though it's no longer the last chapter.

If you have read through to this point without skipping, you have earned a reward. You have learned a great deal, and I know it hasn't all been easy. You have also come to grips with many unfamiliar concepts, not all of which are logical.

The artists and writers interviewed for this chapter were not chosen at random. Their choice was dictated by a desire to present as broad a spectrum of excellence as possible within the space available. Each participant has attained the zenith in his or her respective area of entertainment and each has demonstrated an uncommon ability to communicate his or her experiences and points of view in a manner that is clear, candid, and entertaining. I will be surprised if you don't find at least one you can relate to on a personal level.

If you've been with us from the beginning, sit back and relax: school is out. If you're cheating a bit, that's okay, too; perhaps you will find the inspiration to go back and do your homework.

To speak of the graciousness and sincerity of those who participated would be redundant—the interviews speak for themselves.

INTERVIEW WITH
ASHFORD AND SIMPSON

Established as Gold Recording Artists with more than fifteen LPs behind them, Nickolas Ashford and Valerie Simpson have also written such standards as "Ain't No Mountain High Enough," "You're All I Need to Get By," "Ain't Nothing Like the Real Thing," "Reach Out and Touch," and "Solid." In addition to producing their own albums they also produce artists, including Diana Ross, Stephanie Mills, and Gladys Knight. They have just joined Arista Records and are completing their first album for their new label.

AHS: The title of this chapter is "My Way." Could you very briefly tell me what "your way" was, a short synopsis of how you came to be artists, producers, and writers?

SIMPSON: Well, in short, I think we used the direct approach, which was actually just walking into a publisher's office and saying, "Do you have a piano?" and going over and beating out a song and waiting for approval or disapproval. This actually worked for us because even though we were pushing our writing, we were pretty good singers and we were real good entertainers, so we'd sell people things they didn't even want. . . . So, I think that the direct approach . . . just coming right on, worked for us.

AHS: Was that before Motown?

SIMPSON: Before Motown.

AHS: You were selling songs from one . . .

SIMPSON: One publisher to the next, yes.

AHS: When did Motown come into it, after you had some success?

SIMPSON: Yes. We went from publisher to publisher until we wrote "Let's Go Get Stoned," and our publisher then was . . .

ASHFORD: Ed Silvers.

SIMPSON: Ed Silvers—we signed with him and we'd take two, three songs to him every week, and he would give us an advance. It would keep us going. One week we went there and we didn't have anything. . . . The night before we had been writing to kind of come up with the three songs for the advance, and we just couldn't do it, so we said, "Oh, we'll do it later; let's just go get stoned"—and it was like a big joke. The next day, when we were supposed to present these songs to our publisher, he asked, "Well, do you have anything for us?" and Nick said, "Well, why don't we just strike up that thing we were doing last night?" and we improvised a chorus of "Let's Go Get Stoned," and Ed Silvers said, "You know, I really hear this for Ray Charles." We said "What? Are you kidding?" So we finished up the song and he sent it to Ray Charles and that's how we got our first hit, and that was the beginning of our career.

AHS: Already I have something I think nobody else has . . . this little anecdote. . . . Then Motown picked you up?

SIMPSON: Yes.

ASHFORD: Well, they sent scouts to New York to look for new talent, and someone had given them our names and they called us. I went over to the hotel and they made me wait so long I thought it was bull, so I went to the elevator. . . . I was leaving; then Brian came up to me and said, "Hey, we really want to hear your stuff." So they got me back in the room; they listened to the demonstration record and they were very impressed. They were impressed that we did everything; the lyrics, the background, and the music, because at Motown at that time, they were doing a lot of it separately. That's what they called "producing." We didn't know it was "producing" at the time. They were willing to fly us out to Detroit to talk, so we just went out there and signed the first paper they put in front of us. [Laughter]

SIMPSON: We signed away, quickly signed away, seven years.

AHS: Val, I heard Nick mention that you had a session and that you couldn't go to the Motown meeting.

SIMPSON: Yes.

AHS: Was that as a background singer or doing commercials?

SIMPSON: Oh, yes, a combination of both.

AHS: Was that a factor in sustaining you while you were searching. . . .

SIMPSON: Oh, all in all, I think some of the first money we ever made in this business was doing—remember a hand-clapping session? We got paid $45 to do handclaps. We said, "Well, this is phenomenal." Between that and the background singing and occasionally getting a song published, it was enough to carry you over, and if one wasn't working, the other would kind of hold you over.

AHS: Question: now, looking back—sitting as we are in this most magnificent home, obviously a home of affluence—when you started working in the music business, was it with a profit motive in mind, or did you feel that you just had to do music?

ASHFORD: It was definitely that we just had to do music, because I know I could have done other jobs instead of starving and hoping we could get in the back door somewhere. It was definitely for the love of the music. We would work night and day sometimes, just having fun, because it was something we really loved to do.

AHS: I suspected that would be your answer. Val, when you were at Motown, you had a record or two as an artist.

SIMPSON: Yes.

AHS: Motown didn't bring them home for you, they weren't successful. How did you react to that? Perhaps I should ask Nick how you reacted to it.

SIMPSON: I think it was traumatic, but I always felt that there was an unspoken law at Motown which this kind of . . . just reinforced, that there was only going to be one lady at Motown during that period, and that was Diana Ross. So when my records didn't happen, it just kind of reinforced that idea. I received good reviews and all of that, and people loved the album, but it just didn't really get going.

AHS: You didn't get down on yourself because of it, because you saw other reasons for that happening?

SIMPSON: Yes. I mean by that time I knew how the business worked, and that sometimes for reasons unknown or for reasons known, you just couldn't get your thing across. Also, I had other things to do . . . the writing and producing that we were doing kept me busy. I wasn't depending on being an artist . . . it wasn't as if I was *just* an artist; I think that helped, too.

AHS: Nick, you're not going to get off any easier. The first night I met you, like Harry Truman, you were in the haberdashery business. I met you at an opening of your clothing emporium, and, as I recall, you were very shy and kind of reticent. When I see you on stage now, I don't see the same image. Did you have to change yourself to become a performer, or was it always there underneath that facade?

ASHFORD: I always wanted to perform. I'd had some experience. I sang a lot in the church. . . . I love to sing. I like that kind of freedom of expression; that's why I love to write, but I don't know if I've changed or not. It might have been just lurking underneath somewhere waiting to explode . . . just waiting for the right opportunity.

AHS: The persona was there; you didn't have to work consciously at developing it?

ASHFORD: Entertaining in the pop world, I did.

AHS: That's what I meant, because you struck me as a very private person.

ASHFORD: Oh, yes. Getting out there in front of an audience is totally different from singing in the studio. When I sang in church, I wasn't subject to criticism. When you get out to sing in public, you're up against the critics and what people think of you and all of that. It had been just a spiritual outlet for me; then it became real entertainment for people. . . . That was quite another thing to deal with. I had to learn about that and train myself to be an entertainer, that's for sure.

AHS: Bill Wyman indicated during his interview that the trouble with many young artists today is that they go into a studio and they do an album before they have any idea how to perform, and then it all falls apart when they get out into the world.

ASHFORD: That's usually the case.

SIMPSON: Absolutely.

ASHFORD: That happened to us. You just don't know. You just don't know what it's like until you first do it and then you realize, God. . . .

SIMPSON: It's so different, yes. You might even assume that they're going to fall all over you, they're going to love you because they loved your record . . . and then there's no reaction. . . . You just don't know what to do with yourself!

ASHFORD: Once you get up there you become a visual; they're not just listening anymore, they see *and* they hear, and you have got to fill both of those needs, so it's quite different.

AHS: You have reached the pinnacle in all areas of the music world. You're successful writers, you're successful producers, you're successful recording artists and entertainers. If you had to pick one of the areas that you consider yourself to excel in, which would it be?

ASHFORD: Hmmm . . .

AHS: Do you consider yourself a writer who produces and performs or do you consider yourself a performer who also writes and produces? I told you it wasn't going to be an easy interview.

SIMPSON: A writer who . . . who does the others as well.

AHS: Nick?

ASHFORD: I would say writing, because that's how we started.

AHS: You had been very successful as writers and producers and were, I think, enjoying considerable income when you launched your careers as artists. Didn't you feel it was taking a risk? Did you feel that you were sticking your necks out?

ASHFORD: I really didn't feel we had anything to lose. I thought it was time to grow. Since we had become successful as writers and producers, we needed another outlet for our energies. I think it was a natural step.

SIMPSON: I think too that being a writer and producer is like a backup for being a singer. I always feel on the stage that once you let them know that you wrote some well-known songs, they will forgive you a lot of things. [Laughter]

ASHFORD: They won't forgive some things.

SIMPSON: You know, if you're *just* an artist, they expect you to be *the artist* and you're supposed to be singing impeccably. . . . But because we do these other things, it's kind of like we have this little cushion, you know. . . . "Oh, well, maybe they hit a flat note . . . *but* . . . they really do write well. [Laughter]

AHS: I'm going to ask you a question, and you can cut the answer out of the interview later on if you choose. Was any of your motivation in becoming performers fostered by a sense of frustration that perhaps others obtained fame and glory using your songs?

ASHFORD: I never, never once, felt that way. I mean, I was so honored to have other artists do the material we wrote that it never entered my mind.

SIMPSON: That's right.

ASHFORD: When you're a writer, which we basically started out as being, you don't think such thoughts; you just want to get that tune out there and you want the world to hear something you had to say, and when they hear it, you're satisfied.

SIMPSON: And I think it helps if you have a healthy appreciation of what it takes to be an artist. I mean there's no way we could equate ourselves with Diana Ross. We realized what it took for her to become Diana Ross and knowing what it took . . . I mean, you just don't equate that. There's no way I could feel that we could sing "Ain't No Mountain" and it would have been the same thing. Maybe it would have, but it just doesn't even cross your mind, you know so. . . . It's like a separate hat that you wear.

AHS: You guys are terrific, because you lead right to where I want to go. You've been in the business a lot of years now.

SIMPSON: Yes.

AHS: Have you noticed any particular change in the business as songwriters? Putting yourself in the shoes of a young writer today, as opposed to when you were breaking in, do you perceive a difference? For instance, the availability of prospective users of your songs? What I'm really getting at is: has the advent of the singer/songwriter such as you are now cut the potential market for writers?

SIMPSON: Regular writers?

AHS: Yes. Do you consider that a factor in the industry today?

SIMPSON: I think it has, but . . . I don't see anything the matter with it. I think a singer/songwriter feels a definite emotional need for the public. With the singer/songwriter, you get that two-in-one effect right away, and it does something that maybe just a writer in some respects is not able to do. He's hoping that the artist's talent will blend with him. But a singer/songwriter already has the blending because he is the artist and his is the emotion that created the song, so it comes out right away and there's something very strong there when it works. I just think it's something that the public has been lucky enough to get a lot of, and I think it's been good. But it has cut the market down for just writers.

AHS: What I was getting to really. . . . You indicated before, you took the direct approach, you walked into the publisher and sat down at the piano. Do you think young writers today could pull that off as easily as you could back then?

ASHFORD: I really don't think so because . . . you could call it a writers' inflation. I mean there are so many writers now. At the time when we were coming up and doing the music we were doing, there were relatively few of us. *Now* it's not *just* us. . . . The white writers are able to do black music very well, so that limits the opportunity for other black writers.

SIMPSON: There are just more folks out there doing it.

AHS: When you're putting together an album, do you ever consider doing songs by other writers?

ASHFORD: No, not really.

SIMPSON: Occasionally.

ASHFORD: On occasion, yes. But we prefer to do our own material. I do particularly because it's difficult for me to sing other material. [Laughter] Not being a true singer, being primarily a writer, it's easier to sing your own music. . . . You know how to fluff it up.

AHS: How important do you consider it to have a manager at the inception of your career? I know you're well managed now, but could you have profited by having a manager earlier than you did? How do you feel about management from the perspective of the young artist, or the artist coming up?

SIMPSON: That's interesting.

ASHFORD: You mean as artists, not as writers?

AHS: Yes.

ASHFORD: I think it's absolutely necessary, at least to a certain degree. . . .

AHS: Val, you said it was interesting. I saw wheels turning in your head.

SIMPSON: Gee, I don't know. I think a little bit of fumbling around is not bad, for maybe a year or so, because I know that in the beginning your own ideas aren't formed. To immediately have someone tell you or push you in a direction could be destructive. It depends. . . . Certain people know who they are. Are you going to be somebody else's creation or somebody else's idea or are you strong enough as an individual so young to say, "This is what I want to be, help me be it"? If you can be strong enough, then a manager's good, but if the manager's going to say, "I see you as this," and point you in a direction that might not be right for you, then it's not so good. If you've had time to at least have a hint or a glint of where you're going, then I think management can help you get there, but I don't see somebody just leading you.

ASHFORD: Some artists have a natural aptitude or instinct for their business as well as their art. . . . Others, such as myself, are just really artists—don't care about business and don't want to know about it. I can't deal with it. I can't wake up in the morning and write checks and do things like that; it destroys me.

AHS: What about when you have a record deal? Don't you find that a manager acts as an insulator between you and the record company?

SIMPSON: Oh, yes. I think it's imperative that you always remain the good guy. [Laughter]

AHS: That's why lawyers and managers were invented.

SIMPSON: Oh, absolutely, and I really, really feel that way. Your manager should go in there and fight those battles, and you should still be able to talk to everybody at the record company, even though he's not speaking to half the people at the company anymore.

AHS: Everybody makes mistakes. There must have been some mistakes you made along the way that, if you had the opportunity, you might not make today. Perhaps some young people could profit from your past experiences. Any mistakes you'd like to confess to?

ASHFORD: Don't count any money you haven't got. [Laughter.] You have all these dreams, you're sure this record is going to do this, and so . . . but you just wait and see, because you never know how the tide is going to flow against you. I've made bad mistakes by making plans on the dreams that didn't come true. [Laughter.]

AHS: I don't think that's unique to performing artists. [Laughter] Val, what mistake do you recommend not making?

SIMPSON: Probably fear of high places. I think that in the beginning, you're just so afraid, you want to do something so badly, that you're willing to do it for nothing. You don't realize that when a person or a company is investing money in you, they're investing it because they expect a return. You don't appreciate that you have value. When we did our Motown deal, we didn't have to sign for seven years, but we were so eager . . . and no one told us that we *couldn't* have a lawyer look at the paper, but we were just that green. I can't believe that we ever did that, but we really did do that, and I would hate to think that people would do that today. I mean, if they want you, they will want you even when you suggest the necessary changes to make it right for yourself and to feel like a human being. You don't have to just take the first offer they throw at you. That's the mistake that we made; we just wanted it so bad that we accepted it no matter how uncomfortable it was for us.

AHS: You might have been more prudent had you had a little more experience. Your new album is doing very well. It's on the pop charts, and I believe this is really the first time you're crossing over into the pop field. Is that true?

ASHFORD: There seems to be a strong indication that we are at this time.

AHS: To what do you attribute that crossover? Has your music changed, is there a change in your attitude as performers, or is there a change in your environment professionally, in your record company? To what do you attribute this?

ASHFORD: It's like a song we wrote called "It's the Long Run." I think it's a combination of things. We gathered a following through the years, a following that's started to grow a little, to the point where it's crossing over to more whites.

SIMPSON: I don't even know whether the crossover's really there yet. I think that there are some artists who have such large sales that it seems as if they're crossover sales, but they may not actually be so. Take Rick James, for instance. I doubt that he has a crossover, a real crossover, but he just gets so many sales that it looks like, well, since it's way up on the pop charts, it must be crossed. You know, to some extent it is, but you're never really sure who really is buying those records.

AHS: Do you feel a sense of frustration at not crossing over, at being relegated to a particular market? Does that bother you as performers?

ASHFORD: I hate the labels too, especially this is "Black Music," this is "White Music"; I hate that. And there is a frustration, but I don't think we yield to it. I think we feel strong and confident enough that if we hold on to our brand, our particular feeling about the music, that it will succeed. In other words, we're not going to sell out. We can write a lot of different ways, we can write white or whatever they say is black, but we really go by our own particular feeling as to what kind of ideas we want to offer, and we hope that it will grab and pull the people more or less. We don't say, "Well, this is marketable today, so this is what we'll write." We try to stick to what really moves us, which isn't always going to be commercial.

SIMPSON: But I think you owe it to yourself to do that. We signed with our new record company, Arista, feeling that its president, Clive Davis, was a fan of ours, so I feel like we have to give them our maximum. It's like a God-given opportunity to come up with something that's really *you*, and make that happen. I think that's probably the biggest hit you can ever get, when you really get your identification out there strongly, which is what we're trying to do.

AHS: Is your record company being very helpful?

SIMPSON: Oh, absolutely, absolutely. We go by funny things; it's not so much the deal that's structured—I mean, all that's good . . . once our manager tells me that it is a good deal and he runs the figures by me, I can figure that out, but the most important thing is that the enthusiasm is there, that they really believe. . . .

ASHFORD: In *our* music, not something else.

SIMPSON: Yes, believing that they're going to run with something they like really turns us on.

AHS: I'm sure that as producer, you're very often approached by young people trying to break into the business, and I'm sure you see they're making a lot of mistakes. Are there any particular things you see the youngsters coming up doing that you would admonish them not to do? . . . I'm sure you're deluged with cassettes and requests for appraisals and whatever. . . .

SIMPSON: Oh, yes.

AHS: What are the most universal mistakes that are being made?

ASHFORD: I think the big mistake is to think that there's a format or a set pattern that you can follow. I mean, there's only one heaven, but there are many ways to get there, so you can tell young writers and entertainers a lot of things, but in the long run, it's still the individual endeavor and approach that counts. The basic thing is to really believe that you have the energy to do or die; and sometimes it gets mighty lean. . . . Some people will go off to another side career and it will take over their lives as opposed to standing firm and waiting for that inspiration to get them into their career the correct way. There's no formula, no pattern; you've just got to get out there and say "I believe in this, I'm working on this," and go for it. That's all I could ever tell them. I couldn't tell them to be a busboy and then see the light and then go over here . . . no way.

SIMPSON: I think too that it's gotten to the point . . . I remember from the early days when we first started, there was more respect for what a song is and what a song can do than there is now. I mean, everybody thinks they can write a song. . . . "Well, let me do something that's going to lead me from my mundane life; let me write a song; anybody can write a song" . . . and there are a lot of songs on the radio that sound like anybody wrote them. . . . [Laughter] So I can understand how they get this feeling. There's no quality anymore to the thought, and there should be quality.

ASHFORD: Saying something no one else has said . . .

SIMPSON: Or saying it in a special way, or thinking, Has this been done before? They don't seem to care about these things. It's almost like they do want to copy whatever is out there. That was never our thought; in fact, if we hear something on the radio that sounds like something we're working on, we just say, "Oh, forget it." . . . I think that's the kind of individual feeling you have to have, and it's probably the kind of person you are. It takes a little integrity, I think.

ASHFORD: Look into your own material! After we write our songs, on occasion we've asked ourselves, "Ah, does anybody care?"

SIMPSON: "Who cares about this?"

ASHFORD: We'll analyze the song; we'll listen to it and say, "Um, does anybody care?" And if we both say "No," we just . . .

SIMPSON: We just dump it.

ASHFORD: Dump it, because it's probably not important enough. You can write a thousand songs, but what's the point if nobody cares about what you're saying? Is it important enough to merit attention?

AHS: I think I have a super interview. You mentioned that your energy level drove you to become performers; that you weren't content with just writing and producing. Now that you're approaching your goal as performers, is there anything else percolating in the Ashford and Simpson collective mind?

ASHFORD: Naturally, we have our ideas, mainly because you know you have to grow. One phase was writing and then it was writing and entertaining; now I feel that we should go to musicals. . . . We're thinking about getting our heads into that now because it's another growth; it's another challenge; it's another form of expression that we haven't tried.

SIMPSON: Yes.

AHS: Are you of similar mind, Val?

SIMPSON: Oh, absolutely. The idea of seeing it happen and hearing it at the same time is exciting. I think probably, because of our performing too, we may have a little edge.

ASHFORD: We're not the kind of entertainers who want to be out there past our time. [Hearty laughter]

AHS: I think you still have a lot of time to be out there.

ASHFORD: Yes, but . . . we're always reaching out to try something we haven't tried. It keeps the juices flowing. Even if we fail, we like the idea of being able to say, "Well, we tried to do it."

SIMPSON: Where's the new goose bump going to come from?

AHS: I thank you very much. I think my readers will really enjoy this.

INTERVIEW WITH
MARVIN HAMLISCH

A Chorus Line: *Pulitzer Prize, Nine Tonys.* The Sting: *Academy Award.* The Way We Were: *Two Academy Awards, Four Grammys.* "Nobody Does It Better." "What I Did for Love." *Theme for ABC-TV's* "Good Morning America." *Motion-picture scores. Pop contemporary songwriter. Musician. Conductor. Composer. . . . Gentleman. . . . Marvin Hamlisch.*

AHS: I would appreciate a thumbnail sketch of your career.

HAMLISCH: Around the age of nine or ten, I wrote a song with my cousin and we thought it was a very good song, and we took it to a publisher.

AHS: At age ten?

HAMLISCH: At about ten or eleven or something like that. We made a little demonstration record and we took it to a publisher because that was the way we had heard it was done. The song was called "What Did You Get Santa Claus for Christmas?" It was a very novel idea. Nothing very much happened until months later, when a neighbor said she had heard my song on the radio. I wondered how that was possible. No one told me anything about it. I found out that the song that she'd heard on the radio was called "Let's Give a Christmas Present to Santa Claus." At the age of eleven or whatever it was, I was already the victim of an infringement. . . . As my mother would say, "It was stolen." That was my introduction to the music business and the world of popular music. It became clear very quickly that I was going to get burned a lot unless I could figure out how not to get burned. After I wrote, God knows, two hundred songs and got nothing published and nothing going on . . . just making demonstration records . . .

AHS: At the ripe old age of maybe fourteen?

HAMLISCH: Fourteen, fifteen, something like that. I kept writing songs and nothing really was happening, even though at that time more singers were looking for outside songs. This was before the advent of the singer-songwriter, which has in a way hurt the writer per se (which is one of the points I want to make). In those days, most singers were looking for material. So I went around and I finally found a publisher that I thought was nice, just a nice person. It was Pinkus Music.

AHS: George Pinkus?

HAMLISCH: That's right. He seemed very nice, very reputable. I remember when I finally got a song recorded, it was by a total fluke, having nothing to do with any publisher I knew or anything like that. My ear, nose, and throat doctor knew Georgia Gibbs. She was looking for a very up song. I wrote a song with my cousin called "Sunshine, Lollipops and Rainbows." I presented it to her and she didn't like the song, and turned it down. The doctor was so incensed by the fact that she turned it down after I had written the song and done the demo and worked so hard that it became his mission in life to get that song recorded. He also knew Quincy Jones, and one day Quincy said he was looking for a song for a beach-party movie which could be used to get a girl from one side of the beach to the other. Lo and behold, the girl was Leslie Gore, and that's how the song got recorded. It had nothing to do with the work of publishers or anything like that. It became clear to me even then that the more personal contacts you had, the less you had to depend on publishers. The chances were that if you could meet the right people, the artist, the artist's manager, the producer of the record, whoever, you had a much better shot than if you let your song pile up with the thousands of other songs that were piling up with the publisher. So I wrote a few more songs and the turning point in my career came when I was about eighteen. Having had Leslie Gore's hit, "Sunshine, Lollipops and Rainbows," and then having another hit with her called "California Nights," I walked into her producer's office with the third song that I had written for her, hoping that this would also be a winner. The record producer let me wait in his office for about an hour and a half before he saw me. When I got into the office, I said to him, "I always thought you made me wait because I never had a hit song and I was a 'nobody,' but now that I have a hit song, you still made me wait an hour and a half." I didn't play the song; I left, and I haven't written another song "just for the heck of it" since then. I realized that that was not the business for me. My whole approach to the music business after that was directed to getting projects, to finding movies, to doing a show . . . whatever. What I learned in terms of basic songwriting (and this is not now background; this is more philosophy for today) is that most artists, if they're even accepting outside songs, stick to a certain writer. In order to have that artist continue using their songs, those writers are making deals whereby they're practically selling their souls. Therefore, it's not the most lucrative business to go into if you're just going to be a "writer." If you think there are millions in just writing songs without either producing the record or without being the artist, or somehow having more control, you would be wrong. I don't think you could find a writer to agree that just writing songs is a lucrative business . . . because it isn't, and it's becoming an increasingly difficult business because the number of artists who are looking for outside songs is dwindling. And, of course, as you know, practically no song gets recorded without making some sort of a deal. All of a sudden someone walks in and says, "Well, we'd love to do the song; however, you're going to have to lose some of your 'this' or some of your 'that.' So, by the time you take . . .

AHS: You must have read my book. . . .

HAMLISCH: By the time you take your royalty and you divide it among everyone who was involved, either artistically or not artistically, it becomes rough. So my idea was to circumvent all of that and to determine how I could best get into what I really wanted to do, which was writing Broadway shows. When I was nineteen years old, no one was offering me Broadway shows to write! So I became a rehearsal pianist for Broadway shows and stuff like that. Around the age of twenty-two, I was sent to play at a party for the producer Sam Spiegel. He was producing a film called

The Swimmer and he liked the way I played the party and asked me if I was a composer. He showed me the script, and I went home, and, sight unseen, I wrote the theme music that I thought would be right for that script. He liked it, and he sent me to Hollywood, and that was my first picture. And again, it had nothing to do with agents or publishers. I was at the right place at the right time.

AHS: You saw to it you were at the right place by taking the job as a rehearsal pianist.

HAMLISCH: Whatever. I find that the letters I receive from people who are trying desperately to make it in the music business usually go like this: "Hello. I'm from Iowa and I want to know what I'm doing wrong." And I say, "The first thing that you're doing wrong is that you're not in New York, Los Angeles, or Nashville." I have no faith at all in a song that is just sent to a publisher or to an artist, because I know myself that I get tons of stuff here, and I'm not even an artist, but people want to know my opinion. The truth is you don't have time to listen, and even if you do, let's face it, what are you going to do? Number one, you've got to get to the source; you kind of need a publisher, but what you really need to do is to find the artist, to crack into that wall somehow, and to make sure that at least you were heard on that song. The other thing that I think is very important is to write songs that suit many artists. If you pin all your hopes on a song that would be great for Streisand and if you don't get Streisand, what happens? The song just dies? If the song dies 'cause Streisand said "no," then how good a song could it be? If the song doesn't have a life of its own beyond one artist, you're in trouble, because the minute that artist says "no," you're dead. As you can probably tell, I've been burned a lot. It's very funny; people think I'm a hit songwriter. I'm not. I've had only three or four hits in my life in terms of individual songs. I've had hit projects and hit shows, which I much prefer for about ninety-seven reasons. Because the truth is that the trip of getting a hit song is so fraught with glass on the road that by the time you get to number one, I'm not sure any more how much joy there's left in Mudville. You know what I mean. It's a difficult trail. So I tend to say to upcoming writers: don't make your goal to be just a hit writer. If that's your goal, to just have a hit, then you're going to be in a lot of trouble, because you're not going to be able to sustain yourself financially. There aren't enough pieces of the pie to go around. Get into it in a whole way. I mean get into it as a producer, as an artist. . . . To get into it just as a writer alone is very difficult. And most writers, even hit writers, even writers who've had a lot of hits, tend to agree with me. I would recommend to you, even though you want to get writers that have had hits or that are well known to the public-at-large for your book, that you should interview people who have had hits, but who are unknown to the public . . . real journeymen writers. Yes, Neil Diamond has had hits, but how many hits would he have had if he had been just a writer and not recorded them? I'm always very jealous of, say, Billy Joel. Billy Joel can write whatever he wants to and he knows it will be recorded. Who will record it? Billy Joel! There's no problem. I am always the middleman. I'm the guy who writes it and then has to wait and see who will record it. And I could write what I thought was the greatest song in the world, but if it gets turned down by fifteen artists, it couldn't be the greatest song in the world. Now, if I were Billy Joel, I could just record it tomorrow and it might be a big hit. So, therefore, it's a very difficult road you follow if you are just a writer. I no longer even try going down that road. I don't even write songs per se. I have just written (because my publisher said *please*) two songs out of context, meaning just for the heck of it. These will probably be the only songs I write this year that won't be part of a project such as a show or a movie. So I would suggest to you to see writers who basically do this for a living and nothing else, because I'm very lucky. If you took the money that I made as a "writer of songs" . . . there isn't much of it. Where I made my money was in writing shows, writing movies, and getting involved that way. My actual income from songwriting without those other sources is nearly nil. I got frustrated writing songs for people and then having them constantly either turned down or recorded as other than an "A"-side single. One of the things that's happening in the business now is that there are not so much songs as there are records. I think you should talk about that in your book, about the difference between what a good song is and a good record. Ideally, when a good song and a good record come together, you've got something. Earth, Wind and Fire's last big hit was just incredible, as was "Takin' It to the Streets"—you know, Mike McDonald and The Doobies. A good song stands on its own. You play it—it's a good song. A good record, where the record is just fantastically produced, can be made out of a bad song. I mean, you can have a bad song that is so brilliantly produced that it goes number one because the production values of the record are just incredible. The ideal is to have a good song with a good production. You can start with a good song, and what happens many times is you get a bad production and the song will not become the "A"-side single. They could have gone into the studio thinking

the song is going to be the "A" side, but by the time they finish
at two o'clock in the morning, after making the record, they
conclude, "This just doesn't groove, man; we'll go with the
other song." Well, if you've been the writer who's thinking
you're going to have the "A"-side single and, because of nothing
to do with you, the record just didn't come out well, then what
do you do? There are so many pitfalls that I finally gave up. I
didn't have the stomach for it. I really didn't. I just didn't have
what it took to continue. If I had a son and he said, "Daddy, I
want to be a songwriter," I'd say, "Never; forget it!" But if he
said, "I want to do that *and* I want to produce records," I'd say
"Fine!" Because it's becoming a closed shop. I could write the
greatest song for Stevie Wonder, but what would it matter?
Stevie Wonder does not record outside songs. By the time you
take away Stevie Wonder and you take away Neil Diamond,
Elton John, Billy Joel. . . . Of course, there are always some
people who are going to listen. There are always the Barry
Manilows of the sect, but because there are fewer of them, the
competition has become ferocious. Start looking at records and
see whose names are on what records. It's very interesting. In
fact, take a look at the "B" side and see whose name is on it.
You'll see a lot of familiar names. [Laughter] I would say for a
writer to help himself today, the first thing I would do is try to
have him sign an AGAC contract. I think that is always helpful.
Because, at least, then you can't get totally overrun by the
whims and wishes of everyone else. I think an AGAC contract
is at least a strong, good, minimum basic agreement.

AHS: But most publishers won't sign them.

HAMLISCH: Right; well, that's the other thing. Or then just be in it for the
thrill and not for the money. Just be in it for the fact that your
song got recorded . . . Wow!

AHS: You didn't start off at eleven as an accomplished musician. I
understand that you've had some extensive formal training.

HAMLISCH: Yes, I was a Julliard student, and I studied and everything like
that. But I could play pretty good already at eleven or twelve.

AHS: How important do you think technical training is?

HAMLISCH: I don't think it's important at all. I think it helps if you can put
it down on paper, because you can save some money there. But
I mean most kids pick up a guitar, they learn a couple of chords,
and they start drifting away on their own. I sometimes find that
being able to play well can be a hindrance, in fact, because you
can't "get down" on the piano. Trying to write rock-'n'-roll on
the piano is not an easy thing, you know. It's easier on the
guitar, or a Fender Rhodes piano, or something like that. But I
don't think it matters how well you play. I think having a good

lyricist is very important. I think the big change in music is that lyrics have become much more important in the last twenty years, and having the good hook can be very helpful. When I write, I write to a lyric. But I really think that it would be very helpful if, in your book, you include among the big-name people the journeymen writers, the people who write songs for a living. I think it would be interesting to include some interviews with writers who have not yet made it or have had very scattered success. . . . What are they doing? They've got to be doing something else besides just writing.

AHS: Right. As a matter of fact, I am interviewing a young client of mine this afternoon who just had interest from a record company. He's been supporting himself writing jingles and playing background.

HAMLISCH: Right. It's not an easy task.

AHS: Did you ever do any of that to support yourself?

HAMLISCH: I was a rehearsal pianist for Broadway, and then I became a dance-music consultant, and then I played for ballet schools, and I just kept doing it that way, but I never played in a band or anything like that; that wasn't my thing.

AHS: Was there anybody in your career that you felt helped you a lot?

HAMLISCH: Well, Quincy Jones was very helpful because he went for that song and he was very friendly and very nice. It's nice to meet somebody whose first reaction to a song after they like it isn't "Okay, we've gotta have this and we gotta have that." It would be nice if we could at least have a drink first. It's a very funny thing. I'm not in the business of getting records. The songs that I've had recorded are mostly from movies and shows. To get individual songs recorded requires peddling, and I don't want to peddle songs. You see, the beauty of being Billy Joel is that when you write something, you know it's going to come out if you want it to come out. That's what I do with shows. I know if I write a show and we get a producer, I know on a certain date it's going to be there, and I'm thrilled about that.

AHS: I understand that. One of the points I've made in the book is that if you're not a singer-songwriter, it's very tough.

HAMLISCH: Very tough. I recommend it to no one. I don't care how talented you are. If you're that talented, write a show. If you've got ten great songs, write a show, because at least then it's yours. You're one of the owners.

AHS: You mentioned that you have a publisher. I don't want to pry. . . .

HAMLISCH: Chappell.

AHS: Oh, you work with Chappell. Do you own your own copyrights?

HAMLISCH: Nope. I own some of them, not all of them.

AHS: A piece?

HAMLISCH: A piece of it. Right.

AHS: I would think that Marvin Hamlisch today would own his own copyrights, but those were show tunes . . . you have to give a taste. . . .

HAMLISCH: Yes. Right.

AHS: That is really a problem today for youngsters. They've been taught don't give up your publishing. You have to give to get today . . . at least while you're paying your dues.

HAMLISCH: You're always paying your dues. I know writers who have written big hit songs and have been offered annual advances or guarantees from publishers of no more than $100,000. . . . That sounds like a lot of money, but if that's it after having big hit songs, it's not worth it.

AHS: Publishers are not known to be overly generous.

HAMLISCH: Also, publishers are not doing what publishers used to do. Publishers used to be the people who went from door to door selling the songs and getting records. Publishers basically to me now are huge collection agencies. I mean they just get the checks and then they send you the money.

AHS: In other words, you're questioning, with Harry Fox and with ASCAP and BMI, why do you need a publisher? I mean, they're going to collect most of your money for you.

HAMLISCH: Right, because . . . I guess it's your dream that occasionally, once out of a thousand times, they'll say, "Dionne Warwick's recording; I can get it to her" . . . boom! And they go and they get it. For that one out of a thousand, you stick with them. The reason I'm being down on all this is because I think up to now there has been a tremendous distortion of what young kids think is a glamorous business. Now it may be glamorous for the Billy Joels—I think it's very glamorous—and even then it's hard because they still have to tour like crazy and they have to get on the bus and keep going.

AHS: Do you use an agent when you're doing motion pictures?

HAMLISCH: Yes. I have an agent. That's one thing I do believe in. I have an agent for movies and I have an agent who takes care of me for public appearances. I have been able to divide it up a little bit, and I think that's very important. I don't think one person can do it all. I think it's good to surround yourself with experts. Yes, they get a piece of the pie, but that can be very well worth it. . . . And always have a lawyer around.

AHS: Amen!

HAMLISCH: Always be one step away from a lawyer.

AHS: You've been more than generous with your time. Thank you very much.

INTERVIEW WITH
BARBARA MANDRELL

Consummate musician, established recording artist, television star, peerless performing artist, and best-selling author, Barbara Mandrell has won more awards than can be listed here. She is nevertheless exploring new areas in which to excel.

AHS: Barbara, the title of this chapter is "My Way." I wonder if you could give our readers a brief synopsis of what "your way" was.

MANDRELL: First, I think it was just loving music and wanting to sing music and play music and be a part of anything that *made* music, and it never occurred to me to be doing what I'm doing today or to make *money* doing it. You know that old saying "You have to love this business to be in it"? I really think that's true. At first I just wanted to learn to play instruments. I watched a friend of mine play steel guitar for Merle Haggard. I didn't want to be a singer; I just fell in love with that instrument. I was eleven years old and I asked him to teach me. I started studying, and God had given me an ear and it came sort of easy for me. I had some previous experience with music, because my mother was a music teacher. She taught piano, and she taught me to play the accordion and to read music when I was five. I learned to read music before I learned to read "See Spot run," but I never thought of it as a way of making a living; it was always something I did for the love of it. Then, later, especially as a teenager, I found that it was a good way to make money to buy clothes and to have extra spending money.

AHS: How did you make money as a teenager? It wasn't through records.

MANDRELL: No. I was lucky. I was in a little band. It's as I often tell young people today: be organized, be rehearsed, know your keys, know your numbers, and be as professional as you can, and then find a group that appeals to you, that you think's good, and ask for an audition. Find somebody to work with, or create your own group. I remember in my high-school days, there were always teenage bands that played for dances. Whether it's a dance or a PTA meeting or a church function or whatever, the primary teacher in the music business, as far as I'm concerned, is experience. It's marvelous if you have the time and have the opportunity to go to a university and study music, and I'm not belittling that—that's marvelous and I wish I had that sort of knowledge—but if you want to be a performer, the only school is the school of experience. You learn the most by actually doing. There are so many things that happen to me today— situations that I find myself in—where I know that the only reason I am able to do the appropriate thing in a way that seems to come naturally and that works is because I've been at it so many years.

AHS: You mean, you're not an overnight success?

MANDRELL: I started when I was eleven. I also do a lot of watching. I watch people that I work with. A lot of people won't watch a performer they don't particularly like. I watch every performer that I haven't seen before, whether it's the opening act or the closing act. I watch because I learn by watching. I can learn from a newcomer in the business as well as from veterans. I can learn because you are dealing with a creative subject when you're dealing with music. No two people are alike, and if they're worth their salt, I can learn from them. You sometimes learn what *not* to do as well as what *to* do. I think in the beginning I did it all for the "love of"; now, I am a quote "businesswoman" and I do it for the love of and the profit of, because, unfortunately, sometimes profit is a gauge of success. You know, how well are you doing? How many records are you selling? How many people are you drawing? . . . And that sort of thing. But that love of has to be first, and that's where the heart comes from. I did an eight-day tour one time about four years ago. When I got home, I went into the hospital—I was nearly dead and I didn't even know it was pneumonia. You know, that old thing of "the show must go on"—that's not because somebody *said* it; that's because you love the business and you have a feeling for the audience and you have a feeling for the whole atmosphere of being a performer, and somehow or other, whatever's within you makes you do it.

AHS: I think most people don't realize that Barbara Mandrell had a professional life before EMI, MCA, and ABC. You had an earlier record deal that I recall. The world would certainly not know about it. That must have been a disappointment to you. How did it come about, and how did you react to the fact that nothing happened?

MANDRELL: At first it was a joy just to get a record deal—especially with a major label—but I was really lost in the shuffle, although it never discouraged me. I never had any doubt that it was going to continue, but I'm like everyone else, I get impatient, and I sort of felt like *I* knew I had something to offer. I just wanted the other people who controlled my destiny, as a record label seems to do sometimes, to have as much faith in me as *I* had. I would get on the phone and I would call the disc jockeys and do anything I could think of to make progress. There were times when I was first starting out—my father and I have always been in business together—that we really went through his funds just to pay the bills and to have food and to pay for the diesel for the bus, but I *never*—and I think this is the most important of all the things I could tell newcomers, because it's not press, because it's from my heart and from knowing—I can honestly say, I *never* doubted for one minute that I'd be doing what I'm doing today. I may not have known the path I would take or exactly what the story would be as it unfolded, but I never doubted.

AHS: How did the first record deal with CBS come about?

MANDRELL: Well, each artist has a different story, but if you really analyze each story, you find a lot of similarities. A friend of mine, Gordon Terry, was singing in a small club in Printer's Alley in Nashville. I was living with him and his wife at the time; they were old friends of mine and I couldn't afford my own place. He was appearing and she just said, "C'mon, let's go down and watch Gordon tonight," and we went down there and he asked me to come up and sing, and the club owner liked what he heard and he booked me in there for a week. During that week, different people within the industry—musicians and various people—began to talk a little bit and pretty soon record producers came in to see me. One night there were, I think, representatives from four major labels, and Billy Sherrill of Columbia Records was one of them, and I signed the Columbia contract. It was no big contract, but it was a big label, and it was a chance to make records and to at least have people hear me. It was a shot; it was a chance. I was sitting on top of the world then, but I very quickly found out that just having a record doesn't make for success. Everything happened very slowly for me; I think we're all so impatient today. As a beginner, if you had offered me an overnight smash-hit record—you know, first record out, big hit—I would have said, "Yes, give it to me." But in retrospect I think it was marvelous the way things happened for me, because everything happened very slowly. People within country music knew who Barbara Mandrell was before I had a number-one record, so they weren't going into record stores and saying, "I want such-and-such a song; I don't know who the girl is.". . . You know, sometimes a record gets in front of the artist. I had to *crawl* a lot before I was able to walk in this business, and I think it did two things: it helped establish me on a solid foundation as far as my ability went, and it also made the public more aware of me. Of course, the television show has changed a lot of that; a lot of people have now heard of me who had never heard of me before.

AHS: But you were established before the television show happened.

MANDRELL: Yes. In fact, I won Entertainer of the Year on a Tuesday night and came out to L.A. on the following Sunday to start the show.

AHS: But when things didn't work out on the first record deal and you didn't feel that the record company was doing right by you, you didn't just sit back and lament. You raised hell!

MANDRELL: No! I came off a number-one record and I said I want off the label because I didn't feel I was being treated right. I thought I was a *very* small fish in a big pond, and that I was being very much overlooked. I think no matter what career you choose, but *especially* in the music business, positive thinking is very important. You must never listen to the people saying, "It's too tough; you don't want to do this" or "It's too hard to achieve" or "There are too many people trying for record contracts"— you cannot give any credence to that kind of garbage. It doesn't mean that you walk around being cocky; it simply means that within your inner self, your own feelings about yourself, you believe in yourself and you know that ultimately you will have success. If you don't have that, if you don't have the guts, the determination, and the belief in yourself, you might as well forget it and save yourself the trouble, because you'll never make it.

AHS: Do you feel there are any things in your career that you would do differently if you had to do them all over again? Are there any mistakes that you made? Are there any things you would do differently?

MANDRELL: No. I mean, I've made some mistakes, but I don't think I've made any major career mistakes, because—this is going to sound very philosophical—I followed my instincts, and I surrounded myself with wise people, starting with my father. I didn't have to worry about being swindled or misled or someone choosing things for the wrong reasons. I've been fortunate with my record producers. My lucky breaks have been the people in my life, and one steel-guitar player named Lloyd Green, who's a session musician in Nashville. He is the man who spoke to Billy Sherrill and said, "You've got to go see this girl playing in the Alley . . . she sings, she plays all these instruments, go see her!" After I signed the Columbia deal, I said to him, "How can I ever repay you?" He told me that when he came to Nashville, he was making a living as a shoe salesman, and some guys in the session work helped him, and he asked the same question, and he said he was told that by helping somebody else you sort of repay your debt. There are a lot of crummy people in our business, but the majority of our people care about each other and they help young talent. That's why I get a little up in arms when people belittle show-business personalities and say that they're selfish and self-centered. I think a lot of them try to put back a little bit of what they take out. I've been fortunate in being around good people most of the time, and wise enough to stay away from the ones that were not good people. But I . . .

AHS: That's a little bit what the book is about—how to choose the right people. . . .

MANDRELL: I was approached to do my own session in Nashville and pay for it, but at that point in my life, Merle Travis, who wrote "Sixteen Tons," said to this person, "Aw, c'mon. . . ." People watched out for me, and I had the time to watch out for me, too. I sort of would take each step as it came, or each opportunity, and sort of stand back and look at it and think, Now, should I do this or should I not? Would this be a mistake? . . . And God gives you horse sense, you know, and you just kind of look at the situation. You think, Does it make sense for *me*? I mean, I'm the one that's singing—should I go in and pay for the session? No! If you want me, *you* pay for the session, and if it sells any records, then you give me some money; if it doesn't you don't. Just my horse sense told me that. But unfortunately some people are conned. I think young people are so anxious and so eager that they don't want to take things slowly. I took them so slowly, not necessarily by choice, that it was a struggle just meeting the bills. You beat your brains out and do four or six shows a day at fairs and Vegas and lounges, and have nothing really to show for it as far as profit, but I didn't mind because for some reason I knew that was what I had to do to get where I wanted to be.

AHS: You're highly respected among the professionals in the industry, not only for your vocal talents, but also as a musician. Do you have any sense of how important that was in your development or how important it was to your career?

MANDRELL: In my case, I think it was very important, because I'm not the greatest singer in the world—and I think the fact that I'm a musician and I'm a woman made me different. You see, each of us needs to be unique. That's a very important factor.

AHS: In being successful?

MANDRELL: If you sing just like Ella Fitzgerald, if you sing just like Roy Acuff, we don't need you . . . we've got those people. You've got to be whoever you are and be special and have something to contribute, and if you do, there's room for you and nobody's going to throw you out. I think the fact that I played the instruments and that I had all the years of experience—I had nine years of performing before I ever had a chance to record—was a big factor in my success. I've heard kids say, "Well, I've been playing music, but, you know, I *only* play down at the Elks Lodge," or "I played in a thing over at the city park," like it's nothing. . . . It's *everything*!

AHS: Have you ever had an inclination to write your own songs? To express yourself through writing?

MANDRELL: I really am interested in writing, but I've done very little . . . not even enough to mention. I found that when I did achieve something—you know, to actually finish a tune and record it and everything—it was because I was in a unique situation, where I didn't have anything else to do. I think at this point in my life I probably can't write, because I am too occupied— maybe later. I find that to write I have to be not busy and not preoccupied.

AHS: Are you attuned to the prevalence of singer-songwriters in the business today?

MANDRELL: Absolutely. I was lucky with the instruments and being a woman; it made me different. But if you can write and create your own songs, and if you have a gift of voice, something that makes you sound different, to sing those creations with, I think that is a foot in the door with a record label. But so what if you get a recording contract; so what if you have a hit record; where do you go from there? You better make darn sure you know what to do when you hit that stage. What are they going to do if they can't do something when they hit the stage? You might as well sit there and listen to a record. Now that's my own personal viewpoint, and a lot of people disagree with that, but that's why I say don't underestimate working in drama class in school and working in choir in school. All these things that seem so insignificant are enormously important. I can think back to my school days—I was the first one to raise my hand when it was an oral book report for English, because I wanted to perform, to get up in front of somebody and have their attention. If it was a written book report, I was lucky if it got in on time—and that's the performer in me. Now, as a recording artist, I find I love going into the studio, because it demands something different from me. You have to concentrate on audio, strictly on what those people are going to hear and whether it is commercial—all of those things.

AHS: How do you screen songs, Barbara? How do you decide what you're going to sing, since you don't write most of your songs?

MANDRELL: First impression, really. I've never really thought about this . . . first impression. If I do say so myself, I have a real good ability to listen as a fan. The mistake so many people who are gifted make is the mistake of playing over people's heads or playing things that are non-commercial. I think I have a good ear for what's commercial. Is that what the public will buy? And I don't look for a ballad; I don't look for an up-tempo; I don't look for a positive or negative; I just look for the *magic* in the song. Is it a possibility in the commercial sense?

AHS: This is a tough question. To what extent are songs screened before you ever hear them? I imagine hundreds and hundreds of songs are sent to you and to your producer, and you certainly don't have the time to listen to all of them.

MANDRELL: Okay. I don't sit there and listen myself, so this is based strictly on what people tell me. I'm told that there are many, many of those grocery-store cardboard boxes full of tapes. I'm also told, and I believe, that they are all listened to. Those that surface as having potential and as songs that I should listen to are given to me and I listen to them. At the point I am now in my career, time's the most valuable commodity—and you have to learn how to delegate authority.

AHS: As a rule, you do ten songs on an album. How many songs do you select those ten from? From the hundreds that are submitted, how many ultimately do you listen to in choosing the ten? Ball park figure? I'm not going to hold you to this.

MANDRELL: Well, because I've got a good producer, I would say I probably only listen personally to about thirty, maximum.

AHS: That's about thirty out of hundreds and hundreds?

MANDRELL: Hundreds and hundreds. Young people and older people alike will send me material, and I listen or I make sure it's listened to. What bothers me is that a songwriter may have what I perceive to be a real potential, but *that* particular song may not be it for me. . . . And there is no way to tell them not to be discouraged— that established songwriters send me songs that are not it for me.

AHS: I know—I've sent you those. . . .

MANDRELL: It's hard to choose the words. I think this is important to say to songwriters: don't be discouraged because a certain artist or a certain producer did not take your song if you believe in it, because I—and it's true of every artist—personally turned down hit songs. I think the one that I most regret was a great country hit called "What a Difference You've Made in My Life" that Ronnie Milsap did. I turned it down. I thought it sounded like a Gospel song. . . . I said, "Yeah, when I do my Gospel album, maybe" and then it went on to be a very big hit for Ronnie Milsap. I think every singer you talk to can tell you about a hit song that they turned down. More important than anything— more important than anything I can think of—talent is only 40 percent, maybe—you have to *believe*.

AHS: It's that attitude, plus all of the hard work that you barely mentioned.

MANDRELL: The work is unbelievable, and I wouldn't want any young person to think it's glamorous. It's not a glamorous business. It is *not*; it's just like anything you do. It's not handed to you; you have to make it happen. I don't believe there's so much luck in this business. There's something to be said about meeting the right people and being in the right place at the right time, but I think you make your own luck.

AHS: They say, Barbara, the harder you work, the luckier you get.

MANDRELL: I believe it.

AHS: I think that's your story, really.

MANDRELL: And I also believe that an important factor was that I tried so hard along the way to earn whatever love and affection the audience gave me. I had this need to feel that I could earn their respect. I used to love being the opening act—the challenge of having the audience, who came to see whoever the headliner was, leave talking about you because your show was so good, your music was so good, and you were so together. The next time around, they're going to come back to see *you*.

AHS: Of course you'll not be fronting for another headline act if you're that good.

MANDRELL: Well, another thing—here again I'm skipping around—I'm probably not supposed to tell this, but I'm going to tell it—I don't care—I've had PR people with my record label say that they've had some of my fellow acts on the label complain that I get such good PR with the magazines and the newspapers, etc. Now I'm going back years ago, too, not just today, and they've said that they told them the truth, and the truth was the reason I got good PR was because when they could arrange for an interview or an appearance for me, I did it. A lot of people will have a little bit of success and a little bit come their way and they take it for granted and they feel "I don't need that; I don't need to do interviews." Well, I genuinely feel that I'm fortunate to have a big spread on me in a magazine or an interview on a television show or on a radio station. . . . It's very valuable. I used to—I wish I had the time today, I don't—really visit the radio stations, and they were kind enough to interview me. When I had my first hit on rock stations, I started all over again like a beginner. I knew the country jocks on the major stations, but now I did something like six cities in four days, going to rock stations. Here I was, a fairly major force in country music having to start from letter "A" again with the rock stations, but I think if you think of yourself as a working-class person—and believe me, if you're going to be in show business, that's exactly what you are, a workin' man—you must pay your dues. People pay dues for a reason. It's not because you have to do it to earn the money; it's because you have to do it to *learn your trade*.

AHS: Well, this interview certainly isn't for mass media, so I must assume it's for me, and I thank you very much.

MANDRELL: Is any of that going to work for you?

AHS: I think it's going to work for me beautifully. I thank you very much.

MANDRELL: Thank you.

INTERVIEW WITH
BILL WYMAN

As co-founder and bass player for the Rolling Stones, Bill Wyman needs no introduction. An active and successful record producer, songwriter, solo artist, and composer of film scores, he also enjoys many interests outside the world of music.

AHS: Bill, after a very solid and enduring career, one would think you would be content to rest on your laurels, yet you seem to have chosen to start an entire new career as a solo artist and songwriter. What is your motivation?

WYMAN: In the Rolling Stones, I'm really a bass player, and apart from contributing to arrangements in the recording studio and various business decisions and artistic decisions within the band, there's very little else I can do creatively within the Rolling Stones. I find that my frustrations are building up regarding ideas I have musically for songs of a different kind than the Rolling Stones record. I always found it very difficult to find an outlet for that thing inside me . . . that energy; so one alternative was to go out and try to sell songs to other people, but I didn't think that was going to be very successful, because the obvious reaction would be, "Well, if the song's that good, why aren't the Rolling Stones doing it?" But I thought, Well, I may as well do it myself and see what happens, and I did that reasonably unsuccessfully in the mid-seventies. The records were pleasant to make, and although I had a great time and gained a lot of experience arranging, recording, and working in the studio, they weren't the right kind of songs, and I wasn't singing very well, and I concluded that that was not the avenue to explore. Then I started becoming interested in writing music for descriptive things. I was thinking maybe I could get a small TV special on Stonehenge or some archaeological program like that and I could do the music and slowly work up until maybe I could do a movie score one day. So I started writing descriptive music, and along came a song (completely wrong) called "(Si, Si), Je Suis un Rock Star," and everybody tried to persuade me to record it even though I didn't really want to do solo recording any more. However, everybody was so persistent that it could be a hit (and I did have a gut feeling it might be) that I decided, Okay, well then maybe I won't do another album, maybe I'll just do a single or something and pop that off and see what happens. That's what I did, and it was a success, and consequently there was a need to do another single and then an album, and so on. I'm in that situation now. About the same time, I was offered the opportunity to score the music for *Green Ice,* which I accepted. Suddenly I found that there were a lot of avenues I could explore musically that I hadn't thought about before, such as songwriting for other people with another writer, for instance, and starting to build a music publishing company. More avenues opened relative to various other hobbies that I had. It's just progressed, and of course I *am* a workaholic. I suppose the main reason, to answer your question in a nutshell, is that the Stones don't work as frequently as they did five or ten years ago, and I do have more time on my hands to venture into other things. I do find now that my ventures are successful and that there is a *result* instead of just a chance that something might happen. Now I can see that I'm doing that thing for *that* movie, and I'm doing this thing for *this* album, and I'm doing *another* for a book, and so on. There's always an end product, which so far has been commercially successful.

AHS: Have you noticed an appreciable change in the industry over the last five or ten years, especially from the point of view of somebody who's trying to get a toehold; do you find it more difficult now than it was then?

WYMAN: Well, I find it difficult, yes, and I have a name. I would prefer not to be a name and hope to be successful just on material, but the name is valuable as far as getting TV shows and articles written and going on radio shows and things, but for the average newcomer to music, I think it's *really* tough because of the depression, mainly caused, I think, not by lack of money in the kids' pockets, but probably by the purchasing of tape cassette machines. Who's going to go out and buy the top thirty singles for $30 or whatever it costs, when they can sit at home and tape them off the radio in an hour? . . .

AHS: I know . . . I've fathered two infringers of my own!

WYMAN: [Laughter] Which I don't think really is that bad, because I think if the kids particularly like an artist, then they will go out and buy that artist's album. But they certainly are more selective in what they buy these days. They just don't go in and say, "I want the latest So-and-So album," just because of the name. They really have to like it now.

AHS: Do you feel that the advent of the singer-songwriter, artists who primarily sing only their own songs, has dried up the marketplace for writers who don't perform themselves? Do you think that you as a songwriter would have greater difficulty in placing songs with artists today because they sing their own material?

WYMAN: I think you have to look for the right publishing company. Many publishing companies will not work on trying to get cover versions of songs. Most artists record their own material as much as possible because it's very lucrative, but there is, at least in Europe, which I'm more familiar with than America, still quite a fair number of songwriters who have their material covered by other people and who are not performers or recording artists as such. I think that some of these terrible things that go on, like the Eurovision Song Contest, which I think is really very badly done, do give people a chance of having a song put forward. . . . In England they usually have about six or seven hundred entries from amateur songwriters which get whittled down to thirty, and then twelve and then six, and then one is chosen. So people do get the chance, you know, somebody's mom living in Halifax . . . no, I better not say Halifax . . . [laughter] . . . you'll think it's Canada . . . all right, Huddersfield, in northern England, can write a song, and it could become the biggest record in Europe. A lot of songs are recorded in Europe by people who didn't necessarily write them.

But home recording does hurt the recording companies, who lose an enormous amount of revenue and therefore don't have the money to experiment in other music and new artists. New artists find it very difficult to get recording contracts and advances to buy good equipment and go on the road. That's the problem.

AHS: I find most of the record companies are hurting very badly, or are at least crying "poor boy" and whittling down their deals. The president of a major record company told me today that he made eight deals with new artists in the last nine months, which is really very, very few.

WYMAN: Yes, but don't you think that's also caused by the artists over the last fifteen years "wising up" to what is available in record companies, because in the sixties, when we started, the average artist off the street was getting 1 percent and 2 percent—3 percent, if you were lucky. . . . The Beatles were on 1 percent, I believe, when they first started . . . for five years! We managed to get about 6 percent out of Decca. Now, even a band off the street is going to go in and ask for 12 percent or 10 percent.

AHS: In today's marketplace, I don't think they're going to get it. Maybe a group . . .

WYMAN: They have in the last ten years.

AHS: Oh, in the last ten years, yes. As a matter of fact, it was going up to twelve and fourteen, but this week [laughter], this year, it's gone into reverse.

WYMAN: But the record companies in those days did make an awful lot of money, and although the artist didn't get so much, the record companies were able to experiment and take chances on new acts and now they can't, because everybody's going for the top price when they do a deal.

AHS: I think you've really zeroed in and pinpointed it. I couldn't agree with you more.

WYMAN: It's a shame for the new acts . . . all the young kids out there. . . .

AHS: They have to work harder at it.

WYMAN: Then you get the new little indie labels coming out. In England there are an awful lot of them. Kids just record their single in a back room on a TEAC four-track or an eight-track or something they can borrow for the day or rent for the day, and they go in with a record like they did in the fifties . . . the way all the early rock-'n'-rollers did it, like Eddie Cochran and people like that. Gene Vincent and Buddy Holly went into garages and just cut a dub and sent it to a deejay in those days, and he played it and if it was a hit, then suddenly they had a recording contract. Now they take it to small independent labels like Stiff Records or people like that; there was one just a few months ago who had a really, really big hit home-dubbed, so there's still a chance there for it, but you've really got to come up with the goods now.

AHS: When you said you really have to come up with "the goods," what did you have in mind? Do you believe that the song is the prime factor as opposed to the performance?

WYMAN: That's a tough one. . . . I think a *great* song will always come through. I think an artist, somebody clever, can do a mediocre song, an average song, and make it a great record, as is proven by the Kim Carnes record "Bette Davis Eyes," which was recorded by Jackie DeShannon about five years ago and was a very mediocre, ordinary kind of song as it was rendered. I like it—it's pleasant—because now I know it, but I wouldn't have really gone out and bought it then. Listening to it now, it sounds quite interesting, but the way it was done by Kim Carnes made it a fantastic record, and it made the song sound even better then it probably was. It can go both ways, but I don't think a *bad* song can ever be a hit, a real bad one. . . . Well, there I go; there are are some [laughter]. . . .

AHS: [Laughter] But, in general . . .

WYMAN: The comedy value of the bad ones gets in . . .

AHS: I imagine a lot of aspiring artists and writers try to get your ear. Do you perceive anything in the attitude of today's new artists that differs from the attitude of artists five or ten years ago? What I'm really asking is, do you think they're doing anything wrong?

WYMAN: Yes, they're trying to make records before they tour, before they go out and play in front of the public. They think, Oh, let's get four good-looking guys together . . . he can play bass, he can play guitar, he can play drums, and he can sing, and let's go and make a record. They make a record, and then suddenly it's in the charts and they've never played in front of the public. I'm not saying *everybody*, but it happens quite a lot these days. It doesn't really work that way. I think they have to go out there. Most of the really big acts that have come out over the last twenty years have actually worked a lot in front of the public before they made records . . . including the Rolling Stones. The Beatles were out there four years before they made a hit record; we were luckier than that, but we played an awful lot. We used to play two shows a day, you know, for months. A lot of bands just go in and make a record, have a hit, and then they can't follow it on stage. They go out on stage, and they're a disaster. That also helps to make touring more of a problem these days as well, because touring bands do not sell out, and everybody wants the front line. In the sixties, you'd do anything to go on the road and do a tour with a Roy Orbison or Chuck Berry or anybody that was touring England. You'd give your right arm to be sixth on the bill. We were fifth on the bill, the first tour we did with Little Richard, Bo Diddley, Everly Brothers, and so on, and we thought it was an amazing honor. If that was today and it was a new band that had just made a record like we had then, they'd say, "No, man, we don't want to go out with them; we want to headline our own tour" . . . then they go out there and they don't sell tickets. People don't go out to see bands unless they're really, really top bands, and they know they're going to get their money's worth. Today no one wants to be second on the bill to anybody else. There used to be package tours, but there don't seem to be so many of them now. We used to have four, five really good acts going out together. You could sell out and you could make money. Now you've got one average band backed by a local band, and it doesn't do the industry very much good at all. I saw Crystal Gayle in Australia, who I think is really good, I like her music and she makes great records. She was doing a show of her own in Australia, and she wasn't selling out. In Australia, for instance, people won't go to see a Crystal Gayle concert. Now if it had been Crystal Gayle and Dolly Parton or Crystal Gayle and Jerry Reed, it would have been sold out, but someone of that stature cannot sell out in places like France or Australia or Germany. They might in Nashville. And I felt really sorry for her, you know; it was obviously the mistake of the promoters and management, and it happens all the time. That doesn't help record sales either.

AHS: What I gather you're saying is that the new acts today are not as willing to pay their dues as . . .

WYMAN: They're not as humble as they should be, I don't think. It's the old adage, you know, you've got to starve before you can succeed, and all the great artists, like Otis Redding and Little Richard and Chuck Berry and Marvin Gaye and the Stones and the Beatles and so on and so on and so on, you can name them forever, all starved. . . . They all went through a real tough time at the beginning. They really had to work their asses, you know, to get there. In the seventies, particularly, it was so easy for people just to put a couple of musicians together and get a recording contract, have a hit record, and then . . . nothing.

AHS: I know; it was very easy to make deals then. It's no longer easy to make deals. Tell me, are you thinking now of writing songs for other people as well as for your own performance?

WYMAN: Yes. I think it's an interesting thing to do. I don't write music that is of Rolling Stones style, but I do think I can write songs for many other kinds of artists.

AHS: Do you target your songs? When you write a song, do you think, Hey, this would be great for So-and-So?

WYMAN: No. I just do it and see what it comes out like, and then I think, Oh, that sounds a bit like So-and-So, or maybe that one could have been good if I'd sent it to Ian Dury or whatever.

AHS: I'm going to ask you a kind of loaded question.

WYMAN: Go on then.

AHS: It's really not that bad. In preparing an album, you own album, under what, if any, circumstances would you consider performing somebody else's song?

WYMAN: Only if I like it enough to do a good job on it, really. I don't think of myself as a singer, you see, so my rendering of a song by somebody else would probably not be as good as they might hope. They'd probably sing better on the demo they would give me than I do. Then I have to think, Well, am I going to improve on it musically and get away with not singing it quite as well? . . . And most of the time I think to myself, No, I'm not. . . . [Laughter] So

I tend to stick to material that I find that I can sing successfully. On my new album, I tried a few ballads and things and they came out quite well, and people say, "Hey, he can sing after all," but I never practiced singing like I practiced playing bass and keyboards. I never do it, even in the bath, and you've *gotta* practice if you want to do it. Because I've never thought of myself as a singer and I never wanted to be a singer, I use my voice as an extension of my instrument really, I suppose, as another instrument in the music rather than as a solo thing, and sometimes it's quite difficult to get it together.

AHS: You've been described to me as a true Renaissance man, and I'm wondering to what extent do all your outside interests play a role in your music? You kind of anticipated me and mentioned it peripherally at the beginning of our discussion when you said your "other interests" have caused you to do things. I understand you're a photographer of some reputation. . . .

WYMAN: I wouldn't say "some reputation." I don't think I've got a reputation as a photographer yet, although I've had the opportunity to do a photo- and textbook of Chagall which is coming out shortly, which is very nice. It was a project, and I never had a photographic project before. I've always taken photos, but no one's ever asked me to do anything specifically for a project that was interesting. On my album I've got one song called "Nuclear Reaction," which is really, I suppose, a song about my interest in astronomy because it's factual . . . It's not nuclear *reactors*; it's *reaction*, which is, as we all know, what happens on the sun and in space, and I do talk about all the strange objects in space. I liked very much to do that, because it did express my interest in astronomy, for instance, but my other interests don't really get into my songs apart from the odd time like that. I mean space-sounding music is kind of interesting and it's been popular over the last ten years, so I found that one easy, but I couldn't really write a song about archaeology, could I? [Laughter]

AHS: [Laughter] I don't know; perhaps you could. . . .

WYMAN: [Singing] "I found her in a hole. . . ." [Laughter]

AHS: I don't know what part management has played in your career, or in the career of the Stones. Do you have any opinions or feelings about the necessity of management for new acts?

WYMAN: Yes, management's very important for new artists who are inexperienced in the business. The difficult thing to find is an honest one. I would say the majority are dishonest in varying degrees. Sometimes they're slightly dishonest, but if the group becomes big, the small dishonesty becomes a large one because it escalates with the earnings. Then you have the big dishonest managements that really tie everything up, and the group ends up with nothing after three years, which has happened to a lot of other bands in their careers. You just have to try and find the one you most trust and you think can do the best job for you, and you will always make mistakes. The Stones ended management in 1969 after two attempts and two failures, and since then we've had no management whatsoever, and we find that in our position we can adequately manage ourselves, but of course we do know the business a lot better now than we did in 1963 and '65, when we made the two signings and the two mistakes. It's very difficult to advise or suggest what to do. If you don't know the business, you've got to have somebody. Now we can employ anybody we want for any project we want, and that's a really good way of doing it. If we want a tour done, we employ a tour manager to organize it (or hire three and find out which one's the best), and if we want a cover done, we employ a photographer. If we want anything done like that, we employ a man for the job instead of a manager overseeing all that, because he really only has to follow your instructions anyway. It's strange in our business about management, because if you run any other business, I think I'm correct in saying, your manager works for you, looks after your business, and is responsible to you. In the music industry, it usually turns around after about three months, and you find that the artist is working for the manager, which is a very strange role, and he's not saying, "Would you like to do this show on Thursday night?" He's saying, "I have booked you for this show on Thursday night and you have to be there at 7:30," you know, and "You are on that television show and you will be going in the studio on Wednesday week." It's not an extension of the artist any more, generally speaking; it's a takeover of the artistic decisions, I think, that the artist should really make, and that's not very good for the artist. So you end up working for your manager, and you end up doing things you don't want to do, and going in directions that you don't want to go in as well, and being committed to doing things that you haven't agreed on in the first place. Then you get the frictions and the breakups of the groups and the managements, and the lawsuits and the things that keep you people in business. [Laughter] There's a strange thing in America about lawyers as well. I won't say they're dishonest, but they take percentages of things, don't they?

AHS: We don't.

WYMAN: I know *you* don't. That's why I employ your people to look after me, or one of your people, but many, many do. Many lawyers are very unreliable, and many of them have bad reputations. . . . Am I going to get myself shot here? . . . [Laughter]

AHS: [Laughter] No, because you're going to read it before it's printed, so you don't have to worry. . . .

WYMAN: There are a lot of dishonest lawyers in America.

AHS: I think you use the term "dishonest" almost synonymously with "overreaching" as opposed to actual dishonesty.

WYMAN: Yes.

AHS: I get that impression.

WYMAN: Well, you're probably right, because when somebody walks in and takes a cigarette without asking, I think of that as dishonest, or borrowing a book and never returning it. I mean it's nothing, but it's dishonest. Dishonesty to me includes something that's done without permission and, yes, it's a very general term the way I use it. It's not as heavy and as evil as it might sound or look on notepaper.

AHS: All those fellows who are taking percentages are hurting now because the deals aren't coming through from the record companies.

WYMAN: But even trying to settle things . . . I mean, the European lawyers, mainly English, 'cause I know more about them, are so tied up with their oaths and things that they will ask you (if there's something that they're not supposed to hear that's slightly dishonest), please don't tell them, and they're very, very reliable. They might not be the most efficient lawyers, but they are straightforward, and I would say, as far as principles are concerned, more honest than the average American lawyer, who will . . . (I'm saying honest and dishonest again) . . . who will be in on something for what he can get rather than looking after his client first, and then thinking of his salary. You know . . . "If I settle this lawsuit, I want 20 percent." You never get an English lawyer to say that. He will say, "You will get my fees and charges. They might be a bit expensive, but . . ." And sometimes lawyers and accountants as well, in the music industry in America, do try to get into the same situation as the manager does. That's the rest of what I mean by "dishonest."

AHS: That's my next question. . . .

WYMAN: They like to get involved for a piece of the action, rather than doing a specific job for specific expense and salary.

AHS: I was going to ask you whether you felt lawyers in this country tend to act as managers. . . .

WYMAN: Yes, I know people who have had lawsuits against other people for not being paid for records or for playing in a band, or someone ran off with the advance from the album, and so on, and the lawyers have said to them, "All right, I want that much of the action if you want me to proceed with it, and if I get it for you, you pay me that much," and guys have said, "Okay!" because, you know, a bird in the hand is worth two in the bush. You wouldn't have it that way dealing with it in England, for instance.

AHS: Don't you think that most of those situations arise where the client is bereft of funds and the attorney is taking a risk in expending his time and effort . . . and that would be his compensation?

WYMAN: Yes, sometimes.

AHS: I don't find that as distasteful in those circumstances as . . .

WYMAN: No, he's taking a risk.

AHS: You know, we do have a great deal of experience with not getting paid by artists, especially those who haven't made it or aren't able to make it. . . .

WYMAN: Artists have a lot of experience in not getting paid as well. [Laughter]

AHS: I'm sure they do. . . . [Laughter]

WYMAN: I think there's something on both sides. . . . [Laughter]

AHS: Do you look forward to getting into the business end of the music business?

WYMAN: Not really. I don't consider myself a businessman. I can make artistic decisions fairly adequately, and I can involve myself a little in the legal aspects, but I need experienced people to advise me and suggest what to go for if we're going to do a deal . . . what is possible, what isn't. I have to employ a lawyer to do a deal with a music company for a sound track. I've *no* idea of what's appropriate. I don't know whether I should get $5,000 or $500,000. I just don't know. I don't know what the percentages might be. They know better than I do. They've got similar clients and experience. I'm always ready to listen to professional advice. I mean, that's what I'm paying for when I employ a lawyer or a business consultant or whoever he might be to do a specific job. I'm paying for their advice and experience in a situation I'm not experienced in, so they're very necessary people and some of them do a wonderful job.

AHS: Thank you. You've been more than generous with your time.

nine

ALTERNATE PATHS TO GLORY

This chapter is both unnecessary and terribly necessary. It's point is to underscore the fact that there is life after an aborted or nonexistent career as a recording artist and/or songwriter. Unfortunately this chapter is written with the vast majority of you in mind.

So, you didn't land a record deal, or if you did, you didn't go very far? No publisher was inclined to, or able to, do much with your songs? Maybe the record and publishing pundits were right, maybe they were wrong. In either event it doesn't mean that you can't have a meaningful and rewarding career in the music business. But first, make sure that you love the music business, and that you weren't just turned on by some juvenile fantasy of yourself as a Beatle, a Stone, Billy Joel, or Madonna. It wasn't infatuation, you say, you're really in love with music and this crazy business?

The music industry is very large and becoming larger all the time. It supports thousands and thousands of people, from those who play a word processor or cash register to those who play the synthesizer. If you read the interviews I've included, you can't help but perceive the vast richness of career possibilities available to you. People who have started out as aspiring musicians, singers, and writers have pervaded every craft and position in the music and allied industries. Let's see what's out there.

Think you have an ear? Like gambling your career on each roll of the dice? Like shooting crap with someone else's money? Like the idea of attending the Grammy Awards, or the Country Music Awards, and having your heart pound all evening while you sweat it out with a nominee you discovered and nurtured. Well, there are hundreds of positions in the A&R departments of record companies and music publishers . . . and you can have your choice of N.Y., L.A., or Nashville.

Don't like A&R? How about marketing or promotion?

Think you're a really smart son of a bitch who can chew nails and spit rust? Have a heart so big and tough that it can break in little pieces and still pump enough blood to keep you going? If your answer is affirmative, maybe there is a manager lurking in your psyche.

Really talented musically? A good teacher? Great at bringing out the best in talented people? Want a launching pad for your songs? Capable of enduring abuse and banking large checks . . . maybe? Perhaps you're destined to be a producer.

You're entrepreneurial? Don't mind short rations for a while? Start up an independent production or publishing outfit of your own.

Must perform? The roar of the greasepaint, smell of the crowd . . . and all that jazz. Disc jockey! Dick Clark hasn't done poorly.

I could go on like this endlessly, but I think you get the drift. In this chapter I've included four interviews with people who have all prospered both financially and otherwise in very diverse pursuits related to our business. Read how Larry Rosen, a drummer, became the founder and president of GRP Records, Inc., discovered artists such as Dianne Schuur, exploited the new technology and brought to us such CD masterpieces as *In the Digital Mood*; how John Stix, realizing he was not a world-class guitarist, carved out a career writing about the music he loved and ultimately became the founder and editor-in-chief of the world's leading guitar magazine; how Steve Karmen became "King of the Jingles" after a career as a musician, songwriter, calypso singer, and actor; and how Russ Solomon founded Tower Records and brought it along from an outlet for used records in the back of his father's drugstore to a giant chain employing over five thousand people. I wish you could hear the tapes of these interviews, hear the laughter, the pride of accomplishment, and the enthusiasm each one of these people possesses.

Of course, if you are really bereft of any talent at all . . . you can always go to law school, and ultimately control the music business and everybody's destiny. Only kidding . . . I think.

INTERVIEW WITH
LARRY ROSEN

Larry Rosen started his career as a drummer, evolved into a record producer, and ultimately co-founded the very successful GRP Records, Inc., of which he is President.

AHS: Larry, this is the first time I've interviewed a drummer—a multimillionaire drummer is what I really mean. At the time MCA acquired GRP you said, notwithstanding the riches that were about to befall you, "I'm not giving up my drums!" So the first question is, how did a drummer become the president of a very successful record company, and a very successful man?

ROSEN: Oh, God. You don't kid. You go right to the chase!

AHS: Right to the chase.

ROSEN: Tell me everything about your life from the beginning to the end, you know!

AHS: More or less. Let me explain why to you. This interview is going to serve a dual purpose. It will afford our readers an insight into the record industry, and will run in a new chapter which is called "Alternate Paths to Glory," which is intended to give some hope to those people who don't, for one reason or another, make it as writers or artists, but who are still in love with the music business and want to make it their life's work. This is going to cut two ways. Make it good.

ROSEN: Who's going to play me in the movie? That's what I want to know. Let's see. My mother wanted me to play the accordion. I said if I'm going to play any instrument, I'm going to play the drums—she thought I was crazy. I started taking drum lessons and I got involved and I just loved playing the drums. So that quickly led to all the experiences that you have as a teenager playing an instrument, such as playing in bands. I seemed to excel real quickly and I started playing on a professional level when I was fifteen, sixteen years old. When I was seventeen there was a band in New York called the Newport Youth Band that the Newport Jazz Festival was sponsoring. This was in 1958. All the big bands were kind of falling apart; the whole big band era was over. The Newport Jazz Festival was concerned as to how new young players were going to get the experience of playing in a big band. So the Newport Jazz Festival formed almost a foundation with a guy named Marshall Brown. The concert was to find the best musicians under eighteen in the New York area and form this big band sponsored by the Newport Jazz Festival, have top professional musicians in New York train these young people in this band, and have them perform at the

Newport Jazz Festival and record for Decca Records. I auditioned for this band. There were six hundred kids in the New York area who auditioned, and I was picked as the drummer. This all of a sudden separated me from a lot of other people and kind of put me on a professional level. This band was really intense training. We'd rehearse Friday night, Saturday all day, and Sunday all day, and there were no excuses for not attending a rehearsal. The guy who ran this thing was like a sergeant in the army. Many of the kids in it turned out to be top musicians. A few examples are Eddie Gomez, who's one of the top bass players in the world, trumpet star Jimmie Owens, and Ronnie Cuber, Eddie Daniels, and Mike Abene. So the band was put together, we had all these rehearsals, and we played at the Newport Jazz Festival. They had top writers write for the band. We played with many famous guest artists, such as Lionel Hampton and "CannonBall" Adderley.

We went into the studio and recorded records, and all of a sudden my interest was really sparked in what was going on in that control room. How are they making this record? How does this work? When the Newport Youth Band ended, I was nineteen or twenty years old. Andy Williams came into New York looking for a drummer to go and work with him. Dave Grusin was the piano player and conductor for Andy Williams. Dave knew Quincy Jones, who had heard Newport Youth Band records, and Quincy recommended me to Dave Grusin. I met Dave, who hired me for the Andy Williams gig, and I started working with Andy. So for the next six years, I worked with Andy. Dave was the piano player and the conductor, and I was the drummer. We traveled around the world and recorded records and did television shows with Andy Williams. Very quickly, I started to learn a whole new part of the entertainment industry of which, as a kid from the Bronx, I was totally unaware. I was never on an airplane before in my life, I never was in a limousine before, except if some relative died, I never experienced any of these things in my life. So now we were traveling first class on chartered planes, limousines were taking us everyplace, and I stayed in my own suite in whatever hotel we stayed in. I'd have friends of mine who came out of the Newport Youth Band who were playing with Maynard Ferguson's band and Slide Hampton's band and Count Basie's band, and we'd be in the same town at the same time and I'd go to see these guys, 'cause they were like my idols—playing in a major band in a jazz situation. I'd see they'd be staying in the dumpiest hotel with like a light bulb hanging from a wire, and they were making like $75 a week, and here I was nineteen years old and I'm making like $400 a week and traveling first class and living a lifestyle that I never even knew existed.

I wanted it to continue, so I made it my business to learn about show business, about presentation, about professionalism. Andy Williams was a total professional. He would never sit down in the tuxedo that he was to wear on stage. That was part of his background history of working with the Williams Brothers and Kay Thompson. This was a major learning experience for me. I got very interested in production and how records were made and how a lot of their parts of the business worked. After the Andy Williams experience, I was twenty-five years old. I got married and bought a house in New Jersey. We had no furniture in the house but I built a recording studio in the basement. I did it with the idea of having friends come over and play. I would be playing the drums wearing these headphones and trying to record and play at the same time. Quickly I realized that this wasn't going to work. I was so involved in the recording part of it that I had other friends of mine come over to play the drums while I would record. Then I built a control room and started to really get involved in the recording part of it. Since a lot of my friends were musicians, I decided I was going to form a production company. I started to look at this as a business.

AHS: I want to interrupt you for a second. When you were nineteen years old, you were a successful musician. You were traveling first class, were living in suites . . . you could have gone downhill from there very easily with all of the temptations that were available to you. But you kept your eye on the doughnut, not on the hole, and zeroed in on the business aspect of it. I think that's interesting, and unfortunately not that common.

ROSEN: For whatever reason, I was always interested in the business side of things. When I was in high school, I was going out with this girl whose father was in the vending-machine business. Her father would have all of these vending-machine magazines and I saw ballpoint-pen machines were advertised. I thought, "My God, this is really a neat idea." I could buy these ballpoint-pen machines and put them in high schools, in the school color, and give a percentage of it to the student organization, the S.O. the G.O., whatever they called it. I used to go around once a week and refill the machines, take out the money, and give whoever I had to their 20 percent.

AHS: When you set up this studio in your basement, the object at the time was to do it as a business venture to produce records or as a hobby or . . . ?

ROSEN: When you think of business, you think the bottom line is making money. Making money was never the important issue for me.

AHS: Making music.

ROSEN: It was making music. It was making a record or doing productions . . . it's the excitement of the chase that's more important than the ultimate financial reward. That was never my interest. It was the idea of getting together and making records, and I tried to get involved in the record industry but it was a difficult thing to do. I found out very quickly that it was much easier to get involved in production by doing commercials. I was able to work with local retailers and different department stores, and I would be able to go and speak to them directly, make contact with them, go back to the studio, create a demo, bring it to them and, if they liked it, I would get things on the air. The first thing an agency asks you is to let them hear your other commercials—it's like that old Catch-22—how do you get that first commercial? I was able to put that together and very quickly I started a successful company in New York, doing commercials. I had a partner with me who was a writer and a composer.

AHS: Was that Dave?

ROSEN: No. After the Andy Williams situation, Dave moved to California and stayed there and started to write for television. I came back to New York and was primarily making a living by being a studio player. I got a reputation as a drummer for singers. So when Steve Lawrence came into town I'd play for him. Tony Martin, I'd play for him. I'd play for different singers at different times in New York and in different clubs as well as on recording sessions. I was basically a studio musician in New York. Then I got involved in this production company and creating commercials.

AHS: I've known you for years and I never knew this.

ROSEN: The name of the company was Duo Creatics, it was "two creators." My partner, Shep Myers, was a piano player and a writer. Since I was never a writer or a composer, I always needed that other element. I would do the selling and do the schtick with the agencies. The agencies would assign a project to three or four different companies and say, "Go out and do a demo on this." Since I had the studio in my house, and all my friends were musicians, it didn't cost very much to create these demos. We were able to submit a lot of demos and we started getting more and more of the jobs. Once we got the final production, we would come into New York to one of the major studios. My partner would write the arrangements and I would be the producer. Everybody from the agency would come down; there would be like thirty people in the control room to do a sixty-second spot. There'd be the copywriter, the client, the agency producer, the account executives, and they'd all be in there, we'd record the spot, they'd love it, and we'd be finished.

It all had to be done on a specific budget. So the budget, the business part of it, became real important. Suppose you got paid $5,000 to do two sixties and two thirties for Greyhound buses. We would hire the musicians and pay for the studio, and obviously you had to come out with a profit at the end so you could pay your rent! It really gave me the experience of managing a creative production and at the same time managing its economics. It was really difficult to simultaneously operate the business and to play six nights a week in a club and do recording sessions during the day as a musician. I had to make a decision . . . I had reached a really important fork in the road. I had to decide what I was going to do. Was I going to pursue my career as a studio player and go down that road, or pursue the production side of it, which I loved? I couldn't do both because of the time constraints. I decided to do production on a full-time basis. But to make enough money to support my wife and child I had to play bar mitzvahs and weddings on the weekends. From a musical standpoint, that was a degrading thing to have to do after what I had accomplished as a musician. But I had to do it so I could keep the production company going and strive for what I was really trying to achieve. So I'd be doing production five days a week, and then I'd work Saturday afternoon, Saturday nights, Sunday afternoon, and Sunday nights, and do four weddings and bar mitzvahs or parties or whatever it had to be on the weekend in order to make four or five hundred dollars to be able to pay my overhead. That's the way I paid my dues.

AHS: As a drummer?

ROSEN: Yeah, as a drummer. That's exactly what I did. So whether it's Leonard's in Great Neck or all the country clubs, I'm familiar with these. I know every catering hall, I know every hotel, I know the entrance the bands take in the elevator in the back of the Pierre. I mean I've done it all. Musically, it was a very distressing time for me. I'd come home on the weekends ready to punch my fist through the wall because I hated everything that I had to play. It was very tough because I considered myself as having attained the highest order of musicianship.

AHS: Are you sure you don't want to come to my daughter's wedding?

ROSEN: That's the real reason I'm not coming! It's a flashback—I go to a wedding and I freak out!

As the commercial area got more and more lucrative for us I was able to cut back somewhat on the weekends. The commercial business was an up-and-down kind of thing. You'd do a lot of commercials at one point, and then you'd have a number of weeks where nothing happens because you're out selling the jobs. Also from a musical standpoint, it got to be less and less rewarding. We did sixty seconds' worth of music, which we would hear in the studio through these loudspeakers and you're all turned on . . . then the agency takes it and puts an announcer speaking over the whole thing, and there it comes through the television on tiny speakers. You're trying to figure out what happened to the music you just created in this great recording session! At that point I realized that this is not for me. I really had to move on to the next step, which was records—where the music is what it's all about. People buy the music!

One day, a friend of mine who was a bass player and a singer brought in his guitar and said, "Hey, listen, let me play some songs that I wrote, because I really think they're special." His name is Jon Lucien. When I heard these songs I said, "Whoa, this is the best thing that I've ever heard." I recorded an album of Jon's material in my house and then went around to different record companies and finally made a deal with RCA. That was the first shot that I got at being a producer, producing a record and making a record for a company.

AHS: You didn't do that as an independent producer?

ROSEN: Yeah, as an independent producer.

AHS: Did you own the masters?

ROSEN: No, no, I didn't own the masters.

AHS: RCA took everything?

ROSEN: Yeah, RCA took everything. I got nothing, but it really didn't make any difference. The idea was to go and make the record. That was the most important thing in the world to me. I recorded a lot of the basic tracks in the two-track studio in my house and then brought them to RCA's sixteen-track studio. I would transfer my two tracks to the sixteen-track, and that would leave me fourteen tracks open!

AHS: A lot of great records were made on two tracks.

ROSEN: You bet. Then it was a matter of completing Jon's record. Dave and I always stayed in contact with each other. Whenever he was in New York, I'd see him, and if I went out to L.A. for whatever reason, we would see each other. I sent Dave the tapes of Jon Lucien that we did, and I said I'd love to have strings if you would write them, and he said absolutely. So he wrote the string arrangements, flew into New York, we hired another band, and Dave wrote the orchestrations for the arrangements. Not only was it the first record that I ever made as a producer, but Dave and I were working together right from the beginning on this very first record. And the record won a Grammy Award. It didn't sell very much, maybe 35,000 copies, but Dave won a Grammy Award for the best arrangement accompanying a vocalist. It was the kind of record musicians appreciated, and it became really "culty" and popular among musicians.

AHS: Did you play the drums on it?

ROSEN: No. When I was involved in producing I was in the studio doing that and other people were playing. I got further and further away from playing and more and more involved in production. Then I made another record with Jon. In between, I was still doing commercials and still playing bar mitzvahs and weddings on the weekends. I realized that commercials were really not the thing for me.

I wanted to totally phase out the commercials. I started signing more and more artists to my own production company. I had some associations now with RCA because I made two records for them. Now Bruce Lundval was at CBS and Bruce of course was always interested in jazz. He heard about these records with Jon Lucien through Herbie Hancock. We were very unhappy with the relationship with RCA and what was going on at RCA.

After making two records for RCA with Jon Lucien, Jon had a real strong cult following, a real strong following in New York. In New York he could sell out Carnegie Hall. He could sell out Avery Fisher Hall. We were up to selling about 50,000 units or something like that. We were very unhappy with RCA and worked out a deal with them to get out of the contract. So we decided to put Jon into Carnegie Hall and invite all the record companies to come and see this act and hopefully to make a record deal . . . which was exactly what happened. Well, of all the record companies, very few showed up. But one was a representative from Arista Records who came back to me and said, "I think you really have something special with Jon." His name was Steve Backer. Steve Backer was the head of the Jazz Department at Arista. He brought me to meet Clive Davis. Clive listened to the records that I made and said he'd like to sign a deal. Jon Lucien and I had this production company together, he was the artist, I was the producer. We sat down with Clive to negotiate a deal and we talked about the whole situation. Clive and I were really happy until we reached the point of creative control. Arista was insisting that we couldn't pick a song without their approval. This became a real big problem for us because we felt that Clive Davis knew nothing about this music. How was he going to make a decision on what was right and what was wrong? Well, we went back and forth about this. Just about all of the other points, the advances, the royalties, and everything else in the deal was set. The creative issue went back and forth for four months. While this was going on I got a call from Bruce Lundval, and he said, "I was just talking to Herbie Hancock about Jon. I listened to the records that you guys made and I really would like to work a deal." I said, "Wait a second, I don't know what the ethics are of this thing, but we've been discussing a deal with Arista Records for four months now, we're down to this one point that we're trying to resolve and I really don't know what I should do." He said, "Well, you didn't finalize the deal?" I said, "No, it's not finalized. Look, let me call my attorney and let me get back to you." My attorney said, "I think we should go up and talk to him. The Arista deal's not a done deal." So we went over the next day to see Bruce and as we're walking into the CBS building, I said, "Let's ask for double everything. I just don't want to go through this anymore. I just don't want to go through another trip. Arista was going to pay us $50,000, let's ask for $100,000 and a much higher royalty. If they're not going to do that, let's just get out of here. I don't want to go through this all over again." So we went up there and we sat down with Bruce, told him exactly what we wanted, he said, "Okay." To everything! I said, "Okay, then we've got to get the deal done now. Right now." So my attorney stayed with their people and in like two days finished the entire deal with CBS. We signed the contract . . .

AHS: Who called Clive to tell him . . . ?

ROSEN: . . . okay, we finished the deal in two days with CBS, signed the contract, it was done. So Joe calls up Elliot Goldman at Arista and says to Elliot, "Well, I just wanted to let you know that we just made a deal with CBS. Thanks very much, but it wasn't going to work, and we just decided to forget about it." Well, I just didn't think anymore of it, that was it. About two days later, it's two o'clock in the morning, the phone rings. Hazel picks up the phone and she says, "It's for you, it's Clive Davis." Clive Davis is calling me at two in the morning? We're sleeping! "Hello?" He was very upset. He said, "I have never been so humiliated in my whole life. I told people that Jon Lucien was going to be on Arista Records and that you and I had a deal. This is the lowest thing I ever heard of!" I didn't say one word. He went on and on and on and boom! He hung up the phone.

AHS: He shares this book with you, by the way.

ROSEN: You ask him about this! I said, "My God, I can't believe this! I guess I'm going to make it in this business if Clive Davis bothers to call me in the middle of the night to lay that shit on me! I mean, I must have something going here, I don't understand this!" So we went ahead and we made the record for CBS. The record sold something like 150,000 units on CBS.

AHS: But subsequently you have . . .

ROSEN: Okay, I'll tell you how Clive comes back into the picture again. This was about 1975. In 1976, Dave and I decided to form a record production company together. He's kind of getting bugged with the television scene and the movie thing that he was in, and jazz, with more production elements to it, is starting to become more and more popular. CTI had a real kind of successful run with a "produced" kind of jazz as opposed to what jazz was before. Before that jazz groups would play in a recording studio just as they would in a club. They'd go in for one or two days and make a whole record. The first artist that we had was Earl Klugh, a new guitar player from Detroit. Nobody knew who he was. We made Earl's first record for Blue Note Records. It was very successful. So after we did Earl Klugh and Noel Pointer we did Patti Austin for CTI and then we did Lee Ritenour for Electra. Our reputation in this area of music grew very quickly. We just finished one of the albums out in L.A., this was 1978. The episode with Clive was in 1975 or 1976 . . . like two and a half years later. I had spent a long time in L.A. I did all the engineering on all the records that Dave and I made together. I would do the engineering, Dave worked in the studio with the musicians, and we'd pick the material together and the direction. It was really a good working relationship. So I'm going to come back now from L.A., and I decided I was whipped—I'm going to come back first class. This was the first time I ever went on a plane and paid for first class *myself*. And I said, "The hell with this—I'm going to do this." I upgrade my ticket to first class, get on the plane and sit down, and Clive Davis sits down three seats away. I haven't spoken to him since that night on the telephone. We start flying. So I walk over to him and I said, "Clive, I don't know if you remember me, my name is Larry Rosen." He said, "Oh yeah, yeah, I remember." I said, "I don't know if you're still really mad at me, but the last time I spoke to you it was two in the morning. You called about Jon Lucien and you said that you would never deal with me ever again—do you really still feel that way?" He said, "Oh no, that's ridiculous, I was just upset at that time because of what happened. Why don't you sit down, why don't we talk?" And we sat down and we had this long conversation. He said, "I know about the records that you're making." And he *was* aware of the records that we were making.

AHS: A very bright guy.

ROSEN: Yeah, and he said, "We're having a lot of problems with this jazz fusion–jazz crossover area at Arista, and you're having so much success with this thing, I'd really like to talk to you about it more. Could you send over all your records to me?" I said, "Sure." He asked me, "What do you think we're doing wrong?" And I gave him this whole thing on what I thought he was doing wrong, 'cause he had certain artists, and they were producing them different ways and they were going in all the wrong directions. So, after we got back, I sent all the records. A few days later I get a call from him, and he said, "I'd like you to come over. I'd like to talk to you about a production deal." So I went over there with my attorney and we sat down and Clive said, "I want to talk to you about some kind of a production deal." I said I would like to have our own label, because I feel we have a style . . . that there's something unique about what we're doing. He said, "Okay, fine, let's do that. I have no problem with that." And that's when we came up with Arista-GRP Records. And we made a deal with Clive to find artists and to produce them for that label. He gave us all the freedom we could possibly want, artistic included, to go out and make the records. What I had to do was bring the artist to him for approval. If he didn't want a particular artist, then we would have the right to take that artist to another record company. But he approved every single artist that we brought and we signed Angela Bofill, and we signed Tom Browne, and we signed Bernard Wright, and we signed Bobby Broom, and we produced their records. David and I would just make record after record after record after record. I brought in Angela Bofill's first record to Clive and played it for him, and he said, "This is a beautiful record, but I don't know how we're going to sell one copy of it." I said, "Why?" He said that he didn't think there was a hit single on it. I said, "Yes, but it's a beautiful record." So we put the record out and it sold 280,000 units. He couldn't believe it. Angela's second record sold 450,000 units.

AHS: This is a jazz record?

ROSEN: Well, it's kind of jazz . . . she was a vocalist, not an instrumentalist. Sales were uniquely high. It was like a special kind of adult music product. It wasn't Barry Manilow, it wasn't pop singles, it certainly wasn't rock 'n' roll. It fit someplace in an area that I still can't define. Then we signed Tom Browne, a trumpet player, and he recorded "Funkin' for Jamaica," which sold 700,000 units. It was an absolute number-one R&B single smash. So we had a lot of success with that operation with Clive. But it's just funny, going back to the middle-of-the-night phone call! That was the way we launched GRP Records. It's so ironic. We were with Arista for the next five years. That was a tremendous experience with Clive. He was the greatest teacher in the world when it came to the record industry. I have the highest regard for this guy.

AHS: GRP has a reputation for being on the cutting edge of record industry technology. How did this come about?

ROSEN: We started doing digital recording while we were at Arista. It involved an up charge of $7,000 per album, which did not please Arista because they didn't believe it increased sales.

AHS: Were these CDs?

ROSEN: No, this was pre-CDs. We were doing digital recording way before CDs were ever invented. It was 1979 when we did our first digital recording. CDs weren't introduced to the United States till 1983. We were doing digital recording because we just thought the sound of it was so much better. But ultimately when it came to the consumer it was on a vinyl record or on a cassette or an eight-track.

AHS: Could you hear the difference?

ROSEN: We could hear the difference and of course there was a difference. We saved generations because there were no generations in digital recording as there were in analog recording. We were in the digital domain so the record sounded better. That was part of the image that we were building for ourselves . . . quality of the records that we produced. They always sounded better than anybody else's records. Part of it was that we were doing digital, part of it was also the care and concern that we had for the sonic part of the recording process. At that point Elliot Goldman of Arista took exception to the $7,000 additional cost of digital recording. He didn't think it "sold one more record." I thought that we were building for the future, and that digital recording was the future of the industry. Elliot and I had a couple of world-class battles over this issue, but then the whole thing started petering out because our deal was coming to an end, and Arista had other problems.

When the Arista deal ended we had the choice of going back and being producers for a lot of other labels because every label was calling us to produce product for them, or we could start our own company. And we started to look around. I've always read all of the technical journals and all of the audio magazines, and I felt that CDs were on the horizon. We knew more about digital technology than anybody else and had more experience dealing with it. We said, "Let's focus on digital recording and music in the jazz area."

AHS: With Arista you had a label but not really your own record company. How did the start of GRP Records come about?

ROSEN: Our Arista deal ended in '82. I think we didn't renew because the industry was at a low and because they didn't want us to record digitally because of the extra $7,000 per album. When the record industry goes sour the first artists to be dropped are jazz artists, because they are a luxury, not a necessity. Lee Rittenour and Billy Cobham were dropped from the companies that they were on and Chick Corea was dropped from the company that he was on, so we were able to sign artists to relatively reasonable contracts that we could afford.

AHS: That's lucky for them and lucky for you.

ROSEN: Yeah! It worked out real good. The idea was let's focus on jazz or contemporary jazz or whatever you call this area of music and on digital technology, and get involved in the compact disc market. We coined the phrase "the digital master company" . . . it was GRP, the digital master company. A lot of people thought we were totally nuts. "What do you mean, digital?" This is like an audiophile thing . . . for a few freaks who want high fidelity stuff! We were never mainstream anyway, so it really didn't make any difference to us.

AHS: It's a wonderful opportunity to ask you, what do you think of the future of DAT?

ROSEN: From a technical standpoint I think it's great. How will the public take to this particular configuration? I think we're on the brink of finding out. I think that the hardware manufacturers are coming with DAT players and they're coming with them strong. Every hardware manufacturer that has shipped DAT equipment into the audio

AHS:

environment has sold out. You can't even buy a DAT machine. The production runs have been small but they've all sold out.

AHS: I'm a lousy interviewer—you were hot and I interrupted you. Let's get back to GRP. I'm fascinated.

ROSEN: Now that we determined that we were going to have our own record company, we had to determine how we were going to distribute its product and how we were going to finance the company. We never had to be concerned about these issues before. We had a meeting with CBS about having a P&D deal with CBS. We told them that we had a record we wanted to release in February. They said, "On no, no, no. no. We can't release that for at least six months after that. We have just too much product." We learned very quickly that it made absolutely no sense for us to make a deal with this company because we were going to be totally lost in CBS's huge quantity of product.

It was just at that time that we got calls from the independent distributors. One of the distributors called me up and said, "Listen, I've heard through the grapevine that you and Dave are going to start a record company. For all of the years that you were with Arista we distributed your product." At this time, Arista, A&M, Motown, and Chrysalis all stopped using independent distribution and the independent distributors were losing all the product of their major sellers. This distributor, Jim Schwartz of Schwartz Brothers, tell us that they'd been selling our product for years, and that GRP had a tremendous reputation . . . that the retailers would buy the product just because it was GRP product, even if they didn't know who the artist was. This was the first time I realized that GRP and its music had an identity that carried through the retail environment right to the consumer. The independents were eager to have us because they felt we could build a catalogue. At the time all they had left were dance records, which came and went and had no catalog value. I went to an independent distributor convention and I met all the independent distributors around the country. We put together a system of independent distributors in different territories through the United States. Dave and I put up the money to start the company, to invest in the first recordings. What would we record first? What would be the best demonstration of digital technology and compact disc potential for the area of music that we were involved in? What artist? What band? Our research indicated that the most famous band in the world was Glenn Miller, which really had nothing to do with what we were doing musically. We were doing all these young artists, contemporary jazz, fusion, crossover music, black kinds of things, and now we're talking about Glenn Miller, which is like, before we were born, so . . .

AHS: I beg your pardon!

ROSEN: Well, before I was born anyway. We said, "Let's see how this could work." We worked out an arrangement with the Glenn Miller Orchestra and the Glenn Miller estate to get the original Glenn Miller arrangements, and 3M came out with a thirty-two-track digital recording system. We went into the studio with the top studio players in New York, and we did a rerecording of the original Glenn Miller hits, with the original arrangements, recorded with digital technology. We used the Modernaires to do the vocal parts, and Mel Torme put together this vocal group with Julius LaRosa and others, and we made this record and called it *In the Digital Mood*. That was really the first record on GRP.

AHS: And that was a smash.

ROSEN: When CDs were launched in the United States, Sony came out with the first CD player. They had a CBS/Sony sampler from Japan of pop artists that they were selling in Japan. They had Polygram, of course, who was involved in the technology from the beginning, and they had a classical sampler because they figured the CDs were for the classical market and they had GRP's *In the Digital Mood*. Those pieces of product are what, with the Sony player, Sony sent across the United States to introduce compact discs to the American market. Our product was one of the first pieces of product that was being introduced in this technology. We were in the right place with the right stuff at the right time. Nobody knew what the potential was for this marketplace, but we had the perfect demonstration piece, some music that everybody could relate to and a big band sound that was great, through big speakers! *In the Digital Mood* became the prime sampler for stores all across the country, and as soon as they got in CD players they got *In the Digital Mood*. There was nothing else like this available on compact disc, so it just sold, sold, and sold.

AHS: It's funny, the harder you work the luckier you get.

ROSEN: It's true. Now the independent distributors, who lost all their major labels, had a lot of 12-inch dance labels and GRP Records, and we were the only company that had compact discs. It put the independent distributors into the compact disc marketplace and we had the beginning of a company.

AHS: Now you start a whole new thing . . . and the rest was history.

ROSEN: Yes and no. We had our company launched, but we had all of the new problems that go with growth. If you are in a steep growth curve, as we were, the company eats a tremendous amount of capital. We had to avoid the venture capitalists who wanted to consume us and find other means of getting the capital we needed. As you know, we used every source imaginable. We got advances from the distributors. We made a distribution deal with MCA, which provided us with some capitalization. We used banks, and during all of this we were building a kind of organization a real record company needs. We put together a unique foreign distribution system and ultimately we were acquired by MCA.

AHS: Now that it is part of MCA, is GRP still GRP?

ROSEN: Well, you're sitting in the same office that you've always sat in when we were together. We have the same people and we are operating pretty much as we did in the past. That was our wish . . . and MCA's. Our roster is, of course, somewhat larger, because we have taken over some of MCA's acts that were appropriate for us.

AHS: I think I'm going to put this interview out as a book . . . then we'll fight over who plays you in the movie. Thank you, Larry.

INTERVIEW WITH
JOHN STIX

John Stix is a writer on music subjects and is the co-editor-in-chief of *Guitar for the Practicing Musician,* the leading guitar magazine in the world.

AHS: John, what is your title and job description?

STIX: Co-editor-in-chief of *Guitar for the Practicing Musician.*

AHS: Which is one of the . . .

STIX: Which is really *the* number-one guitar magazine in the world. I say "world" because we are now international.

AHS: I know yours is not the oldest guitar magazine.

STIX: No, it's the youngest.

AHS: It's the youngest and the biggest and the bestest?

STIX: I'll accept that. When you go into business you can do one of two things: you can copy people and take a ride on their comet and see how high you can get on their tail, or you can fill a gap that doesn't exist and invent something new. *Guitar Player* has been out there for over twenty years. Years ago I helped co-found *Guitar World,* another of our competitors, and *Guitar World* copied *Guitar Player.* It was like, "Hey, one person's doing it well. Why don't we just be the second market?"

At the inception of *Guitar for the Practicing Musician* we came up with the idea of putting sheet music in the magazine . . . which had not been done before. Until then, if you wanted to learn a Beatles song or a Rolling Stones song, or a song by any rock group, you would buy a piano/vocal treatment and they'd have little chord boxes on top for the guitar. Instead, we did new Rose Royce transcriptions, exact mirrors of what was on the record, so that a guitarist could finally, as Jon

Gnagy would say, "paint by number" with the tablature, which is a way of reading music if you don't read standard musical notation. No one had ever done this before. We will be able to say: "Hey, we have the whole history of rock guitar–playing from Chuck Berry to Eddie Van Halen to Steve Vai and Joe Satriani now in a way that guitarists can get the most out of it."

AHS: Is there any basic difference between the scope of *Guitar for the Practicing Musician* and its competitors?

STIX: Well, it's a rock-'n'-roll publication. It's not all things to all people. I think there was something else that we scoped out, just like narrow-casting in radio formats. We said, "Let's do a magazine based solely on the excitement and the adrenaline that rock 'n' roll puts out." We were not going to have Joe Pass (who was a great jazz guitar player) on the cover, and inside have Eddie Van Halen! What we did was say to the rock guitarists, "Everything in this magazine will be for you!"

AHS: Would you call yours a metal guitar magazine?

STIX: No, I would call it a rock guitar magazine. There's certainly a lot of metal and hardcore and thrash metal. It's in there, but we have covered Chuck Berry on one end and we have covered Metallica on another and that's all rock 'n' roll. It certainly encompasses metal.

AHS: I'm sitting in your office now and I'm surrounded by cartons of demos and there seem to be hundreds of them. What is a publisher and editor of a guitar magazine doing with literally hundreds of demonstration tapes?

STIX: We're completing the circle. The magazine, through the articles, is directed more to the creative process than are the guitar-tech magazines. We spend less time talking about the equipment than we do about the creative process. We're really concerned with the driver more than just the car. This magazine, with its transcriptions, is helping to bring a whole new level of performance to generations of guitar players. Hopefully more people will get better faster, stick with it longer, and if we're lucky we will help some great new guitar player get started.

AHS: What do you do with the demos?

STIX: As those players get better and better, what are they going to do with their music? We started a guitar recording label called Guitar Recordings, Inc., using the same logo as *Guitar for the Practicing Musician* and saying, "Now we'll give the best of you a chance to actually get yourselves a recording contract and make instrumental rock guitar records." So it's a cycle: helping them get better, and then giving the best of them an outlet. So it's not just a magazine that helps you get better. We're also going to try to help launch your career.

AHS: Was that your idea, John?

STIX: Yeah . . .

AHS: I think it's a brilliant idea. You're going to fall into two chapters now.

I'm going to have to allude to you in the record chapter, because if you think you have a lot of demos now, wait until Simon & Schuster puts your interview into bookstores all over America.

STIX: The first person we signed was a sixteen-year-old named Blue Saraceno, from Middletown, Connecticut, and he has the touch and the feel and the maturity of some players who've been on the circuit for twenty years. He has toured the country with the Jack Bruce/Ginger Baker reunion tour, filling in for Eric Clapton. He's recorded with Michael Bolton, Taylor Dayne, and a cut of his ended up on the last Cher record.

AHS: Is he going to remember you, John?

STIX: I hope so. It's very exciting. So far we've really been able to be a springboard for this young player, and we have a couple of other artists who we are working with, a young man named Mark Bonilla out of San Francisco, and a fine bass player by the name of Randy Coven, who's out on Long Island.

AHS: Does *Guitar for the Practicing Musician* extend to all string musicians?

STIX: Well, no, electric strings. I'd say electric bass and electric guitar.

AHS: No mandolin players.

STIX: No mandolins here. We have another magazine for that. I think your readers will be interested in how Randy Coven got involved with us. People want to start guitar for three reasons: they either saw the Beatles on Ed Sullivan, a generation later they were enthralled by Kiss, and the next generation after that came up with Eddie Van Halen—so showing my age, I started with the Beatles.

AHS: You don't look that old.

STIX: I'm thirty-seven now. I loved the guitar. I wanted to play the guitar, but I had a greater ability to spot talent, shape it, and share knowledge than I did to be a really good player. I could teach a guitarist to be a better guitar player than I was myself in just a month or so. So my point is that even if you can't play, if you love the music, there are, as what we're looking for here, outlets. Back to Randy Coven. I was at a NAMM show, the National Association of Music Merchants, where all the music stores get together and they look at your products. The drummer in Randy's band gave me a record and said, "Hey, give it a listen." The three things you need are talent, persistence, and luck. The individual person, all of us, only has the talent that we are given to develop. And after that it takes persistence to knock on those doors until somebody answers. It could be a secretary, it doesn't have to be the president. Go to whomever you can find. Randy got to Guitar Recordings because the drummer in his band gave me a tape.

I was very impressed with Randy's album called *Funk Me Tender* which we rereleased on the Guitar Recordings label, and I said, "Wow, this is so musical, yet you don't have to be a musician to like it." I think that's one of the keys to Guitar Recordings, that we're not trying to make technical music for musicians. We're trying to sign people who are playing music, not just guitar.

AHS: When you were an aspiring musician did you play in bands?

STIX: I played in bar bands. I played on college stages. This was in the late sixties, early seventies.

AHS: When did you throw in the sponge?

STIX: I threw in the sponge, I think, about '75. When I got out of college I knew that I was not going to be one of the greats, but a friend of mine, Mike English, who was a phenomenal guitar player, asked me to be in a band. I was good at arranging songs, I was good at making things happen, and then I would struggle to get my part perfect and just hope that I would fit in while somebody else could be the star. We lasted about a month and that was the end of my career as a musician.

AHS: How did you gravitate to the magazine business?

STIX: A friend of mine was looking through a magazine one day, and he said, "Holy smoke! I know this writer. I knew this guy years ago. I'll bet you could do better than he could." Well, at the time, I had wormed my way into working with this band called Chick Corea and Return to Forever.

AHS: As a musician?

STIX: No, getting them gigs, things like that. I knew the bass player in the band, Stanley Clarke, and I said, "Okay, I'll interview Stanley Clarke." I wrote up a piece. I sent *Guitar Player* a self-addressed stamped postcard and said, "If I sent you an article on Stanley Clarke, would you read it for publication?" I had little boxes with "yes" or "no." They checked "yes" and mailed it back. I did the interview. I sent it to them. They said, "You didn't write it in our style. Obviously you didn't read enough of the magazine to get it." So instead of changing my style I made a call to a jazz publication, *Different Drummer,* in Rochester, New York, and they loved it and made it a cover story. I started doing jazz things, Dexter Gordon and Betty Carter and Hubert Laws and Ron Carter, Roland Kirk and Herbie Hancock. So I started with this jazz thing and then I went to R&B and ultimately to rock which I always loved. That's how I started working with magazines.

AHS: What happened with Chick?

STIX: He asked me to be the road manager of the band and I said, "No, I don't want to drive around, be in a car for hundreds of miles, every day."

AHS: John, you've been around the music business and around musicians for a long time. What do you think is the key to success . . . besides talent?

STIX: I would have to say persistence. It doesn't matter whether it's music or writing. I wanted to do an interview with Wayne Shorter. The record company PR people said, "Wayne Shorter turned down *Rolling Stone* and *The New York Times*. He's not doing interviews." Here's the lesson. I found out where he was staying. I called him up on the telephone. He was listed under "Wayne Shorter." He picked up the telephone. I said, "Wayne, I'd like to do an interview." He said, "Come on down."

AHS: That's funny.

STIX: So there you have it. There's that persistence, without being a bug. I mean, if the guy had said "no," it would have been all over, but when you want to do something and you really feel it from the gut, then you can very often find a way to get there, if not immediately, maybe down the road a little.

AHS: You seem like a very happy guy. Any sour grapes about not being on stage and not being a performer?

STIX: No, no, because I can still play guitar all I want. I now have the ability to talk to all of my favorite guitarists of any period. I've got a chance to meet my heroes and play with many of them.

AHS: Do you play on any sessions?

STIX: No. Somebody asked me to, once. I practiced for a week in case they were serious but fortunately was able to back out of it.

AHS: Do you play socially?

STIX: Sometimes when we go to an interview I pick up the guitar. I have a great story. Eddie Van Halen is playing the Meadowlands and I'm coming back to see him. I felt wonderful because they're holding back all of the crowds, among them rock stars and big-time reporters, you know, *Rolling Stone* kind of people, and a guy comes out in the whole crowd just to pick me out and goes, "Eddie wants to see you, come on." I said, "Wow, he wants to see me. What does he want to see me about?" I walked in and he said, "Hey, man, how you doing?" I mean, that was it. He just wanted to say hello. I showed him where we ran a transcription of one of his pieces in *Guitar for the Practicing Musician,* and I said, "Isn't it difficult to play?" and this guy who had just gotten off the stage as a headliner goes, "No, man, that's not hard, here, you play it." He hands me his guitar to show me how to play this song. This when he hasn't been off stage for five minutes!

AHS: He enjoys his music too, then? If you don't enjoy it, you don't do that kind of thing.

STIX: Yeah, I mean, you know I feel very lucky that I've been able to do what I've wanted to do. I may have wanted to play on stage, but I knew enough to know that I really didn't have what it takes.

AHS: You know, it's funny. One of the managers I interviewed complained that with all of the inexpensive equipment available today people can go into their garage or their bedroom and put together what passes for a record, and he feels that he—and I guess you and the record companies and the music publishers—are inundated with material that is really not professional, that is amateurish. He felt that in the past, when you had to get up the money for a studio, it kind of filtered out a lot of the people who weren't of professional quality.

STIX: Maybe it means that we get more people that have more energy than talent.

AHS: Okay.

STIX: Or more gumption than talent, but it also means that more people are able to develop their talent, more quickly and to a higher level.

AHS: That's a good place to stop, John. Thank you very much.

INTERVIEW WITH
RUSS SOLOMON

Russ Solomon is the founder of the Tower Record and Tower Book chains.

AHS: I have to tell you that my wife is very excited about your new store in Westchester County, New York.

SOLOMON: Oh, in Yonkers?

AHS: That's a local store for us. We're very excited about it.

SOLOMON: Oh, that's great. Thank you. I'm glad somebody up there cares. That's going to open in another month or so.

AHS: Well, we will be there.

SOLOMON: Good.

AHS: I spoke to Steve Harmen, one of your managers, this morning, and he tells me that you're a terrific listener and a terrific employer in that you listen to your employees and give them their head, so to speak, in running the individual stores.

SOLOMON: I give them their head because I have no idea what they're doing out there, and it's better I don't.

AHS: How many stores are there now, Russ?

SOLOMON: I think—well, it depends on how you count them. I think there are fifty-five or fifty-six record stores in the United States, and fifteen overseas.

AHS: That's a healthy number of stores. I also learned from Steve that you are the founder of the company.

SOLOMON: Yes, I am. That just proves, once again, that I am older than God.

AHS: Well, I think we're about the same age.

SOLOMON: The big-band generation?

AHS: Yes.

SOLOMON: I kind of miss that, though.

AHS: I represent GRP Records.

SOLOMON: They're good guys.

AHS: . . . and they had the Glenn Miller CD, *In the Digital Mood* . . .

SOLOMON: The re-creation?

AHS: Right, and that took me back, I mean, to my childhood.

SOLOMON: I want you to know that I shook Glenn Miller's hand. It's the same hand that shook the glove on Michael Jackson's hand. I thought that's pretty interesting.

AHS: Did you have a musical background? Are you a musician?

SOLOMON: No, I learned how to play a phonograph when I was very young. I was always good at that.

AHS: How did you get into the retail record business?

SOLOMON: It was sort of an accident. I worked in my dad's drugstore in the forties, actually before the forties, and we had a soda fountain. We started selling used records from the jukebox that was in the soda fountain area. We'd buy them from the jukebox operator. My dad was kind of a modern druggist . . . didn't like the medicine part of the drug business as much as he liked the front end, the cosmetics and liquor and cameras and everything else. He said, "Well, shoot, if we can sell used records, we might as well start to sell new records." So we went and got some new records, very few, and started selling them. My background—if there's any real background that I have, because after all I was only sixteen then—is as a retail shopkeeper. No matter what the product, retailing is retailing.

AHS: You know, it's funny, several of my interviewees referred to you and/or Tower Records in the course of their interviews.

SOLOMON: Oh, yes?

AHS: It leads me to believe that you are a force in this industry.

SOLOMON: Well, I think I've been around longer than anybody else. I suppose by virtue of that alone it means something.

AHS: Do you think Tower, or stores like Tower, or chains like Tower, have the capacity or the ability to effect trends in the industry?

SOLOMON: Yes, I believe so . . . only to the degree that in many cases we're the first to carry the merchandise. That in itself is fairly important. There are subtrends that go on as opposed to the real popular kinds of things in the mainstream of pop music. If a buzz happens on the street about that music, and we have it, then the buzz can feed on that. So in that sense we can effect a trend, I guess. That's reaching a little bit, because trends are usually developed by a combination of efforts. The retail stores having the merchandise, the live performances of the music on the street or in the clubs or schools or wherever, and radio play, alternative or otherwise. It's that little magical mix that makes things begin to happen.

AHS: Do you think that a chain such as Tower has the ability to create the buzz?

SOLOMON: I'm not sure we can do it all by ourselves. I think that we need those other ingredients.

AHS: But you could be a factor.

SOLOMON: Well, we'd be an important factor in the whole thing. In other words, we make a specialty of carrying local music. Some cities have got a lot of local music and they're real fountainheads of music, like Boston and Nashville, of course, and in New York to a big degree. Now we're going into Austin, Texas, which I think is another one. Having the local music in the store, just making it available and having it seen frequently by customers, that certainly helps it a lot . . . but I think it needs a little more than just that. It needs some other kinds of exposure.

AHS: But it would appear that you have the ability to reinforce it once it's started.

SOLOMON: Yeah, I think that's true.

AHS: For years I've heard of the value of a window in Tower . . .

SOLOMON: The window displays certainly help a little bit. That's for sure. They create an environment.

AHS: Do your aesthetic sensibilities determine what gets window space, or what gets a front rack, or anything like that?

SOLOMON: Mine, personally?

AHS: Yes.

SOLOMON: No, everything is done locally, but we cooperate with the record companies and we do almost anything they ask to accommodate them. We're unique in one regard at least—we don't charge them for it. We make them pay for our costs of the necessary production or construction, like a billboard on the Sunset Boulevard store, or something like that. They have to pay for that, and they pay for the big transparencies the New York stores use.

AHS: Right.

SOLOMON: We don't charge them for anything else beyond that. We really are providing a kind of space for the companies to exploit their own goods.

AHS: This interview is going to be used in a chapter that's tentatively entitled "Alternative Paths to Glory." It's intended for my readers who can't make it as performers, but do love the business and want to be active in it. It's trying to point out to them alternative ways in which their love of music and the music industry can be manifested.

SOLOMON: One of the lucky breaks that a company like ours gets is that we get a lot of fledgling musicians and actors and other people in the arts, because they like the environment of working in a record store while waiting for their break. Sometimes the break actually comes along.

AHS: And sometimes the break is with you, I guess.

SOLOMON: Yeah, sure. There's certainly a career in retailing. There's no question about that. We have a lot of people who have been around anywhere from five to twenty-five years. It is an interesting and I think ultimately rewarding career to be in record retailing.

AHS: Steve mentioned to me that he learned the business with you in Sacramento.

SOLOMON: Yes.

AHS: . . . and that his assistant manager is now going to be the manager of the Westchester store.

SOLOMON: That's true, he is. In our case, all of our managers come from within. It is so rare for us to go outside for one. We've never gone outside for a record manager. We've gone outside for a book manager for our chain of bookstores a couple of times, because we just didn't have enough bookstores to have the raw material. Basically our entire firm, since its beginning, has promoted from within. All of our managers, all of our buyers, come from within.

AHS: And when you choose your employees, I assume you do it on the basis of a retail background, rather than a musical background. How important is a musical background to you?

SOLOMON: I think the most important thing we look for in an employee—don't forget we have about five or six thousand employees out there—is that they want the job, they want to work in this kind of an environment, and they like music. They have to like it, for God's sake, and be interested in it, and like the idea of working in a record store. Those kinds of things are more important than having any particular educational background or musical talent.

AHS: How did the name "Tower" arise?

SOLOMON: There's a theater still in existence in Sacramento called The Tower Theater, and the name of my dad's drugstore was Tower Drug, so it was simply adopted from that theater name back in 1941. That's how it came about.

AHS: It is truly a story of American enterprise, isn't it?

SOLOMON: It's true. I think even today, people can start very small. If they have good ideas and they have perseverance, there's no reason why they can't start small and ultimately grow. Everybody says it's harder today to start, but it isn't necessarily.

AHS: Thanks, Russ.

INTERVIEW WITH
STEVE KARMEN

Steve Karmen, known in the trade as the "King of the Jingle," is the creator of "I Love New York" and innumerable commercials for some of the leading advertisers in the world. Mr. Karmen is also the author of *Through the Jingle Jungle,* the preeminent book on the jingle business.

AHS: Congratulations, Steve. I just learned that you've become an author. What's your book's name?

KARMEN: *Through the Jingle Jungle.*

AHS: *Through the Jingle Jungle,* by Steve Karmen.

KARMEN: Billboard books.

AHS: I have always thought that you jingle people considered the term "jingle" pejorative, that you didn't like the term.

KARMEN: Most do think it's pejorative, but I think it's exactly right. We write jingles. I was once at a meeting at CBS where everyone was judging the Big Apple Awards, and everyone went around the table, "What do you do?" I'm the chairman of this or I'm the chairman of that. It came to me, and I said, "I write jingles," and everybody laughed. It's perceived as a pejorative term, but it really isn't.

AHS: I never considered it such.

KARMEN: A jingle is advertising in its most memorable form, and it is what it's called. I'm in the jingle business.

AHS: You are known as the "King of the Jingle." Was that a result of a magazine article?

KARMEN: Many years ago.

AHS: Tell me a little about it. Why are you the "King of the Jingles"? Is it because you're the best?

KARMEN: Well, I like to think so.

AHS: I've heard that.

KARMEN: There was a time when almost everything on the air was mine. In every creative field you go through spurts of creativity. I used to think that you were really a star if you could see two or three of your commercials in a row. At the end of a show there's a two-minute break, or four thirty-second spots . . . if you had two of yours in a row, or maybe three, it's nirvana for the jingle writer. There was a time when I had a ton of stuff on the air. When you work for an Anheuser Busch, a Budweiser, they make a ton of commercials. It's not like when you work for a very small producer. The ones that advertise a lot are companies like McDonald's, hamburger chains, soft drinks, beers, automobiles. When you do a perfume or a boutique item, it may be on once every three days or once a week. It could be the greatest piece of music in the world, but you're not going to build a reputation from it. But when you write something that's on the football game, and it's played every fifteen minutes, it helps build your reputation. I wrote "I Love New York," which has become the New York State song, everybody knows it. It is the one that has gotten the most instant recognition. If someone says, "What have you written?" I say, "I wrote 'This Bud's for You.'" Everybody knows it. "I Love New York" is almost universally recognized. I was in Egypt a couple of years ago and I saw a bumper sticker that said, "I Love New York." It has become more than an advertising campaign. It has become almost generic.

AHS: It's taken a life of its own.

KARMEN: It has taken a life of its own.

AHS: I assume it's very lucrative also.

KARMEN: No, amazingly enough, "I Love New York" is not at all lucrative.

AHS: It doesn't get performance credits?

KARMEN: It gets some performance credit out of ASCAP, but as you well know, ASCAP pays only a fraction of a normal credit for jingles. We are still fighting that battle.

AHS: Hasn't it taken a life as a real song, aside from the jingle?

KARMEN: Yes, it has, but it's primarily part of an advertising campaign, and it's a local campaign. I retained the rights to it. I issued licenses to Shea Stadium, Yankee Stadium to use it at the ball park, and the U.S. Open tennis tournament used it. Dollarwise it is not a big money-maker, not like it would be if it was for a network advertiser, some product like an automobile or a beer or something like that.

AHS: When you started out, an adult going to make a living, was it your aspiration to be a writer of jingles, of commercials, or did you have another calling in mind at the time?

KARMEN: I was going to be a performer, initially. I think everybody starts out wanting to be that.

AHS: Well, that's most of the readers of this book. I want these people who are starting out with guitars and hoping to be stars to know that if they love the music business and they can't be performers, that there may be other areas in music that they can pursue.

KARMEN: Well, I started out as a performer, as a musician. I was a saxophone player, self-taught, and when I give speeches on the subject I try to tell people not to be discouraged. You have to have balls of steel in this business. You have to have an infinite tolerance for rejection—otherwise become a civilian and work in something else. But to work in the music business you are going out and saying, "Hey, you love me, don't you, audience? Please love me." It's not, "Here's my book and love me," it's "I'm a performer. I'm up there strumming my guitar. I'm playing my instrument, and I want you to love me." Sometimes they don't love you, and if you make a phonograph record and they don't buy your record, you can't be discouraged. In my book I say it doesn't make you a bad person if you get rejected. I have a good batting average, but there are times I write something that is not accepted and of course I disagree with them. I may think it's a terrific song, but it doesn't work. So as a beginner it's important to feel confident in yourself, and your confidence should not come from your material. Confidence will come from your understanding that maybe you will make it as a performer, and if you don't do that, maybe you'll make it as a writer, and if it's not a writer, maybe you'll be a producer or something, as long as you are in the field.

AHS: How did you segue from Gerry Mulligan to "King of the Jingles"?

KARMEN: I wanted to be in show business and I played saxophone. I started to sing. I started to write songs. I'm an Arthur Godfrey "Talent Scouts" loser. Remember that program back in 1957? I was a calypso singer in those days.

AHS: Belafonte?

KARMEN: I was the white Harry Belafonte. I'm not kidding. I used to do concerts in Carnegie Hall on Saturday nights. They used to introduce me as the most authentic of the nonauthentic calypso singers. I was the Jewish Harry Belafonte, and I sang and I wrote songs and I acted. I went to acting school. If you're in the business you must learn. You have to be versed. Success is not an accident. You have to try; if you're not making it as a singer, you have got to study acting. If you don't make it as an actor, learn to be a dancer, or something! Keep your body in shape. Keep your mind in shape. If you are in the business, one thing leads to another. I sang and acted in a movie, and I went to the producer of the film and said, "Hey, I'm a songwriter." He let me write a couple of songs for the movie. I met the editor of the movie, who was in the advertising business, working as a producer of commercials. He told people, "I know somebody who writes music cheap." I started writing jingles because of that. One thing led to the other, but the main thing that motivated me was the desire to be in the business, and I wasn't intimidated when people didn't like me. I wanted to do this. I really think that if you try and if you have any ability at all, sooner or later, something will stick.

AHS: Did you ever try producing phonograph records, a record as an artist?

KARMEN: I did, but I was unsuccessful at it. I had my own records. I recorded on the Mercury label. I had six single records out in the fifties and early sixties, rock 'n' roll. I was the Frankie Avalon/Bobby Darin type, and I never had any hits—although I worked for almost ten years as a nightclub performer . . . singing and playing guitar.

AHS: While you were doing jingles?

KARMEN: No, this is long before, and I barely eked out a living. Then I got married, and once you have a kid or two and you want to have a house and things like that, you have to do something that provides income. I didn't like being on the road anymore. I was on the road for a long time, singing, working clubs that are now supermarkets. I eventually met a producer who gave me the opportunity to write the background score for a film. I started when I acted in his movie. He was producing low-budget porno films— "nudie movies," they called them—and I started to write the background scores for them even though I had no technique or training.

AHS: Are you going to tell us whether you were acting in them?

KARMEN: I acted in one, but no touching, *no touching,* in those films. But I learned how to write music for movies that way. I sat next to this producer who wanted the job done cheaply, and he showed me how to run a moviola and how to time out the music and where the music would go. If the music was too long, I would edit it. If the picture was not right, he allowed me to edit the film too, to make the music match it, and I sat there and worked for nothing. I received five hundred dollars to make my first score for a movie, which was called *Hollywood Nudes Report.* It was like a travelogue where they showed nude women . . . no touching. This was in the early sixties. The censorship laws were very different then, so it wasn't pornography. *Later,* they started to get a little raunchy. I would learn how to actually edit film and edit music that way, and I scored thirty of those films, over maybe a five-year period. I got five hundred dollars for the first one, and out of the five hundred dollars I had to pay the band and the studio. So I ended up literally with lunch money and we spent it all at lunch; I ordered for everybody . . . all the recording was monaural.

AHS: Two takes.

KARMEN: Yes, two takes. That's it, *maybe* two takes. But I learned the craft by doing that. I always tell people today in the beginning: *take every job.*

AHS: How did the advertising agencies learn of you?

KARMEN: Well, the advertising industry is always looking for something new and different, and the first really big hit that I had was "You Can Take Salem Out of the Country, But . . ." It had an ending that hung, you know, it never ended, and I wrote that and everybody started to call. "Get me the guy who wrote the Salem stuff." I got called by Budweiser and General Tire and Hershey and Nationwide Insurance . . .

AHS: You were making a living.

KARMEN: Yes, that's how it began, but I'll tell you something: the business has changed enormously. If you're going to direct this towards young people, the thing that I would try to impress upon them *most* is that they have to be prepared with a craft. You can't go in and just wing it. Today everyone is an expert. When I started in the business, and I had written a jingle or even a song, if I wanted to present it to you I would say, "Alan, do you have a piano? Here it is and I'll sing it for you." And it's me with my rotten piano-playing and me with my rotten voice, but you get the idea, and "Wait 'til you hear it with an orchestra and we're going to bring in Frank Sinatra to sing it, or Ray Charles or somebody. You're going to love it!" Today it doesn't work that way. Today everyone has a synthesizer. Everyone knows about music. They may not be a trained musician, as such, but they can play out of instinct on the new equipment. It makes everybody an expert. So what has happened in the jingle business, and in the music business, is that there is infinitely more competition than there used to be. It used to be that you could write a song and you would have to convince someone that it was good. "Please invest the money and let's go into the studio." That doesn't happen today. Today they will say, "Well, bring me a tape," and the tape has to be 90 percent finished.

AHS: I've been hearing this a lot. Some years ago the A&R people, the people whose job it is to listen to songs or artists, could listen to a simple demo, create the orchestrations and arrangements in their head, and hear it as finished product. Today your A&R people are very young and they don't have the experience or the training or the ability to do that. They have to hear it pretty much the way it's going to be . . .

KARMEN: Today they expect an almost finished product. We call them demo-finals now. They're not demos anymore. I'm going to go home and work on something now for an airline. They don't just want to hear me on a piano. They want to hear that French horn airline sound, and they want that string section that sounds like an airline.

AHS: You do that yourself on the synthesizer?

KARMEN: Absolutely. I have a studio. It has evolved to the point where you have to have a studio in your house. It doesn't have to be elaborate, but it has to be something where you can produce the sounds of today. You buy a good synthesizer. It's got a drum machine built into it. It's got echo equipment built into it, effects, and things like that, and then you need a little recording machine. Of course, you know, it gets bigger and grander as you go.

AHS: Well, twenty-five years ago that equipment didn't exist.

KARMEN: Right.

AHS: And if you could buy it, you were talking about a hundred to two hundred thousand dollars.

KARMEN: That's right. And there used to be something called the musician.

AHS: Yes.

KARMEN: Today, to be a musician is really very, very difficult. The musicians I know are what we used to call studio players. They were the musicians who would be hired if Frank Sinatra was going to record, "from two to five next Thursday." They would bring in forty musicians . . . the guys would play it, Frank would sing it, and it would be done.

AHS: Session musicians.

KARMEN: Studio musicians, session musicians. Today those people simply do not work. There's a tragedy going on out there. People who spent their entire lives in the music business, people who could sit down, read, and play someone else's music as if they had been playing it all their lives . . . today there's no business for them. The drum parts are done on a machine. The bass parts and 90 percent of the other parts are done on a machine, and you now have the ability even to replace the voice. If you don't like your voice on it, the song is still there. So the whole industry has changed. Young people have to study. You have to learn how to use the synthesizers. I do everything on a computer, and I tell you, Alan, it blows my own mind when I do it. I can sit there and play a piano part and make a mistake and I don't have to replay it. I go into the computer and say, "Find me bar 8, third beat," and if I played an F and it was supposed to be an F-sharp, I push a button and it becomes an F-sharp. And if I want a French horn to play, I push the French horn button. It's incredible.

AHS: We used to have a hell of a lot more fun in the studios . . .

KARMEN: It's still fun—but it's different fun.

AHS: But it's lonely, isn't it?

KARMEN: And it takes five times as long. I mean I am a professional orchestrator. I've written orchestrations and I conducted the New York Philharmonic in my own stuff and I did the entire orchestration for that. Today I don't have to do that. When you don't do it, believe it or not, you lose the craft of doing it. Today I sit down at a computer keyboard and I play my music into my synthesizer and it is now in a computer and I add the drum part and I add the entire orchestra. Instead of writing the entire orchestration out on a score pad and going into a studio and booking forty musicians, I am literally orchestrating onto the computer discs, and when it comes out the sounds will scare you. I mean the technology today is so good that you don't need people anymore.

AHS: Does it miss a heartbeat?

KARMEN: Yes, to a certain degree, but I tell you the layman doesn't know the difference. Now you as a professional and I as a professional know it has engendered its own sound. It has its own sphere, this electronic music, and if you really want to make it terrific you *maybe* bring in a live guitar player, or you bring in maybe one saxophone player.

AHS: I have clients who record and they will bring in live players.

KARMEN: Yeah, but mostly it's a couple of guys to enhance. I'm not saying that you never use live musicians anymore, but less and less.

AHS: You have got to bring somebody to put in a mistake.

KARMEN: Yeah, the mistake is what makes it live. But I have a machine now that's put out by Roland. It's a drum machine called the "living drummer"—a living drum machine—and there is a thing in there that you can program so that it's not quite perfect, and it sounds like a human being. You know, a drum machine would ordinarily be exactly, exactly where you want it, but you throw that little switch and it just gives it that little feeling that it's called the human drum machine. But it's still a machine.

AHS: That's funny.

KARMEN: And the unions of course are up in arms because their people don't work.

AHS: If I were a kid today, and I established to my own satisfaction, for one reason or another, that I really didn't have a future up front on stage or I didn't have the right kind of personality or if I didn't have the looks or I was too shy, or whatever, and I said, "I can write and I'm ingenious and I'm clever, and I think this jingle business might be a good niche for me," how would I start? How would I get going?

KARMEN: You would have to get a piece of equipment that you would be able to express your creativity on, meaning a synthesizer.

AHS: I understand. I'm going one step further. How do I get my feet wet?

KARMEN: I'm going to send you a copy of my book, which I'd like you to take a look at, which will answer a lot of these questions. That's how I directed my book.

AHS: Well, now they'll have to buy two books. My book and your book. *Through the Jingle Jungle,* good title.

KARMEN: I have always looked at my business in a unique way. People ask, "What kind of competition do you have?" I have never felt that I have competition. I have *colleagues* in the business. If you're going to write a song about Pan Am and I'm going to write a song about Pan Am, there are going to be two separate songs. We each approach it with our own personalities and from our own perspectives.

A beginner, to start, has to have the equipment and then he has to put together a tape. The tape is absolutely essential. Then you have to have, as I said before, balls of steel because you have to call the advertising agencies, the music departments. "Hi, I'm Joe Smith. I'm a new jingle writer and I'd like you to hear my reel . . ." Click. They hang up on you. People are lining up in the streets and you have to be persistent.

AHS: One guy who's feeling good that day and magnanimous and . . .

KARMEN: And maybe you happen to know the attorney of somebody who knows somebody, who knows somebody, who knows somebody, who knows somebody, and maybe they'll get you a hearing. Maybe you have an idea to write a song for a beer, for Coca Cola, for McDonald's. People always come up to me and say, "Gee, I have a great idea for Coca Cola," and I say, "Forget it," because Coca Cola has an advertising agency that they're paying millions of dollars to, with floors and floors of people, whose whole job is just to come with an idea for Coca Cola. It ain't going to happen for you, sitting in your living room in Topeka, Kansas. What you can do is to write a sample: "This is a sound that I can come up with. This is a vocal approach." You put it on a tape and you take it to the agency, if you can get into the agency—and there are agencies all over. You keep trying, banging your head against the wall, until ultimately someone says, "We have a new project and we're hiring Joe DiMaggio, Babe Ruth and Lou Gehrig, and we have room for one newcomer. Let's use this kid . . . maybe he'll do it for nothing." As I said before, take the job, and hopefully you come up with something different because you're young, and Babe Ruth knows only how to swing a wooden bat, and you know how to swing a synthesizer bat. Maybe you'll come up with a new sound and then maybe you'll get the job. Then—here's the big point, what I consider is the big point—when you get the job, work under the union, within union structure. What has happened to our industry is that much of the work is done by non-union companies. It has become a business where the advertiser will pay a creative fee of anywhere from $5,000 to $10,000 to $15,000, but they will want to buy it out one time. A friend of mine wrote "The Heartbeat of America," a Chevrolet campaign, and they still use it, but he doesn't participate as a composer. The way everybody makes a living today is by singing on their work. They do not retain an interest in their compositions. Composers want to sing on their work so they can get vocalist residuals, but if you have written this wonderful song and they want to hire Ray Charles and the Raylettes to sing it, the composer gets *nothing*—zip—because he has signed away all rights under a work-for-hire contract! Well, that's exactly what has happened in the industry today. I gave a speech recently at the Long Island Ad Club, for example, and the room was filled with jingle writers. I say, "You have to work union," and they say they *can't* work union. The local savings bank in Syosset does not want to have a residual situation. They want to come to someone and say, "Here's $5,000. Write me a song, produce me a track on your home synthesizer, get your sister and your mother and your brother to sing it. We'll give a one-time payment. Pay them $50 each, whatever you can get away with, but we own it. Period." I was at a dinner with the lady who wrote "Anchor Savings Will Show You the Way to Live for Tomorrow Today." She's a married woman in her early forties, and she wrote this thing about fifteen years ago and got maybe $500 for it on a buy-out basis. It runs to this day and she gets nothing. If I had something like that, Alan, I would slit my throat. A composer must fight to retain an ongoing interest in his work.

AHS: I appreciate what you're saying, but . . . as a beginner, you may not have a choice.

KARMEN: To begin, perhaps, but you must constantly try to raise your price and constantly try to get into a union situation because the unions—as bad as they are, and they are in some ways absolutely terrible—have established the concept of residuals. If you are a songwriter, or an author, you're not going to give your creation away for a one-time fee. They may make a movie out of it. It may become a bigger television series than "M*A*S*H." Talk about it happens to everyone, Neil Simon wrote *The Odd Couple* and they made a television series out of it. This is now fifteen or twenty years ago, and I understand he thought, "Oh, there won't be reruns." So they gave him a big piece of money. My understanding is that he does not participate in the reruns. *Today,* he would never do it. No one with intelligence would ever do it, but in the advertising business that's what they want . . . the advertiser wants to run it unlimited, for one fee. I have always felt that if you write a song or a movie or a book or anything like that, you should never give away all your rights. Always try to keep a piece of the action. I tell young jingle writers, "If you're writing for the savings bank in Syosset and they want to give you five thousand dollars to do it, take the money. Tell them that if you go into the second year, you want fifteen hundred dollars every year they use it." Get something, some sort of an ongoing participation.

AHS: Set a precedent.

KARMEN: It's not really a precedent. It's unusual by current standards. It's only unusual when you ask for it. They may say, "Well, listen, we're going to get the guy around the corner. He'll sign it away."

But if you feel that your work is good enough, the only way that you will ever make progress is to say no. "No, I will not sign a work-for-hire contract," or "Yes, I will sign a work-for-hire contract, but I want an ongoing payment, five hundred dollars a year" . . . *something,* so that you know that if they continue to use your work, you participate in it.

AHS: Jingle writers have a trade association, don't they?

KARMEN: It's kind of moribund at this point. It's unfortunate. SAMPAC is what it's called.

AHS: You were an officer of SAMPAC, as I recall.

KARMEN: I was chairman three times.

AHS: . . . and a young jingle writer who wanted advice or some guidance could get in touch with SAMPAC, and SAMPAC could hold his hand and guide him.

KARMEN: Guide him through it. Right.

AHS: Is there still at least a phone number for SAMPAC?

KARMEN: No, that's one of the reasons why I wrote my book, because I tried to tell people the truth. The advertiser wants your product at the cheapest possible price, and he wants to own everything, whether it's the "Heartbeat of America" or the last McDonald's campaign. The guy who wrote that signed away his rights under the impression that he was going to be able to produce all of their commercials, thereby having the ability to hire himself as a singer, thereby getting residuals. It turned out the agency didn't have the same impression and they let a different music house produce the spots, so the composer/writer gets nothing. I know this writer and I sent him my own contract form where I retain rights. I send it to anybody who wants it, but no one wants to force the issue. Everyone is so afraid today.

AHS: To lose the business?

KARMEN: Yeah. There is no semblance of community in the jingle business. It's unfortunate. It really is, because the industry needs exactly this kind of message, "Don't give up your rights." If you have to, to feed your family, at least try to get some sort of continuing payment or interest. There is no SAMPAC.

AHS: It's funny. Here we're lamenting the fact that the writer of the jingle is not getting any residuals if he does it the way the advertising agencies want, and yet in the pop music area—which this book is really directed towards—it's the songwriter who gets royalties every time the song is played, and the artist, who created the record, receives nothing.

KARMEN: Correct.

AHS: Unless he happens to be the writer.

KARMEN: Well, he gets it from his record sales.

AHS: Yeah, but record sales die within a relatively short period of time, but the performance income on a hit goes on and on and on and on.

KARMEN: A wise man once said copyrights don't talk back.

AHS: I'll buy that.

KARMEN: If you own a copyright, you can pass it on to your heirs. If your song is revived it can go on forever. If you can, as a creator, retain an ongoing interest in your work, that's really where it's at. As a beginner, you have to take every job, but you have to have a goal in your mind, a business goal. When we talk about the music business, there's the music part and the business part. For the business part you need a good lawyer and you need someone who will constantly remind you that your aim is to grow *up,* to grow bigger, and not to remain on one level.

AHS: You need a lot of fortitude.

KARMEN: To repeat: You must be willing to stand rejection. Don't be afraid; it doesn't make you a bad person. This is your business. A career is not one hit record. It's important for people who have made it, who are successful, to pass along at least what happened to them, so that young people can profit from it. The main thing that you have to tell a newcomer is "It ain't easy." Competition is fierce.

AHS: When I asked you to come here and give me this interview, I had no idea that you had written a book.

KARMEN: I'll get you a copy of it.

AHS: It's very important that you wrote it, especially since SAMPAC is not active. If they can't find it in the stores, they can order it from Billboard, I'm sure.

KARMEN: Right. I'd like you to look at it because I think I do for the jingle writer what you are doing with your book. You have to have a tape in the jingle business. If you want to be a jingle singer or writer, nobody will accept a live audition. They want to hear a tape. Tape is what the business is about, to show a potential client that this is how I write, this is how I sing . . .

AHS: I've represented a lot of artists who sing, and I've also represented people who didn't make it big with phonograph records but who have made a very handsome living doing commercials, jingles. As a matter of fact, there are some who do both, who have attained great success as a recording artist and who make a very handsome income doing jingles.

KARMEN: Richie Havens is a very good example.

AHS: Well, I represent Nick Ashford and Valerie Simpson . . .

KARMEN: Great. Valerie sang on all of my Budweiser stuff initially.

AHS: . . . but there are still some people, I think, who are really superb technicians, superb singers, better technically than many of the people who make it big, and yet they don't have that magic that's necessary for hit records.

KARMEN: That's exactly right. The needs are exactly opposite in the jingle business. In the record business they want the personality of the performer. You get a strong sense of personality when you hear Nick and Valerie. In the jingle business they want the singer to subjugate his own personality to that of the product. The singer must be good, but he's not the star. The product is the star, so you'll find that the people who have the tremendous technique and may not have that personality of their own to be a performer, or a solo performer, can do terrifically in the jingle business. There are some singers that I know who have made—and I'm not exaggerating—anywhere from a million and a half to two million bucks a year singing jingles, and you would never know them. They're walking down the street wearing funky T-shirts that . . .

AHS: Would you mention that number again, a million . . .

KARMEN: A million and a half, two million dollars a year, and I'm not exaggerating.

AHS: Singing jingles?

KARMEN: Singing jingles. I'm not even talking about the solo singers, although some of them are. I'm talking about group. They will go from a Pepsi date to a Coca Cola date to a Budweiser date to a Miller beer date to a Cadillac date to a Pontiac date to a Chrysler date, to Datsun. They go from session to session to session. I used to watch Monday Night Football when it first came on, and Datsun and Toyota were the car advertisers. They would take one Datsun track that used to say "We Are Driven" and stick it on every commercial . . . the same music track . . . and for every commercial, the group singers got paid a separate session fee, and they got paid separate residuals. So a singer could come in—and I'm not exaggerating—spend two hours, and over the course of the year make fifty or a hundred thousand dollars from it. But, business has changed. First of all, because what has happened is that a jingle composer is now a singer. There is no longer that elite group of maybe ten or twenty people like Valerie and Nick. Valerie and Nick are the greatest songwriters. They've written hits that everyone will remember forever, but they made a tremendous income, Valerie especially, being the background singer on Budweiser, on General Tire, on "I Love New York," on other stuff that I have done. Valerie is fantastic. Give her a piece of music, she reads it, sings it, and you never know it's her.

AHS: They have an interview in this book also, so you're in good company.

KARMEN: When you see them, please give them a hug for me.

AHS: I will indeed.

KARMEN: Valerie was one of maybe five singers who are really up in that top category. Valerie has a sound of her own, but she also knows how to step back. They don't want to be the solo singers on jingles, they want to be in the group because although the group doesn't pay as well as the solo, it pays *pretty good*—and Alan, I am not kidding . . . a million bucks, a million and a half, two million bucks a year, to sing jingles.

AHS: All over America, little lightbulbs are appearing over my readers' heads.

KARMEN: It's true. But in a union situation only. Nonunion has no residuals.

AHS: It's funny. I used to feel sorry for jingle singers. No more.

KARMEN: Don't. But what has happened is that today there's so much competition for the work. If you are a jingle writer today, you hire yourself, and your secretary, and your sister, and your mother as singers, and then you hire Valerie and Nick to be the two good singers . . . there are many, many more people in the business today . . .

AHS: There's a dilution.

KARMEN: Dilution is the correct word. That's what has happened to the business and it's made it harder. Now every agency wants— instead of paying $2,500 for a demo—to pay you $1,000 or $500. They want it free and the jingle houses are willing to give them demos free, produced on equipment that cost them hundreds of thousands of dollars, just so they can put themselves on as union singers, because that's where the money is. So the industry has changed. There has been a tremendous dilution in the amount of talent that's around, and the creativity has gone down accordingly. I know that when I write a song on the piano, you could not write the same song on the piano as I could, but if you buy a DK7 keyboard or a Korg M-1 keyboard, or something like that, you are producing the same sounds as I'm producing. So the equipment has become an equalizer in the business and created tremendous competition.

AHS: I thank you very much.

KARMEN: My pleasure.

LEXICON PLUS

This section was to be called a glossary, but I was advised that people don't read glossaries. I hope they read lexicons because this one is to the rest of the book what the Rosetta Stone was to hieroglyphics. It is the key!

But take heart. I found the spartan economic style of a true glossary (oops! I mean lexicon) as tedious for me to write as it would be for you to read. Consequently, this lexicon is liberally salted with observations and illustrations which I think make it more readable than it might otherwise have been—hence the "plus."

I recommend that you read it through once, and thereafter use it as a dictionary or glossary or lexicon or whatever.

A

A & R (Artists and Repertoire)—The division or department of a record company traditionally charged with the responsibility for discovering artists and providing and selecting appropriate material for their recordings. The latter function has to some extent been diminished with the advent of the "singer-songwriter."

"A" Side (of a 45-rpm Record)—The side of a single that the record company believes is the hit. It is designated the "A" side on promotional copies distributed to disc jockeys so that they will know which side to play. Most of the time the record company is wrong. Most of the time it

doesn't matter because the disc jockeys don't play it anyway.

Accounting, an—The periodic (usually semiannual) financial reports rendered by record companies to artists and producers and by music publishers to songwriters. In the event all recording costs and advances have been recouped, it is sometimes (depending on the solvency of the company) accompanied by a check in the amount of the royalties shown to be due.

Administration Fee—A fee charged by one music publisher to another for managing and "working" the latter's catalogue of songs. Such fee arrangements vary widely and are subject to extensive negotiation. See Chapter 2.

Administration Rights—The rights granted by one music publisher to another whereby the administering publisher acquires the rights, for a fee, to manage and "work" the catalogue of songs of the music publisher granting the rights. The structure of administration arrangements varies widely, and the contracts governing them are complex and contain subtle nuances with major economic ramifications. Beware! See Chapter 2.

Advance—A sum of money paid to an artist or songwriter in anticipation of, and chargeable against, the artist's or songwriter's future royalties. An advance, if granted, is usually paid on the signing of a contract, the exercise of an option, or on some other event such as asking for it. Advances, though recoupable out of future earnings, are not traditionally returnable if not earned. They are invariably welcomed and fuel the fires of creativity.

AF of M (American Federation of Musicians)—The musicians' union.

AFTRA (American Federation of Television and Radio Artists).

AGAC (American Guild of Authors and Composers)—A national songwriters' association, which performs various administrative, educational, and political functions for its members. It is funded by members' dues and commissions on members' royalties, both of which are assessed on a graduated scale.

Agent—A person or organization licensed under state employment laws to procure employment for clients and to charge a fee for services rendered (usually 10 percent of gross compensation). Eventually artists utilize agents in connection with personal appearances. Songwriters rarely utilize the services of agents. Agency contracts are complicated and deal with many items. They should be carefully scrutinized and negotiated.

Album Cut—A song recorded for an album that is not anticipated to be a "single" or "hit" record. Such songs are not without quality, and are essential to the structure, continuity, and success of an album. All too often singles turn out to be album cuts and sometimes, though rarely, what are thought to be album cuts emerge as singles.

Alternative Music—Alternative music, sometimes referred to as "Neomodern," seems to be new music that can't readily be pigeonholed into an existing and time-honored niche, such as R&B, Pop, or Rock. As an area of alternative music garners a following it acquires its own "label," respectability, and probably its own "chart" in the trades.

AOR—Album-oriented rock.

Approval Not to Be Unreasonably Withheld—Artists and songwriters in their negotiations with record companies and music publishers often ask for and receive the right to approve certain elements involved in the evolution of their work. Artists, for example, may have the right to approve their producers and the songs to be recorded; songwriters may win the right to approve arrangements. No one really knows what "not to be unreasonably withheld" means, but attorneys for record companies and music publishers, with well-earned paranoia, insist on the language in case an artist or songwriter, without any real artistic motivation, refuses approval out of pique or as a hostage in a negotiation.

ASCAP (American Society of Composers, Authors and Publishers)—A performing rights organization whose sole and limited functions are the issuance and enforcement of licenses for the public performance of the nondramatic songs of its publisher and songwriter members and the distribution of the revenues derived from such licenses. ASCAP is not the other things you thought it was. It is not a union, it is not a music publisher, it does not administer or control copyrights. Although they used to give advances, which were a great source of fees for attorneys, neither ASCAP nor BMI now do so. Damn!

Audio-Visual Rights—Rights to couple an artist's visual performance with his vocal performance—sometimes referred to as "Sight and Sound." This fast, maturing bundle of rights is rapidly evolving due to the popularity of videodisc and videotape players. Earlier they could often be reserved to the artist, or at least a "standoff" requiring mutual acquiescence could be won during negotiation of a record contract. Now that what was the future is the present, and the scent of megabucks is high in the air, only established artists with considerable clout can alter what has become intransigence on the part of record companies relative to audio-visual rights.

Audit Clause—The provision in an artist's or songwriter's contract that enables him to have his accountant examine the books and records of the record company or music publisher in order to verify the accuracy of the accounting received. In the not-too-distant past such a clause had to be fought for. Now it is almost universally included as part of the "boilerplate" of all recording and songwriter contracts, although there is wide variety as to their limitations. Some are "cuter" than others. This is a key clause, and you might be advised to consider a change of counsel if a contract not containing an audit clause is submitted to you for signature.

B

"B" Side (of a 45-rpm record)—The "other" side of a single record. It is usually an album cut, since record companies are loath to press two "A" sides on the same single, only one side of which will receive airplay. If an album has two potential "A" sides, one will be saved for release either when the first single proves to be a dud or when album sales begin to flag.

Background Singers—The singers that are heard in the chorus or background of a solo artist's record. If your forte is singing, this is an excellent way to put bread on the table while you are waiting to be a foreground singer. Background singers receive fees for their services but no royalties.

BMI (Broadcast Music, Inc.)—A performing rights organization with the same functions as ASCAP. BMI and AS-CAP are competitors and will fight over the privilege of not giving you advances.

Boilerplate—The provisions that are contained, with little or no change, in all record or songwriter contracts regardless of the luminescence of the artist or songwriter involved. These clauses are probably the only things your contract will have in common with Madonna's or Billy Joel's . . . until your next round of contract negotiations. Boilerplate provisions are usually little negotiated and include such universal things as grants of rights, copyright notices, and other matters considered essential but mechanical, mundane, or otherwise without romance . . . the kinds of things a lawyer can't get a medal or a bonus for.

Bottom Line—No, not the Greenwich Village nightclub. When your lawyer and their lawyer have become sufficiently exasperated with each other in the negotiation of a particular point, one will say, "Enough of this nonsense (euphemism). What's the bottom line?" Depending on what side of the table you're on, it's either the maximum they will give or the minimum you will take.

Budget Line—A record company's line of

records that are priced substantially lower than the company's "top pop" line. A budget line usually consists of albums whose sales have so diminished as to render them no longer marketable as part of a "full price" line. Your attorney will (hopefully) obtain a provision whereby your albums will not be relegated to the budget line until a fixed period of time (12 to 24 months) after they have been commercially released as part of the company's "top pop" line.

Bullet—The black dot, star, or asterisk appearing adjacent to the titles of certain records on the charts of music trade publications. It connotes unusual activity in the growth of a record's popularity. The loss of a bullet is bad news, signifying that the record has peaked and is on its way down or off the chart.

Bump—Bumps are contractual increases that take effect upon the happening of some event. Examples would be royalty increases that take effect upon the attainment of a certain sales level, or upon the exercise of a record company option. Bumps also occur in connection with recording budgets . . . and egos.

C

©—The international symbol for the word "copyright." It must appear with the year date of the copyright and the name of the copyright owner wherever prescribed by the United States Copyright Act and the Universal Copyright Convention. A © is not mandatory on works first published after March 1, 1989, the date the U.S. adopted the Berne Convention. For an example, see the reverse of the title page of this book. I'm unduly impressed by all who have the © on their word processors. Music publishers with such word processors are apt to have more than one writer signed. See *Copyright.*

Capital Gains—A tax term meaning the gain from the sale of a capital asset. Music publishing companies, copyrights, and record masters are capital assets. You will pay a smaller tax on a capital gain than you would on gains that are ordinary income. Let's hope you have to worry about this real soon. Then pay your tax adviser to worry about it for you. His fees are deductible.

Catalogue—A group of songs characterized by something in common such as common ownership and/or common authorship, as in "Chappell Music's catalogue is studded with great show tunes."

Catchall Clause—Most record and songwriter contracts limit the liability of the record company and music publisher to pay royalties only with respect to those income sources specifically set forth in the contract. Since there are few psychic lawyers and an ever-burgeoning technology, it is wise to try to include a catchall clause at the end of the compensation clause. It should read: ". . . and fifty percent (50%) of all other income from all other sources, now known or hereafter to come into existence."

CD—See Compact Disc.

CHR—"Contemporary Hit Radio" is the current nomenclature for stations programming popular hit singles. Also known as "Top 40," this format concentrates, as you may have deduced, on the top forty residents of the "Hot 100" singles charts.

Compact Disc—A 120mm plastic coated disc reproducing sound or sound together with visual images which are read and transmitted from by means of a laser. Great capacity, fidelity, and perpetual life made these rainbow tinged beauties the record of the present more quickly than was anticipated. CDs have all but displaced conventional LPs.

Compulsory License—Under the provisions of the United States Copyright Act, the copyright owner of a nondramatic musical work has the exclusive right to make and distribute phonorecords of such a work *until* a phonorecord of the work has been distributed to the public under authority of the copyright owner. After public distribution, any person may, by complying with the requirements of the Copyright Act, obtain a "compulsory license" to make and distribute phonorecords of the work. In other words, once a voluntary license is issued by the copyright owner, he can't stop anyone else from recording the song. The monopoly supposedly ends. Actually, compliance with the compulsory license provisions is so onerous that few would go this route unless they absolutely had to. When might one have to? When one has followed the tradition of recording first and licensing second, and has pressed and packaged a large quantity of albums containing the unlicensed song. When would a copyright owner refuse a voluntary license? Usually only when he finds the contemplated recording so aesthetically offensive as to be damaging to his valuable copyright.

Controlled Composition—In the parlance of record contracts, a controlled composition is one recorded under the contract and owned or controlled directly or indirectly (as through a corporation) by the artists, his producer, his wife, his parents, his aunts, uncles, cousins, children, or pets. Record companies compete for the most comprehensive and all-inclusive language in this clause. It seeks for the record company a reduced mechanical royalty (music publishing royalty as opposed to artists' recording royalty—don't confuse the two) with respect to controlled compositions and total exemption from mechanical royalties in those instances where there is no requirement to pay the artist a record royalty (for example, on records distributed for promotional purposes or on records given away free). It is a negotiable clause, but how well your lawyer does will be more a function of your clout than his skill (assuming he knows enough to fight like hell on this one). Artists with a track record can usually impose their will. Beginners may have to wait till the next time. There is one new record company which professes to not even ask for a "rate." Is it a trend? Unlikely.

Co-Publish(ing)—The situation that arises when more than one publisher has acquired publishing rights to the same song. This is not at all uncommon, since collaboration in the writing of a song is anything but rare. If the lyricist is signed to one publisher and the music writer to another, both publishers own an *undivided* partial (depending on how the writers agree to share) interest in the song, and each can deal with the song as it sees fit, subject to sharing the income with its co-publisher and subject to an implied obligation not to "waste" or destroy wantonly the value of the copyright. Since each co-publisher can deal with respect to the song, neither can grant exclusive rights or licenses. Since exclusive rights result in the highest advances and other remuneration, it is usually beneficial for the co-publishers to enter into an agreement (a co-publishing agreement) governing how the song will be administered and exploited.

Copyright ©—A limited monopoly granted by Congress as an incentive to creators of certain literary and artistic works so that, subject to certain gobbledygook, they can control the destiny and enjoy the fruits of their creativity. It usually lasts for the life of the creator plus fifty years (séances are helpful). Did you know that you don't have to do anything to get a copyright on your song? That it's automatically granted you when you write your song? Well, it's true. See Chapter 7 on copyright.

Copyright Registration—The legal for-

mality by which the basic facts of a particular copyright are placed on public
record. Registration is not a condition of
copyright protection generally. Registration is, however, considered in the public
interest; therefore the Copyright Act provides certain incentives to encourage registration. See Chapter 7 on copyright.

Coupling—The practice of utilizing cuts
or sides by different artists in conjunction
with each other. Thus are made possible
the plethora of "best of" albums you see
advertised on television. Your attorney
will strive to bar or limit your record
company's ability to thus use your recordings without your approval.

Cover; Cover Record—A recording by
one artist of a song recorded and made
popular by another artist. An artist covers
a record he believes he can improve upon.
Singer-songwriters who sing the definitive
version of their songs are less often covered than singer-songwriters whose singing is weaker than their writing.

Credit, Label—There are two places
where credits appear: on the label in the
center of a record and on the liner notes
on the album cover. While artists invariably receive both label and liner note
credit, producers, if not protected in their
contract, may find themselves relegated
to the liner notes only. Why? Labels have
little space, especially when an independent production company must also receive credit.

Cross-Collateralization—The application
by a record company or music publisher
of an artist's or songwriter's royalties
from one source against unrecouped recording costs or advances from another.
The novice is subjected to cross-
collateralization in two situations. Beginning artists who sign record contracts
with independent production companies
are often required to simultaneously sign
an exclusive songwriter contract with its
affiliated music publishing company. The
artist is very disappointed when songwriter royalties he is anticipating receiving are instead applied against advances
or recording costs still unrecouped by the
sister record company. The other cross-
collateralization snare befalls the songwriter who from time to time assigns
individual songs to a particular publisher.
When at last he meets success and is looking forward finally to paying his lawyer,
both he and the lawyer are chagrined to
find the royalties applied against an unrecouped advance the writer received two
years before and had forgotten about.
The remedy is simple. If you ask for a
"no-cross" clause, you will probably get
it. The trick is to remember to ask.

Crossover Record (or Artist)—A record
destined for a limited market, such as
"R&B" or Country, that finds success in
the pop market. After a few crossover
records an artist may, to his delight, find
himself a crossover artist: one whose
career, though launched in a limited
market, now enjoys across-the-board
popularity. Diana Ross and Kenny Rog-
ers come to mind.

Cut in—The interest and economic benefit derived from the practice of ascribing
to a person (usually an artist) writer
credit with respect to a song not written
by that person. A cut in is usually ex-
tracted as a condition precedent to the
artist recording the song in question. It is
also applied to the practice of assigning a
copyright interest in a song from one
publisher to another for similar reasons.
You may make any moral or ethical judg-
ments you wish, but be assured they will
become tempered with success.

Cutout—A record that has been deleted
from a record company's active catalogue. An artist should strive to have a
contractual provision barring his records
from being cut out until a fixed period of
time after release. Cutouts are sold at
much reduced prices and do not add lus-
ter to the artist's reputation, especially if
they are of recent vintage. To add injury
to insult, no royalties are paid on records
sold as cutouts.

D

DAT—DATs, digital audio tapes, are the tape equivalents of CDs. Housed in tiny cassettes, they are matchless for convenience, and matched only by CD's for sound quality. Slowed in development by industry fear of their duplicating potential, and by industry reluctance to propagate a new media so close upon the heels of the CD phenomenon, DATS are on their way . . . and can't be stopped! They will do to the conventional cassette what CDs did to the vinyl LP: render them extinct!

Demo (Demonstration Record)—A record made by an artist for the purpose of inducing a record company to record him; or by a songwriter or music publisher to induce an artist or producer to record the song "demoed." Demos must be tailored to your talent and their intended purpose. The demo studio is the graveyard of careers. That's why there is a chapter devoted to the demo. It's important. Study it.

Derivative Rights—The rights the Copyright Act of 1976 says remain with the publisher of a song after its writer has exercised his right of termination and has taken the song back. The Copyright Act of 1976 is relatively new and no one is quite sure what derivative rights are. An adjudicated example is the publisher's right to collect mechanical royalties derived from licenses issued prior to termination. Since a writer cannot exercise his right of termination for thirty-five years, there is optimism that the question will be resolved by the time you need to be concerned with it.

Distribution—The process by which a record finds its way from the studio where it was born to the ultimate consumer. Most major record companies have their own distribution systems, and distribute their own product and that of other record companies. Some companies rely on independent distributors. Distribution is a key factor in the success of a record company. Find a record company that doesn't have to worry about it.

Domestic—As used in conjunction with words such as "rights" and "sales," "domestic" is used to distinguish between the United States (and sometimes Canada) and the rest of the world, which is referred to as "foreign." For example: domestic sales as opposed to foreign sales.

Drilled Records—When a record company sells cutout records at a price much below its usual wholesale price, it literally drills a second hole through the label (and through the jacket). This is done to protect the record company from having the record returned for credit at the original or full wholesale price.

E

Earned—Most record and publishing contracts have provisions whereby the artist or songwriter receives as part of his royalties a percentage of the record company's or publisher's income from certain sources. The word "earned" is usually inserted before the word "income" to relieve the record company or publisher from an obligation to pay a share of advances received by it over to the artist or writer until such time as portions of the advances are actually earned. This practice serves the record companies and publishers well on two levels: first, they retain the use of the artist's and songwriter's share of such advances for a period of time at what are today very substantial interest rates; and second, since advances

are often paid with respect to entire catalogues, they avoid the problem of apportioning the advance among many
artists or many writers, which apportion-
ment would be speculative at best and
would assuredly engender the enmity of
certain of their artists or writers.

Educational Music—Usually printed editions of music arranged for and designed
to be used by schools and other educational institutions, either for the purpose
of teaching or for the needs of specialized
users of music peculiar to schools, such
as glee clubs, choirs, school orchestras,
and marching bands.

Employee for Hire—Although a seemingly innocuous term, this one is fraught
with ominous significance for songwriters. If it appears in one of your contracts, it should inspire a knee-jerk
spasm in your colon (no small anatom-
ical feat). The Copyright Act of 1976
provides that if you write a song as an
employee for hire of a publisher, the
publisher, *not you,* is considered the author for the purposes of the Copyright
Act "and owns all of the rights comprised in the copyright." As an employee
for hire you will have forfeited your
right of termination, and neither you
nor your heirs may look forward to the
return of the song at the end of thirty-
five years. If the song has become a
standard, this is a very substantial economic loss. As might be expected, the
Copyright Act of 1976 has prompted attorneys for music publishers to revise
their songwriter contracts so as to cast
their clients as employees for hire. You
are forewarned! But don't lose sleep. A
recent U.S. Supreme Court case will

make it very difficult for anyone to
make Employment for Hire "stick."

Engineer (Recording)—An engineer has
the responsibility for the technical (as opposed to artistic) content and excellence
of a recording. He twists the knobs and
adjusts the levels and does whatever else
is necessary to assure that the tape reflects what the artist and the record producer wish captured. Engineers are
usually employees of the studio in which
they ply their craft, and many studios
owe their clientele to the regard in which
their engineers are held. Engineers often
aspire to become producers—and do so.

EP (EP record)—Extended-play record.
Usually a 12-inch 33⅓ rpm record containing more songs than a single but
fewer than an LP. Never of much commercial significance in the United States,
EPs are popular elsewhere in the world.

Exclusive; Exclusivity—Exclusive means
to the exclusion of all others. You will
meet the term in the form of contract provisions making you a record company's
exclusive recording artist, or a music publisher's exclusive songwriter, or making
someone else your exclusive manager. Although there are songwriter agreements
for individual songs, I have never come
across a nonexclusive recording-artist
agreement or management contact. For
the duration of such exclusive contracts,
you cannot record for another record
company, assign songs to another music
publisher, or use another manager.

Execution (of a Contract)—Legal jargon
for the formal completion or signing of a
contract. A contract drafted but not
signed is termed "unexecuted." A fully
signed contract is termed "executed."

F

**First Record Sold; Payment from first
record sold; Payment from first record
sold after recoupment**—Traditionally, al-

though the record company initially pays
the costs of recording a record, such costs
are charged against the artist's royalties,

if and when earned, as if they were advances to the artist. When an individual producer is lured by a record company to produce an artist's record, he is paid a royalty on sales of that record. For obvious reasons, the record company would prefer not to pay the producer a royalty until after it has recouped its recording costs. The scenario usually goes like this: the record company's first contract draft provides that the producer will receive a royalty only on those records sold after the record company has recouped its recording costs at the artist's royalty rate. The producer's attorney then takes the position that his client insists on receiving his royalty from the very first record sold. The usual compromise results in no royalty being paid to the producer until after the record company recoups its recording costs, at which point he receives his royalty retroactively from the first record sold. Whether the recoupment takes place at the artist's royalty rate or at the combined artist's plus producer's royalty rate (faster!) is the subject of additional negotiation. And you thought it was a simple business!

Folio—A bound collection of songs usually with some common element or theme. "Matching folios" parallel, or match, the contents of particular record albums and usually feature the same cover art. "Personality folios" contain songs, biographical material, and pictures associated with a particular artist and invariably feature that artist on the cover.

Foreign—As used in conjunction with words such as "sales" or "rights," "foreign" is used to distinguish between the rest of the world and the United States (and sometimes Canada), which is referred to as "domestic." For example: foreign sales as opposed to domestic sales.

Free Goods—The term refers to records purportedly given away free by record companies to their customers in proportion to the number of records purchased by the customers—thereby providing the customer with an incentive to buy more records. Your record contract will provide that you will receive no royalty with respect to records distributed as free goods. It is incumbent upon your attorney to negotiate a limitation on the quantity of free goods the record company may distribute (usually 15 percent on albums and 30 percent on singles). Some record companies give no actual free goods, but, instead, reduce their wholesale price by the percentage provided for in the artist's free-goods clause. Such companies nevertheless withhold the artist's royalties as if free goods were in fact given. Where is the sales incentive, in such instances, that is supposed to justify withholding the artist's royalties? The point hasn't been litigated *yet*.

Because of attacks on the free goods system, some record companies have deleted all references to free goods from their contracts and simply state that all royalties will be computed on the basis of 85 percent of all records sold and not returned. (Other record companies "one-upped" their colleagues by doing both! Nice, eh?) This avoids for them the onus of defending an indefensible position.

It is important to note that distinction between free goods and other records given away free for promotional purposes, such as those given to disc jockeys to induce airplay.

Front Money—Another term for "advance." Your lawyer will need little inspiration to pursue front money for you. It is often the only money he can look to for the payment of his fees.

G

Gig—A single professional engagement usually of short duration; a play date. Of jazz origin, gig has come to mean a job, even one not related to music.

Gold Record—A gold *album* is one certified by the RIAA (look under "R") as having had a minimum sale of 500,000 units. A gold *single* is one certified by the RIAA as having had a minimum sale of 500,000 units.

Grand Performing Rights—"Dramatic" rights as opposed to "nondramatic" rights, which are known as "small performing" rights. Simple? Were it so! Unfortunately, it has yet to be determined with any degree of consistency what constitutes a grand performance. The distinction between grand and small rights is important, because if the use to be made is small, the user's already existing AS-CAP or BMI license is all that is needed. If a grand right is involved, a separate license must be negotiated, at additional cost, with the owner of the copyright of the song being used. The courts have from time to time held different and conflicting views as to what constitutes the exercise of a grand right. Different criteria have been applied, such as whether costumes and scenery were used, whether the song was woven into and carried forward the plot. What is thought to be the better view, although it does not dispose of the question, is that a performance of a song is dramatic (grand) if it aids in telling a story; otherwise it is nondramatic (small). In the negotiation of a songwriter contract it is often possible, and always desirable, to reserve to the author the grand performing rights.

Gross Income—The total income from a source without deduction of expenses or other costs of earning that income. Gross income less such expenses and costs is known as "net income."

H

Harry Fox (The Harry Fox Agency, Inc.) —The Harry Fox Agency issues licenses on behalf of its music publisher clients for the use of their songs on phonograph records (mechanical licenses) and in connection with motion pictures, commercials, television films, and videotapes (synchronization licenses). It also collects and distributes to its clients the income from such licenses. Harry Fox charges a commission for its services which ranges from 5 percent to 3½ percent of gross collections with respect to mechanical licenses, and up to 10 percent in connection with synchronization licenses.

I

Independent Producer—An independent producer or independent production company can be thought of as a mini record company in that it discovers talent, signs artists to record contracts, and produces the artist's records. Because it lacks the financial and personnel re-sources of large record companies, it cannot manufacture, distribute, or promote its product. Often it cannot afford recording costs. Consequently, it must obtain those services from a large record company. The usual route is for the independent producer to produce a demo or a few master-quality sides of an artist's performances and to "pitch" these to a record company, which, if it is "sold," will enter into an independent production contract with the independent producer. The record company will provide the funding for an album and its manufacturing, distribution, and promotional services. The independent producer will provide the exclusive recording services of the artist for a period of time measured by years of albums delivered and its production services, in exchange for which it will receive a royalty on records sold. The independent producer pays the artist's royalties out of the royalty it receives. There are infinite variations on this theme, some of which we will explore later on.

Independent Promotion—The practice by record companies of engaging third parties (not employees of the record company) to "promote" their records. "Promote" is a euphemism for "get airplay." The fees payable to independent promoters has been as high as $250,000. The practice is in decline as a result of congressional investigations into its more unsavory aspects. Some recent vintage recording contracts attempted to pass the cost of promotion on to the artist as an "advance." Don't let it happen to you.

Individual Producer—The person who oversees the actual studio recording by the artist. He acts as the artist's coach and director, plans the recording sessions, and helps choose the songs to be recorded. He bears the responsibility for the artistic and commercial quality of the recordings made and for completing them within a prescribed budget. Great producers are rare, highly compensated, and in great demand. They receive royalty on records sold and quite often substantial advances.

Infringement of Copyright—Anyone who violates any of the exclusive rights of a copyright owner under the Copyright Act is an infringer of the copyright. Infringement makes available to the copyright owner one or more of the following remedies: an injunction against further infringement, impoundment of infringing articles, damages and the profits of the infringer, and costs and attorney's fees. In addition, there are infringements that constitute criminal offenses and are punishable by fine and/or imprisonment. I have observed that my clients consider it an infringement of their copyrights when someone else's work bears the slightest resemblance to one of their copyrighted songs—as opposed to an unconscious, subliminal, and minimal borrowing of public-domain material when the shoe is on the other foot. Infringement is "lawyer country" and need not be pursued further here.

J

Jingle—Jingles are musical compositions written for, and as part of, advertising material. The writing and singing of jingles can be a sustaining source of income for aspiring songwriters and artists. Barry Manilow, Melissa Manchester, and Ashford and Simpson are just a few of the "names" who supported themselves by doing jingles until they made it. Some jingles you may recall are: *"You Deserve a Break Today," "Have a Coke and a Smile," "Fly the Friendly Skies," "It's the Real Thing,"* and *"I Love New York."*

Joint Work—A joint work, according to the Copyright Act, "is a work prepared by two or more authors with the intention that their contributions be merged into inseparable or interdependent parts of a unitary whole." If you, a composer, write a song with a collaborator who is the lyricist, you both jointly own the resulting song. You own an undivided half-interest in his lyric and he owns an undivided half-interest in your music. The two are "merged." If, however, a piece of instrumental music had been in existence for some time and the copyright owner caused you to write a lyric for it, the question of who owns and can exercise dominion over the separate elements and the combined elements is still subject to judicial determination. See *Co-Publishing.*

K

K-Tel—K-Tel Music, Ltd., pioneered the practice of licensing record masters from different companies and creating compilation albums. With the aid of extensive TV advertising, the resulting albums were marketed by mail order and through chain stores. The concept proved so successful that K-Tel's name became an almost generic term for that type of record. See *Coupling.*

Key-Man Clause—When you ask for language in a contract whereby you can terminate the contract if a particular executive ceases to be employed by the contracting company, you are asking for a key-man clause. The key-man may be a record executive you think is essential to the success of your career, or a manager in a management company with whom you have a close personal relationship. Although you may ask for it, you won't get it. No corporation will provide an employee with such leverage.

L

Lead Sheet—A copy of a song containing the melody line, the lyrics, and notations indicating the harmonic structure. Prior to the Copyright Act of 1976, lead sheets were required to register a song for copyright. Under the Copyright Act of 1976 a recording can be filed in lieu of a lead sheet.

Liner Notes—The copy on the back or inside cover of a record album. Liner notes are a nice thing to have approval of. They afford you an opportunity to say thanks to people who ordinarily do not receive credit—your musicians, the engineers, background singers, etc. I will confess to an inordinate amount of pleasure at finding I was "executive producer" (without justification) of a client's album. People, including lawyers, love to see their names in print.

Liquidation (of reserves)—In the United States, records (and to a lesser extent printed music) are sold on the basis of "a 100 percent return privilege." If a record seller has bought one hundred copies of your album and it "bombs" and he is left with ninety-five copies, he can return the ninety-five copies to your record company for full credit against his outstanding bill or against future purchases. All record contracts provide that the record company can withhold from the artist's (or producer's) royalties "a reserve for returns." The record company does this so that it will not find that it has paid out royalties that subsequently prove, by virtue of extensive returns, to be unearned. High interest rates provide an incentive to record companies to be quite conservative (pessimistic) in setting up their reserves against returns. It is therefore incumbent upon your attorney to limit the amount of that reserve to a "reasonable" amount or to a specific percentage of the records shipped (30 percent is about right for albums and 50 percent is permissible for singles, which are considered a promotional device more than a profit producer). It is even more important that your attorney provide for the liquidation (the payment to the artist of the unused portion) of the reserve after a specific period of time. Three accounting periods (1½ years) after the reserve is set up is usually acceptable to both sides. Reserves usually provide fertile ground for your accountant to till while conducting an audit of the record company's books. This is a long section of the lexicon, but it will also serve to explain *reserves* and *returns* . . . so read it again!

Litigation—A lawsuit. Although the subject of much posturing, relatively few lawsuits are instituted or progress beyond the initial stages. The risks and expense to both sides usually result in a settlement, either before the suit is started or before the trial itself is commenced. Keep in mind that in the United States, unlike England, the "winner" is not usually awarded attorney's fees. There goes your "profit"!

Loanout—Often, for tax purposes, it is recommended that an artist or songwriter act through a corporation he owns or controls. In such instances the artist or songwriter enters into a personal-services contract with his corporation, which then enters into a contract with the record company or music publisher whereby it "loans out" the artist's or songwriter's services. That contract is called a "loanout agreement."

M

Manager, Business—If you are lucky, you will have need of this chap down the road. He is the expert you will call upon to structure and manage your financial empire. It's his job to make sure you don't end up as the Joe Louis of the music business. Business managers usually have an accounting background and may serve as accountants and business managers.

Manager, Personal—The person charged with the responsibility for molding and overseeing an artist's professional and artistic career . . . the Henry Higgins to your Liza! Your manager can be your salvation or your destruction. This is the key relationship of an artist's career and demands your serious consideration. See Chapter 5.

Master (Record)—The finished, mixed, and polished tape from which the parts necessary to manufacture records are made. It is the ultimate synthesization of everything you've done in the studio.

Matching Folio—See *Folio.*

Mechanical Royalty; Mechanicals—The royalty payable to a copyright owner for the use of its song on a phonograph record. The first "records" were piano rolls for player pianos. These were referred to as "mechanical devices" under the Copyright Act of 1909—hence the term "mechanical royalty." Although player pianos are almost gone, as is the word "mechanical" from the new Copyright Act, the term "mechanical royalties" or "mechanicals" persists in the record industry. Mechanical royalties can be either "statutory" or "negotiated." Statutory royalties are those prescribed by the Copyright Act for those who wish to avail themselves of its compulsory licensing provision. The copyright owner and the user may, and often do, agree to abide by the statutory royalty rate (in cents) without invoking the compulsory license provisions. When the user negotiates a mechanical royalty rate that is less than the statutory royalty rate, the user is said to have received a "rate." A mechanical royalty rate can be negotiated on two levels: a diminution of the statutory rate and/or by exempting from the calculation of royalties certain classes of records, such as records distributed free.

Under the Copyright Act of 1909 the basic statutory rate was 2¢ per song. Under the 1976 Act it was 2¾¢. In 1981 it was raised by the Copyright Royalty Tribunal to 4¢. No, there was no increase from 1909 to 1976. By January of 1990 the statutory rate had risen to 5.7¢. Of course each such rise begets new contract language by the ever ingenious record companies, which is designed to thwart, or at least diminish, the effect of the raise. The statutory royalty rate is subject to continuing change by the Copyright Royalty Tribunal. For the sake of simplicity, we shall assume throughout this book a statutory mechanical royalty of 5.7¢.

Merchandising—The use of an artist's name, fame, and likeness in connection with the exploitation of products and services. If you wish to put this in context, think of Madonna. If that's too oblique, think T-shirts and posters.

Mixing; Mixing Down—The combining or blending of all the "tracks" made during the recording of a record into the final master recording. Most new studios now have the capability to record on sixty-four separate tracks.

MOR—Middle of the road. This is mellow popular music, usually ballads or melodic instrumental music—the music your parents enjoy.

N

Name and Likeness—The term used to describe the exclusive right of an artist, songwriter, or other personality to grant to others the right to use his name and picture in connection with the commercial exploitation or marketing of products or services. A typical example would be the licensing by an artist to a music publisher of the right to use the artist's picture and name on the cover of a personality folio.

Net Income—See *Gross Income*.

New Copyright Act—The Copyright Act of 1976 (which became effective in 1978). Usually the term is used to distinguish the 1976 Act from the 1909 Act. The 1976 Act will probably be referred to as "new" until the next copyright act is promulgated—probably in 2043, if the past is precedent.

O

Old Copyright Act—See *New Copyright Act*.

One Hundred Percent of Sales—The old 78 rpm records were heavy and brittle. Some invariably broke in transit. The shards were expensive to return for credit. The practice therefore evolved of factoring a 10 percent "breakage allowance" into the record company's invoice.

The artist, with justification, was paid a royalty on only 90 percent of the records sold. In 1948 the vinyl, unbreakable record was introduced. Invoicing at 100 percent of sales resumed. Payment of royalties at 90 percent of sales persisted and still persists in some record company contracts to this day. If your attorney requests "payment on 100 percent of sales," it will rarely be refused. The record company's representative may even blush.

One-Nighter—A gig that is limited to one night.

Option—Although there are other options, the one you will be primarily concerned with is the record company's or music publisher's option to extend a contract for additional periods of time, or albums in the case of record companies, should they, *not you,* choose to do so. Today record deals are being cast in terms of albums rather than years. The same principle applies. Record companies uti-

lize this structure to avoid the obligation to spend more money on additional recordings and advances, should they lose faith in an artist's ability to be a commercial success. Understandably, they won't sign an artist for just one year, lest they "break" him in only to find themselves in a bidding war with their competitors for the artist's future services. Songwriter contracts do not usually have option provisions unless the publisher is required to pay an annual advance. When you have some clout as an artist or songwriter, you can insist on "firm" (that is, no options) multiple year or album deals.

P

Ⓟ—The symbol for copyright to be incorporated in the copyright notice appearing on phonorecords of sound recordings. The notice should also contain the year of first publication of the sound recording and the name of the copyright owner. It will be found on the record label: Ⓟ XYZ Record Co. 1990. It is the record company's problem, not yours, since it is their copyright. Your demos should not bear a notice, because they are not "published" in the context of the Copyright Act. You need not worry about a © being included on a record to protect the underlying song. The © is only fixed to visually perceived copies of published versions. If, however, your lyrics are printed on the album cover, they should be accompanied by a © copyright notice.

PA—Personal appearance.

P&D—A P&D (pressing and distribution) deal is one whereby an independent record label, usually small and underfinanced, enters into an agreement with a major label which, for a consideration, presses the small label's records and distributes them through its network. The variations found in P&D deals are infi-

nite and are beyond the scope of this book . . . and your needs.

Packaging Costs—Purportedly, the costs of the jacket in which your album will be marketed. They are set forth in your record contract as a percentage of the retail or wholesale selling price of the album, depending upon which price your royalty is based. They rarely bear any relationship to the actual costs of packaging, and are much higher than such actual cost. This is especially so when an album is successful, and one-time costs such as artwork can be spread over many records.

$9.98	album retail selling price
−2.00	packaging deduction
	(20%, assuming a cassette)
$7.98	
× 5%	your royalty rate
$ .40	your royalty?

Well, almost. There are other deductions factored in, such as "free goods" that we need not go into at this time. The packaging deduction varies from company to company and is not subject to much negotiation, especially at your stage of the game. The record companies take the position that it all "washes"; that it's the way the industry grew and that if they lowered the packaging deduction, they would have to lower the artist's royalty rate to emerge with an acceptable profit. When you're a star, you can negotiate for a dollars-and-cents royalty on a per-album basis and avoid "shrinkage" in the record company's accounting division. If you read your record contract, you will note that packaging costs are deducted from the retail (or wholesale) price before applying your royalty rate to it.

Pass—Congratulations? Wrong! In the music business, "pass" means fail, as in: "Although the artist has talent, we do not hear a hit single, so we'll pass at this time. When the artist has additional material, please do not hesitate to . . ." Record companies never just say "Ugh!"

Pass Through—This expression characterizes a contract or a contract provision whereby one party "passes on" to the other party the benefits contained in the already existing contract. It is a device most often used by independent producers who sometimes pass through to an artist the benefits of the independent producer's negotiations with the record company, or pass through to an individual producer the benefits of the artist's contract with the independent producer. The device avoids embarrassment to lawyers and shortens a forty-page agreement to three pages, since the royalty provisions of the prior contract are "incorporated by reference." Whether a pass-through arrangement is requested or granted depends on the relative strengths of the parties. For example, a very "heavy" producer who is engaged to produce an unknown artist may well feel he can negotiate a better contract than the artist could extract from the independent producer. In such an instance, the producer would be disdainful of a pass-through provision.

Performing Rights—The exclusive rights granted by the Copyright Act to copyright owners of certain works, including musical works, to perform their copyrighted works publicly.

Performing Rights Societies—Organizations, such as ASCAP and BMI, that license to users, on behalf of copyright owners of songs, the right to perform their songs publicly. See *ASCAP* and *Public Performance Right*.

Personality Folio—See *Folio*.

Platinum Record—A platinum *album* is one certified by the RIAA as having had sales of 1,000,000 units. A platinum *single* is one certified by the RIAA as having the sales of 1,000,000 units.

Points—Royalty percentage points. In lieu of saying "3 percent of the retail selling price," the more Runyonesque might opt for "3 pernts."

Pop—Derived from the word "popular," "Pop" refers to the genre of music appealing to the largest listening audience. Pop music is generally youth-oriented and targeted for Top 40 play lists and AM radio. Pop can best be described by what it isn't, for example, jazz, AOR, Country, MOR, R&B, Adult Contemporary, or Hard Rock. A song initially characterized as belonging to one of the categories other than Pop can become Pop if it "catches on" and "crosses over."

Power of Attorney—This has nothing to do with your lawyer's ability. A "power of attorney" is what you give to another person (or business entity) when you authorize and empower him to act for you and in your place, for example, to sign a contract for you. There are limited powers of attorney and general powers of attorney. They are what their names imply.

Rule 1.	Never sign a general power of attorney. Not even for Mom!
Rule 2.	Same as Rule 1.
Rule 3.	Same as Rule 2.

There are two limited powers of attorney

that are legitimate and justified. The first is the one in your songwriter contract that makes the publisher your attorney to sign necessary documents to perfect the copyrights you assigned to the publisher, if you are not available or if you refuse to do so. The second is a power of attorney to your manager to sign contracts for short-term personal appearances when you are unavailable to do so yourself. Most management contracts, which are traditionally prepared by the manager's attorney, contain general powers of attorney whereby, if he chose to do so, your manager could sign you to a ten-year recording contract. Such powers are abusive and entirely unnecessary. They should be deleted.

Premium Records—These are not better-quality records, but, rather, records that are given away with a product to induce sales of that product. The usual record contract provides that the record company may do this. It will also provide that the record company may pay you a much reduced royalty with respect to such records. There are many products on the market with which you may not wish your name or records associated. It is therefore up to your attorney to cause the record company to surrender the right to use your records for premium purposes or to give you an *absolute* right of approval. This is a situation where "not to be unreasonably withheld" is not acceptable.

Print, Print Rights—Printed copies of musical compositions as typified by sheet music; folios; collections; teaching, band, choral, and orchestral editions; books; and an almost infinite variety of other forms. Although somewhat eclipsed by mechanical and performance income, print is a highly underrated source of income for songwriters and publishers.

Producer—See *Individual Producer*.

Product—The creative output of a record company or independent producer, as in "We'll talk about a deal after I hear the product."

Promotional Records—Records distributed for no charge by record companies to disc jockeys, radio and television stations, trade publications, magazines, newspapers, and similar media outlets to stimulate interest in and sales of a record. Promotional records should be distinguished from so-called free goods, which are purportedly given by record companies to their customers for sales-incentive purposes. No royalties are paid to an artist with respect to promotional records.

Public Domain (PD) Works—This is generally how your lawyer characterizes the music you've been accused of infringing. Actually, PD works are works that do not enjoy copyright protection. Works may attain this status in a variety of ways. They could have been created before copyright protection was available. The copyright owner may have failed to observe a formality under the old copyright act or "blown" the renewal under the old act. Or the copyright may have expired by passage of time. Caution, however, must be observed if you intend to use a public domain work. There were extensions of the copyright term under the old act, which make the expiration date of certain copyrights a matter of conjecture. In addition, there are copyrights in arrangements that survive the underlying song's copyright.

Public Performance Right—The Copyright Act grants to the copyright owners of certain works the exclusive right to perform the copyrighted work publicly. Musical works are included but sound recordings are not. Hence the copyright owner of a song on a record would be entitled to compensation for public performance, but the copyright owner of the sound recording (the record itself) would not be. To perform a work publicly means performing it at a place open to the public or at a place where a substantial number of persons outside of a normal circle of a family and its social acquaintances is gathered. The definition also includes transmission of a performance by any means or device to such a place or to the public. "Perform" includes live face-to-face renditions, renditions from recordings, broadcasting, transmissions by cable, microwaves, etc.

Publication—This ordinary word owes its place in this lexicon to the Copyright Act. Many things in the Copyright Act, such as the copyright notice date, and the loss of certain rights, are keyed to the date of publication of the copyrighted work. The Copyright Act of 1976 defines publication as "the distribution of copies or phonorecords of a work to the public by sale or other transfer of ownership, or by rental, lease or lending. The offering to distribute phonorecords to a group of persons for purposes of further distribution, public performance, or public display, constitutes publication. A public performance or display of a work does not of itself constitute publication."

Publisher's Share—The income from a song retained by a music publisher after paying the writer his share. In the traditional deal where the writer assigns 100 percent of the copyright in a song to a publisher, the writer's royalty is supposedly equal to the publisher's share of income. Publishers have rather universally maintained an edge. That advantage is in the area of sheet music (and to a lesser extent in other printed editions), where, although the publisher receives 60¢ or 70¢ from its print publisher, it still offers only 10¢ to 12¢ to the writer. This is negotiable, but not very. It is wise to ask for 50 percent of the publisher's profit from print—with a tight definition of the word "profit."

Publishing—This term has come to mean ownership of the copyright of a song. When you make your first deal, your friends will ask "Did you have to give publishing?" Your answer will be either "No" or "Yes, but . . ." If your answer is yes, they will shake their heads mournfully and seemingly knowingly. Sometimes you just have to give to get. It's known as paying dues. If you're good, you won't have to give for long, and if your lawyer is good, you'll get it back in time for your "prime of life" via the thirty-five year right of termination.

R

R&B—Rhythm and Blues, Black music.

Rap, Rap Music—Recitative of the nineties. A musical style in which the text is declaimed in the rhythm of natural speech with slight melodic variation—street music!

Rate—See *Mechanical Royalty.*

Recording Budget—Pursuant to the terms of an individual producer's contract with a record company or independent producer, he is usually required to prepare and submit for approval a detailed budget setting forth what the project will cost. This will include studio time, musicians, arrangers, instrument rental, background singers, etc. In dealing with independent producers, record companies will sometimes waive a detailed budget and stipulate a sum as the recording budget. Then it is the responsibility of the independent producer to bring the record in under the budget or to pay the excess. Usually, as a practical matter, the record company picks up the excess, too. After all, what good is two-thirds of an album?

Recording Costs—The costs of making a recording. Since all recording costs are charged as advances against the artist's royalties, the record company's contracts have very comprehensive recording-costs clauses. In general, they include all costs of recording that are not part of the manufacturing process—and two that arguably are. These are mixing and mastering. If your lawyer screams, he may get a split: they may delete mastering.

Recoupable—This word invariably precedes or follows the word "advance." It means that when the record company or music publisher gives you an advance, they can recoup it from, or get it back from, your royalties.

Recoupment—If you become an individual producer, you will find the first draft of your contract will state that you will not receive royalties until "after recoupment of all recording costs." Whether there's a second draft, and how it reads, will depend on your bargaining strength and your representation. See *Individual Producer*.

Release Commitment—There isn't any fun in having a record deal, or making a record, if your friends and relatives never see it or hear it—and, even less money. First-draft record contracts usually state that the record company's only liability in the event they don't record you is to pay you union scale for sides not recorded, and they can still keep you under contract! It is incumbent upon you to make sure your contract states that if a certain minimum amount of product (usually one LP) is not recorded *and* commercially released during the initial term, the record company may not exercise its option for a second year. At least then you are free to seek out a record company where you will be more appreciated.

Reserve Against Returns—See *Liquidation (of reserves)*.

Retail Selling Price (RSP)—Most records don't have a marked retail selling price.

Since your royalty may be based upon your record's "retail selling price," it is important that some standard be established in your contract. Since retail selling prices are constantly rising, one would not wish a fixed dollar amount in the contract. The usual solution is to insert "suggested" before retail selling price. For each wholesale price there is an industry-accepted "suggested" retail price; hence some standard is effected. Many record companies are now abandoning even suggesting an RSP, and perhaps wholesale price will replace retail selling price as a royalty standard.

Returns—See *Liquidation (of reserves)*.

Reversionary Rights—Rights that come back to their grantor upon the happening of a certain event or failure. For example, a contract may provide that the copyright in a song will revert to the writer in the event that the publisher fails to secure a commercially released recording within a prescribed period of time. Similarly, under the Copyright Act, a writer may terminate a grant after thirty-five years, whereupon the copyright reverts to him.

RIAA (The Recording Industry Association of America)—The main trade association of the record industry. In general it looks to the welfare of the record industry and serves as its spokesman in lobbying for legislation favorable to the record companies. It also sets the standards for and certifies gold and platinum records.

Royalties—Compensation to the grantor of a right based on a portion of the income derived from the right. We're primarily interested in artist's and writer's royalties for the right to use the artist's performance and the writer's song.

S

Sample, Sampling—A euphemism for infringing copyrights in sound recordings. Sampling is the process whereby a "creator" electronically extracts portions of someone else's sound recording and inserts and incorporates them into his own work. I have yet to hear a persuasive argument as to why this isn't an infringement. The reason is that there aren't any. Of late, because of the threat of litigation, samplers are asking for permission and licenses. Since each label has artists that are sampling from their competitor's product, a sort of gentleman's agreement to "live and let live" has arisen. Don't sample without permission in front. You could be throwing out a lot of time and money.

Scale; Union Scale—The minimum payment a user of talent is required to pay the talent under the rules of the particular union having jurisdiction. If you are a musician, the record company or independent producer is required to pay you scale for your services during recording sessions. If you are receiving an advance, your agreement will state that the scale payments are part of the advance. If you receive no advance, the scale payments will be part of the "recording costs" and recoupable from your royalties.

Showcase—A personal appearance (usually orchestrated by your manager) at a club to which record companies and publishers are invited to send A&R people to see how damn good you are before an audience. Your charisma quotient is important to record companies as a measure of your touring ability and sale potential. Many record companies, even if enamored of a demo, won't sign an act until they see the act perform live.

Sideman Provision—All record contracts are exclusive. There may, however, be occasions when you wish to perform as an instrumental musician (sideman) on another artist's record, either as a source of income or as an accommodation. To be able to do so you will require permission from your record company. It is easier to have such a clause inserted during the initial negotiation of your contract. A sideman provision usually requires that your performances will not be featured and that you will receive no credit or credit

no more prominent than any other sideman.

Sight & Sound—Records or devices embodying both sound and visual images. See *Audio-Visual Rights*.

Small Performing Rights—See *Grand Performing Rights*.

Song Sharks—"Operators" who through small ads in small magazines offer for large fees to copyright your song, print it, and attempt to have it recorded. They may even offer to set your lyric to music. No legitimate music publishers function this way. One might characterize these operations as scams. Many a family has enjoyed macaroni dinners over protracted periods of time as a result of a song shark's efforts.

Soul—R&B, Black music.

Sound Recording—This is the magic expression in the Copyright Act that finally, in 1971, gave copyright protection to recorded works. Sound recordings are defined as works that result from the fixation of a series of sounds (excluding those accompanying motion pictures or other audio-visual works) regardless of the nature of the material objects in which they are embodied. "Phonorecords" under the Copyright Act are the material objects, such as discs and cassettes, from which the sounds can be perceived.

Source, at the—Music-publishing contracts usually provide that the writer receive 50 percent of the publisher's income from territories outside the United States and Canada. It has been not uncommon for the U.S. publisher to assign its foreign rights to an affiliated company in the United Kingdom under an assignment which provided that the U.K. publisher would pay 50 percent of its income to the U.S. publisher. The U.K. publisher then assigned rights country by country to its affiliated publishers, similarly providing for the payments to the U.K. publisher of 50 percent of the income. Thus, if a song earned a dollar in Germany, the German subpublisher sent 50¢ to the U.K. publisher, who, in turn, sent 25¢ to the U.S. publisher, who, in turn, sent 12½¢ to the writer—instead of the 25¢ the writer was anticipating. Finally, the writers' lawyers got smart and insisted on inserting "at the source" at appropriate places in the publisher's contracts. The writer now got his quarter instead of 12½¢, and "Mister In-Between" began to fade. But beware! Although some publisher's contracts have "source" language, others do not.

Staff Writer—A songwriter who is employed by a music publisher. He usually receives a salary and a place to work in the publisher's office. A staff writer is a true employee for hire, and the publisher is usually the "author" of what the staff writer creates in the course of his employment. Relatively few publishers engage staff writers nowadays.

Standard, a—A song of great renown and enduring popularity; for example, "Stardust" or "Bridge Over Troubled Water." One standard puts the kids through college and provides you with country-club membership for life. If you write one, you'll probably write more.

Standard, as in Standard Contract—From time to time you will be presented with printed form contracts bearing the word "standard" in their titles; for example, "Standard Songwriters Contract." Regard this as an attempt by the party proffering such a contract to seduce you into believing that "everyone" signs that same contract and that you needn't "worry about it" or try to better its terms. The word "standard" is also often used to describe a clause or provision you may question. Don't be intimidated by the word "standard." In your business, nothing is standard and everything is mutable.

Statutory Royalty—See *Mechanical Royalty*.

Studio Musician—A musician who earns his livelihood by playing on record dates.

Synchronization License—This is an old motion-picture term which has become of new interest because of the audiovisual explosion in the music business. To use a song in a video, the producer must acquire a license from the copyright owner. That license is called a "synch" or synchronization license. It stems from old copyright language which referred to the "synchronization of music in timed relationships with a visual image" . . . or something like that.

T

Term—The duration of a contract. For example, for a three-year exclusive songwriter contract, the term is three years.

Termination, Right of—The right under the new Copyright Act of the grantor of rights (songwriter) to terminate the grant at the end of thirty-five years, regardless of the terms of the grant. Even if a songwriter assigns his song to the grantee (music publisher) for the duration of copyright (the life of the songwriter plus fifty years), he can still terminate at the end of thirty-five years. The right of termination does not exist if, however, the song was written as an employee for hire.

If the right of termination is exercised, the music publisher is left with only derivative rights. See *Employee for Hire* and *Derivative Rights*.

Tight—Unrelated to alcohol consumption, this term is used to describe a band that is really well rehearsed and playing exceptionally well.

Top 40—Usually the first forty songs on the Pop charts. Most AM Pop stations play a fixed number of songs, repeating them at fixed intervals throughout the day. Stations whose play lists consist of the first forty or so songs on the Pop charts are called "Top 40" stations. "Top

40" has also become an adjective to describe a Pop song that has a good chance of attaining a high chart position.

Tour—A series of concerts or personal appearances through a geographic territory—U.S. tour, European tour, etc. A tour usually corresponds to the release of an album and is usually a device to promote sales of that album. Visits to and interviews by local radio stations usually are part of the tour routine. "Tour support" is the financial aid the record company gives (or advances) to support a tour.

Trades—The magazines devoted to the music business. Notably, *Cash Box* and *Billboard*. Read them. Although subscriptions are expensive, perhaps your library subscribes. They are also found in the reception areas of music publishers, record companies, and entertainment lawyers. Hang out.

Twelve-Inch Single—Also called "Disco Singles," these are twelve-inch vinyl records that feature alternate mixes of the same musical composition. Generally targeted at the dance club market, the mixes vary in length and style to accommodate the taste and needs of the deejay and the club. Labels have found this format a useful device for market testing.

U

Union Scale—See *Scale*.

Unpublished Work—A work that has not been published in the context of the Copyright Act. See *Publication*.

V

Video—See *Audio-Visual Rights*.

W

Wholesale Price—The price at which a record company sells records to its customers. It varies a bit from company to company and is subject to some manipulation. In general, it is approximately half of the suggested retail selling price. Artists' royalties are keyed accordingly; hence the numerical royalty given by a company that pays on wholesale will be twice that of a company that pays on retail. For example, 10 percent WSP roughly equals 5 percent RSP.

Writer's Share—That portion of the income from a song that the publisher pays to the writer under the pertinent songwriter contract; the writer's royalties. See *Publisher's Share*.

INDEX

Van Halen, 92–93
Van Halen, Eddie, 93–94, 300
Variety, 68
videocassettes, 130
"Video Rewind," 127
videos, 125–30
  in contract negotiations, 128–30
  as demos, 156, 161–62
  inconsistent profitability of, 127–28
  as promotional tool, 128
  royalties on, 129
vinyl discs:
  advent of, 123
  CD's supplanting of, 124

Warner Bros., 88, 89, 91, 92–93, 139, 186
Warner Communications, 142
warranties, 33, 36
Warwick, Dionne, 64, 65, 140
Was, Don, 202
Way We Were, The, 255
Weintraub, Jerry, 212–15
  career of, 214
  client list of, 212
  on managers, 212–14
West, Bruce and Laing, 199
West, Leslie, 199–200
"What a Difference You've Made in My Life," 270

"What Can You Get a Wookie for Christmas When He Already Owns a Comb?," 63
"What Did You Get Santa Claus for Christmas?," 256
"What I Did for Love," 255
Williams, Andy, 284–85
writer's mechanical royalties, 21
writing credits, as part of recording deal, 30
Wyman, Bill, 248, 271–80
  on breaking in, 272, 274–76
  on lawyers, 278–80
  on managers, 277–78
  photography by, 277
  on publishers, 273
  on royalties, 274
  on singer-songwriters, 273
  solo career of, 271–72, 276–77

Yeston, Maury, 56–71
  business acumen of, 68
  career of, 56–66, 70
  on copyright, 69–70
  on formal musical education, 58–59
  on music publisher's role, 68–69
  on singer-songwriters, 66–67
"You're All I Need to Get By," 246
"You Can Take Salem Out of the Country, But . . . ," 308

ABOUT THE AUTHOR

Alan H. Siegel, an entertainment lawyer since his graduation from Harvard Law School, began his career as house counsel to a leading international music publisher. He later entered into private practice, and has been a partner in the New York law firm of Pryor Cashman Sherman & Flynn for over twenty years.

Siegel, who confesses to a "healthy schizophrenia" induced by "sitting on all three sides of the bargaining table," enjoys an eclectic entertainment practice. He has represented clients in virtually all areas of the entertainment world, including a galaxy of stars ranging in diversity from rock 'n' roll to grand opera. In addition to his law practice, Mr. Siegel has lectured extensively on entertainment subjects for the Practicing Law Institute, the American Bar Association, and law schools in the United States and Canada.

In addition to *Breaking In,* Siegel's literary efforts include several magazine articles and a screenplay which "taught me to empathize with clients whose talent is not yet recognized." He continues to write fiction "to demonstrate the tenacity I preach in *Breaking In.*"